AF361589

Brazil in the Global Nuclear Order, 1945–2018

JOHNS HOPKINS NUCLEAR HISTORY AND CONTEMPORARY AFFAIRS

Martin J. Sherwin, *Series Editor*

Brazil in the Global Nuclear Order 1945–2018

CARLO PATTI

Johns Hopkins University Press
Baltimore

© 2021 Johns Hopkins University Press
All rights reserved. Published 2021
Printed in the United States of America on acid-free paper
2 4 6 8 9 7 5 3 1

Johns Hopkins University Press
2715 North Charles Street
Baltimore, Maryland 21218-4363
www.press.jhu.edu

Library of Congress Cataloging-in-Publication Data

Names: Patti, Carlo, 1982– author.
Title: Brazil in the global nuclear order, 1945–2018 / Carlo Patti.
Description: Baltimore : Johns Hopkins University Press, [2022] |
Series: Johns Hopkins nuclear history and contemporary affairs |
Includes bibliographical references and index.
Identifiers: LCCN 2021006391 | ISBN 9781421442877 (hardcover) |
ISBN 9781421442884 (ebook)
Subjects: LCSH: Brazil—Military policy. | Nuclear weapons—Brazil. |
Nuclear arms control—Brazil. | National security—Brazil. |
Brazil—Foreign relations—1954–1964. | Brazil—Foreign
relations—1964–1985 | Brazil—Foreign relations—1985–
Classification: LCC UA619 .P378 2022 | DDC 355.02/170981—dc23
LC record available at https://lccn.loc.gov/2021006391

A catalog record for this book is available from the British Library.

*Special discounts are available for bulk purchases of this book. For more information,
please contact Special Sales at specialsales@jh.edu.*

CONTENTS

This book is the fruit of twelve years of tireless and exciting research on the international history of Brazil's attitude toward the global nuclear order since the dawn of the atomic age. Many people helped shape my study. First of all, I thank Alberto Gallo, who introduced me to Brazil's history when I was a graduate student. Since then, Alberto has followed my academic career closely and provided me with constant support and valuable advice.

I owe a debt of gratitude to Matias Spektor, who at our first meeting in Rio in June 2009 suggested that I turn my future dissertation into a book. He kindly agreed to co-supervise my doctoral research. Matias also opened to me the doors to a new Fundação Getulio Vargas (FGV) project on the history of Brazil's nuclear program. My thesis supervisor at the University of Florence, Marco Mugnaini, carefully followed my initial research. I am also grateful to Leopoldo Nuti, a member of my doctoral program and codirector of the Nuclear Proliferation International History Project (NPIHP), an international network established in 2010 by the joint initiative of the Università Roma Tre and the Woodrow Wilson Center for International Scholars. He constantly encouraged me to deepen my research on Brazil and participate in the new historiographical debate on nuclear proliferation. Other NPIHP scholars, such as Christian Ostermann, David Holloway, and Anna-Mart van Wyk, inspired several parts of this book. Thanks to the NPIHP, I was able to discuss parts of my research in the Nuclear History Bootcamps (in both 2011 and 2019) and to spend a predoctoral research period in Brazil doing archival research and conducting oral history interviews. My warm thanks to my friends and colleagues Togzhan Kassenova and the late Nuno Monteiro for encouraging me to publish this book.

A postdoctoral fellowship at FGV allowed me to deepen my studies and conduct archival research in Germany and South Africa. Naike Trincas was a flawless research assistant on my mission to Berlin. At FGV, I found several excellent colleagues and great friends, such as Eduardo Mello, Rodrigo Mallea, and Alexandre Moreli, who made important contributions by discussing different aspects of my research.

In Rio de Janeiro, the Institute of International Relations of the Pontifical Catholic University became my institutional home in 2013 and 2014 thanks to a postdoctoral fellowship provided by Capes (Coordenação de Aperfeiçoamento de Pessoal de Nível Superior). I warmly thank Paulo Esteves, Monica Herz, Márcio Scalércio, and Paulo Wrobel for making PUC a pleasant place to work and continue my research. I am also grateful to the University of Brasília professors Amado Luiz Cervo and Antônio Carlos Lessa for long discussions on Brazil's foreign-policy history. Antônio supervised my research when I spent a short period as a postdoctoral fellow at UnB.

In 2014 I took a permanent position at the Federal University of Goiás. Raquel Campos, Geisa Franco, Jiani Langaro, Ricardo Sapia, Cristiano Rezende, João Roriz, Marlon Salomon, the late Noé Freire Sandes, Alberto Zapatero, and many other colleagues contributed to the friendly environment at UFG. Ana Paula da Cruz Andrade, Ricardo Lopes Esteves, Anna Carolina Arruda Rodrigues, and Rodrigo Sobreira were brilliant research assistants. This research would not have been possible without financial support from the Autonomous Region of Sardinia, the Carnegie Corporation, CNPq (Conselho Nacional de Desenvolvimento Científico e Tecnológico), the British Academy (Newton Advanced Fellowship), and FGV. Several diplomats, politicians, and scientists kindly agreed to be interviewed, providing priceless details and comments on Brazil's nuclear history. Paulo Roberto de Almeida, Pedro Garcia, and Clovis Aguiar made my research at the archive of the Brazilian Ministry of Foreign Affairs easier. Thanks to my friends Flavia Gasbarri, Mara Drogan, and Valeria Benko for sharing important documents. Flavia, Vittorio Felci, and Guido Innocenti turned several research trips into fun adventures in Pretoria, Washington, and London.

In several stages of my writing, I also benefited from comments and suggestions from Renata Dalaqua, Sérgio de Queiroz Duarte, Matteo Gerlini, Togzhan Kassenova, Nuno Monteiro, Benoît Pelopidas, Rubens Ricupero, Cláudio Rodrigues, João Roriz, and Laercio Vinhas. I am responsible for any errors. I had the opportunity to discuss the book's main arguments in seminars at the University of Florence, the Roma Tre University, the University of Bristol, and the University of Cagliari. Special thanks to my colleague Christian Rossi in Cagliari.

Thanks to Johns Hopkins University Press. Marty Sherwin heartily embraced my book project. Laura Davulis and Esther Rodriguez have been very helpful throughout the publication process. Special thanks to the anonymous reviewers of the manuscript. Joanne Allen patiently copyedited the text. Elisa Piras and Jessica Lerche provided a linguistic revision. Matheus Okado created the map, and Fernanda Martins drew the timeline. Earlier versions of sections of chapter 1 first appeared in *Cold War History* 15.3 (2015).

My parents, Cristina and Fulvio, always supported my dreams and taught me to love culture and freedom. Andrea, my brother, always found the right words in the difficult moments of this long intellectual journey. Luciano Guerra was the best partner for travels around the world. My friends in Brazil and Italy made the many years of research a pleasant period. This book could not exist without my beloved wife, Aline. My *porto seguro,* she sacrificed days, nights, and *feriados* so that I could complete this book. I hope to be able to reciprocate her patience. Our daughters, Angela and Clara, both born while I was working on the manuscript, are a never-ending source of joy and energy. This book is dedicated to my *três meninas.*

Brazil in the Global Nuclear Order, 1945–2018

Introduction

On 4 September 1987 President José Sarney announced that Brazil had mastered the sensitive gas-centrifuge method for enriching uranium. This had been achieved through an autonomous effort in national nuclear-research centers, free from international inspections.[1] In less than eight years a collaboration between civilian and military authorities accomplished what had been a goal of Brazil's atomic program since the early 1950s: mastering a key technology for the independent production of nuclear energy. Sarney's declaration surprised both the Brazilian public and the international community, which had been in the dark about Brazil's secret project. Despite assurances from the president and from the chairman of the Brazilian National Nuclear Energy Commission (Comissão Nacional de Energia Nuclear, or CNEN) about the peaceful use of the technology (which was suitable for producing both nuclear fuel and weapons-grade material) and despite a previous communication to the Argentine president, Raúl Alfonsín, doubts existed about the ultimate goal of a technology that was being developed under the military regime.[2] The persistent opposition to the Nuclear Non-Proliferation Treaty (NPT), the defense of the right to manufacture peaceful nuclear devices, and ambiguous declarations by officials of the army only fueled national and international suspicions that Brazil had plans to build a bomb. As noted by the leading Brazilian scientist José Goldemberg, Brazil had the wherewithal to manufacture an atomic device within five years.[3] Exactly three years after Sarney's historic declaration, President Fernando Collor de Mello dramatically closed an atomic shaft and a few days later announced before the UN General Assembly that Brazil had renounced nuclear weapons. It marked the beginning of the path that led Brazil to build a bilateral system of safeguards and inspections with Argentina and to accept regional and global nonproliferation norms. Brazil today still possesses an advanced nuclear complex and aims to create a fleet of nuclear-propelled submarines. It continues to criticize the unfair nature of the NPT, and the lack of substantial steps toward nuclear disarmament justifies its refusal to accept a more intrusive international safeguards system.

This book discusses the historical and political implications of Brazil's place in the global nuclear order from 1945 to 2018. There has been much debate about the changing international role of emerging countries since at least the late 1960s. One of the key areas of discussion has been nuclear nonproliferation. During the Cold War the growing economic and political importance of countries like Brazil, India, and South Africa, mostly within their regions but sometimes with global reach, received increasing attention from both Washington and Moscow. An essential reason for the growing importance of many emerging countries has been their development of independent nuclear programs. Their choices, which were often based on energy demands and strategic considerations, had profound political and strategic consequences for the evolution of the global nuclear regime.

Brazil offers a useful case study for comprehending the attitudes of countries from the Global South toward international norms. Since 1946, when the first international talks about the control of nuclear energy took place, Brazil has consistently sought an *autonomous* position in the nuclear order. In the past seventy years, the country first opposed and then, in 1998, acceded to the international norms after mastering key technologies for producing nuclear energy. Many commentators have maintained a critical view of Brazil to this day and consider it to be an ambiguous player because it opposes the Additional Protocol of the International Atomic Energy Agency safeguards.

Taking into account how domestic and international factors have affected Brazil's nuclear diplomacy, this book aims to answer to the following questions: Why did Brazil oppose nuclear nonproliferation? How did the international context, particularly the United States, limit Brazil's nuclear options? Why did Brazil, in the end, never develop a nuclear weapon? Why did Brazil eventually accept the international nonproliferation norms? What is Brazil's current role in the nuclear nonproliferation regime?

The first major issue is undoubtedly the quest for autonomy within the nuclear order. From the beginning of the nuclear age, Brazil has sought to cooperate with other countries to secure nuclear-fuel-cycle technology. Over the last seventy years, international limitations have constrained the Brazilian quest. Both in the 1950s and in the 1970s, as a part of its strategy to prevent nuclear proliferation, the United States impeded or tried to prevent fruitful international cooperation between Brazil and other countries with advanced nuclear industries, such as

France and West Germany.[4] These foreign constraints were one reason that Brasília decided to create a secret nuclear program in 1978 and to cooperate with other countries outside the nonproliferation regime, such as Argentina and China. Much of Brazil's resistance to the regime is related to its interest in mastering sensitive nuclear technologies, such as uranium enrichment and spent-fuel reprocessing, maximizing autonomy vis-à-vis the major powers, and establishing ad hoc cooperation arrangements with countries willing to transfer advanced nuclear technology.[5]

Specific ideas developed in Brazil about how the international politics of nonproliferation worked. The way in which Brazilian diplomacy framed the nonproliferation "problem" is an essential aspect of how the country approaches the regime. The argument is twofold. First, there is the conviction that the regime is unfair and discriminatory toward emerging states. Second, Brazil would only accept the "rules of the game" once it was able to control the most critical aspects of the nuclear fuel cycle.

Finally, having only limited leverage to shape the institutional framework in which nonproliferation rules are made, Brazil until the 1990s acted mainly as an anti-regime force. It created an ad hoc network of cooperation with countries outside the regime like Pakistan and Israel, as well as with countries within the regime that were willing to transform the rules from within and to transfer technologies, such as Iraq and, to some extent, West Germany. During the 1990s, Brazil adhered to the regime. Rather than signaling a change of heart on the part of Brazilian authorities, acceding to the NPT should be seen as a maneuver to enter the international regime as a nuclear-capable state.

On the basis of many archival sources and extensive use of oral history interviews, this book connects these factors. The book collects and analyzes the available primary sources on Brazil's nuclear policy and represents the first complete account to reply to the questions listed above.

States and the Nuclear Order

There is a growing body of historiographical and theoretical literature on how different categories of countries saw the nuclear order. The *nuclear order* has been studied since the beginning of the atomic age.[6] According to William Walker, it was developed "to address the distinctive set of problems, issues, and goals associated with nuclear technology."[7] Walker elaborated further that it would help to guarantee international security, as well as seek "a tolerable accommodation of pronounced differences in the capabilities, rights, and obligations of states."[8] Walker views the nuclear order as a normative order, a fruit of the Cold War period, based on deterrence ("a managed system of military engagement with nuclear technology") by a recognized group of nuclear-weapon states (NWSs) and abstinence ("a managed system of military abstinence from, and civilian engagement with, nuclear technology") by a group of non-nuclear-weapon states (NNWS).[9] Both groups would be connected by a set of "norms, rules [and] reciprocal obligations, expressed through and not only through the Nuclear Non-Proliferation Treaty (NPT)." The deterrence system also includes mechanisms of communication for avoiding nuclear crises and arms control treaties for limiting the nuclear arsenals. The system of abstinence comprises nuclear umbrellas over the US allies and, during the Cold War, USSR allies. The NWSs ensured that NNWS parties of the NPT would not be attacked or coerced with atomic weapons. Moreover, they committed to ending the nuclear arms race with the ultimate goal of nuclear disarmament.[10] The connecting instrumental and normative tissue for Walker gives the "nuclear order a fragile legitimacy and prevents it from becoming a straightforwardly unjust order."[11]

The nuclear order as defined by Walker was not accepted by the whole international community. As noted by Hedley Bull in the aftermath of the 1974 Indian nuclear test, emerging and developing countries could contest a discriminatory order that had been imposed by the superpowers.[12] In recent years, the availability of primary sources around the world and growing threats to nuclear stability prompted a historiographical effort to track down how different countries viewed the global nuclear order—whether they favored it, objected to it, or eventually accepted it.[13]

The works of Francis Gavin and Shane Maddock are important examples of recent historical analyses of the US effort to promote an order in line with Washington's interests.[14] While other studies shed light on how the Soviet Union and the United Kingdom also sponsored the establishment of the order, it appears important to discuss the cases of countries that still oppose the acceptance of nuclear nonproliferation and disarmament.[15] India, Israel, and Pakistan, three NWSs outside the NPT, have their own view of the nuclear order. All three countries have regional security reasons for keeping their nuclear arsenals. Avner Cohen has demonstrated how Tel Aviv developed a nuclear arsenal but has maintained an opaque attitude toward nuclear nonproliferation.[16] Rabia Akhtar has discussed how Pakistan opposed and had the possibility to defy the NPT, also thanks to the US permissive policy toward an ally.[17] The challenging attitude toward the nuclear order certainly characterized India. Itty Abraham, George Perkovich, and, more recently, Jayita Sarkar, Harsh Pant, and Yogesh Joshi demonstrated how New Delhi contested an unfair system imposed by the superpowers that divided the world into the haves and the have-nots.[18] It is interesting that India first eroded it, with the 1974 test and above all the 1998 one, and later attempted to accommodate the nuclear order to its interests. India's victory appeared clear with the recognition of a nuclear-weapon-country status outside the NPT. It was the case of the Indian-US nuclear deal, the special agreement with the Nuclear Suppliers Group, and New Delhi's acceptance of the IAEA Additional Protocol.

Within the historiography on nuclear nonproliferation a third category comprises countries that shifted from hesitation about or opposition to the regime to adhesion to it. Italy, the Federal Republic of Germany, and Japan were among the countries that signed the NPT immediately but hesitated to ratify it.[19] With an advanced nuclear industry, those countries manifested during and after the negotiations of the NPT their reasons for not giving up the *nuclear option* for security and prestige reasons.[20] A further US commitment to the defense of those allies and direct pressures brought Rome, Bonn, and Tokyo to accept the treaty.

A peculiar case of transition from opposition to adhesion is that of China. In a recent in-depth analysis, Nicola Horsburgh discussed how Beijing first rejected the nonproliferation and arms-control regimes. From the mid-1980s, China embraced and, after its NPT adhesion in 1992, committed to the consolidation of the global nuclear order.[21]

While China and France are NWSs that lately acceded to the NPT, other countries, such as South Africa, Argentina, and Brazil, joined the regime after renouncing their nuclear bombs or the right to develop atomic devices after the end of the Cold War.[22] Anna-Mart van Wyk and Jo-Ansie van Wyk had described, on the basis of primary sources, how Pretoria long opposed the NPT, was an active member of the AIEA, and attempted to circumvent the norms of nuclear proliferation during the apartheid years (when it developed six and a half nuclear devices).[23] Similarly, but before the end of the Cold War, Sweden opted for nuclear reversal. As Thomas Jonter notes, after Sweden reached a state of nuclear latency at the end of the 1960s, the government in Stockholm renounced the atomic bomb, and Sweden was one of the first countries to accede to the NPT.[24]

It appears important to consider the existence of the so-called nuclear-threshold states among the groups of countries that got on board immediately or after a protracted opposition to the NPT. Japan, Brazil, and Germany, for example, "chose nuclear restraint despite having nuclear capabilities."[25] Those countries, as noted by Maria Rost Rublee, had the opportunity not only to promote nuclear disarmament (e.g., Japan's historical call for global nuclear disarmament and Brazil's recent sponsorship of the Treaty on the Prohibition of

Nuclear Weapons, or TPNW) but also to challenge it, given the ownership of sensitive nuclear technologies.[26] Those countries are also defined as nuclear latent since they have technological, scientific, material, and other capabilities to develop nuclear weapons but are not fully weaponized.[27]

Among the members of the NPT, there were some countries that were suspected of having nuclear ambitions. These included Libya, Iraq, and Iran. While Tripoli abandoned its secret nuclear projects through negotiations, Iraq cheated the NPT until the 1991 Gulf War. Both countries demonstrated the weaknesses of the nuclear order in the face of the threat posed by nuclear-proliferation networks and the flaws of the safeguards system, which has been reformed since the 1950s.[28]

Tehran was a different case. At the center of the current international debate over nuclear proliferation for undeclared facilities for enriching uranium, it was suspected to have nuclear ambitions as early as the mid-1970s, before the fall of the shah. While Iran was the target of restrictive US nuclear policies, it also became one of the most vocal opponents of unfair nonproliferation measures that can curtail peaceful atomic projects in the developing world. As Farzan Sabet recently noted, Tehran attempted to adopt a strategy to coalesce the countries contesting the US nonproliferation measures and vindicating fairer access to nuclear technologies.[29]

The literature mentioned above appears essential for understanding Brazil's evolving approach to the nuclear order in the last seventy-five years.

The Nuclear Program in the Context of Brazil's Contemporary and Diplomatic History

This book deals with a period of profound socioeconomic, political, and diplomatic transformation in Brazil. The year 1945 coincided with the conclusion of the Second World War and the fifteen-year rule of Getulio Vargas, opening a short phase of democratization that lasted until 1964.[30] The Vargas era, writes Rubens Ricupero, created the bases of contemporary Brazil.[31] Industrialization, urbanization, centralization, and state modernization, profoundly influenced by the modification of the international system and preponderant role of the United States in Latin American affairs, marked the authoritarian rule of Vargas. Coups or military interventions constantly threatened the democratic governments of General Eurico Dutra (1945–51), Getulio Vargas (1951–54), João Café Filho (1954–55), Juscelino Kubitschek (1956–60), Jânio Quadros (1961), and João Goulart (1961–64). However, the turbulent experiences of Presidents Quadros, who unexpectedly resigned in August 1961, and João Goulart, who eventually acquired full executive powers in 1963 after a short parliamentary regime, culminated in a military coup that inaugurated a twenty-one-year civilian-military regime.[32] Until 1961, the Brazilian government strictly aligned politically with the United States, even though Brazil has never had a formal military alliance with Washington. The Quadros administration radically modified the Brazilian diplomatic tradition. The "Independent Foreign Policy," as the foreign actions of Presidents Quadros and Goulart were labeled, opened the country to new relations exceeding the ideological limits of the relationship with the United States, Western Europe, and Latin American neighbors. Following the activism of other Third World leaders, Brazil's presidents and foreign ministers attempted to expand the country's diplomatic ties to African, Asian, and socialist countries, focusing on themes such as development, decolonization, and disarmament. A poor economic performance (high inflation rates characterized Brazil until 1994), the perception of a possible radicalization of the leftist president Goulart, and social unrest led the conservative and military elites to promote a military coup on 31 March 1964.

The Brazilian military regime of 1964–85, moving between anticommunism and nationalism, followed a nonlinear path in both its domestic and its foreign policy.[33] The first ten years were characterized by repression, which peaked with the Institutional Act No. 5, which suspended habeas corpus. From the moderate general Humberto de Alencar Castello Branco (1964–67) the regime passed to the direction of hard-liners, such as General Arthur da Costa e Silva (1967–69), a military junta, and Emílio Garrastazu Médici (1969–74).[34] The following ten years, with the administrations of Generals Ernesto Geisel (1974–79) and João Batista Figueiredo (1979–85), were a "slow, gradual, and safe distention" toward a re-democratization negotiated by the military.[35] Economically, the initial reforms that characterized the military regime did not eliminate high inflation rates but resulted, even if with deeply unequal income distribution, in the so-called Brazilian economic miracle. In a few years, Brazil boomed, with a growth rate of 11 percent in the years 1969 to 1973, and became the world's ninth largest economy. The 1970s oil shocks and the global economic recession led to an inflationary and debt crisis in Brazil in the 1980s.[36] The foreign policy agenda of the military regime was not monolithic. While in the years of Castello Branco Brazil was strictly aligned with the United States, starting from the time of Costa e Silva Brazil's diplomacy was more autonomous. The country gradually expanded its relations to the Third World, joining with other developing nations in calling for an equal distribution of power in the international system (as was the case in both the nuclear and trade realms). Brazil, which continued its firm stand in the regional cold war (it supported coups in Bolivia, Uruguay, and Chile), played as an "emerging power" with a "pragmatic, ecumenic and responsible" foreign policy, especially in the years of Geisel and Figueiredo.[37] It broadened its collaboration with Western countries (e.g., the nuclear partnership with West Germany) and oil producers (Brazil established preferential relations with Arab countries, which was detrimental to its relationship with Israel). The country also strengthened its ties with communist nations (Brazil was the first to recognize the Marxist government of Angola and engaged in a fruitful cooperation with Beijing). While Brasília-Washington relations deteriorated (because of the rising criticism over human rights abuses, the nuclear program, and colliding interests in the commercial field), the country in the late 1970s transformed its relationship with Argentina from a suspected rivalry to collaboration, above all after resolving a dispute over the rich hydroelectric potential on the trilateral Brazilian-Argentine-Paraguayan border.

Brazil's slow and controlled democratization peaked in 1984 with the indirect election by a congress, still controlled by the military, of Tancredo Neves, one of the political leaders opposing the military government, as the new president of the country. However, Neves's sudden illness and death occurred before he could be inaugurated and take power. José Sarney, his presidential running mate, formerly affiliated to the party close to the military regime, ruled the country until 1990. A Constituent Assembly in 1988 set the rules for the new democratic course. While Sarney's presidency coexisted with the powerful presence of the military in the cabinet, his successor would be free from similar constraints, thanks to a direct popular election. With full powers, Fernando Collor de Melo, a young politician whose career was on a fast track, adopted a liberal plan for significantly reforming the Brazilian state. However, a political scandal led to his impeachment in 1992. Collor was replaced by his vice president, the experienced politician Itamar Franco, who conducted the country through a rigid plan (the Plano Real) for economic recovery and reducing the historical inflation. In 1995, one of the architects of the Plano Real, Fernando Henrique Cardoso (a renowned Brazilian intellectual and leader of the Party for Brazilian Social Democracy), became president. Cardoso's government (1995–2002) would lead the country toward economic stabilization and a consolidation of democracy (despite the need for broad coalitions to gain support from the National Congress). The consolidation guaranteed a smooth transition from Cardoso to Luiz Inácio Lula da Silva, the charismatic leader of the center-left Workers' Party (Partido dos Trabalhadores, or PT), in charge until 2011. During da Silva's tenure, while the country experienced significant social reforms to adjust the high inequality rates, the government kept its goal of a stable domestic economy. A commodities boom led Lula da Silva in the second term to adopt an expansive public economic policy for accelerating growth. While the country experienced a positive economic trend until 2012, Lula's successor, Dilma Rousseff, faced the first signals of a political and economic crisis that after her first mandate (2011–15) led to her impeachment in 2016. She was replaced by her vice president, Michel Temer, who from 2016 to 2019 ruled a country that was profoundly polarized and marked by corruption.

In the democratic years, Brazil's foreign policy was characterized by the quest for autonomy between old and new paradigms and, above all, in the transition to a new international system after the end of the Cold War. The national diplomacy continued to serve the interests of the country but also to follow the political orientation of the government. On the one hand, constant negotiations to resolve the debt crisis characterized the 1980s. On the other hand, Brazil defended its national development from external interference by refusing to accept unfair limitations (e.g., through the law for preserving the national microcomputer sector). From the presidency of Collor through the Cardoso years, Brazil adapted to the new world order and, in a limited way, the liberal recipes promoted by Washington. In this period, Brazil prioritized its relationship with Argentina, establishing the bases for commercial (and nuclear) integration between the two Southern Cone countries. The Mercado Comum do Sul, or Mercosul (Southern Common Market), and the Agência Brasileiro-Argentina de Contabilidade e Controle de Materiais Nucleares, or ABACC (Brazilian-Argentine Agency for Accounting and Control of Nuclear Materials), could be expanded to include the other countries in South America, a continent led by democratic Brazil. While the relationship between Brazil and Argentina strengthened, despite several troubles, Brazil continued to create partnerships with other countries in the Global South. From the early years of the twenty-first century, the nation was recognized as one of the leading emerging countries of the international system. In 2010 the BRICS group (composed of Brazil, Russia, India, China, and South Africa) formed. Brazil adopted an expansive foreign policy, also thanks to the personal initiatives of Presidents Cardoso and Lula da Silva. While in the period 2008–10 Brazil's activism seemed to coincide with its becoming a global player, its role declined as a consequence of the recession during the years of Rousseff and Temer.

Brazil and the Nuclear Order

As previously seen, the literature on the global nuclear order addresses only in passing the importance of emerging countries. Brazil is a case in point. Only a few published works specifically address Brasília's nuclear ambitions, and these works often rely exclusively on journalistic sources to explain Brazil's attitude toward the global nuclear order.[38] There is now an opportunity to carefully examine the history and politics of Brazil's nuclear ambitions and to put them in the global context. Most of the primary sources are now available. Over the past few years I have built up a collection of oral history interviews pertaining to the issue. Furthermore, documents in the United States, Argentina, France, Great Britain, Germany, and South Africa can now be consulted. This allows for a profound reexamination of the main arguments developed over the past decades about the critical role Brazil had in the development of the contemporary global nuclear order.

Research about Brazil's nuclear program has pointed out three possible explanations for the evolution of its nuclear ambitions. The first has to do with how economic considerations pushed Brazil toward an autonomous atomic program. This explanation emphasizes the importance of energy provision for a booming economy that was suffering after the oil crisis because of its strong dependence on the Arab suppliers and rising international prices. Especially from the 1970s onward, Brazilian leaders believed their country had massive potential as a producer of minerals (mostly thorium and natural uranium). The creation of a civilian nuclear industry was seen as part of a plan for providing Brazil with high-technology industry and making the country autonomous from an energy point of view.[39]

The second possible explanation has to do with the growing military ambitions of Brazil, especially during the military regime. During the period from 1979 to 1990 Brazil developed a secret and unsafeguarded nuclear program in order to master the nuclear fuel cycle. Given the secrecy involved, the sensitive technology Brazil developed, and the strong nationalist and militaristic rhetoric that permeated this project, many authors, Leonard Spector for example, believed that Brazil had the ultimate goal of developing nuclear weapons.[40] In principle, that explanation made some sense. Several analysts thought that Brazil's competition with its long-standing regional rival, Argentina, for leadership in South America would lead to the development of nuclear military capabilities by both countries.[41]

The third argument has it that Brazil's nuclear program was connected to Brasília's quest for international status. It was always evident to those in positions of power in Brasília that having nuclear capabilities could allow Brazil to finally join the select nuclear club, the permanent members of the UN Security Council. There is, in fact, much evidence that the quest for autonomy entailed the development of autonomous atomic capabilities.

My research addresses two specific problems with these arguments. First, even though one can find in the available primary sources elements that would support any of these explanations, to date no study has attempted to connect these factors and offer a systematic historical account of the development of Brazil's nuclear ambitions. Second, much of the existing literature only examines in passing the importance of international factors to explain Brazil's role in the nuclear order. A number of systemic forces have pushed for and against indigenous plans for nuclear development. Take, for instance, the US Atoms for Peace program, the rise of a global nuclear-materials industry in the Global North, the rise and ultimate collapse of the Brazil-Germany nuclear deal of 1975, the growing constraints imposed on Brazil by Washington, mainly from the time of the Carter administration onward, or even the increasingly complex relations with Buenos Aires that pushed Brazil more and more toward a bilateral cooperation agreement, especially after the Argentine democratic transition of 1983.[42]

Methodology and Sources

This book draws on and sticks very close to primary sources. Records on nuclear Brazil are now available in specialized libraries around the world. I have spent the last twelve years collecting documents from several countries: Argentina, Brazil, France, Italy, South Africa, the United Kingdom, Germany, and the United States.

In Brazil, the Arquivo Nacional (National Archive) released a great deal of documentation from the National Security Council, which was the core of the Brazilian decision-making process until 1988. In Rio de Janeiro and Brasília, thanks also to recent national legislation over the declassification of public documents, the Brazilian Foreign Ministry allowed me to consult Brazilian confidential and secret diplomatic records until 2003. Despite several attempts, I have not been able to consult the archives of Brazil's air force regarding nuclear activities. In Rio de Janeiro, I researched the documentation present at the Centro de Pesquisa e Documentação da História Contemporânea do Brasil of the Fundação Getulio Vargas (FGV/CPDOC), a repository of the personal archives of many Brazilian presidents, foreign ministers, and diplomats. I have analyzed the personal records of Ernesto Geisel (president, 1974–79); Antônio Francisco Azeredo da Silveira (diplomat and foreign minister, 1974–79); Ramiro Saraiva Guerreiro (diplomat and foreign minister, 1979–85); Luiz Felipe Lampreia (diplomat and foreign minister, 1995–2001); Paulo Nogueira Batista (diplomat and chairman of Nuclebrás, 1974–82); and Rubens Barbosa (diplomat). These collections contain not only diplomatic records but also key documents from presidential administrations, the National Security Council, the National Nuclear Energy Commission, and various ministries.

Materials in the personal archive of Álvaro Alberto da Mota e Silva (the father of the Brazilian nuclear program) at the University of São Paulo helped me to understand crucial aspects of the beginning of Brazil's nuclear projects.

Many diplomats, scientists, and politicians have shared memories of their activities in the nuclear field. This book relies on the results of an enormous task undertaken by the Getulio Vargas Foundation from 2009 to 2012 of collecting and analyzing interviews with dozens of protagonists of Brazil's nuclear history.[43] For granting me personal interviews, I am particularly indebted to Roberto Abdenur, Marcos Castrioto de Azambuja, Fernando Henrique Cardoso, Fernando Collor de Melo, Sérgio de Queiroz Duarte, the late Paul Findley, Ana Maria Gordon, the late Maurício Grinberg, Jan Kalicki, Myron Kratzer, the late Luis Felipe Lampreia, Melvyn Levitsky, Marco Marzo, Rogério Cezar de Cerqueira Leite, the late Robert Pastor, Rubens Ricupero, the late Charles W. Robinson, Cláudio Rodrigues, José Luiz Santana Carvalho, José Viegas Filho, and Laercio Vinhas. Oral history interviews were crucial for comprehending the evolution of Brazilian nuclear activities in the international context.

Outline

Chapter 1 focuses on Brazil's stance during the first decade of the nuclear age (1945–55). The chapter begins with a discussion of Brazil's role as a provider of nuclear minerals to the United States, followed by a discussion of Brazil's position in the UN Atomic Energy Commission from 1946 to 1948, oscillating between preserving the sovereignty of its mineral resources and accepting US proposals. The chapter then sheds light on the origins of the Brazilian nuclear program, focusing on the creation of a nuclear sector and on Álvaro Alberto. This section also discusses the nature of Brazil's nuclear ambitions, emphasizing how international and domestic factors frustrated the first Brazilian attempts to develop nuclear technologies either independently or in collaboration with Western European countries, such as France and West Germany. The chapter closes with the end of the first Brazilian atomic project and a nuclear deal with the United States in the context of the US Atoms for Peace program.

Chapter 2 deals with the redefinition of Brazil's nuclear program from 1956, when CNEN was established, to 1964, when a military coup overthrew the democratic regime. First I discuss the Brazilian nuclear policy of the period, when the country planned to acquire nuclear power plants and autonomously assembled its first research reactor. Then I describe Brazil's position in the negotiations over the IAEA statute and address the debate on why Brazil was chosen as a member of the Eighteen-Nation Disarmament Committee (ENDC) and what its position was in that forum. I note how Brazil promoted nuclear-weapon-free zones, supported complete nuclear disarmament, and attempted to play a key role in order to resolve the Cuban Missile Crisis. I also discuss how the scientific community and the military criticized the Brazilian diplomatic position and demanded the right to develop nuclear energy for military uses.

The third chapter exposes the reasons for Brazil's opposition to the NPT and details Brazilian nuclear policy until 1973. It discusses how the military regime established a nuclear program that aimed at mastering the nuclear fuel cycle with the possibility of building an atomic device in the future. It describes how Brazil reflected this position in the ongoing negotiations in Mexico City and Geneva, defending its right to develop peaceful nuclear explosives. Despite a critical position toward the NPT, Brazil decided to cooperate with the United States, acquiring one nuclear power plant and ensuring the supply of nuclear fuel while forfeiting the technology necessary for developing an indigenous nuclear program. The chapter also considers other attempts at international nuclear collaboration.

Chapter 4 discusses the Brazilian decision to sign a major deal with West Germany in 1975 to acquire eight nuclear power plants and technology that would allow Brazil to master the complete nuclear fuel cycle. I show that Brazil decided to cooperate with Bonn after the new US nuclear policy limiting the export of sensitive technologies and materials to countries opposing the NPT, such as Brazil, was put in place. On Brazil's reaction to the US policy of limiting Brazilian nuclear ambitions, I discuss how at the end of the Ford administration Brazil and the United States reached a secret agreement to find a mutually satisfactory solution. I also detail Brazil's reaction to the hostile Carter administration's nuclear nonproliferation policy. Finally I discuss how Brazil faced the first signs of the crisis in the cooperation with Bonn and conducted the relationship with Argentina, which was supposedly engaged in a nuclear rivalry with Brasília.

Chapter 5 explains why Brazil decided to establish an autonomous civilian-military nuclear program in response to international limitations. This program allowed Brazil to reach uranium enrichment capability. Brasília, moreover, established an atomic partnership with Argentina, ending rumors about a possible nuclear weapons race with its neighbor. With the explicit goal of overcoming the limitations imposed by the nonproliferation regime, Brazil collaborated with other governments, such as the People's Republic of China, in opposing it. The chapter also notes how the Brazilian government discarded the proposal that some sectors of the armed forces put forth to test a nuclear device.

The sixth chapter shows how Brazil's re-democratization affected the national nuclear program, noting that secret plans continued until the eventual announcement of uranium enrichment mastery in 1987. In order to quiet national and international fears, the 1988 Constituent Assembly required that all nuclear activities should be in pursuit of exclusively peaceful goals. We observe how Brazil and Argentina made further progress toward mutual trust in the nuclear realm, not least because of close collaboration between politicians, scientists, and diplomats.

Chapter 7 deals with the first Brazilian steps toward embracing international nuclear nonproliferation norms. It opens with President Collor de Mello's decision to end Brazil's autonomous nuclear program and its international repercussions, followed by the peak in the collaboration between Argentina and Brazil in 1991, when the two countries gave up their right to develop nuclear devices and created a bilateral system of inspections and reciprocal accounting of their nuclear activities. Meanwhile, Argentina and Brazil implicitly accepted important nonproliferation norms, fully acceding to the Latin American nuclear-weapon-free zone and accepting IAEA safeguards, which also covered military facilities. The chapter also discusses how international pressures led Brazil to that decision.

The eighth chapter deals with Brazil's decision to sign and ratify the NPT. I discuss why the Brazilian government gradually shifted toward supporting the Nuclear Suppliers Group, the Comprehensive Test Ban Treaty, and finally the NPT. I show what led the government to make these decisions and how the domestic opposition reacted to them. Overall, the chapter focuses on Brazil's new role in the nonproliferation regime. In the last section I note that by the late 1990s Brazil had decided to resume its nuclear program, with the decision to build a commercial-scale uranium enrichment plant.

Chapter 9 deals with Brazil's stance toward the nonproliferation regime from the beginning of Lula da Silva's presidency in 2003 to the conclusion of the Michel Temer administration in 2018. It discusses how Brazil continues to refuse to accept the IAEA Additional Protocol, which could impose further controls on its facilities for enriching uranium. Although in June 2011 the Nuclear Suppliers Group temporarily accepted the ABACC system pending the ultimate implementation of the Additional Protocol, several countries (including the United States) raised doubts about Brazil's nuclear ambitions, which now include the production of a nuclear submarine, to be completed shortly. This chapter also examines Brazil's activism in the global nuclear order, specifically regarding the 2010 Brazilian-Turkish attempt to propose a solution to the Iranian nuclear crisis and the promotion of the Treaty on the Prohibition of Nuclear Weapons.

TIMELINE OF BRAZIL'S NUCLEAR HISTORY

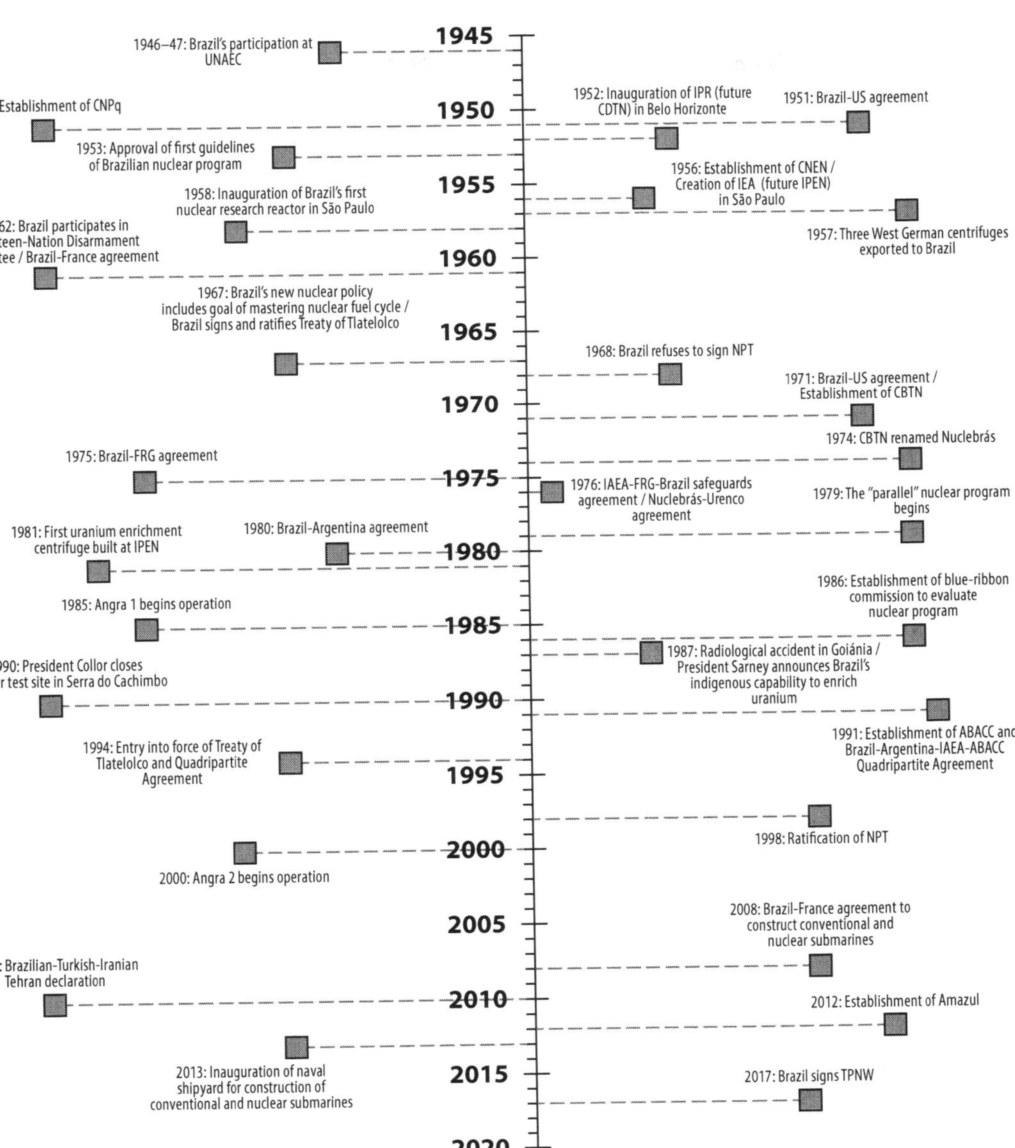

CHAPTER ONE

Origins of Brazil's Nuclear Ambitions, 1946–1955

On 15 August 1946, about one year after the nuclear bombings of Hiroshima and Nagasaki, Alfred Hitchcock released *Notorious*. Conceived in 1944 just months before the explosions in New Mexico and Japan, it was one of the first "nuclear movies" ever made. Brazil is at the center of the plot, featuring as the country where a group of former Nazi officers are accumulating uranium. At the same time, the US government organizes a successful intelligence action to infiltrate the organization. When he was writing the script of *Notorious*, Hitchcock was not completely aware of the high importance of uranium, but suddenly the explosion of a nuclear bomb confirmed his ideas.[1] Above all, the British director did not know that Brazil was one of the leading suppliers of nuclear minerals for the US atomic program and that in the years to come German scientists would indeed be involved in the first project to provide Brazil with a nuclear program.

Notorious premiered in New York, where several delegations to the recently established United Nations were discussing the future of the atom. One of the primary aims of the new international organization was to debate possible international forms of control and development of atomic energy for both peaceful and military purposes. For this reason, the very first resolution of the UN General Assembly (UNGA) in 1946 created the UN Atomic Energy Commission (UNAEC), a body reporting to the UN Security Council (UNSC).[2] Between 1946 and 1949, in the period marked by the beginning of the Cold War, the UNAEC unsuccessfully devoted itself to creating international rules for the use and control of the atom. For two years, during the crucial period of discussions, Brazil actively participated in the forum as a temporary member of the UNSC. It was an important moment not only for the future of nuclear energy in the world but also for the future of the Latin American country.

At the dawn of the atomic age in 1945, certain countries of the so-called Global South had powerful ambitions to master nuclear energy for both peaceful and military ends. Countries like South Africa, India, and Brazil had hitherto been the leading suppliers of nuclear minerals. They began to focus their efforts on nuclear development to achieve energy autonomy.[3] However, as these countries set out to obtain the knowledge, machinery, and technology required to achieve their goal, they faced stiff opposition from the monopolist of atomic secrets. From 1946 to 1951, when the US Atomic Energy Act (the McMahon Act) was amended for the first time, the US government effectively prohibited substantive cooperation with these aspiring nuclear producers in the atomic field.[4] In this context, in 1951 Brazil adopted an explicit nuclear policy seeking to collaborate with countries that both possessed the requisite nuclear knowledge and technologies and were interested in Brazil's rich deposits of atomic minerals, namely, the United States, France, West Germany, Italy, and Norway.

This chapter explains why Brazil participated in the first talks on the international control of atoms and started an atomic program in 1951. Moreover, it sheds light on the reasoning behind its cooperation with international partners, especially Washington, until the mid-1950s. In the period covered in this chapter, Brazil passed through a democratization process that guaranteed a transition from the authoritarian regime of Getulio Vargas (1930–45). Even if Brazil's economy continued to rely on the export of commodities (mainly coffee), the country was transitioning to industrialization, also relying on US assistance. Washington, which imposed its definitive hegemony on Latin America during the Second World War, was the main partner in Brazil's foreign policy. From 1945 to 1960, with few exceptions connected above all to domestic rhetoric, Brazil aligned itself with the United States. Even if several requests of assistance to support Brazil's modernization went unanswered, Brazil followed Cold War thinking that led the government to outlaw the Brazilian Communist Party, to sever its relationship with Moscow (two years after its establishment in 1945), and not to recognize Communist China.[5] The topic of atomic energy became a source of friction in Brazil's relationship with the United States and between nationalists and Americanists among Brazil's scientific, economic, military, and political elites.

Supplying Nuclear Minerals and Participating in the UNAEC (1945–1947)

Brazil's involvement in projects to develop nuclear technology began in July 1945, when it was a supplier of monazite sands—from which thorium and consequently plutonium are obtained—to the Manhattan Project. After more than five months of intense negotiations, the cooperation had been made possible thanks to a secret agreement signed by the US secretary of state, Edward Stettinius, and the Brazilian president, Getulio Vargas.[6] The Brazilian government committed to selling the strategic mineral for three years, with a possible extension to ten years. Beginning in 1940, Brazil provided the United States free access to its mineral reserves and to geological prospecting that led to the discovery of possible reserves of oil and nuclear minerals, such as thorium and uranium.[7] The supply of materials would continue in the context of the war alliance and the inter-American solidarity, as it was established in early 1945 at the Chapultepec Conference in Mexico. At the beginning of the atomic age, Brazil, along with India, was considered a crucial provider of nuclear minerals, especially monazite sands, to the United States.[8]

Even if the flow of atomic minerals to the United States would continue, the Brazilian government instituted a new policy of "specific compensations." No longer content to be a mere supplier of raw materials for other countries' nuclear development, Brazil required that each shipment of strategic minerals be reciprocated with a transfer of technology, training of scientists, geological prospecting, and scientific equipment that would help to develop the country's nuclear sector.

The policy of specific compensations was just one example of the Brazilian government's desire to acquire the same nuclear technologies and knowledge reserved for the great powers. The then Brazilian navy captain Álvaro Alberto, an explosives expert and a pioneer of nuclear energy in Brazil, was a leading advocate of this goal. Alberto viewed uranium mining and the manufacture of fuel supplies for nuclear reactors as the first steps. Alberto represented Brazil on the UNAEC in 1946 and 1947 and was its chair for two meetings. As early as 1946 in this forum, he attempted to preserve Brazilian sovereignty over its nuclear materials.

The Brazilian foreign minister, João Neves da Fontoura, appointed Alberto, who had been chairman of the Brazilian Academy of Sciences (Academia Brasileira de Ciências), to the UNAEC because of his competence in the nuclear field. As a professor of chemistry and physics at the Brazilian Navy School in the early 1940s, he had included nuclear physics in the curriculum. In the 1920s and 1930s he had promoted conferences and workshops on the subject, with the participation of leading scientists, such as Albert Einstein, Marie Curie, and Enrico Fermi.[9] Itamaraty, the Brazilian Foreign Ministry, instructed Alberto and his delegation to align with the United States and "support firmly" the plan that the US representative Bernard Baruch submitted on the occasion of the first UNAEC meeting. The proposal, which relied on the Report on the International Control of Atomic Energy, known as the Acheson-Lilienthal Report, which was written by a committee chaired by Dean Acheson and David Lilienthal, called for the ownership of all sensitive nuclear materials and facilities by an International Atomic Energy Development Agency (IADA), which would both promote the peaceful international use of atomic energy and control all less sensitive nuclear research activities. According to the plan, the United States would give up and destroy its nuclear arsenal after the establishment of the agency.[10] The Soviet Union, which was secretly developing its own weapons, objected to the plan, and its representative, Andrei Gromyko, counterproposed the destruction of all existing nuclear bombs as a condition for imposing any international control over atomic activities. The Soviets, moreover, criticized the American plan as an apparent interference in national sovereignty.[11]

Even though Alberto favored the Baruch Plan, both because of his own political beliefs and because of the instructions he received, he did not accept one of the principles of the US proposal: the establishment of international control over the world's nuclear minerals. The Brazilian delegate reacted by introducing a different formula. On 27 December 1946, in the UNAEC Second Committee, Alberto "won acceptance for an amendment stating specifically that international ownership of mines and ores still in the ground was not mandatory."[12]

Even though Brazil supported all the other aspects of the US proposal and opposed the Soviet Union's counterplan, Washington nevertheless perceived Alberto's position as dangerous for American nuclear policy and the establishment of international control over the use of atomic energy. The US concern was especially evident in August 1947, when a new amendment to the treaty establishing the IADA proposed by Alberto stated "that no restrictions shall be imposed on the nations that hold raw materials relative to the use of material for peaceful ends."[13]

Furthermore, Alberto proposed that while the IADA would be the exclusive purchaser of nuclear raw materials, the supplier should be compensated either with an adequate price or with "specific compensations." As noted earlier, the Brazilian delegate was proposing that the provider of nuclear minerals would receive in return nuclear technologies or nuclear fuel from the IADA, which was supposed to have a monopoly in that field after the international treaty took effect. The negotiation of either a fair price or specific compensation would become a matter of concern in future US-Brazilian relations. At that moment Brazil was the only supplier to claim such a right. The United Kingdom, with the Indian mines still under its temporary control prior to New Delhi's independence, and

Álvaro Alberto chairing a session of the United Nations Atomic Energy Commission, New York, 4 August 1947 (Álvaro Alberto personal archive, AA/foto/043 ONU, Centro Interunidade de História da Ciência, Universidade de São Paulo)

Belgium, which controlled Katanga, did not share the Brazilian position. Even if the increasing tension between the United States and the Soviet Union opened a little room for successful negotiations at the UNAEC, the United States considered the Brazilian reservation dangerous: "If the plan for international control of atomic energy put forward by the majority of the UNAEC delegations were made subject to such, a limitation would become meaningless."[14]

Consequently, Alberto's proposal could undermine international efforts to curb possible "dangerous activities involved in the production of atomic energy," including the mining, distribution, and stockpiling of raw materials. Introducing one of the founding principles of future nuclear nonproliferation policies, the US under secretary of state, Robert A. Lovett, informed Secretary of State George Marshall, then in Rio de Janeiro to negotiate the Inter-American Treaty of Reciprocal Assistance, about the Brazilians' attitude at the talks in New York. Lovett wrote Marshall that the Brazilian delegation must be aware [that] the process[es] for the production of atomic energy for weapon use and peaceful use are throughout most of their courses identical and inseparable. . . . The Brazilian reservation would appear to leave a large loophole in control schemes which would invite evasions and diversions. The country "holding" raw materials would apparently have only to profess peaceful intentions to safeguard itself from strict international control and inspection. The Brazilians have only to ask themselves if they would be prepared to credit such professions if made by any power. Moreover, no security would exist if it were left to each nation to make its decision as to the amount of raw material to be declared or placed under the control of the international agency.[15]

Writing at a moment when Cold War tensions were rising, Lovett concluded that the "Brazil reservation would cloud the record and permit the Soviets, at a crucial state in these deliberations, to point to such departures as lack of confidence in the proposals developed by majority."[16] Alberto's proposal, which gained the full support of the Brazilian National Security Council (Conselho de Segurança Nacional, or CSN), could consequently threaten the solid front against the Soviet Union and the socialist countries existing within the UNAEC.[17] Lovett's telegram appeared to be useful. Immediately after the signing of the Rio Pact on 2 September 1947, President Truman discussed the issue with Brazil's President Dutra, who, familiar with the question, immediately pledged to "take the necessary action to see that Brazil complied with the Baruch proposals to which it had previously agreed."[18] As is evident from both the American and the Brazilian records, "because of the political aspect of the question" the Brazilian delegation immediately modified its position at the UNAEC. It withdrew any possible reservation, even if on the occasion of the 1948 UNGA it raised with South Africa and Costa Rica doubts over the effective transfer of international ownership to the IADA.[19]

In the same period, Alberto submitted a detailed plan for the possible use of atomic energy in Brazil, which also included the full nationalization of the atomic minerals to safeguard Brazil's economic future.[20] The Brazilian government, however, was secretly negotiating a renewal of the 1945 agreement to supply the United States with monazites. In October 1947, a few weeks after the Truman-Dutra talks, both the US State Department and the US Embassy in Rio de Janeiro pressured the Brazilian government to renew the deal and to stop the possible export of atomic minerals to other countries, such as France.[21] Brazil and the United States renewed the agreement in July 1948. The Brazilians, bowing to pressure, decided not to modify the 1945 text and to refrain from exporting fissionable material to other countries. The Brazilian foreign minister, Raul Fernandes, agreed with Marshall that for security reasons Brazil should not ship atomic minerals outside the Western Hemisphere.[22]

This was another setback for Alberto's policy of specific compensations. The renewal of US-Brazilian cooperation was not in line with the new Brazilian constitution of 1946, which prohibited secret agreements, and its approval would be difficult because of the opposition of broad sectors of the Brazilian Congress that wanted to preserve national resources.[23] At the end of March 1950, President Dutra, confirming his pro-American attitude, opposed new congressional discussions about the nationalization of fissionable materials.[24] As we will see in the next section, new legislation over the issue was approved in 1951, after the democratic election of Getulio Vargas as president of Brazil.

While Alberto failed in his attempt to preserve Brazilian national resources, he was successful in securing Brazil's permanent seat on the future IADA. British and American representatives guaranteed their full support for recognizing Brazil's right to a permanent seat because of its status as a major supplier of atomic minerals.[25] The UNAEC negotiations led nowhere—the commission never met after 1949 and was disbanded by the UNGA in 1952—because the United States and the Soviet Union were engaged in a nuclear arms race. Alberto staked out Brazil's future position in the negotiations over the establishment of the International Atomic Energy Agency from 1955 to 1957. The recognition of Brazil's prominence in the nuclear field as a provider of nuclear raw materials would guarantee greater international prestige. It is important to note that in those years both Brazil and India, the world's main suppliers of monazite sands, were aware of their status. Thus, the members of the Brazilian government discussed, albeit without a concrete result, the establishment of a Rio de Janeiro–New Delhi cartel of providers that could create a monopoly in the supply of the mineral.[26]

Despite Alberto's failure to advance his plans for preserving Brazilian nuclear minerals, his action at the United Nations was recognized when he returned to Brazil. In 1949 President Dutra made Alberto a counter admiral, the highest rank for a retired navy officer in Brazil. Almirante (Admiral) Álvaro Alberto, as he was known by the Brazilian public, became the leading promoter of nuclear energy in Brazil, attracting the support of large nationalist political sectors but drawing sharp criticism from the United States and some parts of the Brazilian scientific and diplomatic community. From 1951 to 1955 Alberto led in the creation of the Brazilian atomic project.

The Origins of the Brazilian Nuclear Program

While still in New York, Alberto submitted the first proposal sketching a plan for Brazilian nuclear development to the CSN.[27] The immediate reaction, despite the renewal of the agreement with the United States, was the creation of the Commission of Studies and Control of Strategic Minerals (Comissão de Estudos e Fiscalização de Materiais Estratégicos). Through the participation of nuclear scientists, it would supervise the export also of nuclear minerals. Alberto launched his proposal in the midst of a moment of intense debate among Brazilian scientific and political elites over the future of science and nuclear energy in the country.

The science and technology sectors were expanding in Brazil. Prominent nuclear scientists of the time, for example, the Italian researchers Giuseppe Occhialini and Gleb Wataghin, as well as the young Brazilian physicists Marcelo Damy de Souza Santos, José Leite Lopes, and Cesar Lattes (the latter was, together with Occhialini, in the team that discovered the pi meson), participated in the creation of the Brazilian Department of Physics at the University of São Paulo, founded in 1934. The department, then directed by Damy, acquired from the United States a betatron and sent young researchers to study in North America. Moreover, in 1949 the Brazilian Center for Research in Physics (Centro Brasileiro de Pesquisas Físicas, or CBPF) was established in Rio de Janeiro under the direction of Lattes. Together with several Brazilian politicians, Alberto was working to establish a new centralized system in the country. It would integrate various institutions—in that moment above all military schools, the University of São Paulo, and the University of Brazil (Rio de Janeiro)—involved in the scientific and technological efforts. Like other large developing countries, Brazil sought to create active research centers that would propel the country to a more advanced stage of economic development.[28] Thus, the emergence of a nuclear sector should be understood as part of a wider program of rationalization of scientific research activities undertaken in Brazil at that time.

Discussions about the atomic project started in 1949. In April 1946 the foreign minister, Fontoura, appointed Alberto to chair a commission on atomic energy. He presented the first proposal for the creation of a national atomic energy commission (Comissão Nacional de Energia Atômica) to the Brazilian government headed by Eurico Gaspar Dutra (1945–51).[29] At the same time, a Dutch private company and the French research authorities offered Brazil to sell and produce nuclear power plants in the country.[30] However, the Dutra administration opted to include nuclear energy among the priorities of a national research council rather than to create a national atomic energy commission along the lines of the

Joaquim da Costa Ribeiro and Álvaro Alberto (*front, center and right*) along with others at Catete presidential palace in Rio de Janeiro showing President Getulio Vargas (*front left*) the radioactivity decay rate of minerals found by CNPq in Minas Gerais. (Álvaro Alberto personal archive, AA/foto/050 CNPq, Centro Interunidade de História da Ciência, Universidade de São Paulo)

US model. In April 1949, a commission composed of prominent scientists and chaired by Alberto introduced a bill to the national congress to create such a research council.

The congress passed the bill two years after its introduction, and on 15 January 1951, immediately before finishing his presidential term, Dutra signed it into law, thus establishing the National Research Council (Conselho Nacional de Pesquisa, or CNPq), with Alberto as its inaugural chairman.[31] Accordingly, one of CNPq's primary objectives was to coordinate the domestic development of nuclear energy and to supervise the export of nuclear minerals. The foundation of CNPq came at a critical moment for the Brazilian political system. Getulio Vargas, who had led an authoritarian regime from 1930 to 1945, was democratically elected as Brazil's new president and inaugurated on 31 January 1951. A fierce nationalist, Vargas was an active promoter of the role of the state in economic development. Alberto, who was also the leader of the National Defense League (Liga de Defesa Nacional), one of the main supporters of the Brazilian alliance with the

United States during the war, maintained an excellent personal relationship with Vargas. Since the CNPq chairman reported directly to the president, Alberto found much support for his energy initiatives, thus vaulting the Brazilian nuclear program forward from 1951 to 1955.

The First Nuclear Plan and the Quest for International Partners

The nuclear program began to take shape after Vargas approved the project in mid-1951. Alberto and his closest colleagues began by visiting the main civilian nuclear energy research centers in North America and Western Europe.[32] The purpose of these visits was to find an institutional model for Brazil's nascent nuclear program and to recruit international partners to help bring the effort to fruition. Alberto's tenure as Brazil's representative to the UNAEC had provided him with close working relationships with nuclear scientists worldwide—in Western, socialist, as well as Third World countries—with whom he maintained an extensive correspondence.

In seeking out partners, Alberto considered the United States first. Because it had the most advanced nuclear sector in the world and maintained strong diplomatic relations with Brazil, it appeared to be the best suited to training nuclear scientists and providing crucial technology and materials.[33] The moment was appropriate since in October 1951 the US Congress amended the US Atomic Energy Act, allowing the release of restricted information to other countries in exchange for tangible benefits.[34] Thus, as Brazil was one of the main providers of atomic minerals to the United States, it could easily obtain Washington's cooperation in the nuclear field. However, in an attempt to avoid exclusive dependence on the United States, the CNPq chairman decided to also collaborate with other countries, such as Canada, Norway, France, Italy, and the Federal Republic of Germany.[35] Eventually, it became apparent that Alberto's strategy was prescient. Despite the intense negotiations over trade in nuclear minerals and the supply of nuclear facilities that had been conducted with Washington from 1951 to 1954, the United States chose to limit its collaboration with Brazil to the training of a handful of Brazilian scientists in American universities and the sale of equipment and materials for Brazilian laboratories focusing on uranium research.[36]

The most fruitful collaboration between Washington and Rio de Janeiro was around the purchase of a synchrocyclotron, a particle accelerator that Alberto wanted to install in the new Brazilian nuclear complex to be built in Niteroi, the capital city of the then state of Rio de Janeiro. Emulating the American example, Alberto sought to transfer to Brazil a 72-inch, 25-ton cyclotron similar to the calutron installed at Oak Ridge, Tennessee, which was used in electromagnetic enrichment. It is unclear whether the Brazilian authorities harbored the intention of using such equipment for nonpeaceful ends. The United States, however, did not consider the cyclotron to be a sensitive dual-use technology but exclusively a research tool, so it allowed the construction and transfer of particle accelerators to Brazil. In 1951, Alberto was engaged in setting up a detailed nuclear plan. He decided to follow the suggestion of the Nobel laureate Isidor Isaac Rabi, a physicist based at Columbia University, who warmly recommended that the Brazilian government acquire the equipment.[37] As a consequence, Brazil started negotiations with the United States Atomic Energy Commission (USAEC) to purchase the machinery, haggling at the same time with Canada as well as with the Dutch company Phillips.[38] At the end of 1951, when it appeared clear that Brazil had a good chance of reaching a quick deal with Phillips, the US negotiators decided to ask the American company General Electric to accept the Brazilian cyclotron order. After cordial talks in Rio de Janeiro between the chairmen of USAEC and CNPq, Gordon Dean and Álvaro Alberto, on US-Brazilian cooperation, the US ambassador to Brazil, Herschel V. Johnson, observed that a US denial "would mean that Brazil's orientation in [the] atomic energy field would be diverted from the United States towards Europe and especially [the] Netherlands."[39] CNPq opted to deal with the United States since the Dutch company, fearful of a possible new military conflict on European soil, would not guarantee the cyclotron delivery or the money lost in the event of war.[40]

For financial reasons, CNPq decided to immediately acquire a 25-inch synchrocyclotron, which was eventually shipped to Brazil in 1955, while delaying the acquisition of a 72-inch cyclotron, to be built jointly by the University of Chicago and the Brazilian navy in the Rio de Janeiro shipyards.[41] Furthermore, the US government decided to transfer the blueprints for building the synchrocyclotron to Brazil. It was an outstanding success for Brazil since it represented the acquisition of a significant tool for beginning a research program potentially usable for military purposes. However, the US government could not provide Brazil with nuclear reactors or technologies for the production of fissile materials.

A more substantive outcome of Brazil's quest abroad was Alberto's meeting in the United States with Paul Harteck, a prominent West German scientist who happened to be Alberto's son's professor at the Rensselaer Polytechnic Institute in Troy, New York. Before immigrating to the United States in 1951, Harteck had served as the rector of Hamburg University, and he had been a prominent figure in the Nazi regime's nuclear program.[42] In the mid-1940s, Harteck and his team had developed a process for enriching uranium: the ultracentrifuge method for uranium isotopic separation. This technology, which the American scholars developing the Manhattan Project considered unfeasible, in fact ultimately succeeded in producing enriched uranium in German laboratories.[43] Harteck responded to Alberto's inquiry regarding the best option for Brazil's nuclear program by suggesting that Brazil might use West German reactors fueled with the enriched uranium produced by West German ultracentrifuges if the United States was unwilling to cooperate.[44] When the US option was blocked, the chairman of the CNPq chose to cooperate with the West Germans.

In 1952 Harteck traveled to West Germany on a temporary contract with the Brazilians. He then established a network between CNPq and West German research centers, most notably the University of Bonn and the Max Planck Institute in Göttingen, where Wilhelm Groth and Konrad Beyerle, Harteck's previous collaborators, had secretly resumed their wartime research on ultracentrifuges.[45] It is important to note that according to the available documentation, the West German government was not involved in this collaboration. Harteck's mission was crucial in persuading Alberto and other members of the CNPq, who visited West Germany on several occasions in 1952 and 1953, to join this effort. During the summer of 1953, Groth, Beyerle, and their team agreed to collaborate by training Brazilian scientists in the use of uranium enrichment technologies and in the production of uranium hexafluoride (UF_6), used in the centrifuges for isotopic separation.

While West German research centers were major partners in the Brazilian atomic program, Brazil also set up an important partnership with France to mine and refine minerals suitable for the extraction of uranium. For this reason, despite the reservations of the French ambassador to Rio, Brazilian nuclear scientists conducted their investigations in French nuclear research centers. In July 1953, for instance, Alberto spent fifteen days in France. During his stay, he signed a cooperation agreement with Francis Perrin, the high commissioner of the French Atomic Energy Commission (Commissariat à l'Énergie Atomique, or CEA), and visited the principal nuclear facilities in Bouchet and Saclay.[46]

At the same time, Alberto and other Brazilian nuclear scientists furthered Brazil's collaboration with the Société des Produits Chimiques des Terres Rares (Society for Chemical Products of Rare Earths). It had signed an agreement with the Brazilian government in March 1953 and was considering the possibility of setting up an industrial-scale facility to refine uranium in Brazil.[47] It was the beginning of a fruitful relationship that allowed recognition of the best method for prospecting Brazilian soil.[48] Not only were the US authorities conscious of the French-Brazilian efforts but they were concerned about their strategic implications since the United States had monopolized control of Brazil's atomic rare ores since 1945.[49]

The US State Department, which promoted both a policy of denying exports and a policy of preventing the dissemination of sensitive technologies or materials, was also deeply worried by the Brazilian attempt to acquire heavy water, a crucial element for producing plutonium, from Norway. Brazil had expressed interest in Norwegian nuclear activities since 1951, in particular the heavy-water nuclear reactor that Oslo was inaugurating in collaboration with the Netherlands. Owing to the personal friendship between Alberto and the Dutch physicist Hendrik Kramers, CNPq sent one of its youngest nuclear scientists—Hervásio Guimarães de Carvalho, the future chairman of the Brazilian National Nuclear Energy Commission and another major figure in Brazil's nuclear energy history—to Norway.[50]

Throughout 1952 and 1953 CNPq attempted to acquire a heavy-water reactor and the fuel to operate it from Norway. Alberto was enthusiastic about the possibility of installing a Norwegian reactor in Brazil.[51] However, its high operating costs and also technical advice—provided by Robert Oppenheimer during a meeting in the United States in August 1953 and by Paul Harteck—led Alberto to change his mind and opt instead for the West German reactors and technologies.[52] This endeavor was further hindered in 1952, when the Norwegian company Norsk Hydro, the main producer of heavy water at the time, stated that it would not be able to satisfy Brazil's request for two tons of material. Its annual production had already been contracted to Norwegian, Western European, and American facilities.[53] Brazil was attempting to gain external cooperation to master the complete nuclear fuel cycle. However, the Vargas government and CNPq considered it crucial for the future of the Brazilian atomic energy project that the country not rely exclusively on one partner "even if it is a friend nation."[54]

Prior to Harteck's mission, Alberto had attempted to exploit the international political situation at the beginning of the 1950s by enlisting the aid of several eminent West German scientists in the development of Brazil's nuclear plans.[55] At the end of 1951, a Brazilian delegation headed by Colonel Orlando Rangel, Alberto's chief collaborator and the military's representative to the CNPq, flew secretly to West Germany with the approval of both Vargas and the United States. Their aim was to hire Werner Heisenberg and Otto Hahn—winners, respectively, of the Nobel Prize in Physics for the creation of quantum mechanics and the Nobel Prize in Chemistry for the discovery of nuclear fission—as well as the nuclear scientists Karl Friedrich von Weizsäcker and Karl Friedrich Bonhoeffer, among others.

This was not the first time that a Latin American country had sought to hire important German nuclear scientists. Brazil was emulating Argentina's attempt to recruit Heisenberg, who in 1947 had sought to move to Buenos Aires to establish a nuclear program under then president Juan Perón in concert with other German scientists. At the time, however, the British authorities had barred Heisenberg from leaving West Germany for even a short period.[56] By the end of the 1940s, however, the West had radically modified its policy. Western governments attempted to stimulate the migration of physicists, chemists, and technicians who had been enrolled in the Nazi nuclear program to the Americas, fearing that Moscow would co-opt them to pursue the Soviet Union's atomic goals.[57] So, by 1951 Brazil was considered a safe haven for Heisenberg and his colleagues in the context of a possible resurgence of US-Soviet tensions in Germany resulting from the outbreak of the Korean War.[58]

Although the US authorities supported the attempt to contract West German scientists in the Federal Republic of Germany (FRG), Alberto decided not to involve the Brazilian foreign ministry because of concerns about possible information leaks.[59] Rather, the CNPq chairman sent Rangel as his personal emissary to West Germany to persuade renowned West German researchers to work in Brazil for two years and help establish Brazil's nuclear program. Specifically, they sought out Werner Heisenberg and Karl von Weizsäcker to direct a new Institute of Theoretical Physics in São Paulo, inaugurated in June 1952, to be funded by the state of São Paulo and by the federal military authorities.[60] Their possible arrival did not concern the United States, but it did preoccupy the United Kingdom, which in that very year had become the third NWS. Even if the application of Weizsäcker's and Heisenberg's knowledge and experience to Brazilian industry, military, and defense would not lead to concrete results in the short run, the "evident close association [of the institute] with the military suggests that its research work may prove more 'operational' and less 'pure' than . . . was [then] hoped."[61] The West German scientists dissipated the British concerns when they expressed their interest in moving to Brazil as a desire to work for peaceful uses of the technology and to escape any war that might break out in Europe.[62] However, 1952 found them preferring to continue working in the FRG on the new local atomic research program, as evidenced by the correspondence between Bonhoeffer and Alberto.[63] Although Alberto's offer was ultimately rebuffed, many of the former Nazi scientists, such as Heisenberg, Hahn, and Weizsäcker, did visit Rio de Janeiro in subsequent years to give lectures or for short-term collaboration in Brazilian research activities.[64]

Álvaro Alberto's meeting in Göttingen with prominent nuclear scientists, 11 July 1954. *Front, left to right*: Otto Hahn, Álvaro Alberto, Carl Friedrich von Weizsäcker; *back, left to right*: Bernhard Hassenstein, Karl Wirtz, Karl-Friedrich Bonhoeffer, Konrad Beyerle. (Álvaro Alberto personal archive, AA/foto/075 CNPq, Centro Interunidade de História da Ciência, Universidade de São Paulo)

The year 1953 was crucial for Brazil's nuclear program. On 25 November Vargas approved a plan to acquire all the components of the nuclear energy production process, including the construction of power plants and the training of nuclear scientists from overseas. Developing an indigenous and fully independent nuclear program was an ambition of Brazilian political, scientific, economic, and military officials.[65] However, Brazilian nuclear energy was not exclusively a tool for economic progress. The importance attached to nuclear development for military ends is also evident in several documents from Alberto's archive.

Contemporarily, Alberto received a report on the possibility of creating thermonuclear reactions in Brazil. Local scientists in collaboration with the army ran tests on an implosion bomb that could be used to originate thermonuclear reactions and detonate an atomic device. This implosion bomb, the Bomba Marambaia, was successfully tested in 1953.[66] Echoing the suggestion made by Robert Oppenheimer in a secret meeting with CNPq officers in Rio de Janeiro in July 1953, a confidential CNPq report concluded that the production of a thermonuclear reaction would require plutonium or enriched uranium, elements that could be extracted from minerals available in Brazil.[67] At that moment, the Brazilian government could consider obtaining fissile materials in one of three ways. It could produce enriched uranium using West German technologies;[68] it could produce fissile materials using the synchrocyclotron that Alberto was trying to obtain from the United States;[69] or it could produce plutonium using double-effect reactors that Alberto wanted to acquire abroad.[70]

The report is not the only evidence corroborating the theory that Brazil's atomic ambitions concealed military purposes; for instance, the realization of an implosion experiment can be considered a concrete step toward weaponization.[71] In 1945, immediately after the bombings of Hiroshima and Nagasaki, Rangel insisted in his "Notas sobre a bomba atômica" (Notes on the atomic bomb) that Brazil needed to acquire complete information on the development of an atomic device.[72] The available documentation does not explain Brazil's reasons for weaponizing, nor does it mention any rivalry or competition in the nuclear field with Argentina, which was then developing its own atomic program.[73] Moreover, there is no evidence of presidential approval of the tests.

West Germany had a central role in Brazilian nuclear plans. The cooperation between the two countries was sealed in 1953, when CNPq signed a contract with research centers in Bonn and Göttingen for three centrifuges from the firm Sartorius Werke and Brazilian personnel to receive training to use the equipment.[74] This was just one of the components of a cooperation agreement that also involved geological prospecting and the possible export of Brazilian uranium to West Germany. The secret agreement between West German institutions and Rio de Janeiro was to be implemented in 1954. West Germany, a country still occupied by the Allied forces, and Brazil, a country in the United States' backyard, had excellent reasons to collaborate. They could exchange minerals for technology, and West Germany might restart a research program on sensitive aspects of nuclear energy, such as uranium enrichment, useful for both peaceful and military purposes. As Beyerle would later write to Alberto, the West German–Brazilian deal and the associated financial resources and incentives facilitated the development of research in the field, despite the barriers the Allies imposed on the reactivation of a West German atomic program.[75]

"Atoms for Peace," the Difficult West German–Brazilian Atomic Cooperation, and Alberto's Resignation

In early July 1954 Alberto encountered the first obstacles to Brazil's nuclear ambitions. Authorized by Vargas, he traveled to West Germany to accelerate the construction of the centrifuges and obtain Allied approval for their export. Through the good offices of the former US representative to the UNAEC, Bernard Baruch, on 9 July Groth and Alberto met with James B. Conant, the US high commissioner to West Germany, and inquired about the possibility of building "pilot training laboratorial equipment" for producing reactor fuel for nonmilitary purposes to be shipped to Brazil.[76] Conant's response was negative. Alberto was told that only the USAEC could authorize the shipment. The Americans were fully aware of the real nature of the "laboratorial equipment" and were interested in the work of the German research center, which, unlike the United States, made progress in the ultracentrifuge process.[77]

Following this, the Brazilian government applied to the military security board for a license to export the centrifuges. USAEC technicians communicated to Brazilian authorities that because of the high commission's ban in March 1950, German laboratories could not manufacture the equipment. Specifically, the West German ultracentrifuge would produce an amount of Uranium-235 (^{235}U) higher than that permitted by the US legislation, which could lead to the production of weapons-grade material for military purposes by both West Germany and Brazil. The Brazilians were told that it was not possible to file an appeal against the USAEC decision since it had been imposed not only by the United States but also by France and Great Britain.[78]

In response, the Brazilian government tried to play its last card, setting up a meeting between the chairmen of CNPq and the USAEC. In July 1954 Alberto flew to New York, where he met his counterpart, Lewis Strauss, who subsequently sanctioned the ban on the export.[79] A few weeks earlier, the West German scientists had also received a message from US authorities concerned about the "centrifuge issue."[80] The Brazilian attempts to acquire the requisite equipment had hit an impasse. According to Alberto's files, Groth and Beyerle, who were under contract to CNPq, were available to build the centrifuges in Brazil if the United States prohibited their construction in West Germany.[81] At this time the US State Department became aware of the nature of the secret dealings between CNPq and West German universities. In June 1954 a member of CNPq leaked valuable information to the US Embassy in Rio de Janeiro, revealing that his institution had "four young chemists in Germany participating in a research project on the centrifuge method of U-235 separation" and that "this is regarded as a highly secret matter by the several Brazilians who appear to be in on the operation [since, according to them] the US authorities would otherwise clamp down because the project violates the occupations statutes." Robert Terrill, the economic attaché at the US Embassy, who oversaw the atomic energy portfolio, informed the State

Department that important Brazilian scientists, such as Djalma Guimarães and Francisco Maffei, were at that time in West Germany working under Groth's supervision on the ^{235}U separation project but that the US Embassy had no information about the results obtained from the project.[82] This moment represented the beginning of the end of Alberto's atomic plans. It also marked the start of the US policy of ring-fencing sensitive technologies, such as the centrifuges, to prevent nuclear proliferation.[83]

The ultracentrifuge issue coincided with a period of deep political turmoil in Brazil. After a series of political scandals rocked his government, Vargas committed suicide at the end of August 1954. Vargas had been a strong promoter of Alberto's plan and supported almost all the decisions taken by the CNPq in the nuclear area. Domestic and external factors determined the conclusion of the first phase of the Brazilian nuclear program. One of the first decisions of Vargas's successor, João Café Filho, was to appoint General Juarez Távora as chief of his military cabinet to supervise nuclear activities. Whereas Caiado de Castro, Távora's predecessor, had enthusiastically endorsed the CNPq policies, Távora, who was influenced by some congressional members as well as by several US Embassy officials, took the opposite line.

It is important to note that the international environment changed radically in December 1953, when the US president, Dwight D. Eisenhower, launched the "Atoms for Peace" plan, for international collaboration in the peaceful use of atomic energy, at the UNGA. An international atomic energy agency, according to Eisenhower, would acquire fissile material for peaceful ends from the military arsenals of the United States and the Soviet Union. The proposal was a turning point in the discussion about the creation of a nuclear order and the promotion of nuclear disarmament. It would end the US policy of denial that had led not only to the atomic and hydrogen Soviet bombs in 1949 and 1953 but also to the British bomb in 1952. Moreover, it stimulated cooperation between countries like Brazil and France, frustrated by the impossibility of collaboration with the United States. In August 1954 the US Congress modified the McMahon Act and made cooperation with other countries easier.

Alberto and the Brazilian government immediately perceived the policy as an important opportunity for Brazil's nuclear plans, but they decided to continue collaboration efforts with France, West Germany, and other possible partners. The modified US legislation concerned cooperation in the field of atomic energy research directed toward peaceful ends but excluded dual-use technologies such as those proposed by West German scientists. Brazil's interest in acquiring the gas centrifuge and the uranium hexafluoride plant from West Germany was made clear during the discussions that took place in Washington at the end of September 1954 between Edmundo Barbosa da Silva, head of the Economic Division of Brazil's Ministry of Foreign Affairs, and Gerard C. Smith, special assistant on atomic issues at the US State Department. Barbosa, reflecting Brazil's diplomatic stance, "allowed [Smith] to understand that he thought that [the cooperation with the West Germans] made no sense." Furthermore, the Brazilian diplomat "said he had advised his colleagues in the Foreign Office that such requests would in any event have to go to Washington." At the end of the meeting, Barbosa expressed his negative opinion concerning Alberto's policy, telling Smith "that the Admiral might have to go into dry dock."[84] As noted by the US historian William Burr, one month after the Barbosa-Smith meeting, the Allied High Commission Military Security Board of West Germany finally decided that Sartorius Werke was not authorized to build the centrifuges.[85]

The Brazilian government was informed of the decision at the end of November 1954.[86] Meanwhile, amid the implementation of agreements between Brazil and France and West German universities, Távora requested and obtained a revision to Brazil's atomic energy policy in favor of collaboration with the United States.[87] A secret internal document that he commissioned stated that while on the one hand the scientific community supported CNPq's choices, on the other hand the United States did not appreciate Brazil's nuclear strategy.[88] US diplomats considered Alberto's approach and his policy of cooperation with West German research centers to be obstacles to a possible US collaboration with Brazil. That position is apparent in secret documents that the American Embassy sent to Távora and that were later revealed by a parliamentary commission of inquiry on nuclear energy in July 1956. The US concern also clearly emerges in the internal correspondence between Washington and the American Embassy in Brazil. Terrill considered "the Brazil-German uranium 235 project a waste of resources, a waste of time and a waste of money."[89] Terrill's document also highlighted the possible consequences for Brazil if it chose to cooperate with West Germany. The United States threatened to ban any possible cooperation and considered that "a final reaction . . . is that the establishment in Brazil of a process for the extraction of fissionable uranium, by major interests of a European country that is forbidden by law to manufacture this metal within its boundaries, might be considered as a potential security risk to the United States and to the Western Hemisphere."[90]

The hardline position adopted by Terrill did not seem to be in line with the suggestions received from Washington. As Smith wrote to Terrill, "The Atomic Energy Commission is currently considering the data on the centrifuge as part of a determination of the precise definition of a production facility for the purpose of the Atomic Energy Act of 1954." After the signing in October 1954 of the Paris Agreement, which determined the full sovereignty of West Germany and ended the Allied occupation, the Federal Republic of Germany was finally free to build and export those facilities to Brazil without external restrictions. Smith was inclined not to "press [the Brazilians] for a prompt resolution of these requests" and concluded: "I feel we should not obstruct Brazilian actions in Germany. They do, however, present very real problems and there seems to be a fair chance that the new Brazilian administration will reappraise these actions and possibly cancel them."[91]

Even if Terrill did not follow Smith's advice, the US position prevailed. The Brazilian nuclear policy was reshaped to give priority to cooperation with the United States on the terms that had been discussed by Brazilian and American representatives since August 1953, although Rio de Janeiro's cooperation with European countries was not completely abandoned.[92] Távora, who enjoyed excellent personal relations with US Embassy officials, was inclined to restart negotiations with the United States and accept some conditions that Alberto had opposed, such as the export of nuclear minerals without equivalent compensation. In an attempt to reach a resolution, and echoing Barbosa's sentiments, Terrill wrote that "it would appear necessary to by-pass or eliminate the Admiral who thus far has succeeded in thwarting and obfuscating all efforts to arrive at an understanding with Brazil on the subject of cooperation in the atomic energy field."[93]

Távora fully supported the US position. In May 1955, when the West German equipment was ready to be shipped to Brazil, he forced Alberto to resign from the top post at CNPq after being charged with mismanagement for a financial scandal at the Brazilian Center for Research in Physics. Alberto, who was replaced by José Baptista Pereira, was in Távora's opinion "not only a scientific fake but also playing a dangerous political game."[94] Alberto's resignation represented a victory for the US government, since it had viewed him as a key obstacle to cooperation and, more importantly, to access to Brazil as a supplier of atomic minerals. In March 1953, when Alberto had attempted to impose a quid pro quo for the export of thorium to the United States and begun to negotiate with other countries, the State Department had begun to consider replacing the CNPq chairman with a pro-American nuclear scientist who could reorganize the structure of the council and create a department devoted exclusively to atomic energy.[95] Nevertheless, the Vargas government, in order to give full support to the United States in the Korea War in exchange for economic and military aid, guaranteed access to strategic minerals. On this occasion the government gave Itamaraty control over the export of nuclear minerals, eliminating one of CNPq's prerogatives. The US documents, as well as the report of a 1956 Brazilian parliamentary commission of inquiry, demonstrate that the key figure seeking the resignation of Alberto was indeed Terrill. From his first moments in Rio de Janeiro, Terrill considered Alberto to be anti-American, and he set out to cooperate with Brazilian diplomats in order to find a better counterpart on nuclear energy matters.[96]

In December 1954, when the CNPq began preliminary talks with the American Machine & Foundry Company, which proposed to sell nuclear equipment and possibly a reactor to Brazil, Alberto said that he preferred to negotiate a general agreement on nuclear energy with the US government in the context of the new legislation.[97] A possible "Marshall Atomic Plan," as it was called by Eisenhower's adviser Nelson Rockefeller, could be an opportunity to increase US influence in the Third World, beating the USSR competition. Brazil, a country with imminent political elections, could be a key case of supply of a nuclear research reactor.[98] In January 1955 the Brazilian Foreign Ministry, which was unsympathetic to the bargaining position established by Alberto, with the approval of Távora initiated direct negotiations with the US government.

After five months of negotiations, on 3 August 1955 Brazilian and US representatives agreed, through an exchange of notes, to cooperate on the peaceful use of nuclear energy. Specifically, Washington would export a research reactor and would lend, under safeguards on the peaceful use of the material, the nuclear fuel.[99] The United States, moreover, under a separate two-year agreement would assist Brazil in geological surveys. This was the first nuclear reactor to be built in Latin America. The delivery of this critical equipment as part of the "Atoms for Peace" program to Brazil edged out fellow Latin American competitors such as Argentina and Colombia. It confirmed the special relationship existing at that moment between Washington and Rio de Janeiro. Furthermore, Brazil was also one of the first recipients of US assistance in nuclear matters.

Key members of the Brazilian Atomic Energy Commission (Comissão Brasileira de Energia Atômica, or CBAE), a new CNPq body devoted to nuclear matters that was established by Alberto before his resignation, appreciated the deal.[100] Important Brazilian nuclear scientists such as Francisco Maffei, Marcelo Damy, and Joaquim da Costa Ribeiro discussed the terms of the agreement with an American delegation that visited Brazil at the end of July 1955; the agreement was welcomed because it was consistent with the principle of "specific compensations."[101] The reactor would be built in São Paulo in the new Institute of Atomic Energy (Instituto de Energia Atômica, or IEA), chaired by Damy.[102] It would allow the CBAE, which was considering the type of power plant to adopt, to eventually work with a research reactor in order to upgrade the Brazilian domestic nuclear program.[103]

The agreement with Washington did not represent the defeat of Alberto's plans even if the government decided to freeze the cooperation with West Germany. A definitive decision over the issue would be made, however, by the future president after the general elections of October 1955. The main candidates had a deep interest in atomic energy. Juscelino Kubitschek, the governor of Minas Gerais, candidate of a center-left Varguist coalition, had promoted the creation of the Institute of Radioactive Research (Instituto de Pesquisas Radioativas, or IPr) in his state, which was one of the richest in atomic minerals. On the other side, the conservative candidate was Café Filho's head of the military cabinet, Juarez Távora, a key figure in Brazilian politics since the 1930s and, as seen in the pages above, a protagonist of the imbroglio that led Álvaro Alberto to resign.

The history of atomic energy in Brazil in the first ten years of the nuclear age had been, as in other countries, quite turbulent. The international system, marked by the failed dialogue on the future of the atom, the US-USSR nuclear arms race, and the limitations to international cooperation, explains Brazilian difficulties in developing their atomic program. Brazil's domestic economic, financial, and political troubles also, however, influenced the struggle over the issue. Nuclear energy would continue to play a central role in the public debate in the next years. As we will see in the coming pages, Brazil attempted to establish a nuclear industry and to hold a significant position in the international negotiations for cooperation around the peaceful use of the atom and in the talks on nuclear disarmament.

CHAPTER TWO

Brazil a Promoter of Nonproliferation Norms?, 1955–1964

On 25 January 1958 Brazil's president, Juscelino Kubitschek, officially inaugurated the IEA-R1, the first research reactor in Brazil and one of the first in Latin America. In the presence of delegations from the United States, Argentina, Belgium, Italy, and Honduras, Brazilian nuclear scientists, and Jânio Quadros, the governor of the state of São Paulo, Kubitschek switched on the reactor at the University of São Paulo's Instituto de Energia Atômica (IEA). It was a historic moment for Brazil and Latin America and a promissory gesture by a government that aimed to develop the country through atomic energy with the possible construction of a nuclear power plant in the state of Rio de Janeiro. Many countries were opting for this form of energy, and Brazil could be at the forefront. "Atoms for Peace" and the establishment of the IAEA in that period were stimulating the use of nuclear energy around the world, and it was seen as key for modernization. However, it was exclusively a select club of countries that would eventually opt for nuclear energy. At the same time, the world was experiencing a massive nuclear arms race between the Soviet Union and the United States. The Cold War had the potential to lead to a nuclear holocaust, and in 1962 the Cuban Missile Crisis brought the world to the edge of an atomic conflict. The need to master nuclear energy and avoid nuclear war, one of the main threats to human existence, turned into a goal expressed in a nonlinear way by the Brazilian government. During the years between 1956, when Kubitschek began his term, and March 1964, when a military coup ended the democratic experience, Brazil discussed its possible nuclearization. It also defended full nuclear disarmament and nonproliferation, even in the face of domestic discord. This chapter deals with this intense moment in Brazilian nuclear history.

Brazil's New Nuclear Policy

Juscelino Kubitschek, who defeated Juarez Távora in the 1955 general elections, attempted to resurrect Alberto's strategy by restarting its cooperation with both France and the West German research centers and by strengthening the collaboration with the United States. With few exceptions, Kubitschek aligned with Washington in his foreign policy.[1] He overcame an internal dispute over the modernization strategies, opting for a national development associated with foreign investments (above all North American but also European).[2]

President Kubitschek considered nuclear energy a top priority of his ambitious economic development plan, the so-called Plano de Metas (Target Plan), which sought to industrialize Brazil in a short time.[3] The new Brazilian president, who had previously been governor of the state of Minas Gerais, manifested a keen interest in atomic energy. In 1956 Kubitschek supported the resumption of Alberto's efforts after a parliamentary commission of inquiry on nuclear energy demonstrated the illegal export of nuclear material to the United States from 1953 to 1955. Following a fierce debate in the parliament between deputies in favor of and against Álvaro Alberto, the commission provided evidence that the US Embassy had brought about not only the end of the cooperation with West Germany but also the end of Alberto's career. Juarez Távora was held responsible for the illegal trade of thorium and monazite sands between Washington and Rio de Janeiro. By allowing these exports, the Brazilian Foreign Ministry had not respected the limitations imposed by domestic legislation. Moreover, it had declined to inform CNPq, which was in charge of supervising national reserves of nuclear ores. The inquiry commission's final report suggested (1) a revision of Brazil's nuclear policy; (2) the establishment of a national nuclear energy commission (the Comissão Nacional de Energia Nuclear, or CNEN); (3) the renewal of the collaboration with France and the West German research centers; and (4) the completion of the nuclear equipment purchases ordered by Alberto.

After Kubitschek and the parliament approved the inquiry commission's plan, Brazil finally received the centrifuges in 1957. The renewed collaboration with West German research centers seemed to be working according to the criteria established in the initial agreement.[4] Brazilian scientists visited West Germany to increase their knowledge and enhance their research on nuclear technology. Wilhelm Groth and Konrad Beyerle, the main protagonists of the West German–Brazilian scientific partnership, spent an extended period in the Latin American country. They installed the centrifuges and trained Brazilian officials in the use of this advanced equipment as well as in managing uranium hexafluoride

(UF$_6$).[5] However, CNEN, established in October 1956, which reported directly to the president (until it was subordinated to the newly established Ministry of Mines and Energy in 1960) and headed by Admiral Octacílio Cunha, chose to follow a different path. Domestic nuclear autonomy in Brazil was to be achieved by using different reactors, fueled by its rich reserves of thorium and not by enriched uranium or any of the other technologies envisioned by Alberto. Brazilian nuclear scientists, like their counterparts in countries such as France and India, opted for natural uranium reactors, although they did not discard alternative technologies in the following years.

The debate over the use of natural or enriched uranium would continue until 1969, when Brazil decided on light-water reactors. Because of the choice in the mid-1950s of natural uranium reactors, Brazil would not have to rely exclusively on external collaboration in order to acquire enriched uranium or the technologies for producing nuclear fuel. CNEN also decided to continue to cooperate with the United States in the nuclear field. For these reasons, the centrifuges imported from West Germany were used exclusively for research purposes by a small group of Brazilian scientists at the Institute of Chemical Research at the University of São Paulo until 1967. In October 1958, a team of three Brazilian and two West German scholars began to research uranium enrichment with this equipment.[6] The centrifuge issue continued to be a matter of concern for the US authorities, who would closely follow the activities in that field in Brazil and elsewhere. In the late 1950s, the possible dissemination of nuclear weapons became a major concern in both Moscow and Washington.[7]

Despite Brazil's initial nuclear plans and USAEC approval of the transfer, CNEN decided neither to use the synchrocyclotron finally shipped in 1954 nor to acquire a bigger, 72-inch one thanks to the US companies' approval of the technology transfer.[8] The policy promoted by CNEN was, consequently, only a partial restoration of Alberto's nuclear plans. While the overall goal remained the achievement of autonomy in the nuclear field, the newly established CNEN decided not to follow the direction inherited from the father of the Brazilian nuclear program as far as the means to achieve it were concerned. As seen, those technologies that Alberto considered essential for fostering Brazil's nuclear development both for military and peaceful purposes temporarily lost their centrality in the new atomic plan.

As noted in the previous pages, the new Brazilian plan aimed at achieving autonomy in the nuclear field and providing the country with electric energy through atomic power plants. The official policy to accomplish such goals was clear: safeguarding national resources; acquiring machinery, technologies, knowledge, and nuclear power plants; and building research reactors. Consequently, in the following years Brazil attempted to industrialize the country through nuclear energy. However, the political and economic turmoil that characterized the country from 1961 to 1964 impeded implementation of the project. It also prevented launching international partnerships to build nuclear power plants either with the assistance of the IAEA or thanks to the cooperation of other countries, such as the United States and France. Brazilian efforts in those years were limited to research, focusing mainly on the training abroad of a new generation of nuclear scientists and engineers.[9]

Despite the quest for autonomy, in the first years of the Kubitschek presidency (1956–61) the Brazilian government sought to prioritize and expand the partnership in the nuclear field with Washington. The US openness to cooperation was made clear in early 1956, when the US president, Dwight D. Eisenhower, declared that his government could transfer twenty tons of ^{235}U to friendly countries. It was perceived as a unique opportunity for Brazil. In 1955, having agreed to the acquisition of a research reactor, the government wanted to obtain a nuclear power plant from the United States.[10] However, during the first phase of talks, some US officials in Brazil were cautious about a new agreement. The Brazilian interest in acquiring a reactor fueled by natural uranium was the first matter of concern. According to Robert P. Terrill, this interest indicated that "the Brazilian obsession for producing uranium metal has not changed despite the visit of our [US]AEC people, and that the Canadians and British have probably been giving Brazil some advice."[11]

Immediately after the Brazilian presidential elections in November 1955, several US officials were also worried about the incoming government's political orientation, especially since Kubitschek's vice president, João Goulart, was supposedly supported by the Brazilian Communist Party.[12] For this reason, Gerard Smith informed the USAEC that "it seems advisable to move rather slowly on this at least until there has been more time to form a better evaluation of the plans and policies of Messrs. Kubitschek and Goulart."[13]

The US preoccupation vanished some weeks after Kubitschek's inauguration in January 1956. The new Brazilian president indicated in his State of the Union message that the government planned to build a 10,000-kilowatt reactor. Consequently, at the end of February the Brazilian Foreign Ministry authorized its embassy in Washington to negotiate the acquisition of a 10,000-kilowatt reactor with the US company American & Foreign Power, whose chairman had visited Rio de Janeiro in October 1955 to conduct preliminary meetings with Brazilian authorities.[14] Those talks were successful: from the USAEC Brazil obtained the authorization to acquire a power reactor, beating competition from Italy.[15]

As indicated by the available US documentation, it was clear in the first meeting between the authorities of the two countries that Brazil also desired to procure a small power reactor to develop breeder reactors in order to become "independent of outside sources for fuel materials."[16] In their conversations with the Americans, the Brazilian nuclear scientists admitted their keenness to also acquire the capability to reprocess irradiated fuel.[17] At that moment, the US authorities supported the Brazilian project but imposed some conditions: the whole project had to be internationally safeguarded, and the agreement would be valid for twenty-five years, to avoid any diversion of nuclear fuel by a later Brazilian government.[18] As noted by the American historian Mara Drogan in her detailed study of US-Brazilian cooperation in the nuclear field during the 1950s, the negotiations between the American & Foreign Power Company, the USAEC, and the Brazilian authorities stalemated in late 1956. At the end of August 1956 the CSN nationalized atomic minerals and suspended the export of thorium and uranium to the United States, following the recommendations of the parliamentary commission of inquiry on nuclear energy. President Kubitschek and his foreign minister, José Carlos de Macedo Soares, assured the American government that the decision would not affect their collaboration in the nuclear energy field and extended the uranium prospecting agreement with Washington until 1960.[19]

Despite those problems, in early 1957 the parties were close to signing an agreement for building one nuclear power plant close to Rio de Janeiro and another one, sponsored by the state of São Paulo, in its territory.[20] On 31 July 1957 Brazil and the United States concluded a deal for cooperation in the realization of an atomic power reactor. The US authorized the transfer of uranium to Brazil to fuel its reactor. It also established the purchase of a net amount of 550 kilograms over a twenty-five-year term. It acknowledged the possibility of amending the agreement if the development of Brazil's nuclear energy program generated a need for more fuel.[21] The American & Foreign Power Company was to build a nuclear power plant with a General Electric boiling water reactor fueled by the USAEC. However, the high estimated costs deterred the CNEN chairman, Admiral Octacílio da Cunha, from pressing the Brazilian Congress to ratify the agreement. In 1957 and 1958, the Brazilian government requested financial assistance from the US government, which it denied because of the unfeasibility of the project. Similarly, the project in the state of São Paulo, strongly supported by the state governor and future Brazilian president Jânio Quadros, was also suspended.[22]

Despite the failure of the US-Brazilian agreement, the Brazilian government did not abandon its nuclear projects. During the rest of his presidency, Kubitschek promoted the creation of an IAEA regional training center with the explicit aims

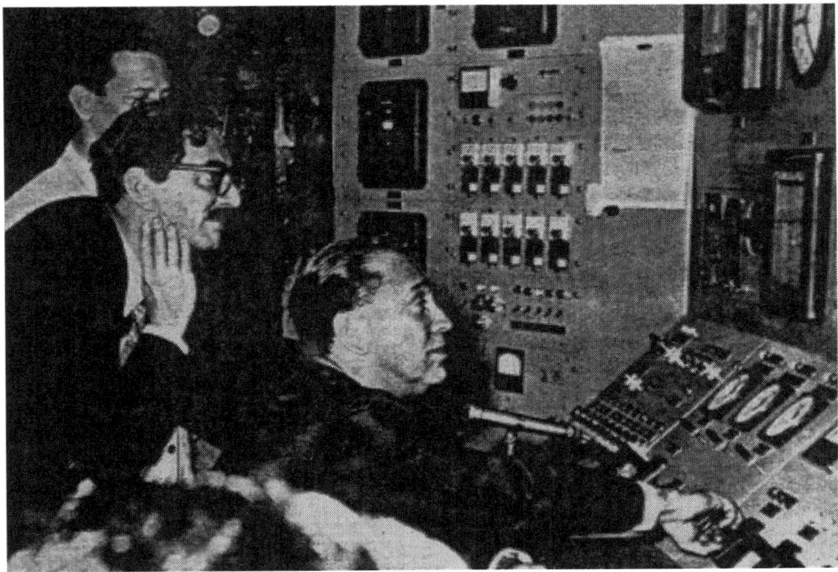

Brazil's President Juscelino Kubitscheck (*right*) and the governor of São Paulo, Jânio Quadros (*left*), inaugurate the IEA-R1 research reactor at the Institute of Atomic Energy in São Paulo, 25 January 1958. (IPEN)

of improving Brazil's human resources and acquiring materials and equipment from the agency for the development of its nuclear sector. Brazil justified its proposal diplomatically by stressing that the country possessed one of the few research reactors in Latin America.[23] The United States and other leading nuclear powers, however, did not support this proposal; their position on the issue remained firm, even when Brazil submitted it to the IAEA General Conference on several occasions during the following twenty years. The refusal notwithstanding, in 1959 the Vienna agency assisted Brazil in choosing the site and type of a future nuclear power plant.[24] However, as in the past, the decision to rely on external collaboration was subject to criticism. During a congress on nuclear energy in Belo Horizonte, young scientists and nationalist congressmen in the Brazilian parliament disagreed with the decision to cooperate with the United States. They denounced the attitude of CNEN and proposed promoting a Brazilian atomic industry exploiting the supposedly rich national reserves of nuclear minerals.[25] The debate provoked the same confrontation that had emerged a few years previously in the 1956 parliamentary commission of inquiry, with a sharp division between nationalists and internationalists. Octacílio Cunha's reply to the critics was in line with the justification given to the Americans when he turned down the proposal to build a power plant: that Brazil lacked the economic and financial resources to support the nuclear project.[26] Even if nuclear energy was at the top of the Plano de Metas, the Kubitschek government did not have the wherewithal to fulfill such a goal.

The year 1961 represented a possible turning point. Jânio Quadros, the histrionic president who succeeded Kubitschek, attempted to reinvigorate Brazil's nuclear ambitions with a plan that included the construction of two power plants in northeastern Brazil (the less developed area of the country); the production of pure uranium; the development of thorium reactors; support of the use and production of radioisotopes; the establishment of a nuclear industry that allowed the country to master different reactor technologies using national uranium resources; and a law regulating the nuclear sector.[27] Quadros's plan would influence Brazil's nuclear policy until 1964, and several elements would also be adopted during the military regime.

A few months before his election, Quadros announced that the University of São Paulo had discovered a method to produce pure uranium for fueling reactors. The IEA, after its foundation in 1956 in the context of the new nuclear policy, had focused attention on, among other things, the study of the nuclear fuel cycle.[28] The news had broad repercussions, even if some commentators doubted that this small group of researchers had pulled off such an achievement. Quadros chose the vigorous Marcelo Damy, former director of the IEA, as the new chair of CNEN. He resumed the 1959 project to build a nuclear power reactor in the state of Rio de Janeiro, the so-called Project Mambucaba, named after the area intended to host the nuclear power plants. The new president also proposed to then president Arturo Frondizi of Argentina the exchange of scientific information in the nuclear field.[29] The Argentine historian Diego Hurtado recalls that Frondizi, like Kubitschek, supported an ambitious plan to modernize and develop the country using nuclear energy.[30] Although the agreement was not implemented, it represented a first step toward collaboration between the two countries on nuclear issues. Quadros's unexpected resignation in late August 1961 sparked a profound political crisis. In the period from 1946 to 1964 Brazil elected its presidents and vice presidents separately. In the 1960 general election the leftist João Goulart, the running mate of Quadros's adversary, was elected vice president. In order to avoid a possible military intervention against Goulart (who was in Beijing at the time), the Brazilian congress in early September 1961 amended the constitution. This inaugurated a short parliamentary period that lasted until 1963, when the full presidential powers were restored.[31]

The political crisis notwithstanding, the debate over the implementation of a nuclear plan continued. Nineteen sixty-two was a crucial year for nuclear energy. At the beginning of the year, President Goulart inaugurated the new Institute of Nuclear Energy (Instituto de Energia Nuclear) in Rio de Janeiro. In a few years it would host the research reactor *Argonauta*, 93 percent of whose components had been manufactured in Brazil.[32] Contemporarily, the IPr, in Belo Horizonte, acquired a TRIGA-MARK research reactor from the United States. While the Brazilian research sector was advancing thanks to its centers in São Paulo, Rio de Janeiro, and Belo Horizonte, the government launched an international tender for the construction of a nuclear power plant. Italian, French, British, and US companies submitted proposals to CNEN in early 1962.[33] Later that year, Brazil selected the French bid to build a natural uranium power reactor. It signed a ten-year agreement with the French government that which included a secret clause to bypass international safeguards.[34] This would allow Brazil to develop nuclear energy for peaceful and military uses free from international controls.

Damy clearly expressed the rationale of the French-Brazilian cooperation in a report to the minister of mines and energy, the nationalist Gabriel de Rezende Passos. It happened in the middle of the discussions over approval of a national nuclear legislation. According to Damy, the natural uranium power reactor to be built in southeastern Brazil would guarantee, thanks to the first unsafeguarded load of French nuclear fuel, the use of the plutonium produced by the reactor to transform the vast reserves of Brazilian thorium into fissile material. Thus, the natural uranium reactors would lead to independence in the country's nuclear development. In the future, as declared by President Goulart in late December 1963, Brazil would also adopt the thorium-plutonium fuel cycle reactors to be built by the domestic industry.[35] Eventually, on 27 August 1962, the Brazilian parliament approved the legislation ruling that CNEN would supervise the nuclear sector.[36] In the same year, the government established a national electric enterprise, Eletrobrás, to coordinate the electric energy sector. The energy plans recognized that the country would rely on vast hydric sources, but nuclear power was needed to complement hydropower. Brazilian scientists and politicians in the years preceding the military coup of 1964 fully supported the option to autonomously develop a nuclear energy sector. France, which tested its first nuclear bomb in 1960, represented the ideal partner for a country with nuclear ambitions.

However, during the period discussed in this chapter Brazil did not concentrate its efforts exclusively on developing and planning ambitious nuclear projects. The country was also very active in international discussions over nuclear nonproliferation and over global control and promotion of atomic energy.

Brazil and the Origins of the IAEA

After Eisenhower's 1953 "Atoms for Peace" speech, Brazil became particularly interested in being involved in the new international debate over the peaceful use of atomic energy. In early 1955, Brazil aimed to engage in the creation of the IAEA. Brazil's posture was not different from the one it had adopted a few years earlier at the UNAEC. The first goal was to preserve sovereignty over its mineral resources in the event of internationalization of nuclear materials. The second was to secure resources for supporting the peaceful use of the atom in the Global South through the creation of an international organization devoted to atomic energy. Furthermore, Brazil aimed to obtain recognition and high status in the IAEA as a major provider of nuclear minerals or as the country with the most advanced nuclear program in South America. Consequently, it was crucial to gain admittance to the negotiations, which until late 1955 had been limited to an Eight-Nation Negotiating Committee exclusively composed of Western countries that had discussed the IAEA draft statute.[37]

The first step toward inclusion was participation in the UN-sponsored Geneva Conference on the Peaceful Uses of Atomic Energy in August 1955. Brazilian scientists actively participated in the conference, and the CNPq member Joaquim da Costa Ribeiro was one of its scientific secretaries. The Brazilians established an intense dialogue with the international scientific community and underlined Brazilian need to adopt atomic energy for supporting the national industrialization. The conference profoundly influenced the country's future choices in the nuclear field.

Brazil's involvement in the talks over the IAEA began on 22 August 1955, when the US State Department submitted the draft statute to all members of the United Nations before the General Assembly's final approval.[38] The Brazilian government paid particular attention to the document and opened an internal debate to define its position concerning the agency.[39] The Brazilian authorities welcomed the US proposal to include Brazil and India on the first IAEA board of governors, the executive branch of the organization. Brazil aimed to become a permanent member of the board, justifying its participation on the basis of its being the representative of Latin America and one of the main suppliers of atomic minerals, such as thorium.[40] According to David Fischer, the agency draft statute had assigned "quasi-permanent" seats to the five largest contributors of technical assistance and fissile materials. The other five seats were to be shared by the leading suppliers of nuclear minerals (uranium, thorium, and other source material that the board could specify). Moreover, a third group, of six members, was to be elected by the general conference.[41]

The government of Rio de Janeiro achieved extraordinary success. The United States proposed Brazil as one of the new members to participate in the next round of negotiations over the IAEA statute. Czechoslovakia, another country rich in atomic minerals, was proposed by the Soviet Union.[42] According to the Brazilian ambassador in Washington, João Carlos Muniz, this was the "first step toward membership on the IAEA board."[43] Thanks to the balance between the two blocs in the negotiations, Brazil's presence was guaranteed and approved by the UNGA in early December 1955.[44] Important issues such as the future composition of the board of governors and the creation of a system of inspections and controls over the peaceful use of nuclear energy would be discussed in the upcoming negotiations in Washington.[45]

Before the meetings, Brazil's diplomats discussed a strategy for strengthening its position within the future organization. Since the existing form of cooperation was considered inadequate for Brazilian needs, the agency should support the development of a national nuclear sector. Moreover, sharing the position of other Third World countries, specifically that of India, the IAEA should be an instrument for fostering economic development and should provide technical and scientific knowledge, nuclear equipment, and materials. The new organization should also establish a new mechanism for defining the international price of nuclear minerals. It was an important issue for the Latin American country, which was providing the United States with thorium. Furthermore, Brazil wanted to amend the draft statute in order not to exclude the possibility of forging bilateral or regional agreements of cooperation in the nuclear realm. Specific responsibilities should be transferred from the board of governors to the general conference. The excessive power of the board could protect the interests of industrialized countries exclusively, marginalizing developing countries that did not have seats on the executive council. For this reason, Itamaraty instructed its delegation to propose the inclusion of two new criteria for admission to the board. The first should be "reasonable geographic representation" in the group of the chief producers and contributors of source materials. The second criterion would be the "fair representation of underdeveloped countries" in the same group and in the group of countries to be elected by the general conference (comprising representatives of different regions of the world).[46]

Some days before the meeting of the working group in Washington, Brazil obtained a significant result: the US government decided to modify the IAEA draft statute to include Brazil in the second group of the board of governors.[47] During the first weeks of the Twelve-Nation Working Committee meetings, the Brazilian delegates were satisfied with their action. According to Muniz's assessment, Brazil was recognized not exclusively as a provider of nuclear materials but also temporarily as the most advanced Latin American country in the nuclear field.[48] It was a victory for Brazilian diplomacy, even if permanence could be threatened by another Latin American country with an advanced nuclear sector, such as Argentina.[49] After a final round of negotiations in Washington, in April 1956 the new IAEA draft statute partially satisfied the Brazilian requests. The text did indeed include underdevelopment as one of the main topics the agency had to deal with. From September to October 1956 a conference in New York would discuss the final IAEA statute. Immediately after the end of the meeting of the Working Committee, Brazil reached a significant result: the choice of Ambassador Muniz (who was particularly appreciated by the US) to chair the conference.[50]

From the Brazilian standpoint, the forthcoming meeting in New York did not represent an occasion to amend the draft statute, since the two superpowers would not accept modification of the text agreed upon in Washington in the spring.[51] Like other developing countries, Brazil believed that the most delicate issue in the draft statute concerned article 12, dealing with the agency's inspections and controls, which could set limitations on the Brazilian nuclear program.[52] Following the instructions from Itamaraty and the approval by President Kubitschek, the Brazilian delegation supported the approval. The international control activities were not to interfere with the development of a national nuclear program, with the important exception of reactor design. On the one hand, the agency would not prevent Brazil from developing a military atomic program. In the case of a Brazilian "weaponization," the country should avoid using the services and the materials of the nuclear watchdog. On the other hand, international control could guarantee Brazil's interests given the difficulty for many countries of developing a nuclear arsenal because of agency interference. The modification of article 12 would risk prompting a withdrawal of the United States, the principal sponsor of the initiative since Eisenhower's speech in December 1953.[53] Despite the instructions finally received, the Brazilian diplomats feared that the United States might impose the application of IAEA safeguards to all the bilateral agreements of cooperation. The US purpose, in the view of one of the Brazilian delegates, was to cooperate with the agency but also to avoid the diversion of peaceful assistance to military aims. The IAEA controls could be "inconvenient" for a country that wished to adopt breeders reactors capable of producing plutonium.[54]

Even if there was little room for modification, the main focus of Brazilian activities in New York was to call the agency's attention to the need to finance projects in underdeveloped areas of the world. For this reason, Brazil struggled to modify article 11 of the draft statute (concerning the projects supported by the IAEA). Besides, the agency should create an information center for spreading scientific and technical knowledge. In order to give equal opportunities to all the regions of the world, the Brazilian delegation should also submit a proposal for creating regional groups. Brazil was able to include in article 3 A.4 the expression "exchange and training of scientists." Despite a critical dispute over safeguards (a French-Swiss solution resolved the issue), on 23 October 1956 UN members approved the draft statute with minimal modifications.[55]

Brazil devoted the first period of the agency's existence to guaranteeing its presence on the board of governors. Argentina, which had initially been perceived as a possible threat by the government of Rio de Janeiro, became an important ally. During and after the work of the Preparatory Commission in New York, there was a constant and frank dialogue between Brazilian and Argentinian representatives.[56] To avoid competition, the Brazilian delegation proposed a diplomatic solution to its Argentine counterpart, launching the idea of the "uninterrupted and simultaneous" participation of both countries on the board of governors. The proposal was that Brazil and Argentina could rotate as members of the board, one as a designated member and the other as an elected member. Brazil requested Argentine support for recognizing Brazil as a designated member in exchange for Brazilian support for including Argentina as one of the two Latin American elected members. Brazil could justify its candidature on the basis of its having been a member of the Twelve-Nation Working Committee, which had negotiated the IAEA statute in early 1956. The formula could guarantee that the two countries would be the representatives of Latin America.[57] The Argentine government, particularly President Pedro Eugenio Aramburu, welcomed the Brazilian proposal. However, the Argentinians disagreed on the reasons for the Brazilian designation. They felt that it should be connected to the state of its nuclear program and not to its participation in the negotiations of the IAEA statute.[58] Brazil agreed on that point and decided, in the final act of the Preparatory Commission, to mention the Argentine support to the Brazilian designation without comparing the two countries' nuclear technological progress.[59] The two governments thus found a modus vivendi within the agency that guaranteed their mutual interests. Except for a crisis in 1962, the agreement of 1957 has always been respected, and it represents one of the foundations of Brasília–Buenos Aires cooperation in the nuclear arena.

Despite the initial enthusiasm, in the following years Brazil's interest in the IAEA declined. As underlined by the Brazilian diplomat Carlos Bernardes when he was appointed chairman of the IAEA board of governors in 1959, the IAEA *momentum* ended because "the agency's future seems bleak to me and with the resurgence of Cold War, the debates in the board are characterized by high tension and verbal violence, at obvious cost to the efficiency and utility of the agency."[60]

The Eighteen-Nation Disarmament Committee, Cuba, and the Early Proposal for a Latin American Nuclear-Weapon-Free Zone

Brazil's diplomatic activism in the nuclear field was not limited to the IAEA negotiations. This became evident in 1961, when the country joined the international discussions on nuclear nonproliferation. They began within the United Nations in 1958 with the creation of a Ten-Nation Disarmament Committee composed of members of the two Cold War blocs. However, the discussions between Moscow and Washington stalemated in 1961 over nuclear tests. After the third Berlin crisis in August 1961, the UNGA, with the full support of the Soviet Union and the United States, approved the expansion of the committee to include eight non-nuclear-weapon countries not aligned with either of the two blocs and representing all the continents. Brazil and Mexico would represent Latin America.[61]

From 1961 to 1964 international disarmament was at the top of the Brazilian diplomatic actions that were labeled by the government as "Independent Foreign Policy" (Política Externa Independente). In the final months of the period, marked by a military coup that overthrew the democratic government, Brazil's foreign minister, Araújo Castro, proclaimed disarmament, development, and decolonization to be the top priorities of Brazil's foreign policy.

Presidents Quadros and Goulart sought a more autonomous attitude in Brazil's relations with Washington, a neutral position in the Cold War, and more global action. They also supported unilateral and multilateral measures for partial or complete disarmament.[62] As noted by the Brazilian scholar Paulo Wrobel, "Brazilian diplomacy, traditionally cautious and firmly allied with the United States, moved to emphasize not only order but also justice as goals worthy to fight for with the arms of international diplomacy. Disarmament was seen as a natural path for a fairer international order."[63] For Afonso Arinos de Melo Franco, the Brazilian delegate to the United Nations, former foreign minister, and one of the principal architects of Quadros's foreign policy, Brazil's support for disarmament was recognized by the international community when it was selected for the

Eighteen-Nation Disarmament Committee (ENDC). Regarding the future effectiveness of the ENDC, in a report to the Foreign Ministry Arinos underlined that "a restricted committee that included some independent voices (not members of the military alliances of the two blocs) could achieve better results."[64]

Brazil's promotion of nuclear nonproliferation was clear in November 1961, when the government strongly supported the creation of nuclear-weapon-free zones (NWFZs). As a reaction to the French nuclear tests in the Algerian Sahara, in 1961 the Brazilian delegation at the UNGA voted to make Africa free from nuclear weapons.[65] It was the first sign of Brazil's support for the idea of NWFZs, a project initiated by the Polish diplomat Adam Rapacki for Central Europe but one that Brasília wanted to apply to areas of the Third World, particularly Latin America. The idea was conceived by Afonso Arinos and Foreign Minister Francisco Clementino de San Tiago Dantas. The proposal received only Brazilian and Cuban support and was not welcomed by the military sectors, which preferred the notion of collective defense through the Rio Pact.[66] In January 1962, at the Punta del Este meeting of the Organization of American States, Brazil, together with Mexico, suggested denuclearizing and prohibiting the presence of nuclear weapons in Latin America.[67]

Even though the proposal led nowhere, Brazil revived the idea in March 1962, during the first session of the ENDC. San Tiago Dantas renewed his support for denuclearized zones and joined the growing international movement to ban atmospheric nuclear tests.[68] Dantas, along with the British foreign secretary, Alec Douglas Home, promoted high-level meetings to discuss the detection of underground nuclear tests. Thus, he warmly welcomed the creation of an American-British-Soviet subcommittee to discuss the issue.[69] However, the Brazilian foreign minister sharply criticized the impasse in the negotiations caused by the renewed lack of confidence on the part of Washington, London, and Moscow. Dantas did not limit his support to discussions of disarmament and inspection; he also supported discussing "a plan for the reconversion of an economy dominated by arms production into a peace economy."[70] Brazil's proposal was supported not only by Third World countries such as India but also by Sweden and Canada.[71]

The rest of the first session of the ENDC was particularly disappointing for Brazil. The ENDC deadlocked over the preamble to a nuclear nonproliferation and disarmament treaty because of persistent Soviet opposition to international controls over its nuclear activities. Nevertheless, Brazil continued to act as a staunch supporter of regional and global disarmament and nonproliferation initiatives. On the occasion of the UNGA in September 1962, the Brazilian delegation proposed establishing a NWFZ in Latin America and attempted to obtain support from all the governments of the region. While Brazil faced opposition from the United States, the idea was supported by Bolivia, Chile, Ecuador, and Mexico (which declared itself a nuclear-weapon-free country on the occasion of the first ENDC meeting).

Because of the Cuban Missile Crisis in October 1962, the initiative gained momentum. As some scholars have demonstrated, Brazil played a meaningful role in trying to solve this crisis, acting as a diplomatic bridge between the United States and Cuba, with which Brasília had excellent relations.[72] Besides direct diplomatic maneuvers aimed at both Washington and Havana, Brazil's diplomatic action at the UNGA became more vigorous.[73] On 8 November 1962 Arinos reaffirmed the denuclearization plan proposed in September.[74] Brazil believed that it could guarantee the efficient removal of Soviet missiles from Cuba and the establishment of an inspection regime for preventing the reintroduction of the weapons. The proposal gained private support from Washington and Moscow. Nevertheless, despite excellent relations with Brazil, the Cuban government continued to oppose the plan and required the removal of all US bases from the Caribbean and Latin America.[75] The United States could not accept these conditions. This meant that the Brazilian proposal, introduced to the UNGA on 15 November, failed.

The death of Brazil's project became evident after a meeting between the Soviet first deputy premier, Anastas Mikoyan, and the US secretary of state, Dean Rusk. The latter confirmed the US interest in approving the Brazilian proposal since "an atom-free Latin America . . . in the long run . . . might provide mutual assurance which could give a feeling of security to these countries."[76] The Soviets, however, set out a different position. Mikoyan defined the Brazilian plan as "good" but, sharing the Cuban position, strongly criticized the unwillingness of the United States to renouncing its bases in Latin American countries. It represented the end of the Brazilian initiative, which eventually lost the support of other Latin American governments, such as Argentina, Venezuela, Paraguay, El Salvador, and the Dominican Republic.[77]

Although all the parties involved in the Cuban crisis had initially agreed to discuss the proposal of a Latin American NWFZ, Brazil was left with no option but to withdraw the resolution from the UNGA agenda in mid-December without a vote. Nonetheless, several other Latin American countries shared the desire to denuclearize the region. For instance, the president of Mexico, Adolfo López Mateos, presented his Chilean counterpart, Jorge Alessandri, with a project for regional disarmament by committing all the Latin American countries to forbid the presence of either atomic weapons or missile bases in their territories.[78] As

Left to right: Foreign Minister José Augusto de Araújo Castro, President João Goulart, and former foreign minister Francisco Clementino de San Tiago Dantas, Itamaraty Palace, Rio de Janeiro, 1963. (ICO 30.195 C23—Ministério das Relações Exteriores no Rio de Janeiro, Seção de Mapoteca e Iconografia)

a Brazilian diplomat involved in the negotiations in New York declared to this author, that was the moment when the leadership of the proposal for disarming Latin America began to shift from Brasília to Mexico City.[79] Furthermore, the Brazilian initiative promoted by the Goulart government was not perceived positively in several countries. The Uruguayan military, for example, firmly opposed the Brazilian proposal to denuclearize the continent.[80]

As recently declassified documents from the Brazilian Foreign Ministry show, the diplomatic idea to denuclearize Latin America also met domestic opposition. This is what was behind the intense reaction of CNEN to the resolution proposed in November 1962. Marcello Damy, chairman of CNEN and a member of the

IAEA board of governors, sent a memorandum directly to President Goulart in November 1962 requesting a radical modification of the Brazilian scheme. It was not the first disagreement between the nuclear authorities and Itamaraty over Brazil's diplomatic decisions in the atomic realm. Damy was particularly concerned that Itamaraty had not consulted CNEN, which was responsible by law for the national nuclear policy and any international agreements regarding nuclear energy. A possible approval of the resolution for denuclearizing Latin America, according to CNEN, could have grave consequences for national security. It would "drastically compromis[e Brazil's] defense possibilities in the event of a nuclear conflict." Moreover, a Latin American NWFZ would, in Damy's words, "impede the development of atomic energy for industrial purposes in our country." The Brazilian scientist also noted that since it was not possible to reach the goal of "integral disarmament" because of the lack of commitment on the part of the great powers, "the system of global security relies on an armed peace." Damy believed that "the international prestige of the countries depends on the 'state of nuclearization' as an expression of the physical power both offensive and defensive." Damy considered the ENDC negotiations meaningless, since countries (e.g., Israel, India, Egypt, and Communist China) would soon join the atomic club.[81] As a result of the several nuclear arms races around the world, Damy thought it "strange that our country assumes an attitude of leading a movement for the denuclearization [*desatomização*] of Latin America, which will definitively place us at the margins of power diplomacy, [in a position] for self-initiative that even the recently emancipated African countries have refused to accept."[82]

Writing about a possible Brazilian weaponization, Damy argued that the "Brazilian atomic development was so significant in Latin America" that the implementation of the power reactor program mentioned in the first paragraphs of this chapter could provide Brazil with the potential to build at least ten plutonium bombs by 1970. Even if the main goal of CNEN was not to use the material produced by the reactors for military purposes, "it is a potential that we can't give up, given the impossibility of foreseeing, with a certain degree of security, what Brazil could face in the next decade, in the event of a new international political situation" and above all a position of inferiority in relation to Argentina. Buenos Aires did not accept the Brazilian proposal and, being a potential nuclear rival with a more advanced nuclear sector, "would not limit its future possibilities in the [nuclear] realm." Damy defined the Brazilian proposal as an "auto-mutilation . . . giving up [Brazil's] future prestige in international organizations, without any compensation but an illusionary influence that leads to victories of purely academic interest."[83]

The chairman of CNEN also strongly criticized the inclusion of international inspections in the proposal for a NWFZ. It would open up the Brazilian nuclear laboratories, facilities, and power plants to international inspectors, "making the [Brazilian] scientific and technological advances accessible to the other countries." Further targets of criticism were "Brazil's commitment not to build, receive or stock devices for carrying nuclear weapons," as well as the impossibility of accumulating plutonium. In Damy's view, Brazil's commitment would impede any future Brazilian research in the field of rockets and missiles, as well as the possibility for Brazil to manufacture nuclear fuel for the thorium reactors since they would also produce plutonium. In conclusion, Damy vehemently criticized the absence of any nuclear-weapon states' commitment to denuclearizing their strategic areas in Latin America (Panama, Guantanamo, and Martinica). The NWFZ would represent a significant threat to Brazilian security. For that reason, Damy recommended a radical modification of Brazil's position within the United Nations. Damy's attitude reflected the position of a scientific community seeking to preserve Brazilian rights to develop nuclear energy for both military and peaceful purposes without international limitations. Damy's position, however, seemed not to prompt the desired effect.

In April 1963 the presidents of Bolivia, Brazil, Chile, Ecuador, and Mexico issued a declaration to create a NWFZ. Through resolution 1911, UNGA approved in November 1963 the proposal submitted by Mexico but originally conceived by Brazil. It paved the way for negotiating Latin American denuclearization. The Mexican government, which led the initiative, convoked a preliminary meeting of all Latin American and Caribbean countries in Mexico City to discuss a possible treaty starting in the following year.[84] In March 1964 the preparatory commission for discussing Latin American disarmament gathered for the first time.

During the same months, the global action for disarmament advanced thanks to the signature in Moscow of the Limited Test Ban Treaty. Brazil signed and ratified the treaty immediately. In September 1963 the Brazilian delegate in Geneva, Josué de Castro, a renowned social scientist, commented on the signature of the treaty as the only reachable result. Even though he had called for an extension of the treaty to include underground tests, the Limited Test Ban Treaty was nevertheless considered a new starting point for further negotiations toward global disarmament and a comprehensive test ban treaty. Despite Brazilian activism, the ENDC remained deadlocked until 1965. The first Chinese nuclear test in 1964, along with the persistent US-Soviet disagreement, froze the work of the committee and halted the general discussions on disarmament and nonproliferation.

CHAPTER THREE

Against the Regime(s) and Brazil's Renewed Nuclear Ambitions, 1964–1974

"The rejection of the atomic agreement between the United States and the Soviet Union defines the Brazilian position and accords with the tradition of defense of the sovereignty of the country."[1] With these words José Honório Rodrigues, a leading Brazilian historian and director of the Instituto Brasileiro de Relações Internacionais, referred to the draft of the NPT as it was submitted by the superpowers in the ENDC in 1965 and to Brazil's position on the agreement. The sentence appeared in the foreword to a special issue of the leading Brazilian journal devoted to international relations, *Revista Brasileira de Política Internacional.* Read and written mainly by diplomats, the journal reflected the position of the Ministry of Foreign Affairs. The special issue discussed Brazil's role in the atomic era. It mirrored the internal debate over nuclear energy and the position to adopt toward the treaty of nonproliferation. Rodrigues, along with many other members of Brazil's scientific, political, military, and diplomatic elites, did not accept a discriminatory treaty that could prevent the country from achieving autonomy in the nuclear field. Brazil promoted disarmament but considered atomic energy to be key to its future role in the international system from the economic, political, and military perspectives. In 1972, after the entry into force of the NPT, Ambassador João Augusto de Araújo Castro (the last foreign minister of the democratic regime, a key negotiator for disarmament, and then ambassador to Washington), proclaimed in a famous article in *International Organization* that the treaty signaled the "freezing" of the international system, as the superpowers imposed it upon the rest of the NNWSs.[2] Like other developing countries, Brazil declared its opposition to a rigid system, a fruit of the Soviet-US agreement. Brazil's position might appear somewhat schizophrenic to an analyst in the early 1970s. While it opposed the NPT, it signed a major agreement with the United States to provide a turnkey nuclear power plant. Brazil defended its right to autonomy but apparently accepted its dependence on Washington. This chapter deals with Brazil's stand toward the international regime of nuclear nonproliferation and with the setting out and initial implementation of a new nuclear policy that would guide the country for the next twenty years.

The Military Coup of 1964: A Rupture with the Past?

On 31 March 1964 a bloodless military coup orchestrated with the support of the governors of São Paulo, Guanabara (now Rio de Janeiro), and Minas Gerais and the US government, overthrew President Goulart, who was accused of being responsible for a possible socialist revolution in the country. The coup was a consequence of the economic, social, and political turbulence that characterized the last years of the democratic period and led to a sharp political polarization. The military-civilian coup should have been a surgical operation that rapidly devolved the power to civilian authorities. However, even if without a preordered strategy by the *golpistas*, the military regime would last twenty-one years. The new administration, headed by Marshal Humberto Alencar de Castelo Branco and supported by the United States, repudiated the country's independent foreign policy and aligned its diplomatic strategy with Washington, at least until 1967. Brazil would adopt economic reforms, but it would progressively restrict social and political freedoms, canceling the 1965 general elections and perpetuating the civilian-military regime. Its foreign policy, led initially by the experienced diplomat Vasco Leitão da Cunha and later by the politician Juracy Magalhães, would follow Cold War thinking even if that meant breaking with the diplomatic tradition of not interfering in the domestic affairs of other countries. Brazil would break off relations with Cuba and participate in the US-promoted Organization of American States Inter-American Peace Force in the Dominican Republic to prevent the consolidation of a nationalist and leftist government in the country. While Brazil agreed with Washington in several areas, its attitude toward nonproliferation would represent a major divergence between the two countries. The literature on Brazil's posture toward the global and regional nonproliferation regime identifies the military coup as a turning point in the country's nuclear diplomacy.[3]

Nevertheless, there had been clear signs of a possible change in Brazil's posture toward the NWFZ as early as December 1963. In May and November 1963 CNEN and the military forces had vehemently criticized the decision to promote and support the UN resolution on Latin American denuclearization.[4] According to the CNEN chairman, Damy, the Foreign Ministry did not respect the national law that gave CNEN decision-making powers regarding atomic policy. Foreign

Minister João Augusto de Araújo Castro guaranteed that the resolution did not represent a commitment on the part of Brazil.[5] The country could reverse that position during the imminent negotiations in Mexico City. On the eve of the military coup, an interministerial working group comprising representatives of CNEN, CSN, and Itamaraty outlined the country's position in Mexico, which strongly reflected the attitude in Geneva. Brazilian negotiators would defend the right to access nuclear technologies and knowledge without international constraints.

Brazil, the NPT Negotiations, and the Treaty of Tlatelolco in the Castelo Branco Years (1964–1967)

The Brazilian representatives in the disarmament forums continued to share the views of the nonaligned countries in the ENDC. Following a stalemated debate over nuclear nonproliferation, in August 1965 the United States and the Soviet Union separately submitted draft treaties that were vague about inspections. In response, on 15 September the eight nonaligned members of the ENDC submitted a memorandum presenting the five basic criteria the NPT should meet. Brazil and the nonaligned members "insisted that the treaty should not be an end in itself but the means to an end," namely, general disarmament. Consequently, the treaty must leave no room for either direct or indirect proliferation.[6] Furthermore, nuclear and nonnuclear countries should share the same responsibilities and obligations. The treaty, the memorandum continued, should be a credible step toward nuclear disarmament and must provide safeguards and inspections to ensure its effectiveness. Finally, "nothing in the treaty should adversely affect the right of any group of states to conclude regional treaties to ensure the total absence of nuclear weapons in their respective territories." The document, approved as UNGA resolution 2028 on 19 November, led the superpowers to withdraw their drafts and was the basis for the subsequent ENDC negotiations.[7]

Brazil criticized the USSR-US proposal, which would crystallize the international community into nuclear and nonnuclear countries. The NPT "should not regard non-dissemination as an end in itself, but it should also take into account the effective security of the non-nuclear weapon states."[8] In March 1966 Ambassador Antônio Corrêa do Lago, Brazil's representative on the ENDC, renewed Brazil's support for the resolution approved several months earlier and declared: "An objective and politically valid treaty should reflect the reality of the power relations between the great nuclear powers and the reality of the power relations between these countries and the non-nuclear world."[9] Corrêa do Lago echoed the position expressed by the foreign minister San Tiago Dantas in 1962 and defended the inalienable right of the developing countries to use nuclear energy for peaceful purposes. "Instead of curtailing the possibilities of economic development of the non-nuclear countries," said the Brazilian diplomat, the treaty "should pave the way for ushering them into the nuclear age."[10]

Corrêa do Lago's words reflected the developing countries' growing demand for nuclear energy. The Brazilian diplomat, however, introduced elements that would define the Brazilian attitude throughout the negotiations. Criticism of an unfair international regime and the defense of the right to develop nuclear energy for peaceful purposes characterized the actions of Brazil not only in Geneva but also in Mexico City, where the Latin American countries (except Cuba) discussed the establishment of a NWFZ from 1964 to 1967.

The negotiations culminated with the signing of the so-called Treaty of Tlatelolco, named for the neighborhood where the Mexican Ministry of Foreign Affairs was located, on 14 February 1967. Brazil, which coordinated its actions with Argentina's (and kept Argentina informed about the negotiations in Geneva), obtained the right to develop delivery systems.[11] It was an astonishing victory for Brazil, which in the early 1960s had created a space commission and was developing the Sonda rockets. Moreover, as stated in a common interpretative note regarding article 18 of the treaty, they could also "carry out the explosion of nuclear devices for peaceful purposes, including explosions involving devices similar to those used in nuclear weapons, or collaborate with third parties for the same purpose."[12] However, Mexico and other countries, supported by the United States, interpreted article 18 exclusively as the possibility to buy nuclear explosives services from NWSs. On 14 March 1967, one month after the negotiations in Mexico City concluded, Brazil's president, Castelo Branco, strongly criticized the Mexican and US positions. He declared that Brazil could not "renounce the peaceful use of atomic energy, a key element for the future of the nation."[13]

In order to defend the right to develop *peaceful* nuclear devices, the Brazilian government aimed to extend the diplomatic success obtained in Mexico. Brasília deployed the arguments made by the superpowers, especially the United States, which conducted the Plowshare Program.[14] Brazil justified subjecting its policy of peaceful nuclear explosions (PNEs) to international inspection as a way to pursue major economic goals, such as "the digging of canals, the connection of hydrographic basins, the recovery of oil fields, and the realization of 'great engineering works.'"[15]

Brazil signed the treaty in May 1967. Still, the acceptance of the regional regime of nuclear nonproliferation and inspection was only a formality and followed specific instructions from the new president, Costa e Silva. At the moment

President Humberto de Alencar Castello Branco (*center, seated*) inaugurates the research reactor at the Institute of Nuclear Energy in Rio de Janeiro, 7 May 1965. (BR RJANRIO EH.0.FOT, PRP.8502, Arquivo Nacional)

of ratifying the Treaty of Tlatelolco, Brazil, along with Chile, conditioned its full accession upon the participation of all Latin American countries in the NWFZ and the ratification of two additional protocols to the treaty designed for the NWSs recognized by the international community and for countries having territorial interests in the Americas. As noted by the US scholar John R. Redick, these protocols (resulting from Brazilian proposals) were included "to assure strong international support for the agreement."[16] According to Additional Protocol I, the "states having territorial interests in the Americas agree to keep their possessions free of nuclear weapons." Through the acceptance of Additional Protocol II, the NWSs (the United States, the United Kingdom, the People's Republic of China, France, and the Soviet Union) would commit "not to use or threaten to use nuclear weapons" against the full parties to the treaty.[17]

The failure of these countries to substantially commit and Cuban refusal to accede to the Treaty of Tlatelolco justified the Brazilian choice not to join the NWFZ until 1994, when Argentina (which had signed but not ratified the treaty), Brazil, and Chile changed their position. It was a victory for the politicians, military, and scientists that in 1962 and 1963 had strongly criticized Brazil's decision to denuclearize Latin America in response to the Cuban Missile Crisis. The Brazilian delegation acted on the suggestion of the then CNEN chairman, Marcelo Damy, to substantially abandon the proposal of denuclearization.

Brazil and the Last Phase of NPT Negotiations in Geneva

Brazil's signing of the Treaty of Tlatelolco coincided roughly with the inauguration of Marshal Arthur da Costa e Silva as the second president of the military regime. A hard-liner, a nationalist, and fiercely anticommunist, Costa e Silva led the country until his death in 1969, when he was replaced by a military junta that would give the powers to General Emílio Garrastazu Médici (1969–March 1974). The two presidents implemented a massive repression policy, abusing both human and political rights (the 1968 Institutional Act No. 5 would suspend habeas corpus). They also experienced a phase of steady economic expansion (the so-called *milagre econômico*) that took the country to an advanced stage of industrialization (despite expanding economic inequality). Costa e Silva and Médici continued their anticommunist crusade in domestic and regional affairs and continued to be key Latin American allies to the United States. However, Brazil's foreign policy under Costa e Silva shifted from an automatic alignment to a more autonomous diplomatic policy that echoed the "independent foreign policy" of the last governments of the democratic experience. The end of the Alliance for Progress experience and the mounting criticism of human rights abuses by the administration of Lyndon B. Johnson and the US Congress partially strained the bilateral relations. Costa e Silva's "Diplomacy of Prosperity" (*Diplomacia da Prosperidade*) aimed at supplying the country with the tools to fight for justice against the inequalities of an unfair international order imposed by the superpowers. It was in that context that Brazil built coalitions not only with the West but also with Third World countries to sustaining its right to access nuclear energy (key for Brazil's future development). Consequently, at the end of May 1967, Brazilian delegates at the ENDC, headed by the ambassador and future foreign minister Antônio Azeredo da Silveira, proposed to amend the draft NPT. Article 1 should mention Dantas's 1962 proposal to oblige the NWS to create a fund (also obtained from the resources liberated by nuclear disarmament) to assist the progress of the developing countries. The proposed article 2-A stated that the NWSs should commit to ending the nuclear arms race and destroying their atomic arsenals in the shortest period possible. Article 4, echoing the text of the Treaty of Tlatelolco, should preserve the universal right to build peaceful atomic devices. Article 5 should oblige the NPT member states to convene five years after the treaty takes effect to evaluate not only the treaty but also the commitment to nuclear disarmament. In Silveira's view, the text did not reflect "an adequate balance of mutual responsibilities and obligations between nuclear and non-nuclear-weapon states." Still, it was merely "designed to maintain the status quo, without taking into account the interests of all the members of the international community."[18] Brazil, mirroring India in its criticism of "atomic apartheid," would not accept a discriminatory treaty. It would split the international community into haves (the countries that had detonated an atomic device by 1967) and have-nots (the rest of the countries, which would be banned from acquiring nuclear explosives). The latter category should also put all its nuclear facilities and material under IAEA supervision, while the NWSs would have no such obligations. As Silveira concluded, "It is thus imperative that the nuclear weapon countries offer an adequate counterpart to the set of obligations that are to be undertaken by non-nuclear countries."[19]

At the end of August 1967 the Soviet Union and the United States separately presented identical drafts to the ENDC. The governments of Washington and Moscow wanted to end the negotiations on the treaty quickly, even if the section about inspections, one of the pillars of the entire disarmament mechanism, was left blank. As a response to possible reservations from either allies or nonaligned countries, the two superpowers, which cochaired the commission, submitted a resolution imposing 15 March 1968 as the deadline for issuing the final text of the treaty to be voted on at the UNGA.[20] Despite the US-USSR ultimatum, many delegates sharply criticized the draft treaty. In early October, Alva Myrdal, the Swedish representative and speaker for the nonaligned countries, hailed an "avalanche of suggestions and amendments worthy of profound scrutiny."[21] India, a country with nuclear ambitions and strongly threatened by the tests of Chinese hydrogen bombs in 1967, considered signing the treaty an act of "political suicide" because of the impossibility of developing nuclear technology for peaceful purposes.[22]

In early October 1967, accepting the draft NPT was not compatible with the Brazilian nuclear policy then under discussion. Renouncing the right to develop PNEs was too high a price to pay. The absence of a real commitment to nuclear disarmament, along with opposition from the People's Republic of China (PRC) and France (two members of the frozen nuclear club) to accession to the treaty, was unacceptable. In an anonymous handwritten note on the document laying out the new Brazilian nuclear policy one can read, "Brazil cannot renounce nuclear weapons."[23] Within the government, some actors in the military and the diplomatic corps saw nuclear weapons capability as a precondition for national security. In 1965 the Brazilian Ministry of War estimated that as a consequence of the inauguration of the three Argentine nuclear power plants, Buenos Aires would be able to accumulate fissile material for building eighty-five 20-kiloton atomic bombs by 1981.[24] Two years later, according to H. Jon Rosenbaun, a feasibility study commissioned by CNEN concluded that it would take Brazil fifteen years to build a nuclear device.[25] However, no direct threat was identified, and a nuclear war with Argentina was considered a remote possibility.[26]

In a top-secret summit of the CSN, Brazil's president, Costa e Silva, and his cabinet defended the right to PNEs to guarantee the country's current and future growth and security. The minister of trade and industry, Brigadier General Macedo Soares e Silva, declared that "saying that Brazil will not produce a nuclear weapon is an illusion." Costa e Silva and the foreign minister, Magalhães Pinto, highlighted the need to emphasize in international negotiations the peaceful essence of Brazilian nuclear activities, which had been allowed by the Treaty of Tlatelolco. Brazil's president underlined that in defending the right to developing the PNEs in Geneva, "we will not call them bombs, but devices that can explode."[27] The Brazilian government wanted to be free from international constraints in the event of nuclear weapons acquisition. Indeed, it had not made the ultimate decision to begin a nuclear weapons program (above all because Brazil would formally test the PNEs under international supervision). In that context, the words of Costa e Silva and those of his minister were meant to justify the country's diplomatic position in Geneva in 1967 and 1968 and the attitude of the country until 1990. Despite the superpowers' concern about Brazil's defense of its right to develop the PNEs, the Latin American country did not have a nuclear complex. As the former CNEN chairman Marcelo Damy publicly underlined, the country was not able to build a nuclear device.[28]

A few days after the meeting of the CSN, the Brazilian delegation at the ENDC submitted its amendments designed to omit any reference to the prohibition of nuclear explosive devices in articles 1, 2, and 10 of the draft treaty. The right to develop PNEs was included within the general rule about the peaceful use of atomic energy contained in an amended article 4. According to the Brazilian delegation, the same right was in line with article 5 of the draft treaty, which recognized "that potential benefits from any peaceful application will be made available . . . to non-nuclear-weapon States Party to this Treaty." This position, shared by India and other countries, provoked a debate over the possibility of establishing a service for PNEs within the IAEA framework. However, the majority of ENDC members agreed that this service should be left to the full discretion of each supplying country through bilateral agreements.[29] As the deadline for submitting the final text of the treaty approached, the Brazilian government instructed its delegation not to sign the agreement if it conflicted with Brazil's national interests.[30]

The draft treaty was discussed during the first part of the twenty-second session of the UNGA in November and December 1967. The United States and the Soviet Union submitted a new draft of the NPT on 18 January 1968. It included a more detailed article on safeguards (to also be applied to the peaceful activities of the NWSs), an offer by the NWSs of potential benefits of peaceful applications of nuclear explosions to NNWSs through bilateral and multilateral agreements, and a more explicit commitment to promote the peaceful use of nuclear energy.[31] In light of the new proposals, the US government in early February 1968 attempted to persuade Brasília to modify its position on the PNEs, considered one of the main hurdles to the successful negotiation of the NPT.[32] The US gesture did not lead to the expected success. The government in Brasília did not modify its previous instructions to its plenipotentiary, Ambassador Araújo Castro, formerly foreign minister, who would represent Brazil at the United Nations in New York.[33]

In the last round of talks, when the success of the US-USSR position was assured, Brazil's firm opposition would consist in "avoiding the ENDC endorsement of the superpowers proposal," which did not respect the five principles of UNGA resolution 2028 (1965).[34] The US representative to the ENDC, Samuel De Palma, attempted to convince Araújo Castro that the "draft before us reflects the broadest area of the agreement now attainable" to decrease the threat of further dissemination of nuclear weapons.[35]

In a lengthy memorandum, Araújo Castro strongly criticized the US-USSR draft treaty, which, with its discriminatory and irreversible features, relied on the idea of a "Super-Directory of Nuclear Powers" that would establish a de facto protectorate over the nonnuclear world. The Brazilian delegate avoided an open confrontation with the United States, choosing to maintain good bilateral relations between Washington and Brasília. William C. Foster and De Palma, the US delegates, personally guaranteed Araújo Castro that *someday* and *somehow* the two countries would resolve the PNE problem.[36] On 11 March 1968, three days before the deadline for the negotiations, the two superpowers presented a revised version of the draft treaty, including three amendments from Sweden and one from the United Kingdom on nonessential points.[37] As a consequence, the text was not the object of further negotiations within the ENDC. It was sent to the UNGA, which could make a decision without the committee's approval or endorsement in April or May 1968.[38]

Brazil's strategy was to delay the action of the UNGA, where in May 1968 Foreign Minister Magalhães Pinto declared that the treaty presented significant limitations and did not satisfy the nonnuclear countries. He proposed beginning a new round of negotiations between the NWSs and the NNWSs to reach a real compromise. According to Pinto, the treaty could be voted on after the Conference of Non-Nuclear-Weapon States ended. The conference, which would begin in August 1968, could help to define a joint position for the two categories of states. A significant number of governments shared this position and raised their reservations and criticism of the proposed NPT.[39]

However, on 30 May 1968 the superpowers appeased the majority of those opposed to the NPT. They promised to undertake "effective measures in the direction of nuclear disarmament," to support the right to acquire peaceful nuclear equipment, to serve the "needs of developing areas of the world" without discrimination, and to start negotiations on spreading the benefits of nuclear technology.[40] Moreover, they offered to provide security guarantees in the event of nuclear attack or threat, as requested by Brazil, which did not feel protected by the Inter-American Treaty of Reciprocal Assistance.[41] This diplomatic demarche was successful. It corresponded with the approval of the NPT on 12 June 1968 despite the abstention of countries such as India and Brazil.[42]

The last decision was taken on 19 June 1968, when the NWSs actively participating in the ENDC negotiations offered negative security guarantees to the NNWSs.[43] As noted by Vojtech Mastny, such guarantees were vague and "far from providing any positive assurance of assistance."[44] With the adoption of the resolution by ten votes to none, and with the abstention of Algeria, Brazil, France, India, and Pakistan, the UNSC paved the way to successful approval of the NPT by the international community. On 1 July, the treaty was opened for signature, and it entered into force on 5 March 1970.

The treaty represented a victory for both Moscow and Washington, which succeeded in imposing an agreement on nuclear nonproliferation after twenty years of impasse, creating an international legal instrument for preventing the spread of nuclear weapons. Furthermore, the subsequent steps for implementing the treaty were left to be decided by the main NWSs. Thus, a comprehensive test ban treaty, the reversal of vertical proliferation, and the IAEA's transformation into an effective watchdog against horizontal proliferation remained unfulfilled proposals presented at the ENDC weeks after the signing of the NPT. The rising disagreement between the superpowers, together with the US Congress's delayed approval of the NPT in response to the Soviet invasion of Czechoslovakia and the delayed West German accession to the treaty, made it difficult to keep to the schedule that had been set by the disarmament agenda.

In this context, Brazil tried to play a critical role at the Conference of Non-Nuclear-Weapon States. The purpose of the 1968 meeting, following the 1965 approval of UNGA resolution 2028, was to offer a response from the NNWSs to the NPT. The Brazilian representatives proposed alternative paths to reaching the general objective of nuclear nonproliferation. They did not share the idea of a global treaty and instead proposed bilateral or regional agreements, such as the Treaty of Tlatelolco, as instruments for controlling the spread of atomic weapons. Moreover, the Brazilian government, not satisfied with the UNSC resolution, proposed a universal convention to be attached to the NPT to obtain further security guarantees from the NWSs. Brazil's goal continued to be to delay any new NNWSs' joining the NPT in order to weaken it.[45]

Brazil's delegation to the UN Conference of Non-Nuclear-Weapon States, Geneva, September 1968. *Left to right*: Antônio F. Azeredo da Silveira, João Augusto de Araújo Castro, and Paulo Nogueira Batista. (Paulo Nogueira Batista Archive, PNB foto 011, FGV/CPDOC)

The conference did not have the expected results. An Indian-Pakistani confrontation over the accession to nuclear technology for any state that refused to accept the NPT safeguards, together with the rejection of a Latin American–African resolution on negative security assurances, led, after a month of negotiations, to the full failure of the conference. The NPT was not undermined at all. The superpowers perceived that failure and attempted to attract new parties to the global regime. Right before the end of the Johnson administration, the Soviet Union and the United States, in private talks, discussed the accession of some key countries, including Brazil, to the NPT.

The US-USSR Reaction to Brazil's Decision

Moscow and Washington had different reactions to Brazil's opposition to the NPT. The Soviet Union considered Brazil to be a *puppet* of West Germany within the ENDC. During a conversation with his Brazilian counterpart, Araújo Castro, the Soviet representative and cochairman of the committee, Ambassador N. V. Roschin, declared that he understood Brazil's opposition to the NPT. Still, he requested that Brazil not delay the conclusion of the treaty. The Soviets believed that Brazil's attitude could strengthen West German demarches against the NPT. Roschin told Araujo Castro: "We are not preoccupied with Brazil, whose peaceful intention we know. We are preoccupied with [West] Germany."[46]

At the time of this writing, there is no evidence of any West German influence on the Brazilian attitude toward the NPT. Recently declassified documents demonstrate that Bonn and Brasília held diplomatic discussions about the issue in Geneva in late January 1968. The FRG ambassador, Swidbert Schnippenkötter, revealed to Araújo Castro Bonn's dissatisfaction with the US-USSR NPT proposal because of the lack of security guarantees. The Japanese and the Italians expressed the same concern to the Brazilians.[47] Despite these attitudes, the Brazilians did not believe that West Germany and Japan would oppose the treaty. While the West Germans continued to express their worries about the treaty in the following months, the Brazilian government did not consider Bonn a key ally for altering the NPT.[48]

Washington took a different position. During the 1960s, Brazil was considered a third-rank threat to the nuclear nonproliferation regime. According to a report by the National Planning Association, although Brazil had the technical skills, it lacked the economic resources to develop a nuclear arsenal.[49] In early July 1967 Glenn Seaborg, the USAEC chairman, visited Brazil to persuade the Brazilians to renounce PNEs in exchange for the sale of peaceful nuclear explosives services by the United States. The mission, however, was unsuccessful, as Brazil continued to defend its right to develop PNEs.[50] Nevertheless, the State Department declared that the United States would continue to cooperate with Brasília in the nuclear field. Its incipient nuclear program was indeed seen as an important opportunity for the US nuclear industry, which aimed at confirming and expanding the 1965 agreement. Brazil did not appear crucial for the US goal of adopting the global treaty, and it was not considered a threat at that moment.[51]

Moscow, on the other hand, showed real concern about Brazil's attitude, fearing that opposition to the treaty by such an important player in the developing world might have worrisome consequences. During a meeting at the UNGA the Soviet ambassador, Yakov Malik, asked the US secretary of state, Dean Rusk, about the prospects of Japan, Brazil, and Argentina signing the NPT. Rusk was optimistic. He believed that both Japan and Brazil would sign the agreement despite the Brazilian foreign minister "having some strange ideas to the effect that Brazil needed to retain the right of developing its own nuclear capability for the purpose of carrying out peaceful nuclear explosions." In his opinion, however, "the main problem was that Brazil's delay created problems for its neighbor, Argentina, and Argentina's delay, in turn, created problems for Chile." It was a chain reaction that Malik compared to the situation existing between India and Pakistan, whose foreign minister confirmed to Rusk that Islamabad could not sign if New Delhi did. Rusk hoped that Gromyko would be able to influence India to sign the NPT. While the United States had to find a solution with Japan, Pakistan, and Latin America, Moscow would use its diplomatic influence with India.[52]

The Brazilian Nuclear Policy in the First Phase of the Military Regime

The Brazilian nuclear policy profoundly influenced the decisions made about both Tlatelolco and the NPT. The first government of the military regime replaced Marcello Damy at the head of CNEN (Costa e Silva rejected his name in both 1964 and 1969 for alleged communist sympathies). Professor Luiz Cintra do Prado (until 1966) and Uriel da Costa Ribeiro (until 1969) led the commission and would follow the general goals of the 1962 nuclear policy. Castello Branco substantially froze the atomic program for financial reasons and because part of the cabinet opposed funding a nuclear power plant. CNEN did not discontinue its cooperation with strategic partners such as France and the United States, with whom it signed, on 8 July 1965, an agreement for the peaceful use of nuclear energy. Following the general debate at the IAEA over the creation of a new safeguards system (set out in Information Circular 66), the cooperation with Washington would be overseen by the Vienna agency, thanks to a trilateral deal.[53] Despite attempting to avoid international control over the received equipment and material (Brazil also agreed to the creation of the new IAEA safeguards system), Brazil's authorities eventually accepted the condition to the collaboration imposed by the United States.[54] As underlined by the interministerial working group comprising CNEN, Itamaraty, the Joint Staff of the Armed Forces (Estado Maior das Forças Armadas, or EMFA), and CSN, the acceptance of that clause could affect the possible future autonomy of Brazil's nuclear sector. Still, in the short term US assistance was needed.[55] Brazil, however, could continue to rely on another partner, France.

In October 1964, during an official visit by the French president, Charles De Gaulle, the Brazilian government confirmed the collaboration in the nuclear field with Paris. France committed to training Brazilian atomic scientists to assist Brazil in developing a national reactor and supporting geological surveys.[56] In the geological field, France had a crucial role in coordinating the third phase of preparing for uranium prospecting. Assisted by CEA, CNEN selected thirty young geologists and established the Section of Mineral Exploration. While the following phase of preparation (1966–70) would be exclusively Brazilian, in 1974 the two countries would resume their collaboration. Scant public resources notwithstanding, CNEN in 1965 created the Thorium Group to design and build an indigenous breeder reactor at the IPr in Belo Horizonte. The Thorium Group, active until 1971, was crucial in those years for training personnel and furthering research in the nuclear field. Thanks to the cooperation with France (a specific agreement was signed in 1966) and the heavy water provided by the United States and Sweden, the IPr could set up new laboratories for studying the physics of the reactors. The breeder reactor, capable of generating more fissile material than it consumed, was supposed to be the basis for future reactors providing Brazil with nuclear energy using the abundant national reserves of thorium.

While it appeared that Brazil would follow the 1962 decisions, the São Paulo Institute of Technological Research (Instituto de Pesquisas Tecnológicas, or IPT) continued the research on uranium enrichment. On 30 March 1966 a team led by Professor Ivo Jordan reached some initial results. The three ZG3 ultracentrifuges designed by Wilhelm Groth enriched uranium hexafluoride, probably at a rate of 0.0175 percent, after previously using argon. Although the research team recorded several technical problems using the equipment, they were working toward resolving such issues. This study was important for the future development of the national capability in the enrichment of uranium.[57] The tiny research group continued to raise suspicions in the United States since it might be concealing Brazil's secret plans to produce fissile materials.[58] Despite rumors to this effect (including the possible construction of a centrifuge cascade in Belo

Horizonte), CNEN suspended the research and gave priority to thorium reactors. Until 1967, atomic activities were limited to research and feasibility studies for building nuclear power plants in southeastern and northern Brazil.[59] After the decision to review Brazil's nuclear policy in September 1966, the government assembled an interministerial working group that recommended the construction of a nuclear power plant in the south-central region of the country. Atomic energy would be the key to future development of the area, since hydroelectric power was projected to become scarce soon.[60]

The government put the atomic sector under the supervision of the CSN. One of the first shifts in nuclear policy concerned CNEN, which was put under the control of the Ministry of Mines and Energy. In May 1968, following the recommendations of the abovementioned working group, CNEN and Eletrobrás (Brazil's national electric energy company) signed an agreement to install the first nuclear power plant. Later Eletrobrás delegated to Central Elétrica Furnas, which created its nuclear engineering division, tasked with conducting the installation in collaboration with CNEN.[61] Until 1979 the nuclear program followed the plan for construction of up to ten nuclear power plants by 1990.[62]

In 1967 the thorium reactor seemed to be the best option for the Brazilian nuclear program, and France's research cooperation was ongoing. The ultimate decision on the reactor line to be adopted would be strongly influenced by the global debate over the choice between breeder reactors—a position supported by France, Canada, and India—and reactors fueled by enriched uranium—as proposed by the United States.[63] The choice had technological and industrial repercussions, as well as military ones since heavy-water reactors could also produce plutonium. The proliferation and industrial concerns would lead the industrialized countries, mainly the United States, to opt for light-water reactors eventually. It was within this debate that Brazil, with a more prosperous economy in 1967, would decide whether to follow the US decision.

To gather the best information in the international realm, diplomacy was crucial. The guidelines of the nuclear policy charged Itamaraty (in strict collaboration with CNEN and under CSN supervision) to secure the cooperation of countries with advanced nuclear programs, to defend the Brazilian right to develop atomic energy autonomously, to protect national resources, and to construct peaceful nuclear devices. According to the new policy, in the short term Brazil needed to obtain external cooperation through technical and training agreements to acquire the knowledge needed to develop a national nuclear industry as well as the capability to exploit and prospect the rich Brazilian mines of atomic minerals. In the longer term, Brazil's primary objective should be to pursue the mastery of the nuclear fuel cycle. It should also aim to develop a nuclear industry for providing energy both to industrial areas and to the poorest regions of the country.[64]

Approaching NPT Opponents about Nuclear Collaboration

As in the past, the Brazilian government adopted a multidirectional approach to acquire technologies, knowledge, and materials for strengthening its nuclear sector. Brazil did not opt to cooperate exclusively with its traditional partners, such as the Western countries, but began discussions with states taking a similar stance toward nuclear nonproliferation. Brazil's rationale was clear. While the United States, France, and Great Britain could refuse to transfer sensitive technologies because of Brazil's opposition to the NPT, Brasília could cooperate with other NPT opponents.[65]

Brazilian authorities attempted to cooperate with India (which exploded the first nuclear device in 1974), Israel (which was supposed to have the bomb), and Argentina. But their efforts had the same result as did their attempted cooperation with Japan and the FRG, which signed but did not ratify the NPT. India and Brazil signed an agreement to cooperate in the atomic realm in September 1968, on the occasion of the visit of Prime Minister Indira Gandhi to Brazil. The possible collaboration was confirmed by the visit of a CNEN delegation to New Delhi and direct talks between Hervásio de Carvalho, appointed as the new CNEN chairman in 1969, and Vikram Sarabhai, chairman of the Indian Atomic Energy Commission and father of the Indian space program. India and Brazil would conduct joint research in spent-fuel reprocessing and heavy-water technologies—India had advanced skills in those areas thanks to Canadian assistance—as well as in nuclear metallurgy and food preservation. Moreover, the two countries with the world's richest reserves of thorium could cooperate in the thorium cycle.[66] Despite the initial enthusiasm, the cooperation was not fruitful, but new efforts would be made during the 1980s and 1990s.

Similarly, Israel collaborated with Argentina in the early 1960s and attempted to implement joint projects with Brazil.[67] After an agreement on the peaceful use of nuclear energy signed in 1966, Brazilian and Israeli negotiators discussed from 1967 to 1973 a possible collaboration in which Israel would train Brazilian personnel in Israeli facilities and transfer a heavy-water plant to Brazil in exchange for nuclear materials from Brazil.[68] Nuclear and military authorities—the Brazilian Military Institute of Engineering (Instituto Militar de Engenharia) had been collaborating with CNEN on heavy water since 1964—strongly supported the agreement. However, the possibility of retaliation by Arab oil suppliers and the superpowers kept Brazil from implementing the deal with Israel.[69]

The quest for a partner in the nuclear field also included Argentina. Contrary to the general impression of the relation between Brasília and Buenos Aires as a rivalrous one, an intense diplomatic dialogue between the leading countries of the Southern Cone also embraced possible cooperation between the Argentine and Brazilian atomic programs.[70] Argentina was more advanced than Brazil in the nuclear realm. Unlike Brazil's government, that of Argentina guaranteed continuity to its nuclear program. In 1968, after the Argentine government had agreed to buy an atomic reactor from Siemens, it was close to inaugurating its first nuclear power plant.

After initial discussions in 1961, the dialogue was resumed in 1967, parallel to the general Argentine-Brazilian coordination over the Treaty of Tlatelolco and the NPT agreed to in February on the occasion of the visit of President-elect Costa e Silva to Buenos Aires. In April 1967, during an inter-American presidential conference in Punta del Este (Uruguay), the Brazilian president declared the need to promote regional integration in the nuclear field and the need to build a nuclear power plant in Brazil.[71] The decision was also connected to the need to maintain a balance in the industrial atomic area with Argentina, which would complete its first natural uranium reactor in a few years. A possible solution would be cooperation between the two neighbors. Therefore, nuclear and diplomatic authorities, with the full support of the CSN and the intelligence service, proposed on two occasions, in 1967 and 1970, a cooperation agreement to Argentina. However, Buenos Aires's reaction remained negative, even if a cordial communication channel was left open for possible future collaboration.[72]

Then, two other actors, Japan and West Germany, refused to accept the NPT. Those two governments (along with Italy) revealed internal divisions over accession to the nonproliferation regime and aimed at mastering sensitive aspects of the nuclear fuel cycle, such as uranium enrichment and spent-fuel reprocessing (a way in the eyes of some to keep the door open to the bomb).[73] Both countries were among Brazil's leading economic partners, and in recent history they had favored the development of important sectors of the Brazilian economy. The Latin American country could provide an opportunity for them. They could import the supposed abundant reserves of Brazilian uranium. They could also cooperate with Brasília, an opponent to the NPT, on secret projects without the interference of the superpowers, which had been particularly concerned since the early 1960s with the development of uranium enrichment facilities around the world. The period 1967–68 was crucial since the global nuclear industry was shifting toward the use of the light-water reactors fueled by 3 percent enriched uranium. In that context, mastering a uranium enrichment method, above all the Zippe method, which had tested successfully in the mid-1960s, would be the key to not relying on external fuel provisions. Security and economic reasons were wedded in a quest for a central technology in the expansion of nuclear energy. Many countries, such as Brazil, consequently promoted their projects to acquire uranium enrichment or sought forms of international cooperation to secure nuclear fuel supplies. At that moment, however, Brazil's technological choice was not clear. In September 1967, Brazil's diplomatic representatives held confidential talks on uranium enrichment with Japanese and West German scientific and diplomatic authorities.

Brazil's ambassador to Japan, Álvaro Teixeira Soares, met on 14 September for this purpose with Ambassador Kumao Nishimura, a member of the Japanese Atomic Energy Commission and responsible for international cooperation. Nishimura, considered to be convinced of Japan's need for autonomy in the nuclear realm, confirmed that the Department of Atomic Energy at the Institute of Technology of the University of Tokyo was working on the development of the centrifuge uranium enrichment method in collaboration with the Toshiba Company. In the recent past, Japan had secretly cooperated with West Germany and the Netherlands. Still, Nishimura underlined the limitations on nuclear activities set by the Japanese constitution, and the United States requested that Japan not share its research on uranium enrichment with other countries. Despite these obstacles, however, Nishimura would assist Brazil's effort to create a communication channel with the Japanese. He also proposed a cooperation to be covered by other commercial activities of the Toshiba Company in Brazil. At that moment, Brazil's and Japan's positions toward the NPT did not diverge significantly, but eventually Tokyo would sign the treaty.[74] Nishimura's collaboration succeeded, and the Japanese nuclear authorities confirmed a few days later Japan's availability to cooperate with Brazil in the nuclear field, including in uranium enrichment.[75] Even though Brazil's ambassador to Japan made all possible efforts to reach an agreement with Japan, including proposing a secret meeting between the Brazilian foreign minister and representatives of Toshiba and scientific institutions, CNEN decided not make a deal with Japan.[76] The available documentation does not inform us about how the talks with Japanese authorities went. The episode shows possible forms of circumvention of nonproliferation norms. Brazil would have new contacts with Japan in 1974, but no cooperation in the enrichment field would be established.

A few days after the meeting in Tokyo, similar talks took place in West Germany between José Leite Lopes, one of the most prominent Brazilian nuclear physicists and chairman of the Brazilian Society of Physics (Sociedade

Brasileira de Física), and Rudolf Schulten, director of the Nuclear Research Center Jülich in West Germany. The purpose of the meeting was to discuss large-scale cooperation in the nuclear field and also to explore the possible acquisition of ultracentrifuges. While a cooperation agreement would be signed in the following years, Schulten explained to Leite Lopes that unlike a few years earlier, international limitations, above all as a consequence of American pressure, imposed secrecy on the possible transfer of information or equipment connected to ultracentrifuge uranium enrichment.[77]

Thus international obstacles impeded transparent cooperation on uranium enrichment. The Japanese proposed to the Brazilians that a possible solution would be to conceal nuclear activities behind other kinds of industrial cooperation. This was the case of a West German proposal that landed on President Costa e Silva's desk in 1968. In September 1968 the Brazilian diplomat Paulo Nogueira Batista visited West Germany to negotiate a broad nuclear agreement. On that occasion the West German government renewed a secret offer made in June. During informal meetings with the Brazilian diplomat, Franz Joseph Strauss, the powerful West German political leader who was then finance minister and had previously headed the Ministries of Defense (1956–62) and Atomic Affairs (1955–56), and Gerhard Stoltenberg, the minister of scientific research, offered a new technology for enriching uranium with a ultracentrifuge isotopic separation method—the Zippe technique, with centrifuges lighter than the Groth-type ones imported by Brazil in the late 1950s—developed by the company Dornier.[78] The West German company was at the forefront of a national nuclear industrial effort that also included two other companies promoted by the West German Ministry for Atomic Affairs for mastering uranium enrichment. Dornier, which worked in the field until 1971, completed a 200-centrifuge test cascade for the Nuclear Research Center Jülich and worked on the design of the needle bearing and the magnetic upper bearing.[79]

The impossibility of enriching fissile material without limits on its enrichment of uranium owing to a provision in the 1954 Treaty of Paris led Bonn to seek a partner for sharing this technology. Despite the strong secrecy and the nonproliferation limitations, West Germany attempted to cooperate again with Brazil. The Dornier factory that would be built in the state of Minas Gerais, mainly for the construction of airplanes and rockets, would revolutionize nuclear activities in Brazil. It would upgrade the studies of the small research group working with the three ultracentrifuges at the Institute for Technological Research in São Paulo. It is not clear whether the cooperation would be subject to international safeguards, but a Brazilian interministerial group was to study the issue. From the perspective of the nascent nonproliferation regime, the collaboration between the then non-NPT members might limit the effectiveness of the treaty and give two countries a crucial tool in the path toward possible weaponization.

The Brazilian decision to cooperate with the United States caused the deal on the centrifuges to fail. However, West Germany and Brazil in June 1969 signed a crucial agreement for scientific and technological cooperation between the two countries. It also included the nuclear sector and allowed the Brazilian personnel of CNEN to be trained at the German Nuclear Research Center Jülich. It was also the basis for the future enlargement of the partnership.[80] The CNEN decision on ultracentrifuge enrichment did not mark the end of Brazil's interest in the technology. On several occasions in the following years, Brazilians and West Germans resumed discussions about the transfer of technologies for enriching uranium to Brazil.

At the time, the West Germans were acquiring a prominent role in the global market of nuclear energy. They eventually merged their capability in the uranium enrichment by the gas centrifuge method with those of the Netherlands and the United Kingdom. In March 1970 they signed the Treaty of Almelo, creating the Uranium Enrichment Consortium (Urenco).[81] The birth of Urenco, whose first samples of enriched uranium would be produced in the early 1980s, allowed Bonn to enjoy the fruits of its technology in the form of uranium enriched abroad. The exportation of both fuel and enriching machinery required a joint decision by the partners. The impossibility of receiving Urenco technologies from West Germany became clear during the negotiations with Brazil for exporting uranium enrichment technologies in 1974.[82]

The Brazilian decision not to acquire the uranium enrichment technologies from West Germany and Japan in 1969, along with the end of the centrifuge project, can be interpreted in two different ways. Maria Regina Soares de Lima, a Brazilian scholar, reveals that the final report of a special working group on nuclear energy, delivered at the beginning of 1968, rejected the domestic production of nuclear fuels as uneconomical and recommended purchasing the fuel abroad.[83] Nogueira Batista, the negotiator with West Germany, wrote that the discussions with the West Germans were troublesome for the reasons expressed in early 1969 by the Brazilian minister of mines and energy, Dias Leite Júnior. A deal with the FRG might harm the ongoing negotiations with the World Bank for financing several hydroelectric plants.[84]

The Initial Implementation of Brazil's Nuclear Policy

The diplomatic action undertaken by Nogueira Batista was part of a broader Brazilian strategy. Brazil's intention was to develop in the long term its natural uranium reactors, to be designed in Belo Horizonte, and to acquire in the short term its first nuclear power reactors from abroad. In fact, the government decided to follow the old plans to build Brazil's first nuclear power plant in the southeastern region of the country through an international tender to companies with proven technology. To choose the technology that was best suited to the nation's needs, Brazilian scientists and technicians visited Canada, Great Britain, Sweden, West Germany, and the IAEA in Vienna. In 1968 a governmental mission headed by the then minister of mines and energy, Costa e Cavalcanti, visited West Germany, France, the United Kingdom, Canada, and the United States.[85] Furthermore, in November 1968 an IAEA commission headed by James A. Lane issued an evaluation report on the Brazilian project to build a nuclear power plant. Both the dossiers following the technical missions and the "Lane Report" defined the kind of reactors that could be described in the international tender and the location of the future nuclear plant: the beach of Itaorna, in Angra do Reis (state of Rio de Janeiro).

To support the Brazilian industrial and economic boom, in 1970 a parliamentary commission of inquiry confirmed the necessity of nuclear energy as a means to satisfy the rising demand for electricity in the country. During the work of the commission, in June 1970, the Brazilian government invited seven companies and consortia involved in the nuclear field to submit proposals before January 1971. Before the deadline, however, three companies—ASEA-Atom (Sweden), Combustion Engineering (USA), and Atomic Energy of Canada Ltd. (Canada)—withdrew. Eventually Brazil received five proposals: Siemens-KWU (Kraftwerk Union) of West Germany and Westinghouse of the United States proposed pressurized water reactors; AEG of West Germany and General Electric of the United States offered boiling water reactors; and NPG of Great Britain proposed a steam-generating heavy-water reactor.

After an in-depth technical and economic analysis, the Westinghouse proposal was considered the most suitable. It beat NPG, whose reactor had never entered into production, and Siemens, which in 1968 was contracted to build the first Argentine atomic power plant (Atucha 1).[86] CNEN made a crucial decision that would be the object of intense criticism from the scientific community. According to several scientists, including Marcelo Damy, the 1969 decision by the CNEN chairman, Hervásio de Carvalho, to go with light-water reactors instead of heavy-water reactors (such as those to be developed in Brazil) would affect the future of Brazil's nuclear autonomy and make the country dependent on external provisions for nuclear fuel.[87]

From May 1971 to April 1972 CNEN and Westinghouse negotiated the contract. The USAEC, which retained the monopoly of uranium enrichment services, approved supplying Brazil with the nuclear fuel needed for its first nuclear power plant, Angra 1. The contract stated that in the event of force majeure, the US government could decide to delay or suspend deliveries.[88] That clause would be applied a few years later, forcing Brazil to seek new external partners for transferring nuclear technology to make the country autonomous with regard to its supply of nuclear material. Moreover, the deal would be subject to international safeguards thanks to a trilateral agreement signed by Brazil, the United States, and the IAEA on 17 July 1972.

A Nuclear Program Dependent on the United States?

Despite the contract with Westinghouse and the fact that the United States was supposed to be its leading partner in the nuclear field and to supply, a few years hence, a second nuclear power plant, Brazil tried to maintain independence from the United States. In 1971 CSN confirmed that it would apply the principle of specific compensations for the export of nuclear material. The Brazilian government decided to keep control over national resources, while specifying a stock of nuclear material (particularly thorium) for the country's needs.[89] Brasília began the phase of the "big investments" in uranium prospecting, which led in a few years to a massive increase in resources devoted to that aim. It guaranteed that from 1970 to 1983 the number of specialists working on the issues doubled (from 60 to 120), and it led to the discovery of large uranium deposits, above all the abundant reserves in Lagoa Real (Bahia) and Itataia (Ceará).[90] As noted earlier, one of the main goals of the 1967 guidelines was to dominate atomic energy, and a consistent increase of the CNEN budget and personnel demonstrated a new trend in Brazilian nuclear policy. Moreover, as prescribed by the first National Development Plan (Primeiro Plano Nacional de Desenvolvimento, or I PND), all the phases of acquisition of nuclear power plants would be accompanied by deeper involvement of private industry. Thus the nuclear complex would contribute to the country's industrial development. Following the French model for the creation of a nuclear sector, in 1971 the Ministry of Mines and Energy established a new CNEN subsidiary, the Brazilian Nuclear Technology Company (Companhia Brasileira de Tecnologia Nuclear, or CBTN), to oversee all the scientific and technological activities of the country. All the research institutes previously under

CNEN (except the IEA, which was under the supervision of the state of São Paulo from 1970 to 1982) would be subordinated to CBTN to rationalize the activities for promoting the emergence of an advanced industrial atomic complex.

CNEN and CBTN accelerated the plans to dominate all the phases of the nuclear fuel cycle, from mining prospection to spent-fuel reprocessing. In 1971 CBTN established a group to study, in constant dialogue with French, Italian, West German, and especially American nuclear scientists (Brazilian technicians were trained at the NUS Corporation), the best uranium enrichment method. It is not clear whether the researchers who had previously worked in São Paulo with the Groth-type centrifuges were involved in those studies. Still, enriching uranium (especially after the choice of light-water reactors) appeared to be a priority. This was clear in a 1971 secret report to Foreign Minister Mário Gibson Barboza from Paulo Nogueira Batista, who suggested that the Foreign Ministry, which was responsible for Brazil's external nuclear relations, should consider alternatives for establishing comprehensive, long-term nuclear agreements between Brazil and a "country to be defined," not necessarily the United States. Nogueira Batista noted that given the trends in uranium production in the United States and Europe, Brazil needed either to associate itself with France to purchase gas diffusion technology or to develop, together with West Germany, ultracentrifuge or jet nozzle technologies. The Brazilian diplomat was worried that Urenco obligations might prevent West Germany from offering Brazil centrifuge technology. However, he concluded that "countries that decide to develop their enrichment capacity will not only occupy a privileged competitive position but also become part of an oligopoly with obvious political implications."[91] CNEN partially shared Nogueira Batista's position and in 1971 sent to Italy professor Ivo Jordan, who had previously headed the small group working with the three Groth-type centrifuges (dismantled and stored in wooden crates at the State University of São Paulo). The Italians, however, demonstrated that they were more interested in the studies the Brazilian chemist had conducted at the Institute of Technological Research and translated Jordan's reports on his research into Italian. Despite the resumption of talks about a possible project for enriching uranium, CNEN eventually decided not to resume the studies that Jordan (who had been attempting to create a new type of centrifuge) had interrupted a few years earlier.[92]

When Washington signed the agreement with Brazil in 1972, the US authorities were conscious of the possibility of other partnerships having to do with the Brazilian nuclear program, above all with West Germany. In an expanding nuclear market—with commercial but also security implications—the administration of Richard Nixon (who took office in January 1969) wanted to maintain close ties with the nascent nuclear Brazilian industry despite Brasília's opposition to the NPT. Washington's intelligence was also aware of the Brazilian attempts to attain uranium enrichment capability. Differing from the two preceding administrations, however, Richard Nixon and his influential adviser Henry A. Kissinger gave low priority to nuclear nonproliferation policy. They supported the US nuclear industry's exporting of technology and nuclear fuel abroad.[93] Differing with the disarmament agencies and the State Department, both Nixon and Kissinger considered the NPT unable to hamper the nuclear ambitions of countries such as West Germany, Japan, India, Pakistan, Israel, Egypt, or Brazil. However, the US National Security Council warned that "the acquisition of nuclear devices by any new state, whether India or some other country, would increase the ultimate possibility of nuclear war and thereby diminish the security of the United States. A new member in the nuclear club would make more difficult the task of holding the line on nonproliferation elsewhere."[94] Until 1974, however, US administrations remained silent on these cases. When the US Congress, with a Democratic majority, assumed major responsibility for nonproliferation issues, the US attitude changed dramatically.

There is no evidence of a Brazilian decision to make military use of the atom in those years, and the US administration's attitude might be attributable to a possible collaboration with Brazil in the area of enrichment. A second aspect of the policy that characterized Nixon's first term as president was the debate over the privatization of the uranium enrichment capability, which until then had been a monopoly of the USAEC, which owned two uranium enrichment facilities, and the security implications of the choice.[95] A radical reform of the 1964 nuclear legislation would allow the creation of private consortiums of companies for enriching uranium in the United States or abroad in order to beat competitors, such as the European Urenco and Eurodif (European Gaseous Diffusion Uranium Enrichment Consortium). It could lead, as emerged from US-Brazilian preliminary discussions in 1971, to multinational uranium enrichment facilities based on the US gaseous diffusion technology.[96]

The possible spread of nuclear technologies in developing and developed countries prompted, however, a rising concern that was also manifested within the US administration. For this reason, in 1972 Washington and other Western countries joined the Zangger Committee (named after the Swiss Claude Zangger, who promoted it), an informal committee for the international control of advanced nuclear materials and technologies. The group issued a list, the so-called trigger list, of materials and equipment that should be safeguarded more strictly.[97] It was an important group at a time of major turmoil in the nuclear field, such as the 1974 Indian peaceful nuclear test and the booming global demand for nuclear energy as a consequence of the 1973 oil shock. It was in the above context that Brazil decided to accelerate its nuclear plans in 1974.

CHAPTER FOUR

The Brazilian Nuclear Program
in the Geisel Years, 1974–1979

On 13 June 1975 the *New York Times* published an editorial entitled "Nuclear Madness." It referred to a nuclear deal that West Germany and Brazil were close to signing and that the American newspaper, among other voices in the United States, considered "a reckless move that could set off a nuclear arms race in Latin America, trigger the nuclear arming of half a dozen nations elsewhere and endanger the security of the United States and the world as a whole."[1] Two weeks later, when the West German and Brazilian foreign ministers signed the deal, the reaction in both countries was very different.

The nuclear cooperation would involve the greatest industrial transfer from an industrialized to a developing country until that time, guaranteeing to Brazil the creation of a national nuclear industry, mastery of the nuclear fuel cycle, and the capability to build nuclear reactors. The transfer would be gradual and internationally safeguarded thanks to the creation of Brazilian–West German joint ventures and a trilateral agreement with the IAEA. Moreover, in a period of deep economic recession and oil crisis, the Brazilian nuclear plans would provide an alternative to Brazil's dependency on Middle East oil supplies and job security for thousands of West German workers in the nuclear industry. Despite a few voices of domestic opposition, the presses of Bonn and Brasília celebrated the agreement as the deal of the century.

This chapter discusses Brazil's decision to sign a major deal with West Germany. Bonn was chosen as Brazil's partner after the new US nuclear policy, limiting the export of sensitive technologies and materials to countries opposing the NPT, such as Brazil, was put in place. It also discusses Brazil's reaction to the US policy of limiting Brazilian nuclear ambitions. While at first, at the very end of the Ford administration, Washington and Brasília reached a secret understanding for finding a mutually satisfactory solution, eventually Brazil resisted the hostile Carter administration's nuclear nonproliferation policy. Third, it discusses Brazil and Argentina's relationship in the nuclear area, and finally it looks at the first signs of the crisis in the cooperation with the FRG.

The New Brazilian Nuclear Policy and the 1975 Deal with West Germany

On 15 March 1974 General Ernesto Geisel, an experienced military man who had previously chaired the oil company Petrobrás, began his term as the new Brazilian president. One of the main goals of his governmental plan was to design and implement a new economic strategy for facing the oil crisis that was threatening the booming Brazilian economy. Highly dependent on foreign oil purchases, Brazil needed alternatives. In that context, Geisel, at the beginning of eleven years of slow, deliberate steps toward democratization, adopted a foreign policy aimed at supporting the national interests and the country's growth free from past ideological constraints. Brazil would collaborate not only with traditional partners (the United States and Western countries) but also with Third World and communist countries (e.g., developing a full relationship with Beijing and recognizing the Marxist government in Angola). The goal was to seek new markets for Brazilian industrial products and establish new partnerships to sustain Brazil's needs. According to Geisel's Second National Development Plan (Segundo Plano Nacional de Desenvolvimento, or II PND) and Plano 1990, a program launched by the Brazilian electric company Eletrobrás, and following the previous developmental policies adopted by Médici, the key to reducing Brazil's dependency on external supplies would be hydropower (with the construction of gigantic dams across the country) and nuclear energy.[2] Brazil's electrical capacity would be expanded in part through the construction of at least eight nuclear power plants and the acquisition of atomic fuel cycle technologies from external partners, complementing its cooperation with the United States.[3] Starting in February 1974, these efforts were strictly supervised by President-elect Geisel, who had also confirmed Brazil's interest in acquiring the ultracentrifuge uranium enrichment technology. After the beginning of the new Brazilian administration, in mid-March 1974, the diplomatic maneuvers (fruit of the collaboration among Itamaraty, CNEN, CBTN, and the minister of mines and energy) were conducted by the new foreign minister, Antônio Azeredo da Silveira, and Paulo Nogueira Batista, head of the Foreign Ministry's Economic Division and a key negotiator in the energy field.[4]

Brazil held discussions above all with West Germany and France. Both countries had a relevant role in training scientists and providing equipment, and in the early 1970s they owned the most advanced nuclear industries in the West after the United States. CBTN's cooperation plans were global; it considered working with Sweden, Italy, the United Kingdom, Japan, and Denmark, along with US private companies. With a detailed schedule, the new nuclear plans, part of the second PND, included not only the 1973 decision to acquire a second nuclear power plant, to be located in Angra dos Reis (probably from the US company Westinghouse), but also the creation of an advanced Brazilian nuclear complex.[5] Accordingly, the Brazilian government would follow the 1967 guidelines for achieving autonomy in the atomic field.[6]

Brazil's nuclear authorities did not involve the academic community in their choice of a reactor type, and their initial goal was to promote a nascent nuclear industry through the active collaboration of private companies.[7] Brazil attracted foreign partners. In fact, in mid-May 1974 the work in Angra dos Reis on the first nuclear power reactor and the declaration of the possible construction of a plant close to São Paulo seemed to confirm a solid nuclear future for the country.[8] Following an explicit decision by President Geisel, the parallel discussions with France and West Germany were kept secret and did not involve military authorities in order not to raise proliferation concerns.[9]

A French-Brazilian Nuclear Deal?

Even if France did not participate in the international bid on Angra 1, since 1971 the French nuclear authorities had been discussing the possibility of resuming their cooperation with the Brazilians on uranium prospection. From 1964 to 1971 more than 60 percent of Brazil's nuclear scientists were trained in France. After that, Brazil (like France) opted to acquire light-water reactors, and CNEN continued the collaboration with the French on new nuclear technologies as well.[10] The abandonment of the thorium line, which relied above all on the cooperation with Paris, was not considered an obstacle by the French authorities.[11]

In 1971, the French and the Brazilians aired a possible trilateral collaboration with Bonn on uranium enrichment, but the idea was soon discarded.[12] French authorities were aware of the competition with Bonn and the trilateral consortium Urenco for a partnership with Brazil. The French Atomic Energy Commission was not available to transfer sensitive gaseous diffusion enrichment technologies, but it proposed to sell Framatome light-water power reactors to be fueled by Eurodif. Paul-Jacques Fouchet, the French ambassador to Brazil, initially proposed that Brazil participate in Eurodif.[13] That would guarantee a promissory market to the consortium for fuel provision, beating out the competition of Urenco, which was not perceived as a threat to Eurodif business, but France ultimately did not endorse the proposal. Paris, on the other hand, was available to

cooperate with CNEN for joint research on uranium isotopic separation, and negotiations continued.[14]

While the West Germans were in advanced negotiations with the Brazilians,
André Giraud, chairman of CEA, visited Brazil for preliminary talks in August
1974 and proposed to collaborate in the creation of a Brazilian nuclear industry.[15] At a preliminary point, Giraud did not exclude possible cooperation in naval nuclear propulsion following the model of cooperation with the Japanese.
Despite his support for the idea, the French government did not authorize him
to talk about the most sensitive issue: supplying a French nuclear-powered attack
submarine.[16] At that moment the Brazilian navy was beginning internal discussions over a project for acquiring such a vessel, but during the talks the Brazilian
authorities were not very explicit.

Giraud offered French assistance at all stages of the nuclear fuel cycle, including establishing a national industry for reactor components and a possible joint
venture for a gaseous diffusion uranium enrichment plant in Brazil, which would
require a considerable amount of energy.[17] For this reason, ministers Ueki and
Giraud agreed on a one-year French-Brazilian technical, economic, industrial,
and financial assessment of Brazil's reserves of uranium. For that assessment, a
group of French geologists would visit the country in October 1974.[18] Confirmation of the richness of Brazilian uranium reserves could justify the transfer of the
uranium enrichment technology and, above all, the French interest in Brazilian
atomic minerals.

Although engaged in advanced parallel negotiations with the FRG, the Brazilian government did not discard the French offer, especially in the field of uranium enrichment, but used it as a possible bargaining chip with the Germans.[19]
Until the conclusion of the talks with Bonn in mid-1975, the Brazilians pushed
France for a broad agreement. Recently declassified documents reveal an internal battle within the Brazilian Foreign Ministry between Silveira, who leaned
toward cooperation with France, and Nogueira Batista, who supported the West
German option.[20]

Eventually, Paris lost the battle with Bonn. Despite a proposal submitted in
December 1974 and Brazil's interest in the French offer to renew the 1962 agreement including new companies for establishing a nuclear complex, Brasília
chose West Germany.[21] On several occasions, Silveira declared readiness to sign
a nuclear deal in Paris, but CEA did not provide a definitive response. Even
though Bonn won the competition with Paris, on 4 July, one week after the signing of the deal with West Germany, Nogueira Batista signed an agreement with
CEA to develop an experimental fast breeder reactor, COBRA, for which the

negotiations started in 1974. This four-year deal, covering areas not covered by the cooperation with West Germany, was inserted into a global Brazilian strategy for managing the complete nuclear sector. Nogueira Batista also manifested Brazil's intention to opt for both the French gas diffusion technology and the dubious jet-nozzle uranium enrichment method to be developed with Bonn.[22]

For the first six months after the signing of the deal with West Germany, the Brazilian authorities continued to assure France that they would establish a similar cooperation with France, one also involving uranium enrichment technologies, in a contract to be signed by February 1976.[23] The French reaction to the Brazilian–West German deal had been negative, and Paris did not accept having been discarded. Moreover, as will become clear in the next pages, the French government criticized the agreement between Bonn and Brasília for its nonproliferation risks. When Silveira presented the deal to the Brazilian Senate, he commented that France could not provide all the technologies proposed by Bonn.[24] Eventually, in December 1975, Silveira was instructed to suspend the talks with the French since it was important to assess the collaboration with Bonn.[25] During the Geisel years the negotiations with Paris continued, but they failed because of the economic crisis and the stronger commitment to the West Germans.[26]

The Cooperation with the Federal Republic of Germany

Relying on a major agreement for scientific cooperation signed in 1969 and previous forms of collaboration, the negotiations with Bonn proved fruitful. Beginning in mid-February 1974, Brazilian and West German authorities considered for more than a year a deal that included binational public-private joint ventures to master the nuclear fuel cycle and train thousands of Brazilian scientists and nuclear-sector personnel and to transfer the capacity to build heavy equipment, turbo generators, and reactors.[27] In exchange, Brazil would provide West Germany with uranium and purchase at least two nuclear power reactors. The contract would benefit the West German economy. It guaranteed jobs for thousands of workers of the West German atomic company KWU (Kraftwerk Union), a consortium of Siemens and AEG-Telefunken, which was facing a crisis and needed to find new markets.[28]

In the negotiations, however, West Germany made an important decision that would affect the Brazilian nuclear program. Despite intense negotiations, Brazil's strong interest, and previous offers of gas centrifuge technology (in 1968 and 1971), the West German government decided not to share such a sensitive method for uranium isotopic separation. Both nonproliferation and commercial concerns justified the West German decision, especially after the Indian PNE.[29] Urenco classified the gas centrifuge technology shared by the nuclear troika, and the West Germans needed to obtain consent from the United Kingdom and the Netherlands.[30] Bonn sent mixed signals to Brasília. In 1973 the FRG was open to collaborating with the Brazilians in the enrichment field despite possible objections from the Urenco partners.[31] The Brazilians were kept in the dark on the issue until early 1975 even though CBTN negotiators expressed their clear preference for the centrifuge method. Immediately after the beginning of the discussions with West Germany, Brazil joined the Association for Centrifuge Enrichment (ACE), an international study association that Urenco promoted in 1972. ACE aimed to examine on an unclassified basis the economics of centrifuge plant construction and operation and to discuss how the countries associated could access Urenco and Centec (the West German firm working in the centrifuge method) technologies.[32]

Even though the parties reached a first understanding over the sale in October 1974, when they signed a protocol in Brasília, the West Germans decided not to specify the method to be transferred.[33] Most likely, the West Germans wanted to save the deal—the Brasília protocol was the basis for further negotiations—and at that moment in time feared the possible competition of other countries (not only France but also the Japanese Mitsubishi) and the potential pressure for preserving the nuclear nonproliferation regime coming from Washington.[34] The Japanese soon lost interest in a nuclear Brazil, and the French were losing the battle with Bonn. Yet the West Germans needed an alternative to save face with the Brazilians and to participate in the construction of new rules over the trade of sensitive nuclear technologies and materials.

In February 1974 the West Germans proposed an alternative method for uranium isotopic separation to Brazil. West German and Brazilian scientists would work together on enriching uranium with the jet-nozzle process developed on a laboratory scale in Karlsruhe by the West German scientist Erwin Becker. After a comparative study in the late 1960s to discover the most efficient enrichment method, the West Germans opted for the centrifuges, a classified technology, and financed Centec and Urenco.[35] Studies on the Becker method continued in the Karlsruhe laboratories, and unlike the gas centrifuge technique, this method was not kept secret but made available in the public literature. The West Germans had already informed Admiral Álvaro Alberto about this method in the mid-1950s. Professor Carvalho, unlike many Brazilian scientists, who thought the technique consumed too much energy and considered it inefficient, was quite enthusiastic about it. It was not the first time West Germans ceded such technology. Secret agreements with Pretoria guaranteed that South Africa could acquire the same equipment from the company STEAG.

Throughout the whole period of negotiations, Brazil received mixed signals from Washington. On the one hand, the USAEC (and after the reform of the nuclear sector in October 1974 the Energy Research Development Agency, ERDA, and the Nuclear Regulatory Commission, NRC) froze a contract that Brazil had signed in June 1974 for nuclear fuel supplies for its future second nuclear power plant. The USAEC decision did not exclusively affect Brazil but applied to the global nuclear market. In August 1974 the US government ordered a temporary suspension of many contracts for the future provision of enrichment services.[36] The cause of this disruption was the unexpected increase in requests in the aftermath of the energy crisis that had struck Europe and the United States the previous winter. The supply shortage led to a lively debate over how to proceed. For some, there was no other choice than to reprocess spent fuel, a technology that could lead to the production of plutonium. Others emphasized the need to bring the private sector on board and let it build enrichment plants to satisfy global demand.[37]

On the other hand, the uncertainty of the US nuclear energy policy led several major American companies in the nuclear field, such as Westinghouse, General Electric, Bechtel, and the Garrett Corporation, to offer reactors, enrichment facilities, and other atomic technologies to Brazil. All the proposals had to be retracted, only increasing the confusion about the US capability to satisfy the rising demand for nuclear energy in the international market. Despite Brazil's willingness to rely on multiple partners, including the United States, Washington's decisions led Brazil to partner with West Germany.

Even though Brazil had defended its right to develop peaceful nuclear explosions in the past, *nuclearização* (nuclearization) for the Brazilian government meant the mastery of atomic energy for peaceful aims and access to the club of industrialized countries.[38] Since the beginning of the negotiations in 1973 Brasília had assured Bonn of its peaceful intentions and agreed to subject the entire cooperation to international safeguards.[39] It would be the first time that a non-NPT member accepted a trilateral agreement with the IAEA and an NPT member (West Germany eventually ratified the treaty in May 1975). The safeguards and nonproliferation clauses of the deal dominated the West German–Brazilian talks in the first part of 1975. In May 1975 the draft treaty was approved. Despite international concerns—the West Germans informed the United States and other Western powers of the ongoing negotiation in August 1974—on 27 June 1975 the West German foreign minister,

Hans-Dietrich Genscher, and his Brazilian counterpart, Silveira, signed the deal in Bonn. It was the largest-ever industrial transfer from a developed country to a developing one. The multibillion-dollar deal would lead Brazil to purchase up to eight reactors (the compulsory minimum purchase was two) and create joint-venture companies to develop all the aspects of the nuclear complex.

Nuclebrás (Empresas Nucleares Brasileiras, Brazilian nuclear companies), which replaced CBTN, was established to supervise all nuclear industrial activities and approved in December 1974 as part of this process. It was the body responsible for Brazil's new nuclear legislation and was connected to Geisel's II PND. CNEN, under the Ministry of Mines and Energy, would retain regulatory powers in the nuclear sector.[40] The centrality of the international cooperation in the nuclear field justified Geisel's decision to appoint Nogueira Batista as the first chairman of the company, which acquired a special status in the Brazilian cabinet.

Private participation in the company was crucial, and the Brazilian state was supposed to retain 51 percent of the shares. Nuclebrás would be at the core of the

Foreign ministers Antônio F. Azeredo da Silveira of Brazil (*left*) and Hans-Dietrich Gensher, of the Federal Republic of Germany, sign an agreement for the peaceful use of nuclear energy, Bonn, 27 June 1975. (Paulo Nogueira Batista Archive, PNB foto 023_47, FGV/CPDOC)

Brazilian civilian nuclear program that arose from the cooperation with West Germany. The company would supervise the national research centers, such as the Rio de Janeiro Institute of Nuclear Energy (Instituto de Energia Nuclear, or IEN) and the Belo Horizonte Institute of Radioactive Research, which in 1977 became the Nuclear Technology Development Center (Centro de Desenvolvimento de Tecnologia Nuclear, or CDTN), and national companies. Nuclebrás also became the holding of West German–Brazilian joint-venture subsidiaries. Nuclei (Nuclebrás Enriquecimento Isotópico, or Nuclebrás Isotopic Enrichment) would manage the jet-nozzle demonstration plant in Resende (Rio de Janeiro), while Nustep (Nuclebrás-STEAG) would develop the method in Karlsruhe, since the patent became part of the deal. Both companies were formed by Nuclebrás and the West German STEAG and Interatom. The heavy components were to be built in Itaguaí (Rio de Janeiro) by Nuclep (Nuclebrás Equipamentos Pesados, or Nuclebrás Heavy Equipment), a joint venture between Nuclebrás and KWU. Nuclam (Nuclebrás Auxiliar de Mineração, or Nuclebrás Mining Associate), in Poço de Caldas (Minas Gerais) and at another Brazilian site, would supervise the uranium ore extraction and mining, while Nuclemon (Nuclebrás de Monazita e Associados) was charged with the monazites. The power plant design would be done by Nuclen (Nuclebrás Engenharia, or Nuclebrás Engineering), while the Nuclebrás fuel factory in Resende would also host the spent-fuel reprocessing pilot plant and the UF_6 conversion laboratory. Even though the Brazilians owned the majority of the companies' shares, West Germans would run the activities. The program Pronuclear, approved a few months later, guaranteed the training of the nuclear personnel in West Germany; eventually more than 500 technicians and scientists were trained in West German laboratories. Brazil would also offer CNPq scholarships for nuclear scientists to train in West German universities and research centers. A future contract with Urenco (signed in 1976) would guarantee the fuel supply for the Brazilian nuclear reactors until Brazil attained autonomous capability. All the activities would be under international safeguards thanks to a specific nonproliferation clause in the treaty and to a trilateral agreement signed with the IAEA in Vienna in late February 1976.

The Brazilian and the West German press enthusiastically welcomed the nuclear agreement, but it was not free from domestic criticism. Both the SBF and the Brazilian Society for the Progress of Science (Sociedade Brasileira para o Progresso da Ciência, or SBPC) criticized the government's exclusion of the Brazilian academic community from the decision over the deal and the national nuclear program for many years. A large proportion of Brazil's nuclear scientists (including the leading physicists Marcelo Damy and José Goldemberg) voiced the opinion that the country should seek autonomy and continue the national research program launched during the 1960s. Franco Montoro, a senator of the opposition party, MDB (Movimento Democrático Brasileiro, or Brazilian Democratic Movement), from São Paulo, supported the criticism and requested the creation of a committee of Brazilian specialists to assess the new Brazilian nuclear policy.[41] Other scientists also questioned the need for a gigantic nuclear program for energy production given the country's huge hydroelectric potential. Furthermore, the scientists denounced the difficulty of running such an ambitious program for a country with just 720 specialists in nuclear energy. Brazil was considered to lack the necessary skills to run the program.[42] After visiting the West German laboratories in September 1978, Goldemberg and another prominent physicist, José Israel Vargas, warned the government about the risks of accepting an ineffective technology such as the jet-nozzle method of isotopic separation.[43]

In this case, both academic and Nuclebrás assessments concurred since Brazil's first choice was for ultracentrifuge technology. From 1975 to 1977 Nuclebrás studied the possible establishment of a centrifuge factory in Brazil through the service of Dietrich Wilhelm Sontag, a West German centrifuge specialist who had previously worked for Centec. However, in July 1977, for unknown reasons, Paulo Nogueira Batista decided to abort the plan.[44] Secret West German documents passed to the Brazilians guaranteed the capability of the method also to produce high enriched uranium (HEU), useful for explosive purposes. South Africa's success in developing a jet-nozzle-derived method, the Helikon technique, was evidence of the technology's effectiveness even if it consumed a huge amount of energy. As noted in the next chapter, the Brazilians would resume their research in uranium enrichment through the use of the ultracentrifuge, and starting in 1974 they studied laser methods in unsafeguarded facilities.

In 1975 all parties in Brazil's Congress approved the deal, even if a representative of the opposition party echoed criticism of the scientific community.[45] A few months later Luís Carlos Prestes, the charismatic leader of the Brazilian Communist Party, then in exile, shared the Soviet criticism, supported Brazil's accession to the NPT, and strongly criticized the deal with the West Germans who, from his perspective, wanted to turn Brazil into a place for increasing rivalries with other Latin American countries and building atomic weapons with an imperialist agenda.[46] In West Germany in 1978 several scientists published a manifesto against the West German–Brazilian cooperation. The main critics of the deal were not in Brazil and Germany; several Western governments and societies and the socialist world suspected that the peaceful agreement concealed Brazilian plans to build a nuclear bomb.

The United States and Geisel's Nuclear Brazil after the "Smiling Buddha"

While one global shock, the oil crisis, accelerated Brazil's nuclear plans, another one threatened to cause them to fail. In May 1974, when the Brazilians were discussing cooperation with foreign countries, India, another fierce opponent of the NPT and a recent partner of nuclear Brazil, tested a peaceful nuclear device, the "Smiling Buddha." The explosion shocked the nuclear nonproliferation regime and the safeguards system. A recipient of assistance from the West had diverted technologies and materials to produce a nuclear explosive. As the global demand for nuclear energy, materials, and technology was rising, the international community faced possible proliferators in the developing world. A year before the first NPT conference review, held in 1975, the government of New Delhi demonstrated the weakness of the nuclear nonproliferation regime, opening the way for new members to the nuclear club. It was a victory for the NNWSs that challenged what the Brazilian ambassador in Washington, Araújo Castro, called a "frozen world's power" and a demonstration of the insufficiency of the safeguards to nuclear activities and the transference of technology. The "Smiling Buddha" had dramatic consequences for the global nuclear order but also for the future of the Brazilian nuclear program.

The United States, the main world provider of nuclear technologies, and the rest of the industrial nuclear suppliers, in both Western and socialist countries, accelerated the talks begun in the 1960s. They continued within the Zangger Committee to discuss setting domestic and common rules to restrict the transfer of sensitive nuclear technologies, such as uranium enrichment and spent-fuel reprocessing. The new US and international measures could target Brazil, considered by US intelligence to be a member of the group of possible future proliferators, including Israel, Argentina, South Korea, and South Africa.[47] The Latin American country could emulate India. As one of the leading Brazilian dailies wrote, it could turn into the "seventh nuclear weapon state" in the wake of India's having shifted from an "almost-nuclear" to a nuclear country.[48]

Until the Indian PNE, the United States was Brazil's main partner in nuclear activities. However, as seen in the previous section, the new restrictive US legislation, along with multilateral talks between nuclear suppliers in London (the so-called London Club) about stricter rules for sensitive exports and reaction to the Indian PNE, contributed to Brazil's decision to collaborate with another country. In a dispatch to Brasília, Araújo Castro described the congressional decisions as "legislative weapons" in the nuclear field that aimed at limiting horizontal nuclear proliferation even if that meant the United States would sacrifice its cooperation with other countries. Both Washington's and the London Club's decisions could hinder the complete nuclear development of Brazil. According to Araújo Castro, the possible acceptance, even if not direct, of the NPT and stricter international safeguards could threaten the national security and future nuclear autonomy of Brazil.[49]

Brazil resisted all the requests to accede to the NPT and found a partner in Bonn, which was a member of the London Club and reflected its commitment imposing strict export safeguards that were more comprehensive than those in the NPT, and decided not to cede the sensitive ultracentrifuge technology.[50] The West Germans would also share in the control of all activities connected to the cooperation for at least fifteen years. Any export by Brazil of nuclear material or equipment to third parties would be subject to FRG authorization. The Brazilians implicitly limited the nuclear activities to be developed with the West Germans, accepting nuclear nonproliferation norms, and they carefully avoided mentioning PNEs and noncivilian uses of the atom.

The lack of agreement among the nuclear suppliers, which began at their gathering in London in November 1974, impeded the application of stricter rules to the Brazilian–West German deal. Exporting the whole nuclear fuel cycle was a dangerous precedent that West Germany and France wanted to emulate in agreements with Iran, South Korea, and Pakistan (countries that unlike Brazil had security reasons to pursue nuclear weapons capabilities). Despite all the guarantees offered by the deal, the international community, above all the United States, remained concerned about a possible diversion of Brazil's nuclear technologies for nonpeaceful ends. West German pressure notwithstanding, the country retained several unsafeguarded laboratories and facilities that refused to enter into the deal with Bonn.[51] The United States, especially Fred Iklé, director of the US Arms Control and Disarmament Agency (ACDA), was mainly concerned about the Brazilian decision to acquire spent-fuel reprocessing plants that could conceal military uses. The decision, commented Iklé, covered a possible Brazilian desire to produce plutonium for military purposes and lacked "economic rationale" since the United States "had over fifty reactors, but no reprocessing plant now in operation."[52]

The US Attempt to Accommodate Nuclear Brazil

Nevertheless, in June 1975, when news about the possible deal began to circulate, key members of the US administration, including Secretary of State Henry Kissinger and President Ford, were not worried about the nonproliferation implications.[53] They wanted to avoid clashes with Brazil (a traditional friend of

Washington) and with a crucial ally such as the FRG. Still, several US congressmen urged the administration to intervene. According to the congressmen, the safeguards were not sufficient to deter Brazil. Senator John Pastore (D-RI), chairman of the special committee on atomic energy, wanted to block the deal, which he said "could contribute to the fabrication of an atomic bomb if [Brazil] desires."[54] Senator Walter Mondale (D-MN), who would be Carter's vice president, also called for "an immediate [international] moratorium on the transfer of enrichment and reprocessing technology and installations."[55] The State Department diverged from Mondale and Pastore's position, although it agreed that Congress should expand its role in regulating nuclear trade.[56] The US press echoed the view of the two senators and a segment of the national disarmament agencies, including the ACDA.[57] Kissinger and Ford avoided mentioning the nuclear issue when they met the West German president Walter Scheel in Washington a few days before the signing of the agreement. In further contacts with both Brazilians and West Germans, Kissinger denied the possibility of any interference.[58]

After the deal was signed, several critical voices on both sides of the Iron Curtain arose against it. The French, as seen earlier, and the Soviets, even if Moscow offered unsuccessfully to sell nuclear fuel to Brasília, criticized the deal as a "dangerous precedent" for the nonproliferation regime.[59] During a meeting with Kissinger the Soviet foreign minister, Andrei Gromyko, said that he thought "Brazil [was] on the path to the production of nuclear weapons and want[ed] to use the help provided by West Germany. . . . Incidentally, [West] Germany is a party to the NPT, but Brazil is not."[60] Kissinger "did not believe that Brazil has decided to build nuclear weapons," but he manifested his concern by guaranteeing action toward a multilateral solution, such as attaching conditions to the trilateral safeguards agreement, to be approved by the IAEA board of governors.[61]

The domestic American, French, and Soviet concerns notwithstanding, Washington did not retaliate against the Brazilian–West German nuclear cooperation. The Brazilian minister of mines and energy, Shigeaki Ueki, confirmed to Charles W. Robinson (deputy secretary of state and charged with nonproliferation issues) Brazil's interest in continuing collaboration with Washington, above all in the area of high-temperature gas-cooled reactors (HTGRs), fast breeders, and fuel supplies for Angra 1, since the deal with Bonn "was not so great."[62] In Washington's view, however, the transfer of atomic technologies from nuclear suppliers to countries with atomic ambitions endangered the survival of the nuclear nonproliferation regime. A possible solution could rely on the creation of IAEA regional enrichment and reprocessing centers in the five continents

(Brazil could host the Latin American one).[63] However, the initiative never gained traction.[64]

The decision of the IAEA board of governors would be decisive for the future of the Brazilian–West German nuclear deal. The vote on the trilateral safeguards agreement was scheduled for late February 1976, and an adverse decision could postpone the implementation of the cooperation. Probably because of pressures coming from the United States and other nuclear suppliers, Bonn and Brasília agreed to report the transfer of materials and sensitive technologies from West Germany to Brazil.[65] Brazil's national facilities and its nationally developed technologies would not be subject to international safeguards.[66] When Brazil and West Germany submitted the text of the trilateral agreement to the IAEA, several actors, such as France, criticized it for not complying with the London Club suppliers' guidelines under negotiation. The main problem had to do with the notification of the transfer of equipment and the absence of safeguards on the enrichment process, the Becker jet-nozzle method, which the Brazilians and the West Germans considered a technology available in the open literature.[67]

Even if some sectors within the US government were against the approval and the Soviet Union proposed to delay the vote, the Ford administration preferred not to risk undermining the relationship with Bonn and Brasília. Following an interagency report, it recommended to its representative in Vienna and the British government support of the deal.[68] From President Ford's standpoint, a good relationship with Brasília could guarantee resumption of nuclear negotiations with the Latin American country.[69] On the eve of the approval, Henry Kissinger flew to Brasília to sign a memorandum of understanding that improved the bilateral relationship. On that occasion, he gave Foreign Minister Silveira personal guarantees of a positive outcome in the vote in Vienna.[70] Despite a negative French vote, on 26 February 1976 the IAEA board of governors approved the deal.[71] It was an astonishing victory for Brazil, even if new troubles would come from the United States.

While the administration approved the vote, a stronger nuclear nonproliferation regime was under discussion in the US Congress. After the Indian "Smiling Buddha," Capitol Hill advocated tighter controls over nuclear exports that would also affect Brazil. The lack of consensus among nuclear suppliers led Congress in June 1976 to approve a proposal by Senator Stuart Symington (D-MO) to amend the 1961 Foreign Assistance Act. The measure prohibited US economic and military assistance to any country supplying or receiving nuclear enrichment or reprocessing equipment materials or technology unless the supplier and recipient agreed to accept IAEA safeguards on everything transferred and on all nuclear fuels and facilities in the recipient country.[72] The Symington amendment affected the actions by Ford and Kissinger, who lost their room to maneuver with Brazil and other countries with nuclear ambitions. The measure threatened not only Brazil's nuclear program but also its economy, which was showing its first signs of crisis with an increasing inflation rate.

A new US nonproliferation policy could deeply modify the attitude toward Brazil. During the 1976 presidential campaign, the democrat candidate, Jimmy Carter, sharply attacked Ford's policy, which he said by 1985 would lead to "20 nations [with] the capability of exploding atomic weapons." [73] In October Carter proposed a "voluntary moratorium" by supplier countries on future and existing agreements for transferring reprocessing and enrichment technologies.[74] In response, Ford said that as part of a deep revision of the US nonproliferation strategy, in his second term he would apply stricter safeguards on nuclear exports by limiting them, except in rare cases, to countries that had signed the NPT or had accepted full-scope safeguards.[75]

Both Carter's and especially Ford's proposals would revolutionize the US nuclear nonproliferation policy and have deep consequences for the Brazilian nuclear program. The threats on the Brazilian–West German nuclear deal led the Brazilian government to contemplate two options for saving its atomic projects. Minister Ueki suggested that President Geisel "accelerate the national [and unsafeguarded] projects of enrichment and reprocessing (if possible, with naturalized West German expats), or . . . consider the possibility of [developing] natural uranium reactors [which would not create dependence on enriched-uranium imports]." The second option was to face a diplomatic offensive from President-elect Jimmy Carter for guaranteeing the implementation of the deal with Bonn.[76] Brazil's attitude toward saving the nuclear deal was firm. Should the Brazilians not receive the West German assistance, they would develop their own nuclear program. Eventually, they opted to negotiate a solution with Washington through discreet and secret channels.

A negotiation team led by Charles Robinson (but also made up of persons close to the new administration) offered to provide economic assistance and nuclear fuel should Brazil agree not to acquire sensitive technologies from West Germany. Washington would resume the provision of nuclear fuel suspended in 1974.[77] In a personal meeting with Robinson, General Geisel agreed on a possible moratorium on the acquisition of sensitive facilities, but he conditioned the success of the deal on American discretion in order not to face opposition from the military hard-liners.[78] While the Brazilians were taking the first steps toward commitment (in late January Senator Virgílio Tavora declared that the construction of the reprocessing plant would be suspended), problems appeared on the US side.[79]

Carter's Opposition to a Nuclear Brazil

Members of the new US administration enthusiastically praised Robinson's diplomatic maneuvers.[80] However, the State Department publicly declared that the West German-Brazilian nuclear deal would not involve dual-use technologies.[81] Having agreed to probe the informal agreement through official channels, Brazil was furious. The retired ambassador Vasco Leitão da Cunha, former foreign minister and appointed as an unofficial representative of the Brazilian government on the issue, informed the American emissaries that the Brazilians were no longer interested in talks over the possible suspension of part of the deal with the FRG.[82] It was the end of the discretion that Geisel had requested when he met with Robinson.[83] Brazil's authorities agreed to receive a US nonproliferation team in Brasília in early March, but they would only discuss general nonproliferation issues, avoiding dealing with the nuclear program's future.[84] At that time, the Brazilians no longer believed in the possibility of US nuclear fuel supply in exchange for the renouncement of reprocessing technologies. Consequently, meetings between Silveira and US Deputy Secretary of State Warren Christopher in March 1977 came to nothing. The two delegations talked over each other, and the Brazilians made it a point to state clearly that Christopher's trip need not have taken place and that it should be cut short. Whatever room for accommodation there had been now disappeared, leading to bitterness and long-lasting friction between the United States and Brazil—but also between the United States and West Germany—over sensitive nuclear exports to Brazil.[85]

In a personal letter to the US president, Geisel criticized Carter's aggressive and discriminatory nuclear nonproliferation policy.[86] On other occasions, Brazilians and American authorities attempted to resume talks over the nuclear program, but all the initiatives failed.[87] It was in fact at that moment that Carter, following his electoral promises, began a review of the US nonproliferation legislation. Brazil was deeply affected by the review, which had a "policy of no nuclear fuel to those who reprocess to see what we can do towards those who refuse to sign the NPT."[88] Carter's global nonproliferation strategies included sponsoring the International Nuclear Fuel Cycle Evaluation (INFCE) and strengthening the Nuclear Suppliers Group (NSG).

The Carter administration promoted an international debate over the best fuel cycle for guaranteeing the peaceful use of the atom avoiding the "plutonium economy" and the diversion of reprocessed spent fuel for military uses.[89] In

Front, right to left: Nuclebrás president Paulo Nogueira Batista, Minister of Mines and Energy Shigeaki Ueki, President Ernesto Geisel, and Foreign Minister Azeredo da Silveira looking at a maquette of the future Angra 2 power plant reactor, Brasília, March 1977. (Paulo Nogueira Batista Archive, PNB foto 045_4, FGV/CPDOC)

mid-April 1977, under the auspices of the United States, the main actors in the nuclear field gathered in Salzburg, Austria, and decided to begin a permanent conference on the fuel cycle. Ambassador Gerard Smith, who became Carter's ambassador-at-large for nuclear nonproliferation and US representative at the IAEA in June 1977, was to direct INFCE from the first meeting in Washington, in November 1977, on.[90] Brazil, Japan, and the European countries defended spent-fuel reprocessing and opposed the US theses. As Arnaldo Barbalho, the Brazilian delegate and deputy minister of mines and energy, explained to Joseph Nye (deputy to the undersecretary of state for security assistance, science, and technology), Brazil's participation—which also represented the Argentine position—in the evaluation program would not mean the suspension of the nuclear activities of the countries present in the working groups, as the United States expected.[91]

During the period of international negotiations, Brazil sought to avoid direct consultation with the United States on nuclear issues and defended INFCE as the proper forum for talks. The defense of the nuclear program led Brazil to adopt a low-profile strategy in the technical groups it was part of. Gerard Smith flew to Brazil in 1978 to persuade the nuclear authorities to find viable alternatives to the costly enrichment and reprocessing technologies.[92] INFCE did not have a fruitful outcome. Experts from forty-six countries failed to find a solution to the plutonium economy. When the evaluation ended in February 1980, there were no agreements that supported the Carter administration's attempt to delay or eliminate the use of plutonium. The success of INFCE, from the Brazilian perspective, relied not only on the United States but also on other nuclear suppliers.[93]

Carter's second front of international action was the NSG. The strategy adopted toward Brazil and other countries would affect the multilateral export control policy. The US administration, after an internal debate in late March 1977, decided not to include countries such as Brazil (which had attempted to be added since 1975), South Africa, and Argentina. They were possible proliferators but also recipients of nuclear sales.[94] Their inclusion could undermine the effort to strengthen the nonproliferation regime and the imposition of stricter rules on nuclear trade. West Germany, which supported Brazilian inclusion, eventually confirmed the export of sensitive technologies to Brazil, thereby derailing the Ford and Carter efforts to downscale the Brazilian–West German deal. Brazil's inclusion in the group would be mentioned again in April and June 1977, but both Brazilian and American intransigence led to another failure.[95] The NSG was eventually expanded in September 1977 from the original members (the Group of Seven: the United States, the Soviet Union, Great Britain, France, Canada, West Germany, and Japan) to include new associates of both the socialist and Western countries that were acquiring nuclear industrial capabilities (Belgium, the Netherlands, Italy, Poland, East Germany, Czechoslovakia, Sweden, and Switzerland). Moreover, the group was discussing the approval of a new, more stringent legislative framework on nuclear exports that would impose full-scope safeguards. It would create a regime stricter than that established in the Brazil–West Germany and France-Pakistan cases. From the Brazilian perspective, the US objective was to transform the NSG into the operational tool of the NPT, effectively strengthening the nonproliferation regime. Participation in the NSG could provide Brazil with a new status in the international arena and an active role within the main forum of nuclear discussion.

Brazil's nuclear plan continued to preoccupy the US government. In a memorandum addressed to Warren Christopher, Paul C. Warnke, director of the ACDA, underlined that "indigenous unsafeguarded development may prove to be the larger non-proliferation problem in Brazil in the long run, given the high political cost to Brazil of violating international safeguards obligations, the absence of near-term compelling security motivations to tempt Brazil to undertake such violations, Brazil's considerable indigenous capabilities, and her interest in holding open the unsafeguarded facilities upon."[96] Warnke's apprehension proved to be right since Brazil was already discussing the possibility of indigenous nuclear projects free from international safeguards. The United States should adopt a more incisive policy toward Brazil and also Argentina. (The final section of this chapter deals with the effort to find a regional solution to what Carter perceived as a nuclear race in the Southern Cone.)

At the beginning of 1978, the CIA reported that "if [Argentina and Brazil] continue to develop reprocessing capabilities as planned, Argentina will be within reach of nuclear weapons by 1981, and Brazil by 1983."[97] The White House and the State Department did not succeed; their most effective measure was the approval of new nonproliferation legislation. In May 1978, more than a year after the beginning of the Carter administration and as a consequence of four years of talks on Capitol Hill, Congress passed the Nuclear Non-Proliferation Act (NNPA).[98] The most severe outcome for Brazil was the requirement of full-scope safeguards and stricter rules for importation and US assistance. Similar to what Gerald Ford had proposed in his last statement on nonproliferation, the act determined that cooperation in the nuclear field with the United States would be conditioned on the acceptance of inspections of all the facilities of the recipient countries except the NWSs recognized by the NPT.

As the Brazilian government had expected, the act deeply affected the future of the national nuclear program, which relied on international assistance. The new US legislation imposed strong limitations on the international trade of nuclear technologies. As had been proposed by Minister Ueki immediately after President Carter's election, Brazil could follow an alternative path to "nationalize" the nuclear program free of international constraints. On the one hand, Brazil was suffering the global consequences of the new US legislation; on the other, the country was experiencing the first failures of the cooperation with West Germany. So Brazil's authorities began to design new strategies to save the nuclear project and guarantee the country's future nuclear autonomy.

The First Signs of Crisis in the Agreement with West Germany and Doubts about the Jet-Nozzle Method for Enriching Uranium

While the US administrations were attempting to downplay the sensitive aspects of the Brazilian nuclear program, the cooperation with the FRG was suffering from the first signs of crisis. The construction of Angra 1, expected to be completed in 1978, and that of Angra 2 and 3, the fruit of the cooperation with West

Germany, were delayed because of miscalculations by the construction company and geological problems in the region. Moreover, the rising cost of the deal and a series of scandals exposed by the West German magazine *Der Spiegel* provoked a wave of criticism from the public and in the Brazilian Senate, which established a parliamentary commission of inquiry led by the MDB senator and future Brazilian president Itamar Franco.

Several factors, both external and domestic, explain the problematic implementation of the 1975 deal. Nuclear nonproliferation concerns about the aim of the Brazilian projects had been relevant since both US pressures and the outcome of the NSG meetings affected the implementation of the deal. As seen in the previous pages, the US administration had consistently attempted to modify the terms of the nuclear deal, proposing that Brazil freeze the acquisition of reprocessing technologies. It also pressured the West German Urenco associates not to provide Brazil with the fuel for the nuclear plants to be built in cooperation with Bonn (Angra 2 and Angra 3). While London, albeit reluctantly, accepted the sale to Brazil, Dutch approval was problematic. In early 1977 the antinuclear wing of the Dutch parliament attempted to block the sale. Relying mainly on the US accusations of diversion of low enriched uranium (LEU) for nonpeaceful uses,

Foreign Minister Azeredo da Silveira (*far left*) before the US delegation, headed by Undersecretary of State Warren Christopher (*far right*), Brasília, 1 March 1977. To Silveira's left are Ambassador Geraldo Holanda Cavalcanti and the CNEN chairman, Hervásio de Carvalho. (BR RJANRIO EH.o.FOT, EVE.13106, Arquivo Nacional)

Christian and other political movements denounced the possible military ends of the Brazilian nuclear program since its military regime refused to accept the NPT. Part of the Dutch parliament was not satisfied with the international guarantees, mainly because of the lack of an international agreement for the storage of plutonium. The crisis was an additional factor in the context of the US attempt to negotiate secretly with Brazil in February 1977. It contributed to a climate of acrimony between Brazil and West Germany, on the one hand, and between the United States and other NSG members, on the other. Eventually, in 1978, the Dutch approved the Urenco supply, but the episode illustrated the difficulties that Brazil might have in obtaining nuclear fuel for its power plants.[99] The cooperation with West Germany and Urenco had been considered a reliable alternative to the dependency on a partner such as the United States (even if in 1978 the Carter administration confirmed the supplies for the Westinghouse nuclear power reactor Angra 1). In 1977 Brazil began to be uncertain about the cooperation with the European consortium and with West Germany. How could Brazil rely on partners that could question the provision of nuclear material for the country's energy needs? The 1976 Urenco contract with Brazil was one of the firsts the troika had signed, and its future could be considered crucial for the real implementation of the 1970 Treaty of Almelo.

From the Brazilian standpoint, the crisis within Urenco over the supply to Brazil could turn into an opportunity. Diplomatic, technical, and political authorities discussed submitting a proposal to their West German counterparts on the occasion of President Geisel's visit to Bonn in March 1978. Discussions about the nuclear cooperation would touch upon the effective implementation of the nuclear deal but also on a possible addendum to the collaboration with West Germany over the sensitive aspect of the nuclear program: the transfer of the ultracentrifuge method for enriching uranium. Even if Brazil and West Germany were expected to produce low enriched uranium through the jet-nozzle method, the Brazilian scientists and technicians were dissatisfied with a technological option that many had considered ineffective.

During a top-level meeting at the presidential residence in Brasília, the Palácio da Alvorada, President Geisel discussed a possible request to West Germany with his closest advisers in the military, nuclear, and diplomatic areas.[100] Dutch concerns over the Brazilian contract could keep West Germany and the United Kingdom from renewing Almelo's treaty.[101] On the visit to Bonn Silveira planned to express Brazil's concern over the dangerous effect the Dutch attitude could have on the future of the Brazilian nuclear program. Silveira's strategy was to explore the possibility of West Germany's withdrawing from Urenco and sharing the ultracentrifuge method with Brazil. If the Urenco agreement were not to be renewed, West Germany would be able to transfer such sensitive technology to Brazil. The minister of mines and energy, Shigeaki Ueki, shared Silveira's position and underlined the benefits of acquiring this technology, which was much more viable than the jet nozzle. He also noted that the construction of a commercial plant with that technology could be fast. Moreover, according to Ueki, the West German company Interatom, partner of both Urenco and Nuclebrás, could ease the withdrawal.

The proposal prompted various reactions. A stronger nonproliferation regime could limit any possible West German sale of the ultracentrifuge method to Brazil. President Geisel doubted that the NSG would approve such a transfer from the FRG. Carvalho, CNEN chairman, recognized that such technology was ideal for "war aims" and that it could be transferred only if the NSG recognized Brazil as a "nuclear-capable country." The available transcripts of the meeting do not explain what Carvalho meant by this phrase, but it may have referred to a country able to master the whole nuclear cycle. As seen earlier, it was in that same period that the NSG expanded to include new actors that would acquire industrial nuclear capabilities. Acquisition of the ultracentrifuge technology could elevate Brazil's status in the international nuclear market but also lead the country to revise its attitude toward the NPT. Brazil would not join the regime as a have-not but in an intermediary category between haves and have-nots, a country with full industrial nuclear capacities that chose not to develop nuclear weapons (like Japan and the FRG). Several governments, mainly Italy, were discussing the possible creation of a new category of states within the NPT, and Brazil could be part of it.[102]

Against this background, Foreign Minister Silveira suggested that if the condition for acquiring the ultracentrifuge method were acceding to the NPT, Brazil could commit to the treaty. President Geisel supported Silveira's position and added that Brazil should make every possible effort to obtain a more advanced technology than the jet nozzle, whose failure could be quite embarrassing both for Brazil and for the FRG. The meeting appears to have influenced Brazil's attitude toward the development of its nuclear program and possible full participation in the nuclear nonproliferation regime. President Geisel's attitude seems to confirm his possible decision to sign the NPT under favorable conditions for Brazil, such as acceding to an effective and sensitive technology that could provide the country nuclear autonomy. The meeting mirrored the ongoing internal debate over the future of nuclear energy in Brazil. The option for the jet-nozzle process was not definitive, and since the beginning of the Geisel administration Brazil had been attempting to acquire the centrifuge process.

The 1978 meeting did not have tangible and immediate results. The West German and Brazilian documentation currently open to researchers does not mention whether Bonn was ready and able to withdraw from Urenco to collaborate with Brazil. It was a critical moment for the international uranium enrichment consortia, above all for the downscaling of nuclear power projects around the world. The French-led Eurodif, for instance, was offering company shares to new associates because of the defection of several partners, and Italy offered a part of its future Eurodif fuel to Brazil. Urenco, as mentioned earlier, was facing an internal crisis that was eventually resolved.

In direct meetings with Geisel and Silveira, West German authorities pledged to supply Brazil with nuclear fuel. The fuel for Angra 1, to be provided by the United States, and for Angra 2 and 3, from Urenco facilities, would be guaranteed on the condition (posed by the Dutch parliament) of sufficient guarantees against possible misuse of the supplied materials for military purposes.[103] In 1981 Urenco circumvented the potential Dutch opposition and moved the production of the enriched uranium of the Brazilian contract from the Netherlands to Great Britain.[104]

Nevertheless, Brazil's government decided to continue the debate over alternatives to the jet nozzle. The review of Brazil's technological possibilities coincided with increasing public criticism of the deal.[105] The solution to the troublesome implementation of the West German–Brazilian deal, also affected by new international nonproliferation norms, could lie either in cooperation with other countries or in the quest for a purely national nuclear program. A possible partner for Brazil's nuclear projects could be Argentina, perceived by many as a rival, which was engaged with Brazil in a dispute over water sources but also targeted by the US nonproliferation policies and having ambitions similar to Brazil's to attain national nuclear autonomy.

Brazil and Argentina during the Geisel Years: Between Rivalry and Rapprochement

During the 1960s and 1970s, mainly after the Indian explosion and the signing of the Brazilian–West German deal, the Brazilian nuclear program was perceived internationally as a form of engaging Argentina in a nuclear race. As seen in the previous pages, the United States attempted to attract NPT opponents, such as Brasília and Buenos Aires, into the international regime. Membership in the regime would allow the acquisition of nuclear technologies and materials. During the Carter administration, the United States tried several times to make the cooperation between Argentina and Brazil dependent on their entrance into the regime of nuclear nonproliferation.[106]

As recently declassified documents show, Brazil and Argentina in those years were suspicious about each other's nuclear programs, but they also discussed possible ways to cooperate in the nuclear field. Geisel's entire administration was marked by a dispute over the hydroelectric plant on the Paraguayan-Brazilian border, affecting the course of the Paraná River, which was also shared by Argentina in its downstream stretch. Immediately after the Indian "Smiling Buddha," Geisel was concerned by the Indian-Argentine nuclear cooperation, above all after the Argentine press interpreted the Delhi–Buenos Aires agreement as a possible way to weaponize.[107]

But it was in the United States that concerns were the deepest. The real danger lay not in Brazil or Argentina but in the dynamics between the two. They were tied together in the minds of decision makers in the United States. Not only did they share a subcontinent; they also shared nuclear ambitions, which were met with growing suspicion. Both were considered possible threats to the nuclear nonproliferation regime. According to US intelligence estimates, within a period of three to ten years the two countries could reach nuclear weapons capability. Argentina had a more advanced nuclear sector and was thought to be in the forefront of those constructing atomic devices. Brazilians were aware that the option for a natural uranium reactor, along with reprocessing and plutonium purification facilities, could give Argentina the possibility to produce, starting from late 1974, 150 kilograms of Plutonium-239 (^{239}Pu). It would correspond to fifteen nuclear devices of 10 kilotons each that Argentina could explode in the atmosphere, since it was not a signatory of the Treaty of Moscow.[108] In response, according to the United States, Brazil could speed up its plans, accelerating a nuclear arms race with its neighbor.[109]

Akin to the Brazilian fears, the United States thought the Indians might "share their explosive technology with the Argentineans."[110] The US preoccupation increased when the Indian ambassador to Brazil affirmed that India was "prepared to furnish its Brazilian friends the technology which permitted it to build an atom bomb."[111] The Brazilians also knew that the Indians could make the 1968 cooperation effective, including spent-fuel reprocessing and heavy water, since officials of the Military Institute of Engineering (Instituto Militar de Engenharia, or IME) had begun negotiations in India on the issue in 1973.[112] The cooperation eventually turned out to be ineffective, and the agreement expired in 1975. It did not help that within weeks of the explosion the Indian deputy foreign minister, Pal Singh, visited Buenos Aires before arriving in Brasília.[113]

As the Brazilian historian Elio Gaspari has noted, on 10 June 1974, a few weeks after the Indian test, in a meeting with top-level army officials President Geisel "showed his interest in developing a project for producing nuclear fuel . . . because he believed that the Argentines were ready to 'make their weapon in the future.'"[114] However, Brazilian and Argentine nuclear authorities continued their dialogue about possible collaboration, with reciprocal invitations to visit the nuclear facilities and with a proposal of cooperation. Silveira informed Geisel that according to the Argentine authorities, financial problems, lack of technology, international safeguards, and growing pressure from Canada would prevent Buenos Aires from building a nuclear device, at least in the next twenty years.[115] Besides the existing common Brazilian and Argentine positions toward the NPT, Tlatelolco, and international safeguards, the path for establishing mutual trust began to be mapped out in those years.[116]

Washington's fear of a possible rivalry and Brazil's fear of an Argentine nuclear bomb were quieted in 1974 by a proposal for a Brazilian-Argentine integration of nuclear and hydroelectric sectors. The Argentine minister for the economy, José Gelbard, presented the idea in a private meeting with Arnaldo Barbalho, the Brazilian deputy minister of mines and energy.[117] The agreement was not reached, largely because of the turbulent political situation in Argentina, which led to a military dictatorship in 1976. A deal would have resolved the Paraná River dispute, as well as the integration of the two nuclear sectors. In June 1975, on the eve of the signing of the West German–Brazilian deal, the United States was aiming to dispel Argentine-Brazilian mutual suspicions, an issue that kept arising in the FRG-Brazil and US-Brazil nuclear cooperations. From the US perspective, a potential way for dealing with proliferation concerns was a possible Argentine-Brazilian agreement "according to which all facilities would be safeguarded, and conceivably to coordinate reprocessing plans on a regional basis."[118]

The US concern, however, was not a misinterpretation of the Argentine position. With a more developed nuclear program, the government of Buenos Aires did fear that Brazilian superiority in a sector dominated by Argentina could prompt the end of the strategic balance in the region. In a confidential talk with a West German official, a high-ranking Argentine diplomat expressed his government's preoccupation with the possibility that Brazil might acquire a nuclear weapon.[119] Argentine nuclear authorities feared the potential drain of nuclear scientists (several of whom had been investigated by the new regime) from CNEA to the Brazilian nuclear sector in growing numbers after the contract with Bonn.[120] However, the Brazilian government attempted to divert the US preoccupation with nuclear proliferation toward Argentina, which was, in the words of an authoritative Itamaraty high officer, "the country that will be the first in Latin America to set off a nuclear explosion because the Argentines need some dramatic action to regain the prestige they have lost because of domestic political problems."[121]

The conflicting opinions of Brazilian and Argentine diplomats over their respective nuclear programs did not prevent Buenos Aires from showing solidarity when the Carter administration attempted to downgrade Brazil's nuclear plans. In February 1977 Esteban Takacs, the Argentine ambassador to Ottawa, affirmed in a talk with his Brazilian counterpart that "the Argentine government should officially support Brazil in the issue of the nuclear agreement with the FRG." He correctly predicted that "if the United States succeeds in impeding or limiting the German-Brazilian agreement, the next objective will be the sabotage of the Argentine nuclear program."[122] In 1976 the CNEA multibillion-dollar 1975–1985 Nuclear Plan aimed at building several nuclear power plants and mastering the nuclear fuel cycle. Argentina needed to protect its atomic projects from external pressures, and sharing a common position with Brazil could be the key to such strategy. It was not the first time that Argentina had proposed to Brazil a common stance for facing the US nonproliferation policy. In November 1976 the Argentines offered to issue a joint declaration on a possible renouncement of nuclear explosives, but the Brazilians declined.[123] A possible engagement between Brazil and Argentina on nuclear issues was not just the subject of the conversations in Ottawa. It was also discussed in Brasília, where Itamaraty told the West Germans that it was not negotiating with Buenos Aires in the nuclear field.[124]

Both the Brazilian and Argentine military regimes were targets of the Carter nuclear nonproliferation policies. In the US internal debate, Paul C. Warnke proposed full Brazilian and Argentine accession to Tlatelolco and hoped for a successful outcome concerning Brazil. It "should also help lay the groundwork for a favorable settlement to the Argentinean problem. The situation in Argentina . . . is, in a number of aspects appreciably worse than that in Brazil, since their program is further along, and they intend to acquire a full, unsafeguarded, fuel cycle based on the Indian model. Moreover, it appears highly unlikely that Brazil would find it acceptable to give up the acquisition of a safeguarded reprocessing facility while Argentina was indigenously building an unsafeguarded facility of the same approximate size."[125] For the first time, the United States involved the Argentine factor in resolving the Brazilian issue. It was the first step of a strategy to reach a regional solution, and it lasted until the end of the Carter administration.[126] In response, the Argentine ambassador to Brazil, Oscar Camilión, in a meeting with a high-level Brazilian military officer proposed bilateral cooperation in the nuclear field to resist the United States.[127] From May to August 1977, US representatives (including the First Lady, Rosalynn Carter) pressed President

Geisel to accept the Treaty of Tlatelolco. Geisel reacted by criticizing the failure of both the Americans and the Soviets to accept the protocols of the treaty, and he refused to fully accede to the Latin American NWFZ.[128]

The White House was not the only player seeking to persuade the two countries to commit to nonproliferation. Capitol Hill continued to act to limit the spread of nuclear weapons and sensitive dual-use technologies. After the 1977 Glenn Amendment increased the restrictions to the trade of sensitive materials, Congressman Paul Findley (R-IL) took a personal initiative toward Brazil and Argentina. On the occasion of a congressional mission to the two Latin American countries in August 1977, Findley, in private meetings with Brazilian and Argentine authorities, proposed the adoption of a bilateral safeguards system and the renouncing of PNEs. At present, the framer of this initiative is not known, and Findley's action was not part of an action of the Carter administration, despite the friendly relations between the Republican congressman and the president. Adopting a bilateral safeguards system and renouncing PNEs became the core principles for ABACC, established in 1991. Findley made his proposal public through articles in the Brazilian and US press. The initiative was also conveyed to Argentina's president, Jorge R. Videla, and Brazil's vice president, Adalberto dos Santos, on the occasion of the ceremony in Washington for the signature of the Torrijos-Carter agreements on the Panama Canal. Although Argentina responded favorably to the idea and indicated its possible accession to Tlatelolco, Brazil rejected it.[129]

When Findley's action failed, the White House fashioned a new initiative to try to persuade Brazil to renounce sensitive technologies. During a visit to Buenos Aires and Brasília in November 1977, Secretary Vance negotiated an agreement according to which Argentina would abandon reprocessing technologies in exchange for greatly increased US assistance in heavy-water technologies. The condition that Vance proposed to Videla was that Brasília would give up the same technology to guarantee a "nuclear" equilibrium between the two countries. Vance made a similar proposal in his talks with Foreign Minister Silveira and President Geisel. The initiative would offer leverage to force Brazil to change its nuclear policy despite the government's public statements about defending the atomic project. When Vance met with President Geisel a few days later, he was surprised that Brazil was aware of the advancement of Argentina's nuclear program and its (possible) capacity to produce an atomic device. Still, Geisel did not consider its neighbor a threat and criticized the US nonproliferation strategy, which limited the transfer of technology rather than fully committing to a stronger international regime and disarmament. In an organizational lapse, Vance left a paper with the instructions for negotiating with Brazil and Argentina in Silveira's office. It exposed the American strategy of using a supposed arms race to enforce its nonproliferation policy. Vance's bluff showed the US lack of awareness of Brazil and Argentina's ongoing discussions about possible nuclear cooperation. The US pressure eventually had the effect of accelerating the Brasília–Buenos Aires rapprochement in the nuclear realm.[130]

Geisel's words were probably part of a strategy for resisting Vance's action to get both countries to accept Tlatelolco and other nonproliferation initiatives. Minority elements in the military circles and several voices among the public of both Southern Cone countries were convinced of the need for nuclear weapons to control their neighbor. Leonel Brizola, one of the prominent voices of Brazil's opposition in exile, revealed in a meeting with Robert Pastor (Carter's national security advisor for Latin America) his conviction "that the military wanted the bomb for reasons of prestige and because of Argentina" and thought "that they could be diverted from their objective."[131]

Despite those external and domestic perceptions, the available documentation does not indicate relevant top-level discussions about a possible Brazilian military nuclearization to face Argentina. A hypothetical "small nuclear bomb," according to several members of the EMFA, could deter the small countries around Brazil, but this position remained vague and never received the support of the cabinet. On the contrary, economic matters and poor water resources control were the only hurdles to cooperation between Argentina and Brazil. For this reason, President Geisel consistently refused to begin advanced talks with the Argentines on atomic cooperation. US pressure and the growing international isolation of Brazil in the nuclear realm led both countries to adopt similar strategies to develop their nuclear programs and cooperate mutually.

CHAPTER FIVE

Between Autonomy and International Collaboration, 1979–1985

In 1978 the US Congress approved the Non-Proliferation Act, ruling that the United States could export nuclear materials and technologies only to countries accepting the full scope safeguards. . . . The same supply for Angra 1 (the recharge), even if contractually guaranteed, was conditioned on Brazil's acceptance of additional requirements. That law was enforced in the first months of 1979.[1]

With these words, general Danilo Venturini, secretary-general of the CSN from 1979 to 1985, explained to a parliamentary commission of inquiry how international constraints (e.g., the Nuclear Non-Proliferation Act) and the difficulties of the deal with the FRG led Brazil to establish and implement an autonomous, unsafeguarded civilian-military program. The final aim was to provide the country autonomy in the nuclear field. This chapter explores how Brazil began a nuclear program "parallel" to the civilian one through the active collaboration of civilian and military institutions. It also discusses how Brazil collaborated with other NPT opponents, especially Argentina and China. Furthermore, the following pages document how the Brazilian government discarded the proposal by some sectors of the military to test a nuclear device.

Brazil, the United States, and the Non-Proliferation Regime

On 15 March 1979 General João Batista Figueiredo began the last and longest administration of the military regime. This period concluded the democratization process inaugurated by his predecessor, Ernesto Geisel. Figueiredo and his foreign minister, Ramiro Saraiva Guerreiro (former secretary-general, with long experience in nuclear negotiations), would continue a similar diplomatic program, even if Brazil would face more critical situations, such as a dramatic debt crisis. Brazil did not modify its attitude toward international nonproliferation norms.

After several episodes of divergence, Washington and Brasília attempted to improve their relationship in the nuclear field.

To ease the tension with Brasília, Jimmy Carter, who considered the new president more flexible than Geisel, sent his vice president, Walter Mondale, to Figueiredo's inauguration.[2] The Department of State wished "to reach a *modus vivendi* on a myriad of trade problems and nuclear policy."[3] For the rest of the Carter administration the Brazilian and US governments discussed the nuclear fuel supply for the US-provided reactor Angra 1.[4] US nuclear authorities eventually provided the fuel in 1983, when the unit entered its power ascension (Angra 1 began its operation in 1984, but with technical problems). With a more cordial climate, the Reagan administration established a bilateral working group with Itamaraty to discuss nuclear issues.[5] However, Washington continued to criticize the Brazilian stance toward the regime, and US legislation led countries such as Brazil and Argentina to develop indigenous nuclear strategies within an unfavorable international environment.[6] In this period, Brazil continued to oppose the NPT. It assessed, as an observer, the second NPT review conference (RevCon), convened in Geneva from 11 July to 7 September 1980, as a complete failure owing to the persisting discriminatory nature of the treaty and the NWSs' lack of commitment to disarmament.[7]

Brazil's "Parallel" Nuclear Program

From 1978 to 1982 a parliamentary commission of inquiry headed by Senator Itamar Franco listed the flaws of the nuclear program, especially those connected to the deal with West Germany.[8] The difficulty of obtaining enriched uranium from Urenco, stricter international safeguards, the lack of valid technology coming from West Germany, the rising cost of the civilian project run by Nuclebrás (US$4 billion to $18 billion), and the wave of internal criticism of the agreement with Bonn derailed Brazil's nuclear plans with West Germany inaugurated by Geisel. In the early 1980s, budget restrictions justified the Brazilian decision not to build two of the four reactors in Angra (Angra 4 and 5) and the two reactors in the state of São Paulo (Iguape I and II). Nuclebrás, moreover, faced an internal crisis that in 1983 led the czar of nuclear energy, Nogueira Batista, to resign. According to Cesar Cals, Figueiredo's minister of mines and energy, Brazil's main goal was to master the nuclear fuel cycle.[9]

At the peak of the Carter offensive, the Brazilian CSN identified the main deficiency of the 1975 nuclear deal as the absence of the transfer of technology for converting yellowcake into uranium hexafluoride (UF_6). Despite initial promises, Bonn would not transfer one of the key aspects of nuclear fuel production. France and the United Kingdom, two countries that produced UF_6, declared that they were willing to transfer this industrial capability, but only if Brazil would accept safeguards.[10] Even though Nuclebrás had initially accepted the agreement with the French company UPUK, this was a resounding setback.[11]

The Elaboration of a New Nuclear Project: Project Autônomo

The deficiencies of the Brazilian-FRG deal and the impossibility of acquiring the conversion technology in the international market, given the new nonproliferation norms, led Geisel to make a forceful decision. At the end of 1978 he commissioned CNEN to coordinate the activities of research centers in São Paulo, Belo Horizonte, and Rio de Janeiro, all part of the National Nuclear Energy Plan, to develop such technology.[12] In a few months, the Nuclear and Energy Research Institute (Instituto de Pesquisas Energéticas e Nucleares, or IPEN), formerly the IEA, under the direction of Professor Rômulo Ribeiro Pieroni, fulfilled the order. Pieroni headed a research center free from international safeguards (with the exception of the research reactor) and dedicated part of the IPEN activities to the study of the nuclear fuel cycle. Through a massive effort, in February 1979 the IPEN research group, led by the chemist Alcídio Abrãao, presented to Geisel the first samples of uranium hexafluoride produced in Brazilian laboratories.[13] This outcome led the minister of foreign affairs and the minister of mines and energy, along with the secretary-general of the CSN, to suggest that Geisel establish a working group to allow IPEN participation in the development of UF_6 production, a key phase of the nuclear fuel cycle.

At the very end of his presidency, on 14 March, Geisel approved the working group, made up of representatives of the Secretariat of Planning of the Presidency of the Republic (Secretaria de Planejamento da Presidência da República, or SEPLAN); Itamaraty; the Ministry of Mines and Energy; CNEN; CNPq; and the state of São Paulo, which oversaw IPEN.[14] After three months of intense activity, the working group submitted to the new president, Figueiredo, two possible alternatives: Project Integrado (Integrated Project) and Project Autônomo (Autonomous Project). The first option, proposed by Nuclebrás, would create a partnership between IPEN and Nuclebrás, which would collaborate in that field with the French company UPUK. The second alternative would establish an autonomous national project that would guarantee IPEN, under the supervision of the CSN, full capability to produce UF_6. At that moment, with the decline of the Nuclebrás project and in the face of domestic criticism, the working group chose Project Autônomo. Although the project would be more expensive than Project Integrado (200 million Brazilian cruzeiros compared with 140 million), it had more advantages. Project Autônomo would increase Brazil's bargaining power with foreign nations and maximize in the long run the use of scientific, technological, and financial resources available in the country. Moreover, it would guarantee the development of national nuclear technologies free from international safeguards with the active involvement of the Brazilian academic and scientific communities. The endeavor, even if secret, could be immune to the rising criticism of the nuclear program. It would answer one of the requests of the Brazilian scientists, who vehemently protested against the Brazilian–West German nuclear deal. This aspect appeared to be particularly important in this last phase of the military regime, which was moving the country in the direction of re-democratization.

President Figueiredo approved Project Autônomo. In a few years, IPEN completed a pilot plant for converting uranium dioxide, producing 180 tons of UF_6 per year.[15] The goal of the project was to produce UF_6 on an industrial scale to satisfy Brazilian needs, especially when the UPUK-Nuclebrás agreement was not implemented a few years later. Project Autônomo was one the first acts of a secret nuclear program parallel to the official one but without the constraints posed by the 1975 deal and by the international context. For similar reasons, Buenos Aires had made a similar decision a few years earlier, making Argentina the first country in the region to have the ability to produce uranium hexafluoride.[16]

Economic motivations also explained the Brazilian choice. The second oil price shock, the rising debt, and the economic crisis led President Figueiredo to adopt Project Autônomo along with other strategies for nationalizing key sectors for domestic development. The initial IPEN project for UF_6 conversion, better known as Project Conversão, constituted the basis for a larger rationalization of all the nuclear activities external to the civilian nuclear projects, fruit of the collaboration with West Germany or other countries participating in the nonproliferation regime. The new national nuclear policy would guarantee the coordination of all the autonomous and unsafeguarded projects that had been developed since the 1950s by civilian and military nuclear institutes. Project Autônomo would be one of the first steps toward the Autonomous Program of Nuclear Technology (Programa Autônomo de Tecnologia Nuclear, or PATN). The ultimate purpose was to give Brazil total control of the nuclear fuel cycle and of peaceful uses of nuclear energy, from naval propulsion to PNEs. By choosing Project Autônomo, the Brazilian government gave IPEN the responsibility of producing uranium components (either natural or enriched) useful to the other projects.[17] Furthermore, IPEN could guarantee the "development of [uranium] isotopic enrichment processes alternative [to the German jet nozzle and] autonomous and independent of international safeguards."[18]

The program, which became known during Brazil's re-democratization as the parallel program (*programa paralelo*), was kept top secret to avoid possible criticism from the public, and, above all, to escape foreign interference (even though from the very beginning rumors about its existence appeared in the press).[19] As one of the protagonists of the program and former chairman of CNEN, Rex Nazaré Alves, has recently noted, the research groups worked on items included in the 1977 NSG guidelines. Brazil was pursuing domestically what international constraints impeded them from acquiring abroad.[20] From the beginning, however, the Brazilian authorities declared that the final outcome of the national research would respect the international commitments of the country and would be shared with other Latin American countries to guarantee the region's development. PATN was a joint effort coordinated by the three armed forces (army, navy, and air force), CNEN, and IPEN (which was put under the supervision of CNEN in 1982).[21] The three military branches and the civilian institutions had different tasks. The next section discusses in depth how Brazil acquired command of a technological method for enriching uranium, crucial for both peaceful and military uses.

The Quest for an Indigenous Technology for Enriching Uranium

The Brazilian government had never digested one of the primary deficiencies of the West German deal: the transfer of the unproven jet-nozzle technology. As seen, since the beginning of the negotiations with Bonn in 1973, Brazil had been attempting to acquire the ultracentrifuge method for isotopic uranium separation. The Becker method's imposition was highly criticized, not only by the scientific community (it was particularly clear during the hearings of the parliamentary commission of inquiry) but also by the technicians who negotiated the agreement with the West German authorities.[22] The Brazilian nuclear research centers and, at the beginning of the cooperation with West Germany, Nuclebrás continued to study alternative uranium enrichment techniques possibly free from international controls.

The Laser Project

One of the first efforts to enrich uranium autonomously in Brazil (after some attempts in the 1960s) was a product of the collaboration between military and civilian nuclear scientists. In 1974 they started a research group to look at a promising method for isotopic separation that used electromagnetic radiations generated by a laser. Alongside the international quest for a partner in developing a nuclear complex, this project was approved in 1974 by the Institute of Advanced Studies (Instituto de Estudos Avançados, or IEAv), of the Aerospace Technical

Center (Centro Tecnológico da Aeronáutica, or CTA), and the Ministry of the Air Force after an agreement with the Ministry of Mines and Energy. CNEN was aware of this study conducted at the State University of Campinas (Unicamp), established a few years earlier by the state of São Paulo.

Unicamp's scientific environment was appropriate for conducting such research. The new Unicamp Institute of Physics was initially directed by the former chairman of CNEN, Marcelo Damy, who secured rich resources for creating one of the most advanced research institutes in the country from the president of the new university, Zeferino Vaz.[23] Despite the possible constraints of the military regime, Unicamp became an oasis of well-funded research for scientists with an ideological position different from that of the government. The institute would focus on solid-state physics and quantum mechanics. To pursue this endeavor, and within a strategy agreed upon between the Brazilian Ministry of Education and the United States Agency for International Development in 1968, Damy (and later his successor, Rogério Cerqueira Leite) and Zeferino Vaz decided to hire the best Brazilian scientists working in foreign countries (including those previously purged by the Brazilian universities for ideological reasons).[24] The commitment was to replicate in Brazil the research conducted abroad. It was the continuation of a strategy that Damy had helped create in the early 1950s, while he sat on the executive committee of CNPq. Among other prominent scientists, Zeferino Vaz invited Professor Sérgio Pereira da Silva Porto. Porto, who had studied in the United States and had been a researcher at Brazil's Aeronautics Institute of Technology (Instituto Tecnológico da Aeronáutica, or ITA) from 1954 to 1960, was lecturing at the University of Southern California (USC) after pioneering work on laser technology at Bell Laboratories. Thanks to a government contribution of US$2 million, Porto had built at Unicamp a research team with advanced equipment for working on laser research. Porto's project was realized thanks to constant interaction with foreign universities, mainly USC. Unicamp could fund foreign researchers to spend long terms in Brazil, and vice versa.

One of the team's areas of interest was laser enrichment of uranium, building on Porto's work at USC.[25] The studies on that method of isotopic separation were at an early stage in the United States, and Porto was one of the world's leading experts on the method. As noted by Steven Hargrove, the technique was developed initially as a "cost-effective, environmentally friendly technology to supply enriched uranium for nuclear power plants and special nuclear materials for national security needs."[26] In the early 1970s, the United States was investing heavily in this field. The laser enrichment technique, if proved to be viable, could reduce the environmental and economic cost of producing nuclear fuel in a period of booming demand for nuclear energy. Brazil was particularly interested in such a technique, and Porto's interest in developing this research in the country offered a significant opportunity. The idea arose during Porto's stay in California, where he met two Brazilian researchers. The first was the air force lieutenant colonel José Alberto Albano Amarante, who worked at the IEAv and was finishing his PhD. The second was the IPEN researcher Cláudio Rodrigues, a former Unicamp student who was completing a postdoctoral fellowship at the California Institute of Technology.[27] Geisel's minister of planning, João Paulo dos Reis Velloso, allowed Porto to return to Brazil. He promised abundant financial resources to the Brazilian scientist and his team for the laser project.[28]

In 1974, after Porto and Amarante returned to Brazil, the IEAv and Unicamp decided to join forces through an agreement supported by civilian and military authorities. The study was conducted in Campinas, and after the project received government approval, it was given the highest priority by CNEN. The ultimate purpose of the research was to confirm that the separation of isotopes of uranium by the use of monochromatic radiation could succeed in Brazil. Professor Carvalho, then chairman of the CNEN, in a secret letter to minister Ueki wrote that "the possibility of obtaining the isotopic separation autonomously and without international controls" could not be ignored. "Such an achievement will give Brazil the possibility to increase our negotiation capability in the economic and political areas and, perhaps to meet national needs, in special circumstances."[29] What was meant by "special circumstances" is not clear. Probably it included the possibility of producing not only nuclear fuel for power and research nuclear reactors but also material for a peaceful nuclear device.

The conclusion of the first three years of research saw promising results. It led the Brazilian government to discuss the next phase for Porto and Amarante's research, whose scale was to be upgraded.[30] In the Unicamp laboratories, Porto's group had been able to separate spectroscopic lines of different isotopic molecules of uranium hexafluoride. It was an important achievement, and the research had to continue and to be preserved.[31] In September 1977, after Carter's diplomatic attacks on the Brazilian nuclear program, the Geisel administration considered it vital to obtain enriched uranium, above all for the country's security and development. Hervásio de Carvalho believed that "the development of national technology resulting from Brazilian research, parallel to that resulting from the adjustment and transference through the agreement with the Federal Republic of Germany, will be decisive for turning the country into an emerging nation, peaceful but sovereign."[32] Here, for the first time, we see the use of the term *parallel*, which would come to characterize the autonomous nuclear program. Carvalho and the Brazilian authorities were aware of the growing international political and commercial constraints on Brazil's nuclear program. A parallel program was indispensable for many sectors that had difficult or no access to technologies and knowledge. Carvalho recommended stricter security measures for the laser enrichment project, allowing curious or foreign people no access. CNEN did not have such laboratories, and the Nuclebrás-controlled institutes—IPr, IEN, and the Institute of Radiation Protection and Dosimetry (Instituto de Radioproteção e Dosimetria, or IRD)—had low levels of security and were subject to international safeguards.[33]

The best option was the IEA, free from international safeguards. At the time, any use of military research centers could raise suspicions that a project had military aims. The CSN council shared Carvalho's concern about the future of the project, including its security. Moreover, in May 1977 the journal *Science* had published an article entitled "Laser Enrichment of Uranium: The Proliferation Connection." Because of the possible international reaction to the research, the Brazilian government supported Carvalho's proposal.[34]

Porto and Amarante would continue the research begun at Unicamp facilities at the IEA in 1977. Their partner, in new facilities to be built on the São Paulo campus, would be Claudio Rodrigues. When Rodrigues returned to the São Paulo institution, he worked in the area of special projects, established by Rômulo Pieroni. IEA's research on nuclear fuel would give the team useful material for studying laser enrichment of UF_6. In 1977 CTA, CNEN, Unicamp, and the state of São Paulo signed a special convention (o8 IEA/77) with the IEA for participating in the laser enrichment separation project. The IEA, like Project Conversão, was crucial for the success of the endeavor, which constituted the enlargement of a civilian-military nuclear collaboration. The research on laser enrichment continued in the IEA facilities until 1981. It was eventually transferred to São José dos Campos, a city in the state of São Paulo where CTA was based in a new IEAv building inaugurated in 1982. Between 1979 and 1981 the research team lost two protagonists. Sérgio Porto died prematurely in 1979 as a consequence of a heart attack he suffered during a stay in the Soviet Union, and José Amarante died in 1981 of leukemia.[35] Before his death Porto achieved an important scientific result: the development of a new process for producing heavy water through laser irradiation. Porto revealed the outcome during a talk with the US Embassy's scientific attaché in Brasília, underlining that obtaining heavy water with his technique would be less expensive than conventional methods.[36]

It is not clear whether the research on heavy-water production continued in São José dos Campos, but laser enrichment did constitute one of the three aspects of the atomic project (Project Solimões) and part of the autonomous program, conducted by the air force at the IEAv under the coordination of Brigadier Reginaldo dos Santos and Hugo Piva. The enrichment effort (even if slowed down after Porto's death) was wedded to the second part of the project, the development of peaceful nuclear devices to be assembled with enriched uranium. It was the most sensitive aspect of the Brazilian project, which, as we will see in the next pages, did not lead to the construction of a Brazilian PNE but to the building of a nuclear test shaft in the early 1980s at the air force base in the Serra do Cachimbo in the state of Pará, in northern Brazil. The last research area of interest at IEAv was fast breeder reactors. As we will see, the research on laser enrichment continued after the Figueiredo years.

The IPEN-Navy Centrifuge Project and the First Uranium Isotopic Separation

After the laser project moved in 1977 from Unicamp to the IEA, which since 1970 had not been subordinated to CNEN and had changed its name to IPEN, the São Paulo institute took the lead in the effort to master nuclear enrichment. In the late 1970s, through an agreement between CNEN, the air force ministry, and the navy, IPEN would also work on the possible development of Brazilian ultracentrifuges, useful for producing the fuel for a nuclear-powered submarine.

In the early 1970s, the Brazilian navy manifested its interest in developing small nuclear reactors for naval propulsion.[37] Despite the agreement with West Germany and the possibility of collaboration also with France, the Brazilian government limited its attention to the nuclear propulsion of civilian vessels. Geisel decided to exclude the possibility of nuclear-powered submarines in the official discussions with the West German authorities, even if he did not exclude the possibility of the navy's future participation in nuclear projects.[38] The navy's decision to enter the nuclear field is attributable to Captain Othon Luiz Pinheiro da Silva. After earning a master's degree in nuclear engineering at the Massachusetts Institute of Technology and a short period at Nuclebrás, Pinheiro da Silva served at the Directorate of Naval Engineering (Diretoria de Engenharia Naval, or DEN). He worked on a river vessel and in the nuclear area. Understandably, the navy gave low priority to nuclear energy. Still, a report submitted to the directorate at the end of May 1978 paved the way for a deeper engagement in the atomic field. Pinheiro da Silva proposed focusing on mastering the nuclear fuel cycle and, in a second phase, developing a system for applying nuclear propulsion to submarines. And he proposed that the work be done indigenously, without collaborating with Nuclebrás, in order not to threaten the West German–Brazilian agreement and not to be subject to international safeguards.

Following the initial support of Rear Admiral Mário César Flores, the admiralty approved the proposal in December 1978. After an agreement between the Ministry of the Navy and the Ministry of the Air Force, Pinheiro da Silva began to work at the IEAv with Lieutenant Colonel José Amarante in the field of uranium laser enrichment. Despite the promising achievements obtained by the research team, laser enrichment was not considered an isotopic separation method capable of producing remarkable amounts of enriched uranium in the short term. In June 1979 Pinheiro da Silva submitted a new report to EMFA in which he recommended starting a project on gas centrifuge uranium isotopic separation. EMFA backed his recommendation. Pinheiro da Silva also obtained the support of Professor Alberto Pereira de Castro, supervisor of the Institute for Technological Research (IPT) at the University of São Paulo, and Cláudio Rodrigues, who, as head of special projects at IPEN, was already collaborating with him on laser uranium enrichment. Rodrigues, even without the support of his institute, shared Pinheiro's concern about the immediate viability of the technique Porto and Amarante were developing.

In July 1979 the Ministry of the Navy approved the creation of a special project for enriching uranium with a budget of 15 million cruzeiros for the first two years.[39] In the same period, and thanks to the collaboration and mutual support of Pinheiro da Silva and Amarante, President Figueiredo approved the joint request submitted by the Ministries of the Air Force and the Navy. Starting in 1979, the enrichment project would be divided between the navy, with a specific project on gas centrifuge, and the air force, which would continue its research on laser enrichment in the CTA facilities. The navy, which did not have its own nuclear research center, joined IPEN in the study of the nuclear fuel cycle in the unsafeguarded facilities in São Paulo. The civilian-military interaction would be crucial.

Despite Hervásio de Carvalho's initial refusal to provide CNEN financial support to the project, Rex Nazaré Alves, a CNEN executive director who had actively participated in the elaboration of Project Autônomo at IPEN, personally sustained the plan in September 1979. Alves's support was important for the future of the project. President Figueiredo appointed him as a special adviser to the secretariat of the CSN; Alves became the civilian responsible for nuclear energy.[40]

The project began on 2 February 1980, and its civilian and military researchers worked with enthusiasm. The aim was to master the technology needed to build the ultracentrifuges. In the late 1970s, Pinheiro da Silva, Amarante, and Rodrigues required Professor Ivo Jordan's expertise. Jordan, who had publicly criticized the choice of the jet nozzle, would participate on the research team developing the gas centrifuge isotopic separation process and above all the separation cascades.[41] Despite their technical obsolescence and the difference between Groth's technique and Zippe's, Groth's centrifuges were reactivated in order to study his technical process. Two of them were actually used, while one was taken apart for the purpose of extracting knowledge and design information through the process of back engineering.[42] IPEN and navy researchers needed to master the newest techniques and more sophisticated materials and machinery. More than 150 Brazilian companies secretly collaborated with IPEN to provide the industrial basis for mastering the ultracentrifuge technique and UF_6 production. The São Paulo institute, in exchange, assisted private industry with research oriented toward meeting the needs of the companies.[43] In other cases, the solution had been to acquire components on the international market, useful also for other purposes.

As already noted, the main problem the Brazilians faced was how to acquire and control the magnetic suspension bearings of the centrifuge. As Jordan described, IPEN partially resolved the trouble through the reverse engineering of German Leybold high-vacuum pumps with magnetic rotor suspension available on the open market.[44] Like many other countries that suffered international limitations to the development of indigenous technologies, Brazil had to purchase elements in an unconventional way. On one occasion, for example, the Brazilian authorities acquired the switches for the centrifuges in France from the company Thomson and shipped them through the diplomatic pouch.[45] Moreover, there are rumors of the possible acquisition of technical and scientific secrets either by industrial espionage or by hiring foreign experts.[46] The existing literature on the Brazilian case excludes the involvement in the Abdul Qadeer Khan network, not least because, as will be noted in the next pages, Pakistan probably rejected the offer to collaborate in the nuclear field.[47] According to Mark Hibbs and Daniel Horner, two West German engineers would have provided technology, expertise, and design to Brazil. A former H + H Metalform employee, Dietrich Hinze, would have sold a vertical flow-forming machine to Brazil in early 1984, and a former MAN Technologie engineer, Karl Heinz Schaab, would have ceded the centrifuge bearing design.[48]

There is no hard evidence of external collaboration to master the centrifuge technique, and the Brazilian authorities insisted that the project had indeed been indigenous.[49] After three years of work in the laboratories at IPEN, in September 1982 the researchers assembled the first Brazilian ultracentrifuge prototype and realized the first uranium isotopic separation. It was a remarkable achievement for the secret nuclear project and constituted the first success of the autonomous effort to master the enrichment technique. As Cláudio Rodrigues has recently observed, the outcome was achieved in the laboratory, and the research group then still had a lot to accomplish.[50] In 1982, IPEN was eventually integrated by CNEN after an agreement between the federal government and the state of São Paulo. Despite the initial difficulties, the first cascade began to operate in September 1984.[51] Even if the IPEN-navy effort produced only a few centrifuges before the end of the military regime, the supporters of the autonomous program could present results superior to those of the official program with West Germany.

Other Civilian Projects within the "Parallel Program"

IPEN's participation in the parallel program was not limited to the UF_6 conversion and the studies on uranium enrichment. CNEN and IPEN also contributed to PATN in the metallurgy field (in the preparation of metallic uranium and the mastery of the technologies for its application) and in the radiometric and environmental control of facilities. Another critical aspect of the nuclear fuel cycle was spent-fuel reprocessing, which according to the guidelines of the autonomous program would guarantee Brazil the production of plutonium. The effort, known as Project Celeste, began during the 1970s. Even at the scale of the laboratory, it provided Brazil with expertise in a sensitive area. The project was parallel to a similar one begun at IEN in the mid-1970s (with IAEA assistance) and to the reprocessing plant to be developed with the West Germans. While in 1983, according to US sources, Nuclebrás abandoned the reprocessing project, the IPEN activities evolved, with scientists trained in the FRG, until the first years of the

Figueiredo's visit to IPEN. *Left to right*: Rex Nazaré Alves (CNEN chairman),
Franco Montoro (governor, state of São Paulo), President João Batista Figueiredo, and
Dr. Constância Pagano Gonçalves da Silva (IPEN), São Paulo, 10 October 1984. (IPEN)

twenty-first century, when the partnership was dismantled.[52] In the early 1980s there were rumors about the imminent capability of the Celeste unit to produce plutonium using the spent fuel to be produced by a breeder reactor. It was to be built in Rio de Janeiro in CNEN facilities through the cooperation of Italy, which replaced France in the project.[53] In 1983 the CIA reported that the spent fuel could be extracted by a natural uranium research reactor that IPEN would build. However, IPEN never built such a reactor. Except for Project Celeste, those projects continued after democratization, although some were later dissolved or ceded to the navy's research center.[54]

Other Military Nuclear Projects

Uranium enrichment was not the autonomous nuclear program's only activity. The three military branches, even if coordinated by the CSN, had their own specific projects. During the military regime, a bureaucratic contest reflected existing rivalries between the three military ministries, each having its own ambitions. In the early 1980s, this competition was also on the level of the official program. The navy program was by far the most successful, but in discussing Brazil's role in the global nuclear order from the late 1970s to the early 1990s it is important to mention the military projects and their possible international repercussions.

The Army's Atomic Project

The army had been interested in atomic energy since the inception of the Brazilian atomic program. In the mid-1950s the Military Institute of Engineering started the first academic program in nuclear engineering. Thanks to a 1972 agreement with CNEN, the techniques for heavy-water production were studied in its laboratories.[55] Many protagonists of the Brazilian nuclear program received their training in army facilities and continued to collaborate with the military forces. When the CSN approved the PATN, the army integrated it into Project Atlântico, which was to be implemented by the Army Technology Center (Centro Tecnológico do Exercito, or CTEx), in Guaratiba, close to Rio de Janeiro. The Institute of Special Research (Instituto de Pesquisas Especiais, or IPE), inaugurated in the early 1980s, would conduct the project, with two interconnected aims. The first was to develop the technology to produce pure nuclear graphite for moderating a natural uranium reactor. The second was to build a small natural uranium reactor, capable of producing plutonium.[56] Beyond the resumption of Damy's research interests, the project's final aim was to manufacture material that could be used in a nuclear device. Even though CTEx was not successful in its project, which was developed in association with CNEN, the army received the blueprint for a natural uranium reactor from a civilian engineer.[57] Hypothetically, the army could pursue a nuclear weapon option since CTEx was also working on a rocket program at Marambaia, where thirty years earlier the army had conducted the first experiment on implosion bombs. The army nuclear project also continued during the democratic transition until 1990, without, however, achieving concrete results.

The Air Force Project and Potential Delivery Systems

As seen in the previous pages, the air force played a crucial role in beginning the autonomous uranium enrichment. While Project Solimões involved both laser isotopic separation and the development of nuclear explosives, nuclear test shafts were projected and built on military bases in northern Brazil. A side project to the nuclear one, a project that raised foreign concern, was the research and development in the field of missiles and rockets. According to US evaluations, during the military regime the aerospace research centers (such as ITA) and companies (such as Avibrás) were able to develop sounding rockets (such as Sonda I, II, III, and IV). They were test-launched from the Barreira do Inferno Launch Center in northeast Brazil. While the official justification of the program directed by the Complete Brazilian Space Mission (Missão Espacial Completa Brasileira, or MECB) was to coordinate launch vehicles, the United States was concerned about a possible diversion of the technology for a ballistic missile.[58]

The Navy's Project

The origins of the naval nuclear project have already been described here in part. Unlike the air force and the army, until 1986 and the creation of Special Project Coordination (Coordenadoria para Projetos Especiais, or COPESP) the Brazilian navy did not have its own research center. The research group already existed under Othon Pinheiro da Silva and had executed two projects. Project Ciclone, developed in collaboration with IPEN, aimed at mastering gas centrifuge enrichment and assembling a demonstration facility. It is important to note that the ultimate aim was not to maintain the navy nuclear activity at IPEN but to set up a navy research facility for mastering the nuclear fuel cycle. Producing nuclear fuel was crucial for the development of the second project, Remo, which aimed at developing nuclear propulsion technology to build nuclear-powered submarines. A third, connected project, Chalana, was focused on the development and construction of the submarine hull.[59] In contrast to the army and the air force, the navy did not have a nuclear explosive project. Better funded than the other projects, the project led by Pinheiro da Silva was the most successful. The Brazilian presidency gave the navy plan priority.

International Cooperation and the Partnership with Argentina

After establishing the autonomous program and parallel to the cooperation with the FRG, Brazil collaborated with countries either opposing or breaking the NPT rules. The country also cooperated with individual entities through unseen purchases on the black market.[60] During the Figueiredo years, Brasília established fruitful nuclear cooperation with the People's Republic of China and Iraq, discussed possible collaboration with South Africa and Pakistan, and created a partnership with Buenos Aires. Foreign governments such as the United States and probably France and West Germany were aware of Brazil's autonomous effort and in several cases were concerned about it. To understand how "atomic assistance" was relevant for Brazil, the following pages deal with cases of cooperation or negotiations for collaborating in the nuclear field.[61]

A Pragmatic Cooperation: Saddam's Iraq

Nineteen seventy-nine began with a new energy crisis that deeply affected Brazil. The Iranian Revolution prompted a new oil price shock that led Brasília to accelerate a diplomatic strategy to seek commodities at a low price in the Middle East. The dependency on external supplies and the expansion of the Brazilian goods market gave the Latin American country the opportunity to expand its relations in the region, above all with Arab countries. Libya, Algeria, and Iraq became important partners for the Brazilian economy. The skills and goods that Brazil could export included nuclear materials and machinery. The expanding Brazilian nuclear sector, along with the capability to produce nuclear components and materials, attracted the attention of Baghdad, a key supplier of oil to Brazil.[62]

Despite its accession to the NPT in the early 1970s, the Iraqi government set up a secret nuclear weapons program.[63] The vice president, Saddam Hussein, who would become president in 1979, was the head of the Iraqi atomic project. In 1978 the Iraqi government requested Brazilian assistance in developing an ambiguous nuclear program that was at the center of international suspicions about Iraq's nuclear ambitions. In July 1978 an Iraqi delegation of nuclear experts visited the Brazilian atomic facilities, and a few months later Baghdad submitted a proposal for cooperating on uranium enrichment and spent-fuel reprocessing. The price of nuclear cooperation would be Iraqi oil and the expansion of Brazil's presence in the Iraqi economy.[64]

Despite Brazil's initial skepticism, the first negotiations took place in May 1979, when the vice president of the Iraqi Atomic Energy Commission, B. A. Maarouf, visited Brasília. A more productive dialogue started in October 1979, when a Brazilian delegation flew to Baghdad. Following the instructions of Foreign Minister Saraiva Guerreiro, the cooperation was to be public and subject to international safeguards, and in response to West German pressures, it could not involve sensitive technologies included in the FRG-Brazil agreement.[65] Brazil was available to collaborate in the technical field and supply of uranium dioxide. The industrial cooperation could last ten to fifteen years and would respect the principle of specific compensation.[66]

After several months, in October 1979 the two governments signed a protocol for the peaceful use of nuclear energy that the Brazilian Congress ratified in 1981.[67] The cooperation, which served as the model for the deals with Somalia, Saudi Arabia, and Libya, would last ten years, guaranteeing the supply of natural or LEU for fueling the Iraqi nuclear power and research reactors.[68] The nuclear ambitions of Iraq—whose Osirak reactor was bombed a few months before the deal with Brasília—were suspected by the United States and Israel, as Brazil's would be. The suspicions were particularly strong after the two countries also began to cooperate on missiles for military purposes. The nuclear cooperation with Baghdad was not as effective as expected. One of the Brazilian diplomats responsible for the deal recently revealed that Brazil received the payment in a secret bank account in New York and shipped sixteen of the eighty tons of uranium dioxide to Iraq before the official agreement and free of international safeguards.[69] The Baghdad-Tehran war kept Brazil from exporting the rest of the material. Suspicions of such cooperation remained high until the eve of the Gulf War in 1990, when Brazil, under international pressure, suspended its troublesome collaboration with Hussein's regime.

Cases of Missing Cooperation? South Africa and Pakistan

Despite Brazil's need for collaboration in the nuclear field, Brasília has rejected proposals of possible agreements with certain countries for political reasons. This was the case with South Africa, which offered Brazil components and knowledge to improve the jet-nozzle uranium enrichment method in exchange for heavy components for South African reactors.[70] The priority given to the autonomous program and the downscaling of the official nuclear project can explain Brazil's decision not to negotiate with Pretoria.[71] A few years earlier, similar political reasons and the proximity to the Arab countries had impeded cooperation with Israel, even if in the early 1970s Tel Aviv and Brasília had been close to reaching an agreement.

Brazil's nuclear authorities also considered a partnership with Pakistan. As in the case of South Africa, the two potential partners had been subject to new, stricter nuclear nonproliferation norms and above all of limitations on the trade of sensitive nuclear material and technologies established through the nuclear suppliers' guidelines. In a very different regional context, Pakistan mastered uranium enrichment in the period 1976–80, facing the same technical troubles that Brazil had faced in developing ultracentrifuges.[72] Pakistani assistance could be valuable for acquiring full enrichment capability. In early 1984, on the occasion of a meeting of the IAEA board of governors in Vienna, Muniz Khan, the chairman of the Pakistan Atomic Energy Commission (PAEC), approached his Brazilian counterpart, Rex Nazaré Alves, who had become head of CNEN in 1982.[73] The Brazilians were aware of the rumors about a possible Pakistani nuclear bomb project. Moreover, they knew of the efforts to conduct centrifuge research thanks to the action of the former Urenco nuclear physicist Abdul Qader Khan, who had been appointed head of Pakistan's enrichment project in 1975. CNEN and Brazil's foreign ministry, however, were not fully informed about the stage of advancement of the uranium enrichment program.[74] During their talks in Vienna, Muniz Khan informed Alves that Pakistan had mastered all the phases of the nuclear fuel cycle and built a 60,000 rpm centrifuge. The machinery was more advanced than that created by IPEN. Like the South Africans, the Pakistanis were interested in Brazil's capability for constructing heavy components for the reactors. In 1984 Pakistan was planning to acquire a new reactor from either France or West Germany. The Brazilian company Nuclep could be the appropriate partner in an international market that set numerous limitations on Islamabad.

Formal talks could be established in a future visit to Pakistan that Foreign Minister Guerreiro had planned for April 1984. Muniz Khan's offer had immediately caught the attention of Brazil's nuclear and diplomatic authorities. In a personal dispatch to President Figueiredo, Saraiva Guerreiro, who was particularly concerned with the evolution of the Brazilian nuclear program, set out the advantages of a possible technical collaboration with Pakistan, especially in the area of uranium isotopic separation. Even though the Navy-IPEN effort had led to the enrichment of the first milligrams of uranium in 1982, the Brazilian scientists had to improve the equipment before they could assemble the first centrifuge cascade. The solution could be in Pakistan. Brazil, according to the foreign minister, would be cautious. Initially it would accept a cooperation through Nuclebrás, and later it would involve CNEN, which was running the autonomous project. A high degree of discretion was recommended, since rumors about

IPEN's activities could endanger Brazil's quest to master uranium enrichment. For Saraiva Guerreiro, who was responsible for all the foreign collaboration in the nuclear field, it was crucial to acquire nuclear autonomy before the end of the military regime. Probably he feared the possible dismantling of the nuclear program under a democratic government. Moreover, he wrote explicitly to Figueiredo that reaching autonomy was essential vis-à-vis Argentina, which had a more advanced nuclear sector. The Pakistani collaboration could be more than useful for achieving that goal, but secrecy was also required in order to avoid Indian criticism.

President Figueiredo gave his foreign minister the green light to take part in preliminary talks in Islamabad. A delegation made up of representatives of Nuclebrás, CNEN, and the Foreign Ministry discussed the issue with Pakistani officials, but the secret aspect was left for discussions in Vienna between the heads of the national nuclear commissions during the meetings of the IAEA board of governors. The talks probably were not as successful as had been expected.[75] While Islamabad, presumably, did not become a partner, Brazil established a new, solid collaboration with Beijing.

Trading with Beijing: The Purchase of Enriched Uranium and the Nuclear Cooperation with the People's Republic of China

A significant nuclear cooperation in the last phase of the military regime was with Beijing. The PRC, one of the five NWSs recognized by the NPT, was not part of the nuclear nonproliferation regime and shared Brazil's criticism of the norms imposed by the industrialized countries.[76] Despite the rapprochement with the United States, Communist China did not share Washington's nuclear nonproliferation concerns, and it was not yet a member of the IAEA. It did not impose international safeguards on its program and its international partners. Because of its advanced nuclear sector and its pragmatic policy, Beijing collaborated in the atomic field with several countries, including ones not participating in the NPT. It became an important provider of nuclear material and technologies.[77]

As part of Brazil's pragmatic and universalist foreign policy inaugurated by President Geisel in 1974, Brasília established diplomatic relations with Beijing in August of that year. The military regime, which abandoned almost all its ideological objections to cooperating with a communist country (a significant exception was its refusal to purchase nuclear fuel from the Soviet Union in the mid-1970s), aimed at expanding the market for national commodities and industrial goods. China could be a relevant partner for Brazil.[78] The bilateral trade jumped in ten years from US$17 million to almost US$1 billion. Brazil was Beijing's main commercial partner in Latin America. Nuclear fuel, a promising export item for China, was not excluded from the trade with Brasília. In December 1981, following a proposal from Beijing, consultations began about the possible supply of enriched uranium for peaceful purposes. During the preliminary phase, it was not clear whether the nuclear fuel for the reactors would be 20 percent or 93 percent enriched uranium. A few weeks later, Brazil's interministerial working group on nuclear issues welcomed the Chinese offer. Unable to enrich uranium in Nuclebrás and IPEN laboratories, Brazil could obtain nuclear fuel for its reactors from China at a competitive cost and free from international safeguards. Politically, concluded the working group, cooperation with China would increase Brazil's bargaining power vis-à-vis the NSG members within the IAEA.[79]

The consultations began in March 1982 on the occasion of the visit of Brazil's foreign minister to Beijing. The discussions were not limited to diplomatic representatives but also involved members of other ministries, such as the Ministry of Mines and Energy in Brazil and the Ministry of Industry and Mechanics in China. The role of the recently established China Nuclear Energy Industry Corporation (CNEIC), which was seeking new markets for China's nuclear fuel, appeared fundamental in the talks.[80] An assistant to Saraiva Guerreiro discreetly discussed the issue with representatives from the abovementioned Chinese agencies. The PRC could sell both enrichment services and 20 percent enriched uranium in the form of metallic uranium, UF_6, and uranium dioxide (UO_2). The Chinese negotiating team underlined that it would offer enriched uranium to friendly countries and for peaceful aims exclusively, but it would prohibit reexporting the material to Israel, South Africa, and South Korea. Brazil accepted China's terms and proposed to purchase up to 200 kilograms of 20 percent enriched UO_2 in powder and other amounts of the same material enriched at 3 percent.

Both countries considered the transaction to be the first step of a broader cooperation, avoiding the nuclear nonproliferation regime's restrictions. The negotiations were concluded in December 1982, during a visit to Beijing of a delegation headed by CNEN chairman Rex Nazaré Alves.[81] When Alves visited China, Brazil's nuclear research center had just produced the very first samples of enriched uranium. Nevertheless, the atomic sector was facing an important crisis: the lack of fuel for the IPEN research reactor. Traditionally fueled by US 20 percent and 93 percent enriched uranium, the research reactors had been victims of Washington's decision not to export the material for research purposes. Collaboration with China would significantly reduce Brazil's dependence on external nuclear fuel supplies.[82] Alves's mission was successful. According to the instructions drawn up by the CSN, CNEIC would provide the enrichment service for one ton of 3 percent enriched uranium, 100 kilos of 7 percent enriched uranium, and 200 kilos of 20 percent enriched uranium at a cost of US$5.5 million. The supply would guarantee Brazil's national research needs for ten years.[83] Through a simple exchange of notes, the Brazilians promised the peaceful use of the material. Brazil's UF_6, the fruit of the IPEN activity, was shipped to China in 1983 and returned in the form of LEU one year later. According to a Brazilian diplomat who was then a member of the CSN, the enriched uranium shipped from China included a very small amount of HEU, useful for the research reactor. It was the most sensitive aspect of the trade, with possible negative consequences for the nonproliferation regime.[84]

Western countries were aware of China's collaboration with Brazil. Bonn was conscious of the transfer of 20 percent enriched uranium but also of the possible acquisition of HEU useful for the research reactor.[85] The US public reaction was more hostile. In 1984 Beijing was slowly complying with the international nonproliferation rules thanks to a nuclear agreement with the United States and its entrance in the IAEA in 1985. However, US senators accused Beijing of providing assistance to possible proliferators.[86]

After the purchase of the enrichment services and on the eve of the enriched uranium shipment, Brazil decided to expand its cooperation with China. The initiative gained momentum in 1984 after the visit to Brazil of the Chinese minister of water resources and electric energy, Qian Zhengying, and after an evaluation of the advantages of the cooperation with Beijing carried out by the interministerial working group on atomic energy. Moreover, Figueiredo was about to be the first Brazilian president to visit China. Invited by the Chinese government in 1983, he approved the discussions of an agreement for collaborating in the research and development of reactors, exchanging information about the nuclear cycle, producing material, and eventually collaborating on nuclear security.[87] The cooperation was agreed upon in a memorandum signed by Presidents Figueiredo and Li Xiannian on 27 May 1984.[88] The treaty of cooperation, finally approved in October of the same year, raised some international suspicions. Relying on the intelligence data of an allied West European country, West Germany, the main partner in Brazil's civilian nuclear program, suspected that the agreement concealed a secret clause for guaranteeing Chinese assistance in assembling a nuclear reactor for naval propulsion. The PRC-Brazil public agreement, according to a German document, included the collaboration in the construction of nuclear reactors, but a secret clause would make it possible for Brazil to train IPEN scientists in China in the construction of research reactors and for Brazil's navy research center to receive assistance in constructing the reactor for future Brazilian nuclear submarines.[89]

For now, the possible secret aspects of the Brazilian-Chinese cooperation have not been confirmed by further evidence. Even if the agreement was not as fruitful as expected, the immediate and secret outcome of the cooperation and of Figueiredo's visit was the shipment of the uranium enriched in Chinese nuclear facilities.[90] As already noted, other countries, such as West Germany, knew about the Chinese-Brazilian transaction and were also aware of the possible transfer of HEU to fuel the research reactors. The West Germans and the Chinese (with the latter guaranteed that the enriched material would be used for peaceful purposes) probably were not, however, conscious that the final use of the enriched uranium, unsafeguarded until the late 1980s, would prompt a debate within the CSN.[91] Another new partner of Brazil's nuclear program would be Argentina, its historical rival.

A First Step toward Collaboration in the Southern Cone: The Brazilian-Argentine Nuclear Deal

After many years of controversy over the construction of a colossal hydroelectric plant at the Brazil-Argentina-Paraguay border, in mid-1979 the three countries recognized their respective rights in the rich hydrographic area of the Paraná River. Such rapprochement was the end of a long period of tension that eventually reopened a nuclear dialogue that had begun in the late 1960s. The common position toward nonproliferation norms, the need to develop nuclear technologies free from international constraints, and the positive aspects of a bilateral collaboration led the two countries to sign a nuclear cooperation agreement in May 1980.[92] The core of the deal was Argentina's supply of fuel fabrication services and the lease of uranium concentrate to Brazil. In return, Brazil's Nuclep would manufacture heavy components for Argentine nuclear plants. Moreover, a supplementary agreement provided for cooperation on regulatory matters and nuclear waste. It was the beginning of a possible integration of the nuclear sectors of the two countries. The cooperation between Buenos Aires and Brasília was the result of years of dialogue between Argentine and Brazilian diplomats and scientists. The change of government in Brazil created a favorable environment for negotiations, as both the new president, Figueiredo, and his foreign minister, Saraiva Guerreiro, were sympathetic to Argentina.

From mid-1979 to January 1980 intense discussions between the two countries' diplomatic and nuclear authorities set the basis for the agreement. Brasília made the first move. A few months before the signing of the Corpus-Itaipú agreement in October 1979, Buenos Aires rejected an offer to collaborate in the nuclear area. Despite some criticisms of Brazil's nuclear ambitions, the refusal did not represent the end of the talks. High-ranking Argentine officials, especially the ambassador to Brazil, Oscar Camilión (later Argentine foreign minister), delivered an offer of nuclear cooperation.[93] From January to March 1980 the heads of Brazil's and Argentina's nuclear sectors—Admiral Carlos Castro Madero (CNEA), Carvalho (CNEN), and Nogueira Batista (Nuclebrás)—met several times in both countries.[94] Suspicions about each other's atomic projects did not keep the two countries from reaching an agreement to begin their collaboration, which received informal approval from West Germany. As a clear signal of growing trust, Nogueira Batista and Carvalho visited the nuclear plant Atucha 1 and the reprocessing pilot plant in Ezeiza.[95] Castro Madero wanted an agreement that would go beyond a formal declaration of intentions. The forthcoming visit of President Figueiredo in May 1980, according to the Argentine foreign minister, Pastor, highlighted the political importance of the possible collaboration.[96] The Argentine-Brazilian cooperation could serve as a model for cooperation with other countries, overcoming, for example, the traditional rivalry between Chile and Argentina. From the Brazilian perspective, the cooperation with Buenos Aires would dissipate potential suspicions over the intentions of the main Southern Cone countries. A future agreement could also be fruitful for West Germany, partner of both countries in the nuclear realm, since it would eliminate any international accusations of fueling a possible atomic weapons race in the region. Bonn's affairs could, as a result, be free from international suspicions, even if a new agreement with Argentina was far from being signed because of NSG limitations.[97]

The collaboration between the Argentine and Brazilian nuclear sectors would be profound. During the talks, five areas of possible cooperation were indicated. Brazil's Nuclep could provide heavy components for the future Argentine plant Atucha 2, while Brazil could receive the technology for the lixiviation of uranium. The third area of cooperation, which reveals Brazil's lack of yellowcake production, was the leasing of uranium concentrate from Argentina, along with the service of building zirconium alloy cladding tubes. The final agreement would also include a contract of sale for 200 tons of yellowcake annually.[98] Eventually, as soon as the Nuclebrás facility in Rezende was operable, Brazil would provide the uranium 20 percent enrichment service. The talks suggested each country's hope of complementing its own nuclear programs with the skills of the new partner.

The partnership was cemented by a common position toward the nonproliferation regime. Castro Madero guaranteed to Nogueira Batista that like Brazil,

President João Batista Figueiredo (*right*) meets Kang Shi'en, vice premier of China, Palácio do Planalto, Brasília, May 1979. (BR RJANRIO EH.o.FOT, PRP.10827, Arquivo Nacional)

Argentina would not accept full-scope safeguards and that the terms for Argentina's ratification of the Treaty of Tlatelolco would be the same as the Brazilian conditions for the waivers.[99]

On 17 May 1980, after almost five months of discussions and building on the several attempts of the previous thirty years, Presidents Figueiredo and Videla signed the first Brazilian-Argentine agreement for the peaceful use of nuclear energy. The signing took place on the first visit to Buenos Aires by a Brazilian president since 1935. Even though the deal faced the opposition of ultranationalist groups in both Argentina and Brazil, it demonstrated, in the words of the Argentine diplomat Julio César Carasales, "that the nuclear competition of nearly three decades was being restrained."[100]

The importance of the bilateral agreement and of the similar positions adopted by Buenos Aires and Brasília toward the international nuclear nonproliferation regimes is paramount. Differing from agreements signed recently with other countries, it aimed to establish joint projects for technological development, with joint working groups and the reciprocal supply of equipment and services. In line with the reorientation of the foreign policies of the two countries toward a prioritization of Latin America, the Brazilian-Argentine cooperation aimed to contribute to Latin American development. Moreover, Buenos Aires and Brasília committed to impeding the proliferation of nuclear weapons through nondiscriminatory measures to obtain general and complete nuclear disarmament under strict international oversight.[101] In the following years, members of the diplomatic, political, and scientific communities several times proposed giving up the right to develop and build nuclear explosives. The public agreement was approved by the legislative branches of the two military regimes and allayed international worries about the nuclear programs of Buenos Aires and Brasília. It also contained an implicit criticism of intrusive international nonproliferation norms. The government in Washington, which remained the main promoter of Argentina's and Brazil's signing on to the NPT and the Treaty of Tlatelolco, partially praised the deal. According to the US administration, "Although limited, the agreement should help to reduce mutual suspicions between these traditional rivals . . . no militarily sensitive technologies will be shared. At present, the two nations have little motivation for a nuclear arms race, although both are trying to maintain the option of producing PNEs, which would involve nuclear weapons technology."[102]

The two South American countries strengthened their relationship during and after the Falklands War, between Argentina and the United Kingdom, in mid-1982. Brasília chose an "imperfect neutrality" in the conflict. It supported the Argentine historical claims to the islands, represented Argentinean interests, and guaranteed material and military support of its neighbor.[103] During the war, the Argentines denounced the British violation of international norms regarding the peaceful use of the atom. The CNEA chairman, Castro Madero, in fact accused London of failing to respect the Treaty of Tlatelolco as it deployed nuclear submarines in the conflict. Castro Madero's public reaction was furious and confirmed that the fact that Argentina's nuclear projects had peaceful aims did not mean that the country lacked the scientific and technological capability to build an atomic device.[104] The British use of nuclear vessels led the Argentines to confirm to Brazil their project to build nuclear-fueled submarines.[105] It thus became clear that Argentina and Brazil had similar plans for providing their navies with strategic deterrents.

The Falklands War did not stop the Brazilian-Argentine nuclear cooperation. On the contrary, it paved the way to mutual trust. In November 1982 Brazilians visited the CNEA reprocessing plants.[106] Argentines and Brazilians strengthened the collaboration, with Buenos Aires confirming its interest in Nuclebrás slightly enriched uranium (1.7%) for fueling the natural uranium reactors. Argentina would be one of the first foreign customers of the Nuclebrás fuel facility inaugurated in 1982 and would be able to satisfy the Argentine needs from 1988 on, since the enrichment plant was supposed to be operational in 1987.[107] The Nuclebrás enrichment services made the integration of the Brazilian and Argentine nuclear industries seem possible.

The Broken Nuclear Balance? The Argentine "Parallel Program" and the Announcement of Buenos Aires's Uranium Enrichment Capability

The nuclear balance between Brazil and Argentina was suddenly broken in November 1983. Buenos Aires claimed that it had mastered the uranium enrichment capability thanks to a gaseous diffusion plant in Pilcaniyeu, in the southern Argentine province of Rio Negro. The Pilcaniyeu facility was part of the Argentine "parallel" secret nuclear project, headed from 1978 by CNEA, which aimed to master all the phases of the nuclear fuel cycle but did not involve active military participation. Having a pilot reprocessing facility in Ezeiza, in Buenos Aires Province, Argentina needed to master another sensitive technology, uranium isotopic separation. It is not clear whether the Brazilians were aware of the secret aspects of the Argentine nuclear program. However, Brazil's government was conscious of the public elements of the program and of the Argentine strategy to diversify its partnerships, such as acquiring a heavy-water facility from Switzerland and purchasing enriched uranium from the Soviet Union and China.[108]

The uranium enrichment capability would be a key aspect of the Argentine nuclear program. The declaration that it had mastered the technology would prompt different reactions in the international community, above all after the Argentine defeat in the Falklands War. For this reason, the Argentine government, after the democratic election of Raúl Alfonsín and with the consensus of the president-elect, decided to adopt a cautious attitude in announcing this technological and scientific achievement.[109] The announcement could strengthen the country's international image after the war. Brazil's positive attitude toward Argentina during the conflict created a more trusting relationship and avoided generating suspicions of Argentine intentions.

Thanks to a letter from President Reynaldo Bignone to Figueiredo, Brazil's government became aware about Pilcaniyeu before the rest of the international community.[110] On 18 November 1983, a few hours before the official announcement, Buenos Aires presented a diplomatic note to the representatives of four NWSs (the United States, the Soviet Union, France, and China) and the IAEA and informed the Latin American ambassadors. Castro Madero explained that the 1978 decision to construct an enrichment facility was a direct consequence of

Carter's Non-Proliferation Act, which impeded acquiring that capability on the international market. In a meeting with Richard Kennedy, the US ambassador-at-large for nonproliferation, and Hans Blix, the IAEA director-general, Castro Madero underlined the peaceful purpose of Argentina's nuclear program. The enrichment facility constituted an alternative to the technological dependence on the North.[111]

Brazil's reaction was unclear. President Figueiredo, who had not expected the Argentine declaration, celebrated the success of Brazil's neighbor and declared to be "aware that the Argentine intention is exclusively peaceful and the same as the one that animates Brazil." The available documentation shows that Brazil was unofficially working on an indigenous enrichment technology, but at that moment the official civilian effort of Nuclebrás, whose first chairman, Paulo Nogueira Batista, had been forced to resign in late 1982, had not been completely abandoned. Saraiva Guerreiro requested Figueiredo's support of financing the jet-nozzle project, whose laboratory in Rezende was supposed to produce the first samples of LEU by 1987. According to the foreign minister, Nuclebrás and the civilian program needed to achieve Brazil's goal of enriching uranium to reestablish the nuclear balance with its neighbor.[112]

The United States, by contrast, reacted cautiously and moderately to the Argentine announcement. The State Department and the CIA affirmed that it was not possible to verify the Argentine declarations. As Richard Kessler noted, the announcement "came as a complete and utter surprise to everyone in the US government" and "represent[ed] a startling and dismaying failure of intelligence gathering."[113] Washington considered the Argentine action a further step toward proliferation. The CIA believed, in fact, "that Argentina's development of its own uranium enrichment technology has strengthened the commitment to nuclear development in Brazil, which has privately begun to accelerate its indigenous nuclear program."[114] US intelligence saw it as evidence of a new level of competition in the Southern Cone, prompted by the growing distrust of long-term Argentine intentions and capabilities to develop nuclear explosives.[115] However, despite US doubts about the solidity of the future Argentine regime, the re-democratization process and immediate Argentine diplomatic maneuvers explain why the cooperation between Brazil and Argentina was not derailed.

With the first free general elections in Argentina in over ten years, President Raúl Alfonsín was inaugurated on 12 December 1983. He renewed the Argentine effort to cooperate with Brazil. The purpose continued to be to dispel the view held in Europe and the United states of rivalry between the two countries. Alfonsín and his foreign minister, Dante Caputo, confirmed that Buenos Aires would share Brazil's position toward the nonproliferation regime as it was structured at that moment.[116] On 3 December 1983, a few days before Alfonsín's inauguration, Caputo proposed to his Brazilian colleagues a joint declaration renouncing atomic explosions. The Brazilian government apparently favored such a declaration, but the military hard-liners firmly opposed it.[117]

Obtaining the Bomb? An Atomic Farewell to the Military Regime?

Brazil's response to Caputo's proposal was probably connected to the internal debate in Brasília over the construction of a bomb. As it would be exposed by international and Brazilian reports since the mid-1980s, the most sensitive aspects of the autonomous programs were coordinated by the air force, which was working on the development of PNEs. In December 1983 Brigadier-General Hugo Piva, recently appointed CTA director, declared to Folha de São Paulo (but in contrast with CIA estimates) that Brazil's scientific community had the necessary knowledge to build the bomb. Accordingly, if the government were to give the go-ahead, the country would need five years to manufacture the device.[118] From 1984 to 1990 there were many rumors of a possible *peaceful* Brazilian nuclear test.

It was in that context that in 1984 Délio Jardim de Mattos, minister of the air force, proposed to build a nuclear explosive using the nuclear material (probably the HEU) imported from China. According to the proposal, the explosion should take place in March 1985, on the eve of Brazil's first democratic presidential inauguration after twenty years of dictatorship. It could be the "celebration of the end of the military regime." The rationale behind this was to give Brazil international prestige vis-à-vis Argentina, the international community, and the Brazilian people, who in late 1984 were demanding more transparency regarding the research conducted at IPEN.[119] The proposal was contradictory, since the Chinese HEU was not considered useful for a device and, as recognized in the proposal, Brazil lacked the technical capability to assemble it.[120] As recently underlined by ambassador Luiz Augusto de Castro Neves, the country was not able to produce weapons-grade material. The civilian and autonomous projects "did not succeed in enriching uranium to an explosive grade, and in reprocessing plutonium from irradiated material (because all of the irradiated material was under safeguards and only a few milligrams were reprocessed)."[121]

The cost of Brazil's decision, both internally and externally, risked being particularly high. The demonstration of nuclear capability would prompt negative consequences for the country's relations with Argentina, which might interpret such an explosion as an offensive action. In a context of close diplomatic, scientific, and technical cooperation in the nuclear field with Buenos Aires, a Brazilian nuclear deterrent was meaningless. The bomb would abruptly end the cooperative dialogue in the Southern Cone. In 1984 Brazil had no security reasons for building a nuclear device. Even if the country could acquire the capability to build and explode a device, it lacked a strong motivation for paying such a high economic and political price.

Furthermore, the consequences for the international regime of nuclear proliferation eleven years after the Indian explosion could be significant. It would mean that 1985, the year of the third NPT review conference, might be marked by a Brazilian bomb. The reaction of the international community could consist of severe sanctions on the Brazilian government, and it could mean a crisis for the Brazilian economy. The relationship with the United States could dramatically worsen, and Washington had the wherewithal to punish Brazil severely, both economically and politically, at a moment when the country was negotiating its international debt. In addition, the Brazilian generals had been aiming since 1974 to achieve a soft transition from the military regime to a democratic one. Consequently, Brazil's government could not risk international, regional, and domestic isolation.

General Figueiredo, who sponsored the rapprochement with Buenos Aires, and the CSN therefore firmly rejected the proposal.[122] As a US document reported, "Brazilian leaders are not persuaded today that nuclear explosives are necessary to their national security or prestige."[123] Here, one of the protagonists of the debate confirms Washington's perception of the Brazilian attitude in the nuclear field. Even though Brazil continued its diplomatic campaign against the discriminatory nature of the nuclear nonproliferation regime, the CSN and Itamaraty replied to Jardim de Mattos's proposal underlining the dangerous consequences of the nuclear test, above all for the relationship with Buenos Aires.

So the military regime did not end with an atomic bomb but with a nuclear program that had rapidly approached the capability to enrich uranium and to master several phases of the nuclear fuel cycle.[124]

CHAPTER SIX

Brazil's Re-democratization and Continuation of the Nuclear Program, 1985–1989

On 8 April 1988 President Raúl Alfonsín of Argentina and President José Sarney of Brazil inaugurated the Brazilian navy's Aramar Experimental Center in Iperó (state of São Paulo) with the activation of the uranium enrichment facility Almirante Álvaro Alberto.[1] It was a landmark in the relationship between the two countries and a crucial step toward nuclear autonomy for Brazil in a context of external pressures constraining its atomic activities. Both Argentina and Brazil thus mastered a key sensitive technology after efforts on their own and free from international controls. Alfonsín was reciprocating the visit Sarney had made to the Argentine uranium enrichment facility in Pilcaniyeu, and in Iperó he confirmed his country's commitment to cooperation with Brazil. In 1987, after the re-democratization in both countries, Sarney and Alfonsín continued to oppose a global nuclear order they considered unfair.

Neves's Election, the First Scandals, and the Vargas Commission

With the first Brazilian democratic elections in 1985, Tancredo Neves, who had been prime minister during the short parliamentary period in the turbulent early 1960s and was one of the leaders of the PMDB, was elected president of the republic. Neves's illness before his inauguration and his sudden death immediately after it meant that he never took power. His vice president, José Sarney, formerly affiliated with the party close to the military, the Democratic Social Party (Partido Social Democrático, or PDS), became the first Brazilian president in twenty-four years to be chosen democratically, albeit through an indirect election with a congress still sympathetic to the military regime. Democratization might have prompted a rethinking of the nuclear program. Neves and his running mate, however, decided not to dismantle the country's nuclear projects but to review them.[2] Despite growing criticism from large segments of the population, the nuclear activities remained partially secret.[3]

Following the elections, Tancredo Neves decided to strengthen the cooperation with Argentina, and he did not take a different position toward the parallel program. Neves considered the NPT and the international safeguards regime unfair.[4] In February 1985, during a visit to Buenos Aires as president-elect, Neves agreed to discuss mutual inspections of the countries' nuclear facilities with Alfonsín.[5] According to recently declassified US intelligence estimates, Neves reprised the opposition of the last democratic government to the possible development of nuclear weapons and was sympathetic to the position of the scientific community. Notwithstanding, Brazil's controlled process of democratization maintained key members of the military regime in the cabinet, including former vice president Aureliano Chaves, who was appointed head of the Ministry of Mines and Energy, which oversaw the civilian nuclear program.[6]

President Sarney had to face the first crisis of the nuclear program in April 1985, when *Folha de São Paulo*, one of Brazil's main newspapers, revealed the existence of a secret nuclear program whose aim was to develop and explode a possible Brazilian atomic bomb in 1990.[7] After the first revelations of the early 1980s, *Folha* reported that according to a former military minister, IPEN and IEAv would supervise the development of a bomb that could be exploded either at the air force base of Serra do Cachimbo, in the south of the state of Pará, or on the Atlantic Ocean island of Martim Vaz, close to Trindade. At the same time, a Brazilian deputy from São Paulo's state assembly who was a member of the opposition Workers' Party (PT), denounced in West Germany the continuation of the military regime's projects.[8] The scientific community did not have a cohesive position on the issue. The Unicamp professor Rogério Cerqueira Leite, who had strongly criticized the West German–Brazilian agreement in the past, declared that the political will to build an atomic bomb was lacking. On the other side, Ennio Candotti, of the Federal University of Rio de Janeiro (UFRJ), and Luis Carlos Menezes, of the State University of São Paulo (USP), defended the aim of the parallel and unsafeguarded atomic program to build nuclear explosives.[9] These positions reflected the debate that characterized Brazilian society until the eventual decision to give up the right to nuclear explosions in 1990. It is not clear who leaked the information to *Folha*, but the new democratic government had to react to rising domestic and international criticism of the nuclear projects.

The deep financial crisis that affected Brazil at that moment also demanded action from the new administration. The rising cost of the nuclear program with West Germany, the existence of a partially secret autonomous and unsafeguarded nuclear project, and the suggestions coming from the scientific community led Aureliano Chaves and President Sarney in September 1985 to appoint an independent blue-ribbon commission, the Commission to Evaluate the Brazilian Nuclear Program (Comissão de Avaliação do Programa Nuclear Brasileiro), to assess Brazil's nuclear activities.[10] Known as the Vargas Commission, after its president, José Israel Vargas, a prominent nuclear scientist, the commission, unlike the military regime, included members of both the government and the scientific community.[11]

The final report contained several recommendations for future nuclear activities that the government partially implemented in the years to come. The commission endorsed the maintenance of a Brazilian nuclear program, given the strategic importance of mastering nuclear energy completely and autonomously for the production of electricity and for the peaceful use of the atom. Although many commission members had criticized the 1975 deal with West Germany in the past (and they confirmed their criticism of the negotiators of the agreement with Bonn for their lack of technical knowledge), the report suggested continuing the cooperation with Bonn, adjusting the program to meet the real energy needs of the country. It reflected the path indicated a few years earlier by the 1978 parliamentary commission and suggested postponing the decision about future nuclear plants. It recommended continuing the construction of the Angra II and Angra III power reactors and building in Brazil heavy components to sell on the national and international markets in cooperation with the private sector. The commission supported the exploitation of Brazil's uranium (above all from the mines of Itataia and Lagoa Real) and recommended reactivating the nuclear mineral prospection. The fruits of Pronuclear (the training program of the deal with Bonn) and the past technology choices were criticized. Brazil, according to the report, needed more technicians with PhDs and MSs, more competitive scholarships, and more active engagement in the debate over technology transfers.

The commission did not criticize the parallel program but praised the national efforts at IPEN to master the nuclear fuel cycle in national research centers, even though Vargas and his colleagues advocated continuing the laboratory studies on the jet nozzle.[12] The commission thought the spent-fuel reprocessing program should be postponed, given its high costs, but recommended building the fuel fabrication plant (the Fábrica de Elementos Combustíveis), along with a nuclear-waste disposal site. The Vargas Commission's recommendations also included reframing the entire nuclear sector, transforming Nuclebrás into an enterprise focused on fuel-cycle activities and closing subsidiaries such as Nuclam, Nuclei, and Nuclep, as well as privatizing Nuclemon. Eletrobrás should create a subsidiary for managing the construction and operation of Brazil's nuclear plants, absorbing Nuclen and the nuclear sector of Furnas. Moreover, following other international examples, the functions of CNEN should be divided between a regulatory body and an agency promoting research and development in the field of atomic energy under the supervision of the Ministry of Science and Technology. With the clear exception of the last one, the Brazilian government followed the recommendations of the Vargas Commission. The commission suggested that in addition to continuing the cooperation with Bonn, Brazil should strengthen its cooperation with Argentina by gradually establishing mechanisms for mutual inspections of the nuclear activities in both countries.

It was the first time that an official Brazilian commission had recommended that its government adopt such a system, after several proposals from Argentina and the United States and, as already seen, a convergence between Alfonsín and Neves. This commission report's impact would not be immediate, but it would encourage the ongoing dialogue with Buenos Aires.[13]

Brazil's Announcement of Its Enrichment Capability

The final report of the Vargas Commission, which remained secret until 1990, influenced President Sarney and Brazil's future nuclear program. Despite the beginning of commercial operations of Angra 1 in 1985, the civilian program suffered continuous delays connected to the deep financial crisis the country was experiencing. Sarney, who considered the agreement with West Germany a failure since the completion dates for the Angra 2 and Angra 3 nuclear power reactors was unclear, requested that the deal with Bonn be renegotiated and that Nuclebrás be downscaled.[14] The transfer of sensitive technologies was particularly slow. All the technologies that Bonn had proposed to Brasília in fact remained unproven, and the machinery exported by West Germany had been only partially utilized.[15] These problems might have constituted the rationale behind the parallel and unsafeguarded nuclear program during the first years of democracy. Sarney, most likely to avoid facing the still powerful military wing of the cabinet, decided to keep the program secret. Despite a few leaks by the Brazilian and the international press, the program remained secret until its main achievement: the enrichment of uranium through the ultracentrifuge process.

The available documentation reveals that the United States was aware to a certain extent of Brazil's secret program. In 1982, after the meetings between Presidents Figueiredo and Reagan, Brazil and the United States established a working group to discuss cooperation in the nuclear field and avoid major crises.[16] The experience of the Carter administration and the existence of a faction within the Reagan cabinet that favored the nuclear industry were good reasons to avoid a bilateral crisis over nuclear energy. However, the cautious US attitude toward a nuclear Brazil did not amount to a laissez-faire approach to the autonomous nuclear program. Washington's ultimate goal was to impede the spread of sensitive technologies and to follow the NSG and Zangger trigger lists. It was not the only country that followed such a strategy toward nuclear Brazil. France, for instance, refused to sell to Nuclei compressors for use in the civilian enrichment facility. On the other hand, the United States decided not to transfer to the Brazilian navy supercomputers and a mass spectrometer, useful for detecting the rate of uranium enrichment. Even though Brazil's authorities justified the purchase as functional, for implementing the national system of safeguards, the United States did not authorize the transfer.[17] The US policy, together with the United States' renewed relationship with the Soviet Union around banning nuclear tests and peaceful nuclear explosions, was tailored to reinforce the system of safeguards and the regime of nuclear exports control after the NSG impasse. Despite the gestures and joint declarations of Brazilian and Argentine authorities, international observers were skeptical about the peaceful nature of the activities developed in the secret civilian-military nuclear program. Ambassador Richard Kennedy, special US representative for nuclear nonproliferation, requested a list of the sensitive activities developed in Brazil. However, Brazil resisted the external pressures until September 1987, when President Sarney announced to the world Brazil's mastery of a uranium enrichment technique that differed from that developed jointly with West Germany since 1975.

As seen in chapter 5, IPEN and navy researchers were able to test the first uranium-enrichment gas centrifuge cascade in 1984, but it was not definitive evidence of mastery of the technique. In 1986, Brazil's nuclear authorities suggested waiting for a year to be sure of the nation's capability in manufacturing the centrifuges.[18] In December 1986, after new rumors about the Serra do Cachimbo nuclear test site as part of Project Solimões, the CNEN president, Rex Nazaré Alves, publicly revealed the existence of a "secret" nuclear program, but he denied that the ultimate purpose of the project was to produce nuclear weapons. In that same period, an Argentine delegation visited IPEN unsafeguarded facilities and the enrichment laboratories.[19] The aim of Nazaré Alves's declaration was to allay suspicions about the parallel program and, above all, to reply to declarations made by military officers. The Alfonsín-Sarney dialogue notwithstanding, the powerful army minister, General Leônidas Pires Gonçalves, publicly declared several times in that period that Brazil needed to manufacture nuclear bombs in order to deter "potential aggressions" from its neighbors.[20] On another occasion, General Haroldo Erichsen da Fonseca, the army science and technology secretary, stated that producing a bomb was not Brazil's goal but that it would consider doing so if necessary.[21] All these declarations were immediately denied in public statements by the Brazilian government.

On 4 September 1987, after first informing Argentina's President Alfonsín, Sarney, surrounded by political, military, and scientific leaders, announced to the world that Brazil had developed a method for isotopic separation autonomously and had manufactured the centrifuges in unsafeguarded Brazilian nuclear research centers.[22] The national reaction was enthusiastic, although several journalists and members of the civil society saw in the autonomous effort the confirmation of Brazil's ability to build a nuclear bomb in the short term. President Sarney and Nazaré Alves gave guarantees that the sensitive technologies would be used for peaceful purposes. However, the doubts were not completely dissipated until 1990.[23] As noted by José Goldemberg, Brazil was capable of manufacturing an atomic device in five years but lacked the political will to pursue the option.[24]

The international reaction was one of general surprise. In Vienna on 13 September Nazaré Alves officially announced Brazil's technological achievement. He cabled Brasília about the impressions of the other members of the IAEA board of governors. As expected, Brazil was perceived as a new actor in the international system that had the capability to join the select club of suppliers of sensitive nuclear technologies. Many countries, including the United States and West Germany, demanded that Brazil adopt full-scope safeguards, but they also requested Brazil's collaboration in the nuclear field. Discussions were taking place between representatives of the Soviet leader, Mikhail Gorbachev, and of President Sarney to come to a far-reaching agreement on Brazilian-Soviet collaboration. The Soviet Union did not demand Brazilian compliance with the NPT nor the adoption of full-scope safeguards, but it did request that Brazil not reexport the technology developed. China and France were interested in broadening the collaboration. Great Britain and West Germany aimed to keep the Urenco contract with Brazil alive. However, Nazaré Alves saw other avenues of expansion for the Brazilian nuclear program, above all, for the possible future export of nuclear fuel.[25] On the same occasion, the CNEN chairman agreed to the future visit of the IAEA director-general, Hans Blix, to the Aramar Experimental Center in Iperó. It was a gesture toward transparency in Brazil's nuclear activities.

Despite Brazil's public announcement, the United States grew more suspicious about the final scope of the nuclear program. Washington refused to export machinery and materials useful for the gas centrifuge program even if the Brazilians stated that they would be used for other purposes. Washington pressured other NSG members, such as West Germany and the United Kingdom, to avoid allowing equipment useful for Brazil's unsafeguarded military-civilian nuclear activities to circulate.[26] This was the case, for example, with a UF_6 mass spectrometer, a crucial tool for Brazil's nuclear program that was on the centrifuge trigger list (INFCIRC/209/Mod.2). Washington first refused to sell that equipment and then demanded a similar stance from West Germany, where the firm Finnegan Mat GMBH was to export the item for the German-supplied enrichment plant, which was under international safeguards.[27] The US authorities were concerned about the possible diversion of the equipment and technology already transferred to Brazil from the safeguarded facilities to Brazil's unsafeguarded program. The US government asked West Germany to determine what equipment and technology sent to the Resende jet-nozzle facility could be used in a centrifuge enrichment plant and how to ensure that no diversion to Aramar occurred.[28] There had been rumors about the phasing out of the nozzle enrichment program and the possible transfer of the Resende equipment to Iperó.

The rumors were justified. Following Sarney's announcement, Bonn received guarantees that the nuclear collaboration would continue. However, reframing the scope of the collaboration appeared unavoidable because of the Nuclei isotopic uranium enrichment effort.[29] Twelve years after the signing of the nuclear deal in Bonn, the activities had not produced the promised results, and no technology had been transferred. As a German report makes clear, the West Germans transferred know-how and equipment from the Karlsruhe Nuclear Research Center (Kernforschungszentrum Karlsruhe, or KfK) to Nuclebrás/CDTN (the former IPr in Belo Horizonte), and an advanced separation stage was finally sent to Brazil in September 1987 for use in April 1988. During the experiments at a pilot plant in West Germany, the West German-Brazilian team had been able to produce just 55 grams of 0.87 percent enriched uranium.[30] The continuing funding problems explain the slow pace of the implementation of the plant. Also, the reprocessing pilot plant, based on unproven technology, was demonstrated not to work. Although Brazil had never given up on this technology, as Argentina did in the mid-1990s, no fruitful research with West Germany has been developed for reprocessing spent nuclear fuel and extracting plutonium.[31] If one compares the results obtained at IPEN with those obtained at military research centers, the more successful autonomous projects made the most sense. Despite the rumors, however, Sarney did not dismantle the jet-nozzle demonstration plant in 1987.[32]

A Constitutional Ban of the Atom?

After twenty-one years of a military regime, Brazil's re-democratization process prompted convening an assembly to discuss a new constitution.[33] After the explosions in Hiroshima and Nagasaki and the nuclear arms race, many countries included a ban of nuclear weapons in their constitution. A global movement called for nuclear disarmament, and after the 1986 nuclear disaster in Chernobyl a rising number of states also renounced nuclear energy for peaceful aims. The members of Brazil's constituent assembly could offer up valuable reasons for prohibiting nuclear energy and atomic devices.

In September 1987 the mishandling of a medical radioactive device not under radiation protection surveillance made Goiânia, a city two hundred kilometers west of Brasília, the theater of one of the worst civilian radiological accidents in nuclear history. It originated in the handling of the remnants of a capsule of a caesium-137 teletherapy unit abandoned in a building no longer in use of a private radiotherapy institute, which had not notified the licensing authority, CNEN, as required by the institute's license. The accident resulted in four deaths and many others injured and led to the radioactive contamination of parts of the city. Once the accident was made known, local and international authorities contained the contamination and protected the population.[34] The rapid response, in strict cooperation with the international community (especially the IAEA and Argentina), avoided an accident of major proportions. Still, it strongly affected the image of nuclear energy in Brazil, above all because of the spread of wrong information, which caused misperceptions about the real effect of the episode.[35]

The Goiânia accident—which happened during the constituent assembly discussions—was not the only source of mistrust toward the atom. As seen in the previous pages, the national press had denounced secret military efforts in the nuclear realm, and many international and local commentators suspected the existence of a covert plan to build a bomb. The exposure of the existence of nuclear boreholes coupled with the recent announcement by Sarney of Brazil's mastery of enrichment thanks to a civilian-military effort made the purpose of the atomic project unclear. A global movement to abolish nuclear weapons, along with the public statements of US and Soviet leaders about nuclear disarmament, strengthened civilian and political groups' call for the abandonment of nuclear energy. The final word in Brazil would belong to the constituent assembly.

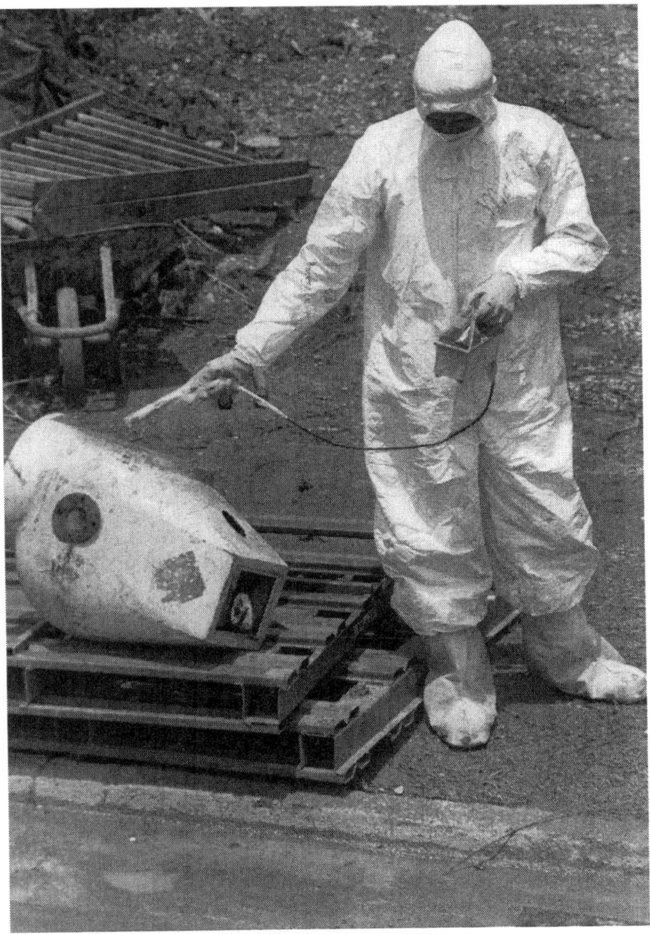

A technician measures the radioactivity of the source involved in the 1987 radiological accident in Goiânia, Brazil, on 6 October 1987. (Lailson Damásio, *O Popular*)

A few weeks before the radiological accident in Goiânia, some members of the constituent assembly supported by José Goldenberg, Brazilian scientific associations, and petitions signed by sixty thousand persons proposed banning the fabrication, transportation, and importation of nuclear devices. According to the proposal, Brazil's president would ultimately be responsible for seeing that the prohibition was carried out. The new constitution should also explicitly impede "governmental members with megalomaniac and warmonger attitudes" from building nuclear bombs.[36] The recent nuclear accidents in Chernobyl and Three Mile Island prompted a request to invoke a plebiscite over the continuation of a nuclear program. A softer proposal, presented by the Brazilian Society of Physics and the Brazilian Society for the Progress of Science, suggested unifying the civilian and parallel nuclear programs. By contrast, other members of the assembly, respecting the original draft of the charter, proposed limiting the use of the atom to peaceful aims. Any activity in the nuclear realm would be conditioned on the approval of congress.[37] The original draft of the constitutional article did not mention a ban on PNEs, so that the air force project could continue to build nuclear devices. An organized lobby representing the interests of CNEN, the military, and the nuclear industry pressured the assembly to guarantee the continuation of the nuclear projects begun during the military regime.[38]

A decision of the constituent assembly could lead Brazil to stop its nuclear activities and abandon any plan to build a nuclear device. Pressure from civilian movements, such as those calling for the closing of the military nuclear facility in Aramar, and the support of important political figures such as the future presidents of Brazil Fernando Henrique Cardoso (PMDB) and Luiz Inácio Lula da Silva (PT) suggested a victory for the antinuclear movement. However, not all the amendments prohibiting nuclear weapons, military research centers, and nuclear power plants were passed. A majority of 223 to 168 eventually rejected the amendment to an article of the Brazilian constitution that would limit "all nuclear activity in the national territory to peaceful aims."[39] The nuclear program would continue, and Brazil would keep the door open to PNEs. It was a clear victory for the military and other defenders of the Brazilian nuclear program. In a recent interview, a prominent member of the scientific community reported that CNEN enthusiastically welcomed the constituent assembly's decision: the parallel nuclear program could continue without legislative constraints.[40] Fábio Feldmann, a congressman who was part of the antinuclear group and a strong supporter of the constitutional amendment, revealed that General Leônidas Pires Gonçalves, the minister of the army and one of the pillars of the Sarney government, had told him that Brazil needed the bomb.[41]

Despite the victory of the nuclear lobby, the atomic program underwent its first reorganization. Following the final report of the 1986 Vargas Commission, the Brazilian congress decided to dismantle Nuclebrás and to dissolve some of its subsidiaries, such as Nuclei and Nuclam. CNEN would control the remnants of the company that had been the symbol of the ambitious 1975 West German–Brazilian nuclear deal and would replace Nuclebrás with Indústrias Nucleares Brasileiras (Brazilian Nuclear Industries), or INB. The new company would manage the production of nuclear fuel for the Brazilian power plant and also oversee Brazil's uranium mines. Furnas and Eletrobrás would control the nuclear power reactors.[42]

The 1988 Brazilian constitution also eliminated elements of the security services. The National Information Service (Serviço Nacional de Informação, or SNI) and the CSN, key institutions during the military regime, were dissolved. The latter institution had promoted and coordinated the parallel nuclear program and was replaced by another body directly connected to the presidency of the republic, the Strategic Affairs Secretariat (Secretaria de Assuntos Estratégicos, or SAE). Headed by a civilian, the office would supervise important aspects of Brazil's security system. Until 1988 the process of re-democratization depended on the support of the military. The first general elections following the new constitution's approval, in 1989, would instate a president directly elected by Brazil's population. With full powers and free from military influence, the president would rule the country for the next five years. With a nuclear program mastering key sensitive technologies, Brazil's new president would be able to decide whether to keep the parallel project and the traditional Brazilian stance toward nuclear nonproliferation or to adopt a new posture. However, a new Brazilian nuclear position in the global nuclear order would depend on the relationship with Buenos Aires. While the period from 1979 to 1985 led to a rapprochement, the Sarney years saw an acceleration in the nuclear relationship between the two countries.

Toward a Deeper Cooperation with Argentina

The partnership with Argentina was crucial for Brazil's foreign policy and any possible plan for Latin American integration. President-elect Tancredo Neves decided to continue the strategic partnership that Brazil had begun during the latter years of the military regime. He discussed a renewed cooperation in the nuclear field with President Alfonsín. They sought to create a climate of mutual trust between the two countries and to resist the external pressures to accede to the global nuclear nonproliferation regime. After Neves's sudden death, President José Sarney decided to continue on the path chosen by his predecessor. In February 1985 Alfonsín had suggested to Neves that they begin talks on the creation of a bilateral, exclusively Brazilian-Argentine system of mutual control of nuclear activities.[43] The idea was not new; it had been proposed repeatedly by the United States and Argentina in the late 1970s and early 1980s. After the beginning of Argentina's democratization, Alfonsín's foreign minister, Dante Caputo, and Argentine and Brazilian scientific societies resubmitted the plan.

During the final year of the Figueiredo administration, Alfonsín proposed that the governments of the two countries issue a joint declaration on the creation of a Latin American safeguarding mechanism during a visit to Brazil that was planned for January 1985.[44] It would mark a turning point in the relationship between the two countries in Brazil's democratization process. The Brazilian authorities opposed making such a declaration, however, because it could constrain the government both domestically, owing to the opposition of the still powerful armed forces, and internationally, because it might bring increased pressure for further Brazilian nuclear nonproliferation commitments. Alfonsín's proposed statement in favor of nuclear nonproliferation and inspections was in line with the Declaration of New Delhi in January 1985, when the heads of government of Mexico, India, Greece, Tanzania, Sweden, and Argentina requested a commitment on disarmament from the NWSs.[45] Brazil was not ready to accept a new safeguards system, and immediately after Sarney's inauguration Itamaraty organized a visit between the new foreign minister, Olavo Setúbal, and his Argentine counterpart in Buenos Aires.

Caputo renewed the idea that Alfonsín and the Argentine diplomats had proposed in both 1984 and early 1985. He underlined the advantages of common technological and nuclear capability. While the Argentines requested Brazil's clear political commitment to the proposal, Setúbal's reaction was cautious. Brazil would only accept the Argentine initiative after careful analysis. The proposal would have a clear consequence for regional integration since the system of mutual inspections could be expanded to include other Latin American countries.[46] Itamaraty, CNEN, Nuclebrás, and the CSN studied the proposal for several months.

While the Brazilian government was studying the Argentine plan, another suggestion for a joint declaration with Buenos Aires came in the form of a personal initiative by the physicist José Goldemberg, who wrote to President Sarney about the Brazilian-Argentine nuclear collaboration. Goldemberg shared Brazil's and Argentina's aspiration to master nuclear technologies, but he underlined that the international community could perceive such mastery, suitable also for military uses, as dangerous because both countries had refused to make nonproliferation commitments. In the view of the scientist, Argentina and Brazil could be recognized as a pole of international instability, alongside conflicts in the Middle East and between India and Pakistan. In order to eliminate negative international misperceptions of the aim of their nuclear programs, Goldemberg proposed to President Sarney that he issue a joint declaration with President Alfonsín stating that neither country had decided to produce nuclear weapons and that they had no intention of doing so but were seeking to stimulate mutual cooperation in the nuclear field. According to Goldemberg, the declaration would not commit Brazil and Argentina regarding their future decisions in the nuclear field, and it would increase Sarney's prestige in the international context. Brazil, the physicist proposed, should give a clear signal about the peaceful aims of its nuclear activities before the third NPT RevCon, which would convene in Geneva in September 1985 and would deal specifically with the spread of nuclear weapons.[47]

Itamaraty's reaction to Goldemberg's proposal was negative. Its view was that such a joint declaration would not increase the two countries' prestige but rather would be a signal of subservience to a discriminatory regime of control and an unfair nonproliferation treaty. In its assessment of the first fifteen years of the NPT, Brazil's Foreign Ministry concluded that accession had provided no advantage to the nonnuclear countries. A declaration submitted on the eve of the NPT RevCon, moreover, would deal a blow to Argentine and Brazilian chances of reaching nuclear autonomy. International pressure was aimed at forcing them to abandon the mastery of dual-use technologies, even though, as Itamaraty observed, both countries lacked the political will to build nuclear weapons. In the view of Brazilian diplomats, a stronger signal to the international community would be a strengthening of the bilateral relationship with Buenos Aires.[48] Strong action from Alfonsín and Sarney was relevant internally for relations between Argentina and Brazil since some sectors of the public and the armed forces were suspicious about the nuclear projects of the neighbor. In internal analyses of the possibility of an Argentine bomb, the Brazilian Foreign Ministry confirmed in May 1985 that "nothing leads us to believe that the current Argentine government . . . will take such a grave decision."[49]

Even though Goldenberg's suggestion was discarded, Brazil resumed the strong disarmament efforts made under the previous democratic government in the early 1960s and partially continued during the military regime. While the foreign actions of Presidents Quadros and Goulart promoted the Latin American NWFZ, eventually established in 1967, Sarney took the lead on an initiative to turn the South Atlantic Ocean, a strategic area for Brazil, into a NWFZ through the creation of the South Atlantic Peace and Cooperation Zone (Zona de Paz e Cooperação do Atlântico Sul, ZPCAS or ZOPACAS). Following the 1978 UN resolution on the creation of "zones of peace," the Brazilian president vehemently criticized the proliferation of nuclear weapons and proposed a South Atlantic zone of peace to the UNGA in September 1985.[50] The area was officially established in October 1986. The proposal was significant for the relationship with Argentina because it aimed to avoid the development of nuclear weapons in the area—one reference was to South Africa—and prohibited the use, or threat of use, of such devices by external countries, such as the United Kingdom. The only opponent to the initiative was the United States, and Argentina supported the Brazilian proposal in the years to come.[51] ZOPACAS was a victory for Brazilian diplomacy and inaugurated a new course of activism by Brazil in the Atlantic region (including both Africa and South America) and in disarmament forums.[52]

The Brazilian-Argentine nuclear cooperation would evolve further during the historic meeting between Sarney and Alfonsín in Foz de Iguaçu, in the Brazilian state of Paraná, on 29 and 30 November 1985. The Brazilian interagency group that assessed the Argentine proposal of early 1985 found in the period after the 1985 NPT RevCon the most appropriate moment for a joint declaration by the two presidents. Possible pressures from NWSs for Brazil and Argentina's accession to nonproliferation and stricter safeguards systems led the Brazilian government to discard the possible establishment of a system of mutual inspections, but it supported the creation of a bilateral political-diplomatic and technical working group to discuss the strengthening of the nuclear collaboration established in 1980. It would follow the model of the two-year US-Brazilian working group on atomic issues established after the Reagan visit to Brazil in 1982, which guaranteed that the Latin American country would obtain important results in the bilateral nuclear trade. The working group, which would meet alternately in Buenos Aires and Brasília and would be cochaired by Argentine and Brazilian diplomats, would guarantee a regular dialogue between the scientific, technical, diplomatic, and political communities of both countries. The meetings would dissipate external suspicions about a possible nuclear race. Such a Brazilian counterproposal would ward off external pressure such as that suffered by Islamabad and New Delhi on the occasion of the US mission that attempted to force them to negotiate on nuclear affairs in September 1985. The declaration, as noted in the evaluation of the Goldemberg proposal, would strengthen the cooperation and highlight the peaceful nature of both programs aimed at mastering nuclear energy.[53] Sharing a concern of many nuclear authorities, Brazil would aim in the meeting to guarantee the parity of the nuclear sectors of the two countries.[54]

Alfonsín and Sarney's choice of Foz de Iguaçu for the location of their first meeting was particularly appropriate. It would finally confirm the end of the dispute over water resources, with a historical encounter in the middle of the Tancredo Neves Bridge, linking the Argentine city of Puerto Iguazú and the Brazilian Foz de Iguaçu. It also marked the beginning of a close personal relationship between the two presidents. While both diplomatic teams were preparing for the meeting, a Brazilian military aircraft overflew the Argentine Pilcaniyeu

President Raúl Alfonsín of Argentina *(left)* with President José Sarney of Brazil, Foz de Iguaçu, 30 November 1985. (Orlando Brito, Acervo histórico do Presidente José Sarney)

enrichment facility, but Argentine authorities decided not to freeze the dialogue with Brazil. It would be the first of a few incidents that might have hindered the consolidation of the nuclear relationship.[55]

The final declaration in Foz de Iguaçu proposed a broad cooperation between the two countries with the ultimate aim of integrating Latin America and turning the region and the South Atlantic Ocean into a zone free from external economic, military, and political interference.[56] Specifically, the parties issued a joint declaration on nuclear policy regarding the need for a stronger collaboration that would also be open to other South American countries. Argentina and Brazil also established a joint working group to promote technological development and create "mechanisms that will guarantee the peace, security, and development of the region."[57]

The declaration showed how the 1980 agreement had evolved. In that moment, Brazil could not go further, given the military opposition to a broader cooperation and to the creation of a system of mutual inspections. Differing from the scientific community—the Vargas Commission manifested support for enlarging the collaboration with Argentina—the CSN, an institution dominated by the military and dismantled only in 1988, saw the Argentine offers of cooperation as an effort to acquire a deeper knowledge of the Brazilian nuclear capabilities in order to freeze the Brazilian nuclear program. Despite the negative military perception, Brazilian diplomats recognized the Argentine offer to establish mutual safeguards as a way to dissipate any "mutual suspicion" in the area. The force of trust would replace the mechanism of competitive dissuasion through nuclear devices being built by Argentina and Brazil.[58]

The main challenge for Brazilian and Argentine authorities would be to implement the declaration, resisting domestic and external pressures and avoiding crises created by mutual distrust. The joint working group (JWG) was the best mechanism for deepening the mutual knowledge and confidence between technicians, scientists, and diplomats of the two countries. It functioned as a model for groups working on the broader Brazilian-Argentine integration. Both countries' diplomats relied on the good experience acquired at the IAEA, where the two countries represented Latin America and took identical positions toward the international regimes of nonproliferation and safeguards.

In August 1986 the whole collaboration seemed at risk again when *Folha de São Paulo* published a detailed article on the Serra do Cachimbo air force base and the possible presence there of "pits and cisterns whose features are adaptable for several kinds of nuclear tests and for the storage of nuclear waste for industrial plants."[59] The article, which appeared after the recent Chernobyl accident in the Soviet Union and whose reception differed from that of a similar article published one year earlier by *Folha*, gained more attention from the domestic and international public over the aims of the Brazilian nuclear program. The Unicamp scientist Rogério Cerqueira Leite supposed that the site was useful for nuclear tests, but along with other geologists, he considered the area unsuitable for nuclear waste. Despite the guarantees of the local governor, environmental NGOs, indigenous communities, and political parties protested over the presence of a dangerous site for nuclear waste and demanded the immediate suspension of the work of the underground facilities.[60] The presence of a test site that according to *Folha* could be ready by 1991 could damage the relationship with Buenos Aires. As noted by Michael Barletta, declarations of the army minister, Leônidas Pires Gonçalves, about the need to dominate the nuclear fuel cycle in order to make Brazil into a country of preeminent greatness prompted a reaction from Argentina. Defense Minister Horácio Juanarena, Intelligence Chief Facundo Suárez, Foreign Minister Caputo, and CNEA Chairman Alberto Constantini met to discuss the issue.[61] Argentine nuclear authorities were concerned that some military sectors might decide to take over the control of the Pilcaniyeu enrichment facility.[62]

Itamaraty, after a specific request from Buenos Aires, tried to reassure the Argentine government that the site's purpose was peaceful.[63] According to a Brazilian aide-mémoire, the former test site had been chosen to stock the nuclear waste of the Angra 1 nuclear power plant after opposition from the local population in other locations.[64] Moreover, Sarney guaranteed in a group interview that Brazil did not aim to build an atomic bomb.[65] The Argentine government was satisfied with the Brazilian communications, according to CNEA and San Martin's officials, and despite the initial apprehension did not voice further doubts about the nature of the test site.[66]

Serra do Cachimbo's issue was not a topic of conversation during the third meeting of the Brazilian-Argentine joint working group, which focused on the implementation of the Foz de Iguaçu declaration in order to guarantee mutual trust but also to defend the right to master the nuclear fuel cycle. During the first meetings of the JWG, Argentine representatives proposed adopting a mechanism, such as a new safeguards system, to extend to all Latin American countries. It could create the conditions to overcome the main obstacle to Buenos Aires's full accession to the Treaty of Tlatelolco, the safeguards system imposed by the Latina American NWFZ. Argentina, like Brazil, considered the Tlatelolco safeguards system to be as strict as that adopted by the NPT members. The new system would not replicate the IAEA system. Brazilians presumed there would be no inspections of sensitive facilities, but the Argentines did not provide more details.[67] It was an important evolution in the position toward Tlatelolco, but it would probably prompt a revision of the agreement existing in Latin America. The discussion of the future mutual inspection system would be crucial for the continuation of the dialogue. Both sides opted for complete coordination in international forums over disarmament, where Argentina and Brazil had been particularly active since 1985. Their goal was to allay fears of a mutual arms race and defend the right to fully develop nuclear energy.

From a concrete point of view the two programs were benefiting from the cooperation. The third meeting, in Rio de Janeiro in late November 1986, led to collaboration in the area of nuclear instruments and detectors. After the US refusal and pressure upon other suppliers over the sale of mass spectrometers for the Brazilian nuclear program, the mutual cooperation could guarantee more autonomy. Moreover, Nuclebrás confirmed its strict cooperation with CNEA to produce low enriched fuel elements suitable for Argentine research reactors.

With that purpose, CNEA representatives visited the Resende Nuclebrás uranium isotopic separation facility, while a CNEN delegation visited the top-secret INVAP (Investigación Aplicada) Pilcaniyeu enrichment plant. The JWG drew up protocols for nuclear cooperation in the areas of uranium enrichment and fast breeder reactors, a promising area in the development of future reactors that could be crucial for the Argentine-Brazilian collaboration. Both areas were sensitive, and the group created a subgroup to discuss the cooperation and the safeguards to be applied to those facilities, which were to be excluded from inspections at the beginning. As a consequence of the IAEA effort after the accident in Chernobyl, the JWG set up a system of immediate notification and assistance to be used in the event of a nuclear accident or radiological emergency.[68] Presidents Sarney and Alfonsín approved all the decisions on 10 December 1986, when they issued in Brasília a "Joint Declaration on Nuclear Policy" and a protocol for nuclear cooperation.[69]

The years 1987–88 would see a strong acceleration of the collaboration. The two presidents reached a peak in mutual trust. While the working groups negotiated the details of the cooperation, Alfonsín and Sarney showed their interest in overcoming all the hurdles to convergence and made symbolic visits to the enrichment facilities in Pilcaniyeu and Iperó, where the Brazilian navy inaugurated an enrichment plant. The first move was made by Argentina. In June 1987, on the occasion of Sarney's visit to the country, Alfonsín invited his counterpart to visit the Bariloche nuclear complex, in southern Argentina.[70] It was the first visit by a Brazilian president to the main Argentine nuclear facilities. At the last moment, moreover, Alfonsín decided to further demonstrate his openness toward Brasília. The two presidents and a delegation of Brazilian scientists and diplomats also visited the uranium enrichment laboratories in Pilcaniyeu.[71] For the first time, a foreign delegation was given full access to the secret nuclear plant; it was allowed to see all the equipment and materials, including the barriers manufactory, of the gas diffusion plant.[72] The Argentine gesture astonished the Brazilian president and his delegation, who were positively impressed by the Argentine facility. It was a fundamental step toward removing the last hurdles to full trust between the two Southern Cone giants.

In July 1987, following the visit to Pilcaniyeu, the two presidents met in Viedma, which had been proposed as the future Argentine capital city, and jointly declared, among other things, that they would emphasize fluid dialogue in the nuclear field.[73] The "spirit of Viedma" characterized the months to come. As seen in the previous pages, the Brazilian scientific, military, and political authorities were ready to announce to the world the mastery of uranium enrichment through an indigenous gas centrifuge method developed jointly by IPEN and the navy. To reciprocate Alfonsín's openness, Sarney decided to inform his Argentine colleague in advance. Consequently, on 3 September his special adviser for foreign policy, Ambassador Rubens Ricupero, made a secret visit to the Olivos presidential palace to inform Alfonsín of all the details of the Brazilian nuclear achievement ahead of the announcement. The reactions of Alfonsín and the deputy minister of foreign affairs, Jorge Sábato, were enthusiastic, and the president sent a message of warm congratulations to Brazil for the historic success of the domestic nuclear community. It could have positive repercussions also for the Argentine nuclear program and for Latin American independence in the peaceful use of nuclear energy. In a letter that Ambassador Ricupero delivered to Sarney, Alfonsín declared his and his population's "confidence about the peaceful nature of Brazil's nuclear activities" and underlined that the "intensification of [the Brazilian-Argentine] cooperation in the nuclear field cemented the trust and fraternal friendship that unifies the two countries."[74]

The mastery of the gas centrifuge method did not change the partnership between the two countries, but it did change the terms of their collaboration. It immediately became more helpful to establish cooperation with the research centers working with a proven technology than with the Nuclebrás facility developing the jet nozzle. Secrecy also dissipated when the Brazilians opened all their facilities to Argentine visits. In 1987 the JWG decided on the first round of mutual visits to sensitive facilities. Unlike today, when panels hide the centrifuges from IAEA inspectors, Argentine scientists and diplomats had full access to Brazilian technology. The system of mutual visits and inspections evolved in a way that would have been considered impossible in countries that previously had secret nuclear projects. It was the beginning of a practice that would be institutionalized in a few years and that would create an original system of bilateral accountability and inspection.

It was the peak of a confidence-building process that was strengthened not only by Argentina's immediate assistance on the occasion of the Goiânia radiological accident but also by another highly symbolic move. Some months later, in April 1988, the two presidents together inaugurated the uranium isotopic enrichment facility Almirante Álvaro Alberto at the navy's Aramar Experimental Center in Iperó, close to São Paulo. In a joint declaration, Alfonsín and Sarney highlighted the full convergence of positions on international nuclear issues. They noted the advances in the cooperation in areas from fast reactors to safeguards. On the same occasion, the status of the Argentine-Brazilian JWG was upgraded: it became the Permanent Committee on Nuclear Policy (Comitê

Permanente sobre Política Nuclear, or CPPN). In contrast to the JWG, the CPPN also involved nuclear scientists and committed to meet at least every 120 days.[75] The body confirmed the Brazilian-Argentine rejection of IAEA full-scope safeguards and continued to discuss bilateral mechanisms for inspecting each other's nuclear activities.

On the occasion of their last presidential meeting, in late November 1988, at the sensitive Ezeiza reprocessing facility near Buenos Aires, Alfonsín and Sarney pledged to continue their collaboration.[76] Brazilian and Argentine scientists, as they had immediately after Alfonsín's election, continued to push for transparency, civilian control of nuclear activities in both countries, the creation of bilateral safeguards, and ultimate accession to the NPT.[77] The imminent elections in both Argentina and Brazil would leave the final decision to other protagonists, such as Carlos Saúl Menem and Fernando Collor de Mello, who gave the final input to create a bilateral safeguards system and to pave the way to joining the regional and global nonproliferation regimes. In two years, the Brazilian president would make important decisions for the future of the Brazilian nuclear program.

CHAPTER SEVEN

Giving Up the Bomb, 1989–1994

On the morning of 19 September 1990 Brazil's president, Fernando Collor de Mello, flew to the Serra do Cachimbo air force base in the Amazon state of Pará. Collor symbolically threw whitewash into a 1,050-foot-deep borehole that he declared to be a shaft for nuclear tests.[1] Surrounded by a delegation of journalists and military and civilian ministers, Collor had decided to make such a gesture as an overt action against past nuclear ambitions. A few days later, at the UNGA in New York, Brazil's president declared that "Brazil today discards the idea of any experiment that might involve nuclear explosions, even if only for peaceful purposes." Probably referring to Argentina, he continued that he "trust[ed that] other nations [would] consider the possibility of following the same path."[2] A few months later, Buenos Aires reached an agreement with Brasília to renounce the right to develop nuclear devices. While Collor's words echoed globally, Brazil's congress was investigating the parallel nuclear program that had led Brazil to master uranium enrichment a few years earlier. Secret bank accounts had financed the secret nuclear program, and Brazil's public demanded transparency.

Brazil's democratization and the end of the Cold War, along with the country's stance toward international nuclear nonproliferation norms, were affecting present and future Brazilian nuclear activities. In 1988 the Brazilian constituent assembly guaranteed the continuation of a national nuclear project, but there were suspicions about the country's real military atomic ambitions. In 1990, at the beginning of Collor's tenure, the new Brazilian president became fully aware of all the aspects of the military nuclear program. The following pages discuss Brazil's steps toward abandoning the nuclear weapons option. The government depended on external and internal pressures to dismantle the heritage of military rule and accede to the international regime of nuclear nonproliferation. Following the path begun in 1980, Brasília and Buenos Aires decided how to create

President Collor fills one of the nuclear boreholes with lime, Serra do Cachimbo air base, 19 September 1990. To Collor's right is José Lutzenberger, secretary for the environment. (Acervo histórico do Presidente Fernando Collor de Melo)

a bilateral system of safeguards, inspection, and trust in the nuclear field. Their rapprochement produced the conditions for an eventual acceptance of IAEA-promoted full-scope safeguards and of the Treaty of Tlatelolco. After more than twenty years of opposition, Brazil, with the capability to master the entire nuclear fuel cycle, was ready to accept international nonproliferation norms, to renounce the right to develop PNEs, and to show the world a new face.

The End of the Parallel Nuclear Program and Brazil's Decision to Abandon the Right to Peaceful Nuclear Explosions

On 17 December 1989, after a two-round presidential race against the charismatic leftist leader of the Workers' Party, Luíz Inácio Lula da Silva, Fernando Collor de Mello was elected president of Brazil. For the first time in almost thirty years, Brazil's population directly chose its chief of state. From the small Party for National Reconstruction (Partido da Reconstrução Nacional, or PNR), Collor was a young politician who in the space of a few years had reached the dizzy height of becoming the successor to President José Sarney. His platform relied on a liberal agenda that involved structural economic reforms, the privatization of big public companies, and the reorganization of the state. His foreign policy, even if he continued many of his predecessor's programs, would be open to the major changes in the international order that coincided with the end of the Cold War and the fall of the Berlin Wall.[3] The young president, whose father was a senator who had participated in the delegation that discussed the NPT in Geneva in the late 1960s, did not support a possible Brazilian nuclear bomb and criticized the expensive nuclear program. His popular mandate allowed him to ignore the suggestions of the military and the former government about Brazil's nuclear plans.

Prior to his inauguration on 15 March 1990, the military ministers of Sarney's government and the chairman of the CNEN briefed Collor and his closest advisers in detail about the parallel nuclear program and the military projects.[4] The construction of peaceful nuclear devices, through Project Solimões, continued to be a goal of the air force. Collor's immediate reaction after his inauguration was to replace Rex Nazaré Alves, CNEN president and one of those in charge of the autonomous program, with José Luiz de Santana Carvalho, a CNEN official who had the trust of the new president. Brazil's new cabinet also included José Goldemberg as secretary for science and technology, who profoundly contributed to the modification of Brazil's nuclear posture. Another key figure was Collor's minister of the environment, José Lutzenberger, an activist against nuclear energy and winner of the Alternative Nobel Prize for his environmental campaign. Both strongly opposed a Brazilian nuclear bomb and participated in the discussions promoted by Collor on reorganizing the national atomic program.

Following Collor's decision to reorganize the program, in April 1990 Paulo Pedro Leoni Ramos, the secretary of strategic affairs, convoked a working group to examine the national nuclear energy program, the Grupo de Trabalho sobre o Programa Nacional de Energia Nuclear, or GT-PRONEN. The ultimate purpose was to provide an assessment of the Brazilian nuclear program and indications for its future. After discussions that engaged the military (air force, army, and navy), civilian ministers (foreign affairs, infrastructure, science and technology, environment, strategic affairs), and the CNEN, the working group recommended continuing the nuclear program under the supervision of the secretariat of strategic affairs.[5] Unlike in the past, civil society was involved in the discussions through the active participation of academic organizations and NGOs that favored and opposed nuclear energy.[6] The final report mirrored the position of the ministries: it suggested concluding the construction of the two nuclear power plants Angra 2 and Angra 3 and maintaining the activities of the parallel nuclear program with the construction of six nuclear reactors under military control.[7]

The working group was not the only institution established to assess the nuclear program. After an exposé in the Brazilian press, a scandal about a secret financial channel for the autonomous nuclear program arose. As noted by the

American scholar Michael Barletta, Brazil's CSN and its successor agency kept funding the parallel program with "money hidden from congressional scrutiny" as part of a strategy "adopted to circumvent cuts in commercial energy funding imposed under an austerity plan reached with Brazil's international creditors."[8] The scandal led to the establishment of a parliamentary commission of inquiry. The nuclear authorities were accused of violating the 1988 constitution, which required congressional approval of the nuclear activities promoted by the executive power. Chaired by Ana Maria Rattes, a senator of the Party for Brazilian Social Democracy (PSDB), the commission gathered in June 1990 and had to produce its final report within 180 days, that is, by December. The members of the commission heard from all the protagonists of the secret program. Among them, the former CNEN chairman Rex Nazaré Alves and Figueiredo's CSN chief, Danilo Venturini, revealed the goals and the activities of the program in secret sessions. Members of Collor's cabinet such as Leoni Ramos and Goldemberg told the commission that there had been a declared intention to test a nuclear device at the Serra do Cachimbo air force base during the military regime.

Despite this and other revelations, the final report of the commission did not criticize but praised the outcome of the autonomous effort, which was mastery of crucial aspects of the nuclear fuel cycle. The commission proposed to protect the technology developed at IPEN and at the Aramar Experimental Center, but it recognized the existence in the past of a project to build a nuclear device. The secrecy of the project that led to the design and construction of the IPEN-navy ultracentrifuges was justified at the time because it had been conceived within another institutional framework. The commission recommended that the nuclear technologies, a product of the indigenous effort, be protected. Any act to safeguard Brazil's national technologies should guarantee that its nuclear centers, which had not been part of the agreement with West Germany, would not be subject to IAEA inspections.[9] This constituted an important point of continuity with the previous regime and a strong signal of resistance to conforming to more intrusive international inspections. The congress would supervise all the nuclear activities. Consequently, the undeclared "black" budgeting, through a bank account with the code name Delta, was eliminated, and the parallel and official programs were unified. The strict control of the nuclear program's financial resources deprived the secretary of strategic affairs of fundamental supplies for the three military branches, which became self-reliant in conduct and funding their atomic research.[10]

When the report was submitted in November 1990, the main action concerning Brazil's nuclear activities was taken by President Collor. International, domestic, and personal factors led him to halt Brazil's activities to develop atomic devices. The end of the Cold War, the superpowers' effort toward disarmament, and the eventual absence of international support for PNEs probably all influenced Brazil's attitude.[11] Brazil, which confirmed its staunch opposition to the NPT in answer to a new US request to join, would be one of the few countries defending the right to develop those devices.[12]

Brazil's drastic decision to abandon previous nuclear plans can also be explained by the international scandal over Brazil's atomic cooperation with Iraq and the transfer of sensitive material and technologies. At the end of July, a long *New York Times* piece exposed Brazil and Baghdad's collaboration.[13] Brigadier Hugo Piva, a retired Brazilian air force officer and former director of CTA, was helping Iraq to build long-range missiles. The involvement of one of the former leaders of the air force Project Solimões was considered dangerous. The US sale of supercomputers for the Brazilian air industry could indirectly favor the nuclear plans of both Brasília and Baghdad. Starting in 1987, Brazil was already suffering US retaliatory measures against the nuclear projects, with the suspension and cancellation of a minicomputer sale for the Aramar Experimental Center.[14] The US action was not isolated; it was part of a general limitation on the export of sensitive technologies agreed upon by NATO countries (excluding Iceland) and Japan within the context of CoCom, NATO's coordinating committee on multilateral export controls.[15] Brazil's situation worsened after Iraq invaded Kuwait on 2 August 1990. The FRG, its main partner in the nuclear field, also questioned Brazil's action in Iraq. During a high-level meeting between German and Brazilian nuclear negotiators, Brasília's representatives remained evasive on the cooperation with Baghdad.[16]

A rapid action would dissipate any doubt about Brazilian's nuclear intentions. Collor and Itamaraty informed the US president, George Bush, of Brazil's efforts to strengthen its collaboration with Buenos Aires and to place its nuclear program under full civilian control. They emphasized that Brazil would take significant steps toward the full implementation of the Latin American NWFZ.[17] As the Brazilian emissaries were delivering Collor's message to the US government, the Brazilian president was just about to perform a spectacular *coup de théâtre*.

After informing the Argentine president, Carlos Menem, about his decision on 17 September, Collor summoned the Brazilian press to join him on a flight to the Serra do Cachimbo air force base in Pará.[18] A few years earlier, the *Folha de São Paulo* and the *Jornal do Brasil* had exposed the existence of boreholes for testing nuclear weapons.[19] However, on 18 September Collor announced that he was closing the shafts. Contrary to the previous government's declarations, he declared that they had been designed to test nuclear devices, and in a symbolic ceremony he personally filled one of the holes. It was a slap in the face to those who wanted to maintain control of nuclear projects and leave the door open for the construction of a nuclear device, even if peaceful. The three military ministers who accompanied Collor had to stand and watch as the hole was filled. They had been to Cachimbo just a few months earlier to inspect the shafts. The high level of secrecy guaranteed that until the visit only the air force minister, Sócrates da Costa Monteiro, had been aware of the final purpose of the shafts: testing a nuclear device. The military ministers considered Collor's trip to be an act of political marketing hostile to the armed forces. However, it is known that an unnamed air force officer indicated the wrong hole to the president. If any successor to Collor were to change position about nuclear devices, the test shaft would still be there, ready to use.

The action of the Brazilian president was strong and had domestic and international repercussions. Filling the hole represented the end of the military-led nuclear program and clearly indicated that the president wanted civilian control over all the projects. The timing was apt, as Collor was about to leave on his trip to the United States, where he would present Brazil's new credentials and the country's stance toward the nuclear bomb.[20] The action was a firm response to military sectors that thought the president should maintain the Solimões PNE air force project. The response was needed following a specific request of the Brazilian military. In a recent interview, José Luiz de Santana Carvalho, chairman of CNEN during Collor's term, declared that the Brazilian armed forces had planned to explode an atomic device on 7 September 1990, Brazil's Independence Day.[21] No official document confirms Santana's declaration, and it has been refuted by Sarney's air force minister and, in a recent interview with the author, by the former Brazilian president himself. Collor recognized the existence of Project Solimões but vehemently denied the existence of fissile material that could be used to build a bomb.[22] Brazil's capability to launch a PNE in 1990 was significantly more advanced than in 1984, when the air force minister had proposed building a nuclear device. At present no document confirms the presence of both fissile material and designs for nuclear explosives. Sócrates da Costa Monteiro has recently given his final word on the issue. The military forces during the military regime had a plan to design and build a nuclear device for peaceful purposes, and in the early 1980s they built the boreholes for testing it. The project, confirmed Costa Monteiro, had been abandoned several years before 1990.[23] In 1992 the air force eventually informed the president of the still existing boreholes, which were eventually destroyed. Collor's decision was respected: the bomb was given up.

The new Brazilian attitude reverberated on 24 September, when Collor confirmed Brazil's decision to abandon the right to develop PNEs at the 1990 UNGA.[24] Brazil did not give up the idea of mastering nuclear technologies, but it did acquire new international credentials and left behind a small group of countries, such as India, that still defended the right.[25] Collor's decision, which ended a long quarrel with the United States, gave Brazil the possibility to acquire highly sophisticated technologies after several years of restricted trade. Above all, as the secretary-general of the Foreign Ministry, Marcos Castrioto de Azambuja, wrote to Brazil's president, Collor's announcement was extremely relevant for "Brazil's image and insertion in the new world after the Cold War."[26]

In conjunction with the recommendations of the parliamentary commission of inquiry, the presidential decision led to the first modifications of Brazil's nuclear projects. The main victim would be the unviable jet-nozzle enrichment plant. After huge investments in the West German–Brazilian effort to produce enriched uranium using the Becker method, the technique and equipment would eventually be abandoned. In 2001, after an agreement with the Germans, all the equipment and laboratory machinery imported from Germany were destroyed under international supervision.[27] A risible amount of uranium had been enriched at high cost. All the efforts in the enrichment area would be focused on the centrifuge method. Brazil's navy facilities at Aramar would guarantee the production of ultracentrifuges, enriched material, and mastery of the nuclear fuel cycle. In the period 1990–97, some IPEN activities to produce nuclear fuel (e.g., UF_6 conversion and UO_2 production) would be transferred to Aramar, while Project Celeste, to reprocess spent fuel, would be ended.[28] The civilian nuclear program would enjoy the fruits of the autonomous effort, and Brazil would be able to produce enriched uranium on a commercial scale in the future. The only condition, both within and outside the country, was that the congressional recommendation must be followed and industrial secrets must be kept. Despite the suggestion to cede technological control to civilian authorities, the centrifuges would remain under military supervision.

The activities of the military nuclear projects would proceed jointly with the civilian ones. Collor and the Brazilian congress reorganized and cut the costs of the nuclear program, but they did not abandon the plans to build new nuclear power plants and a nuclear-powered submarine. Despite the Serra do Cachimbo episode, the Brazilian press criticized Collor for only closing Project Solimões, while the rest of the military projects could continue their research in sensitive areas, such as uranium enrichment and plutonium production.[29] The official response to the external criticism came from CNEN. In order to reduce the cost of

Brazil's nuclear program, the commission decided to stop funding the military projects. The reduction affected both the autonomous project and the the civilian one. In the years of Collor's presidency, from 1990 to 1992, the construction of Angra 2 and Angra 3 was suspended. Financial constraints led the government to discuss new solutions with the West German partners.[30] Eventually, work in the nuclear power complex at Angra dos Reis would continue, but slowly and with several interruptions.

Collor's action in Cachimbo and the confirmation of the end of Brazil's ambitions to build a nuclear device were positive notes in a period in which the fourth NPT RevCon did not reach a consensus on strengthening the nonproliferation regime.[31] Brazil quieted many doubts about the collaboration with Saddam Hussein's Iraq and above all about the bomb project. In order to consolidate Collor's decision, the Brazilian government designed a strategy for approaching the nonproliferation norms. Even if it represented the ultimate goal of Collor and several Brazilian politicians and scientists, Brazil was not ready to accede to the NPT. It would find its own way to accept international full-scope safeguards and conforming in full to the nonproliferation regime.[32] The US policy and the West German decision to require full-scope safeguards of all nuclear partners within five years, starting in August 1990, could have constrained the future of the Brazilian nuclear program.[33] Brasília, together with Buenos Aires, would finally decide to give up the right to build PNEs and accept full-scope safeguards in its nuclear activities.

Buenos Aires and Brasília Renounce the Right to Develop Nuclear Devices and Create Their Own Nuclear Nonproliferation System

Brazil was not the only country to hold a presidential election in 1989. After the end of the military regime, Argentina's second general election brought to power Carlos Saul Menem, an initially conservative politician who after his inauguration shifted to a liberal agenda that did not diverge from Collor's. Brasília and Buenos Aires decided to continue and strengthen their intimate collaboration in the nuclear field within the framework of a broader Argentine-Brazilian integration.[34]

Collor's revision of the nuclear projects led to parallel talks on revision of the common position toward the nonproliferation regimes and international safeguards. Any move toward a new system of inspection and safeguards depended on the previous application of Brazilian national safeguards to all the nuclear facilities and materials. Even though CNEN safeguards regulations had existed since 1982, civilian inspectors only monitored the installations covered by IAEA safeguards. Following growing public pressure, the announcement that Brazil had mastered uranium enrichment, and the accident at Goiânia, CNEN decided in 1987 to place all Brazil's nuclear facilities under national control and make them accountable. However, the 1982 regulations were not fully implemented until May 1990, and they ended in November of the same year, when a first complete inventory of all facilities suspected of containing nuclear materials (including enriched uranium imported from China) was completed. For the first time, CNEN inspectors were granted access to military nuclear facilities.[35] Implementing national safeguards in Brazil and having a full account of the nuclear material present in the country was a preliminary and necessary step before the possible creation of a bilateral system with Buenos Aires could be discussed.

This was where things stood in July 1990, when Presidents Collor and Menem met for the first time at a summit in Buenos Aires and committed to strengthening the relationship between their respective atomic sectors.[36] The main issue since the first meeting between the two foreign ministers in early June had been Argentina's preoccupation with the creation of a Latin American system of safeguards that could be a clear signal to the international community of the peaceful goals of the Argentine nuclear program.[37] Buenos Aires, like Brasília, wanted to preserve its technological secrets but did not want to be excluded from the market of advanced technologies.

At the end of July 1990, the Brazilian-Argentine talks progressed toward making a proposal for complete accession by both countries to Tlatelolco. The main hurdle was to accept IAEA full-scope safeguards, as requested by article 13 of the treaty. Moreover, some articles needed to be modified. For Argentina, as became clear in meetings of the binational working group on nuclear energy in late June, the acceptance of a stricter safeguards regime would depend on a system of mutual trust and bilateral inspections with Brazil. The Argentine foreign minister, Domingo Cavallo, delivered to Azambuja an aide-mémoire with an innovative proposal. Relying on a solid relationship in the nuclear field and on a shared political will, "the Argentine government proposes to the Brazilian government to examine the possibility of celebrating a bilateral agreement on reciprocal safeguards between them . . . [in order] to establish mechanisms for exchanging information, joint accounts and mutual guarantees on nuclear programs, activities, facilities and materials of the two countries."[38] A new bilateral system of accounting and control and the protection of both domestic nuclear secrets and the right to develop nuclear submarine propulsion would be the preconditions for accepting Tlatelolco.[39]

The system, according to the Argentine diplomats, could follow two different models. The European integration process provided the first example. Euratom in 1958 developed its own system of safeguards (excluding the NWSs France and the United Kingdom) and negotiated safeguards agreements with the IAEA after the establishment of the NPT. The IAEA inspectors would see that the Euratom commitment was respected but would not have access to industrial secrets of the member countries.[40] The second model, suggested by a US technical team led by Dr Jörg Menzel, head of the nuclear safeguards staff of the ACDA, was Japan. After years of negotiations with the agency, in 1983 through a hexapartite safeguards agreement (between the United States, the Troika states [West Germany, the Netherlands, and the United Kingdom], Japan, Australia, Euratom, and IAEA), the IAEA inspectors guaranteed Japanese industrial secrets.[41] The most advanced South American countries in the nuclear area could follow in the footsteps of Japan and the European Community, setting up a system of reciprocal safeguards and control and, later, negotiating an agreement with the Vienna agency. The urgency was evident, since France, Cuba, and Chile could accept the Treaty of Tlatelolco and its protocols, leaving Brazil and Argentina in the undesirable position of not being full members of the Latin American NWFZ and having their real nuclear ambitions suspected.[42] The discussions between Argentine and the United States evinced the latter's comprehension of the need to keep industrial secrets and provided a model for a solution to the Brazilian-Argentine safeguards problem.[43]

Brazil's government reacted positively and was interested in the agreement as a mechanism of reciprocal safeguards.[44] For the first time since the initial proposal made by former Argentine foreign minister Caputo in 1983, Brazil welcomed the idea. Celso Amorim, one of the main Brazilian negotiators and head of Itamaraty's Division of Economic Affairs, suggested a possible revision of the Treaty of Tlatelolco to make it relevant to the reality of the continent.[45] Eventually, at the end of August 1990, the Brazilian-Argentine Permanent Committee on Nuclear Policy began talks on the adoption of the Argentine proposal. The Brazilian authorities were aware that international pressure on both countries to join the NPT would not end, but they expected a positive repercussion regionally, in Latin America, and domestically, in both Argentina and Brazil.[46] Negotiations actively involved diplomats and nuclear scientists (responsible for the national nuclear energy commissions).[47]

The political climate between Brasília and Buenos Aires also improved after Collor's communication to Menem about the imminent public announcement of giving up the right to PNEs. In early November, after almost two months of discussions by the permanent committee, a high-level Brazilian delegation composed of Goldemberg, Leoni Ramos, and Azambuja met with the Argentine foreign minister, Cavallo. Brazil and Argentina agreed to create a Common System for Accounting and Control of Nuclear Materials (Sistema Comum de Contabilidade e Controle, or SCCC), to be applied to all nuclear facilities and activities, including the spent-fuel reprocessing and enrichment plants. Both countries would continue their negotiations with the IAEA for a new tripartite safeguards agreement that would incorporate the SCCC. According to the discussions, the IAEA-Argentine-Brazilian talks would last until the IAEA general conference in September 1991. The trilateral agreement, along with further talks on the Latin American treaty, would lead to Brazil's and Argentina's full accession to Tlatelolco.[48]

On 29 November 1990, five years after the historic Alfonsín-Sarney agreement, Fernando Collor and Carlos Menem met in the Brazilian city of Foz de Iguaçu.[49] The presidents, in the presence of the IAEA director-general, Hans Blix, and the secretary-general of the Agency for the Prohibition of Nuclear Weapons in Latin America and the Caribbean (Organismo para a Proscrição das Armas Nucleares na América Latina e no Caribe, or OPANAL), Stempel Paris, issued the Argentine-Brazilian Declaration for a Common Nuclear Policy (Declaração sobre Política Nuclear Comum Brasileiro-Argentina). Relying on previous bilateral declarations, Menem and Collor confirmed the decisions taken in early November and agreed to implement the SCCC through the exchange of descriptive lists of each country's nuclear facilities, the preparation of initial inventories, and the first inspections. In Foz de Iguaçu the two presidents decided to negotiate with the IAEA for a common agreement that relied on the SCCC as a precondition for the future accession to Tlatelolco.[50] After Brazil and Argentina publicly declared the peaceful nature of their nuclear programs, several countries—such as Australia (a traditional NPT supporter), the United States, Chile, and Uruguay—welcomed the Iguaçu Declaration and asserted their interest in cooperating with Buenos Aires and Brasília and supporting their action toward acceptance of Tlatelolco. Santiago and Montevideo wanted to be part of the new system proposed in Foz de Iguaçu. Chile's reaction was particularly relevant since it was a country that conditioned its full participation in Tlatelolco on Brazil's and especially Argentina's commitment.[51]

The IAEA considered the declaration a "very encouraging step and a good example for other regions," but it noted the implicit rather than declared Argentine renunciation of PNEs.[52] It was what kept Argentina from achieving the same position as Brazil in the global nuclear order. As a condition for acceding to the Latin American NWFZ, Buenos Aires had been negotiating with the IAEA since

1982 for a safeguards system that would preserve Argentine industrial secrets and guarantee the right to pursue PNEs, as allowed by the Treaty of Tlatelolco.[53] In mid-December 1990 Argentina disagreed with Brasília and insisted in the bilateral discussions on seeking a compromise with the Vienna nuclear watchdog that would permit the two countries to have the material for PNEs but not for the construction of nuclear devices. Argentina was prepared to give up its rights to develop nuclear devices but not its right to PNEs.[54] Buenos Aires held that position, and the issue would be central in the negotiations toward a formal agreement that would substantiate the Declaration of Iguaçu.[55]

Some months later, in May 1991, Ambassadors Azambuja and Juan Carlos Olima (undersecretary of Argentina's Foreign Ministry) settled on an imminent agreement between the two countries and on the creation of a binational agency, with the status of an international organization, supervising the SCCC: the Brazilian-Argentine Agency for Accounting and Control of Nuclear Materials (Agência Brasileiro-Argentina de Contabilidade e Controle de Materiais Nucleares, or ABACC). Its headquarters would be in Rio de Janeiro, and the agreement would be signed in a city that could be a symbol of Brazilian and Argentinean integration.[56] The deal would mark the integration not only of Brazil and Argentina but of all Latin America. On 18 July 1991 Menem and Collor signed the agreement in Guadalajara, Mexico, on the occasion of the first summit of the twenty-three Ibero-American countries. Moreover, the two presidents made the historic decision to renounce PNEs definitively and ban nuclear bombs. After more than twenty years, Brazil and Argentina accepted the argument of the NPT that it was not possible to make a technical distinction between nuclear explosives for peaceful purposes and those for military purposes.[57] ABACC, inspired by the Euratom, was initially conceived as an instrument for implementing the SCCC and as the basis for an agreement on full-scope safeguards with the IAEA, and it was open to expanding the nuclear cooperation to include the rest of Latin America.

The bilateral pact and the constitution of ABACC were followed on 13 December 1991 by the Quadripartite Agreement, between Brazil, Argentina, ABACC, and the IAEA. After almost five months of negotiations and with the SCCC as a basis, the four parties reached an agreement to apply international full-scope safeguards to Brazilian and Argentine nuclear activities.[58] The Quadripartite Agreement would replace the trilateral agreements with the IAEA. ABACC would cooperate with the Vienna agency to guarantee that no material was diverted for the construction of explosive devices. Non-weapon and safeguarded military activities could continue. Buenos Aires and Brasília could keep their plan to build nuclear-propelled submarines, and they could maintain safeguarded military

Signing of the safeguards agreement between Argentina and Brazil in Vienna, 13 December 1991. *Left to right*: Dr. Hans Blix, IAEA director-general, President Fernando Collor de Mello of Brazil, and President Carlos Saúl Menem of Argentina. (Rodolfo Quevenco, IAEA, IAEA Image Databank)

atomic facilities, such as the Aramar Experimental Center. Consequently, Brazil's navy project and the development of high-level technologies could continue.

The US government praised the new Brazilian attitude toward the nuclear non-proliferation regime and in 1991 began to consider Brasília as a model to follow and a possible recipient of sensitive technologies.[59] Collor's goal during his term was to propose, similarly to South Africa, a new position for promoting nonproliferation norms. As a part of the dismantlement of the recent Brazilian nuclear program, as in the case of the cooperation with Iraq, Collor declared to President Bush that he had "sent a proposal to the Brazilian Congress which would prevent any present or retired government employee of Brazil that had access to secret or top-secret information from using that information in cooperation with any government in the development of a nuclear program or other proscribed weapons development program."[60]

In those years the profound changes that occurred in the international context played a relevant role for Argentina and Brazil, which within a few months renounced their right to develop peaceful nuclear devices and accepted international safeguards. Other actors outside the international nuclear nonproliferation regime took similar decisions. The end of the apartheid regime in South Africa coincided with the dismantling of its nuclear arsenal and its accession to the NPT. In early 1992 France and China accepted their role as military nuclear powers, signing and ratifying the treaty. Moreover, the NSG, after fifteen years of impasse, adopted full-scope safeguards, considerably strengthening its control on the trade of nuclear material and dual-use technologies. Brazil was aware of the radical changes in French and Chinese foreign policy since mid-1991. South Africa's nuclear rollback and the eventual accession of two NWSs to the NPT were important in a period when Brazil and Argentina were creating their bilateral nuclear nonproliferation agreement.[61] At that moment, ABACC became an example for other areas to follow. India and Pakistan, which were discussing a nonproliferation plan in South Asia, demonstrated interest in the Brazilian-Argentine deal, as did Israel. Even if the Middle East and South Asia did not constitute NWFZs, ABACC served as an extraordinary model for curbing military nuclear ambitions. Senior international analysts retained their doubts over the real elimination of military nuclear projects.[62] Brazil and Argentina would take two years to ratify the international agreements.

In that state of flux, in their acceptance of full-scope safeguards Brazil and Argentina implicitly recognized the international regime. Following an idea of President Collor and some members of the Brazilian scientific community, the ultimate act would be accepting the NPT. However, political turmoil in Brazil that led in 1992 to President Collor's impeachment slowed down the pace of assuming international nonproliferation commitments. Domestic constraints, such as congressional skepticism toward ratifying the Quadripartite Agreement and strong military pressure, prevented quick acceptance of the decision adopted by the Brazilian government.

Accepting Tlatelolco and the Quadripartite Agreement

At the beginning of 1992, immediately after the signing of the agreement in Vienna, Buenos Aires and Brasília began to discuss the last point contained in the 1990 Declaration of Iguaçu: full participation in the Treaty of Tlatelolco. Both governments wanted to discuss several articles of the treaty, such as how to protect their industrial and technological secrets and how to send the information to OPANAL and the IAEA with the establishment of a mechanism for special inspections.[63] In February 1992 the two countries agreed on the points to modify. Technical amendments did not change the principles or the goals of the treaty. Collor and Menem sent a historic joint declaration to the OPANAL plenary on the Brazilian-Argentine decision to participate fully in the Latin American NWFZ.

The announcement coincided with the celebration of the twenty-fifth anniversary of the treaty on 14 February.[64]

Following the Brazilian and Argentine example, Chile, another country opposing both Tlatelolco and the NPT, participated in the revision of the treaty. The seventh extraordinary general conference of OPANAL approved the modifications in August 1992. As a consequence, the three countries declared that they would waive "all the requirements which have not yet been met and which are referred to in Article 28, paragraph (1) of the Treaty."[65] The joint declaration was the final step before the treaty's ratification and before it entered into force for Brazil. France, because of the Foz de Iguaçu declaration, acceded to Additional Protocol I. Cuba, after preliminary talks with the Brazilians in 1991, announced its intention to join the treaty in 1994 but did not do so until 2002.[66]

Domestic troubles impeded Brazil from taking that decision. Itamar Franco, an experienced politician who had chaired a parliamentary commission of inquiry on nuclear energy in 1978, replaced Collor after his impeachment and resignation in 1992, but the ratification of both Tlatelolco and the Quadripartite Agreement was problematic. ABACC was working, but since the senate's rapporteur reported that the body was opposed to the ratification of the acts, the Brazilian government decided to postpone the vote in order to avoid the senate's refusal. Luiz Felipe Lampreia, secretary-general of the Foreign Ministry from October 1992 to June 1993, recently revealed to this author that the main hurdle was not in fact, the opposition of Brazil's senators but that of the military ministers, who did not want to accept external constraints to the nuclear program.[67]

According to the US scholar Mitchell Reiss, international pressures led the senate to eventually ratify the treaty. One of the threats, as perceived by Brazil's congressmen, was the loss of jobs with the privatization of the nuclear program and possible dependence on external supplies of sensitive technologies. From 1990 to 1992 several decisions, such as suspension of the construction of the power plants and the threat to national efforts in the nuclear field, indicated the possible end of the atomic program. As in 1990, Germany contributed to Brazil's final decision. In 1993, at the moment of negotiating the continuation of the 1975 nuclear deal, Brazil agreed to conclude the Angra 2 power plant. The foreign minister and future president Fernando Henrique Cardoso believed that the Brazilian government should demonstrate its place as a reliable actor in the international system, respecting the pact with the Germans and a recipient of advanced technologies.[68] Bonn wanted to be a central investor in Brazil and Latin America, but the condition for cooperating was Brasília's acceptance of full-scope safeguards. As Reiss and the Brazilian historian Luiz Alberto Moniz Bandeira noted, during his visit in early October 1993 Klaus Kinkel, the German foreign minister, "reminded Brazil of the 1995 deadline for terminating all technical cooperation and financial assistance in the nuclear field." Kinkel had probably also requested Brazil's acceptance of the NPT, but he only succeeded in contributing to the final ratification of the Quadripartite Agreement.[69] Following an agreement signed in early 1994 with Cardoso's successor at Itamaraty, Ambassador Celso Amorim, Germany continued to finance the Brazilian nuclear program.[70]

Reiss's and Moniz Bandeira's interpretations should be considered alongside the suggestions received from Washington. In August 1993, in fact, President Bill Clinton sent a personal letter to Itamar Franco praising Brazil's recent nonproliferation policy but suggesting the implementation of such decisions through a congressional ratification of the Quadripartite Agreement and the amended text of the Treaty of Tlatelolco. In his reply, President Franco said he hoped for an imminent conclusion of the process of complete accession to full-scope safeguards.[71]

While the pressure from Bonn and Washington was relevant, the Chilean and Argentine actions mattered. In fact, Santiago, Brasília, and Buenos Aires intended to jointly formalize the enforcement of the treaty during the eighth extraordinary general conference of OPANAL in January 1994. The Franco cabinet decided to give full support to the ratification in mid-1993 after convincing the congress.[72] According to Barletta, the secretariat of strategic affairs, led by Admiral César Flores, persuaded the military and later the congress that "ABACC would carry out all inspection activities, and the IAEA, would merely assure 'quality control.'" This thesis undermined the opposition of a left- and right-wing nationalist coalition within the congress, which was convinced that "IAEA safeguards would impinge on Brazilian sovereignty and expose industrial and commercial secrets to foreign espionage." The establishment of a bilateral regime was one of the main factors in winning congressional approval.[73] The Brazilian congress eventually approved the Quadripartite Agreement on 9 February 1994 and then ratified the amendments to the Treaty of Tlatelolco on 11 May. After twenty-seven years, Brazil eventually became a full member of the Latin America NWFZ.[74]

Both external and domestic factors explain Brazil's decision to give up the bomb (or not to opt for the bomb) in the period from 1989 to 1994. The constitutional ban of nuclear weapons and the democratic participation in the political arena are important elements that justify the decisions taken in the early 1990s. The continuation of the joint Brazilian-Argentine effort to establish a system of mutual safeguards, along with global efforts in the nonproliferation and arms control fields—linked to the end of the Cold War—were other crucial factors that pushed Brazil toward accepting, reforming, and creating international, regional, and bilateral nonproliferation rules. Despite Collor's decision to give up central aspects of the nuclear fuel cycle, Brazil accepted full-scope safeguards, preserving the capability to enrich uranium and leaving the door open to the future construction of a nuclear submarine. The Brazilian navy continued Project Uside for enriching uranium, Project Proter for building a prototype of the submarine reactor, and Project Costado for mastering the technology for conventional and nuclear submarines. The Brazilian nuclear program did not end in Cachimbo but would continue in the following years, if at a slower pace. Civilian-military collaboration would continue. Re-democratization also led to the redefinition of the space program and the creation of a Brazilian space agency with the final purpose of launching a satellite vehicle from a Brazilian base.[75]

Sensitive technologies were needed by a country that wanted to own an advanced nuclear and space program. Brazil, no longer considered a pariah state in the global nuclear order, became an example of nuclear reversal. And its construction together with Argentina of mutual trust in the nuclear field was a model to be followed by other supposed rivals. The country accepted having the most intrusive measures placed on its atomic activities but continued to criticize the unfair nature of the NPT. Although Amorim defended disarmament as one of Brazil's foreign policy pillars, several countries wished that Brazil's commitment to disarmament forums could coincide with the eventual acceptance of the NPT. Some observers considered accepting Tlatelolco and the Quadripartite Agreement insufficient for silencing the doubts about Brazil's military nuclear ambitions.[76] On the eve of the 1995 NPT RevCon, the Brazilian government did not declare itself open to a possible accession to the global treaty. The 1994 general election would be crucial. It would install a new president who would mark the future of the Brazilian stance toward global nuclear norms. Even if, according to the 1988 constitution, decisions in the nuclear realm belonged to the congress, the fact remained that the main foreign policy decisions were made at the Palácio do Planalto.

CHAPTER EIGHT

Brazil's Accession to the Nuclear Non-Proliferation Treaty, 1995–2003

"For joining the NPT and ratifying the CTBT, Brazil has hit what any baseball fan on any continent would call back-to-back home runs. Mr. Foreign Minister, today you are the Sammy Sosa and the Mark McGwire of international diplomacy."[1] With these words Madeleine Albright, the US secretary of state, welcomed her Brazilian counterpart, Ambassador Luiz Felipe Lampreia, to a ceremony at the State Department on 18 September 1998 to celebrate the end of thirty years of Brazilian opposition to the NPT. It was the last step toward acceptance of the non-proliferation regime. Some sectors of the Brazilian government believed that it would give the country more credibility on the international stage. In 1998, new shadows loomed over the future of complete nuclear disarmament. Despite Brazil's accession to the NPT, nuclear weapons tests in India and Pakistan and the threat of an atomic bomb in North Korea weakened the efforts to curb new states that wanted to join the nuclear club. Brazil would have a new role in the global nuclear order. Even if Brazil continued to point out the unfair nature of the regime, the country would redouble its effort toward full nuclear disarmament. Acceding to the NPT was part of a new course in Brazil's domestic and foreign policy. Brazil renounced nuclear devices and accepted international safeguards but retained its right to maintain an advanced industrial program as well as its state of nuclear latency.[2]

The following pages discuss Brazil's decision to accede to the NPT, its gradual shift toward entering the NSG, its negotiation of access to the Missile Technology Control Regime (MTCR), and its signing of the Comprehensive Test Ban Treaty (CTBT). The decision to accede to the NPT was made by the Brazilian government during the presidency of Fernando Henrique Cardoso. Joining the NPT was Cardoso's wish during his short tenure as foreign minister in 1992–93. External factors in the region and in the broader international system can explain the choice. Cardoso and his cabinet faced opposition not only from nationalist political and military sectors but also from some traditionalists in the Foreign Ministry who believed that acceding to the treaty would mean accepting the international system imposed by the superpowers during the Cold War. Brazil vehemently criticized India and Pakistan for testing nuclear bombs, but it refused more intrusive aspects of the regime, such as the Additional Protocol to the IAEA safeguards agreement negotiated and proposed to the international community in the Cardoso years. During the final phase of Cardoso's presidency, Brazil revitalized its nuclear energy program with the conclusion of Angra 2 and the decision to build a commercial-scale uranium enrichment plant.

1995: Fernando Henrique Cardoso, the NPT Review Conference, and the Gradual Change in Brazil's Attitude toward the Treaty

Fernando Henrique Cardoso, a renowned social scientist and politician, became Brazil's president in the general election of 1994. Starting in 1995, he would give a new direction to Brazil's foreign relations. He inaugurated fifteen years of "presidential diplomacy."[3] He and his successor, Luiz Inácio Lula da Silva, even with their different aims, would be protagonists in leading the country's foreign policy. Their common goal was to project Brazil as a new actor in the international community. Cardoso and his cabinet, above all his foreign minister, Luiz Felipe Lampreia, drew up and implemented a strategy for modifying the country's diplomacy. Both were aware of the deep changes that had taken place in the international system in the last years and aimed to adjust Brazil to the new reality, giving the country more international credibility. The new Brazilian president, one of the leaders of the Party for Brazilian Social Democracy considered not only an East-West confrontation but also the North-South divide obsolete. The end of the Cold War and the strengthening of multilateral forums could permit major countries from the South to play a new role in global decisions.[4]

Cardoso made all efforts to promote integration with other Latin American countries and improve relations with Washington. Bill Clinton's administration recognized the structural reforms as worthy, above all the Plano Real monetary stabilization plan. The new Brazilian president, former minister of economy, was one of the authors of the new Brazilian course. According to Cardoso and his foreign minister, a possible new role in the international community met with Washington's acceptance. Acceding to the NPT and other regimes with regard to sensitive technologies and eliminating the last doubts over now past nuclear weapons ambitions could increase, for example, the possibility of Brazil's acceptance as a new member of the UN Security Council.

At the beginning of Cardoso's presidency, Lampreia recognized that the important changes in Brazil's foreign policy (including in the nuclear realm) were part of an international, continental, and domestic modification.[5] Cardoso and Lampreia would follow the path of the previous two governments, which had given preeminence to global disarmament and built up a bilateral regime with Argentina. After a wave of accessions to the NPT, Brazil's activism in the disarmament field could lead to the eventual acceptance of the treaty. The country abandoned its dogmatic position against the global agreement. Brazil's authorities were doubtful about the real effectiveness of the treaty, since Iran and North Korea were cheating the regime and France and China were performing new nuclear tests. Moreover, Brazil's diplomats kept up their criticism of what they saw as the unfair nature of the treaty. The new Brazilian government had an additional reason for approaching the NPT: the Argentine accession to the agreement. Unlike in the very recent past, Buenos Aires did not agree to modify its stance toward the nuclear nonproliferation regime, nor did it notify Brazil before actually making the decision. Argentina signed and ratified the treaty in 1994, a few months before the beginning of the NPT review conference.[6] As noted by Julio Carasales, the Argentine decision was a "surprising about-face" that ended twenty-five years of staunchly opposing and criticizing the treaty. According to the Argentine government, joining the NPT after being admitted to the NSG and the MTCR would facilitate the transfer of sensitive technologies. Within a few months, Argentina became one of the "most vocal supporters of an international instrument which it opposed during such a long time."[7] The decision surprised the Brazilians. During Lampreia's first visit to Buenos Aires, in late January 1995, Guido Di Tella, his Argentine counterpart, explained that acceding to the NPT had, above all, a political meaning, since the country had already accepted the most intrusive measures through the ratification of the Treaty of Tlatelolco.[8] Accepting the NPT was part of the convergence between Buenos Aires and Washington. It was, however, the first time in many years that Brazil and Argentina did not assume the same posture toward the nuclear nonproliferation regime.

Cardoso wanted to follow the example of Buenos Aires. A strong opponent of nuclear weapons, the new Brazilian president wanted to inaugurate his administration with a declaration on the forthcoming accession to the NPT. However, Lampreia persuaded him to adopt a different strategy.[9] Brazil would join the NPT gradually, waiting for two important negotiations: the 1995 NPT RevCon and the discussions on the CTBT within the UN Conference on Disarmament.[10] During the preceding months, several countries, including NWSs, had questioned Brazil's possible acceptance of the NPT. Some sectors of the new Brazilian government—an exception was the secretary of strategic affairs, Ambassador Ronaldo Sardenberg—were in favor of changing the traditional policy concerning the treaty. However, such a decision required domestic political and bureaucratic support. Several sectors of Brazilian society, from the more conservative military to the leftist Workers' Party to a large faction among Brazil's diplomats, maintained a nationalist position toward the international regime. In Lampreia's opinion, the goal of joining the NPT needed to be approached with caution.[11]

Despite Brazil's bilateral nuclear nonproliferation agreement with Argentina, some countries were doubtful about the two countries' real intentions. The Russian secret service reported the continuation of Argentine and Brazilian projects to develop nuclear weapons through parallel programs. The air force and navy research projects particularly concerned Moscow.[12] The autonomous Brazilian missile program was particularly criticized by several countries, and that was the reason for the Brazilian effort to join the MTCR.[13] Because of these few persisting suspicions about Brazil's quest for the bomb, Lampreia began to implement his strategy in the first days of Cardoso's administration. On the occasion of the presidential inauguration, Lampreia confirmed Brazil's interest in successfully negotiating the CTBT and guaranteed that it would be "open-minded and undogmatic" about the NPT.[14]

Brazil's new stance in the nonproliferation regime bore its first fruit: both nuclear superpowers recognized Brazil's efforts and signed agreements for the peaceful use of nuclear energy. After several years of a cold relationship with the United States in the atomic field, on 6 March 1995 Lampreia signed an agreement to cooperate in the peaceful use of nuclear energy with John Holum, director of the ACDA. The agreement took effect in 1997; it was a historic step and a clear signal that Brazil had not renounced its nuclear activities.[15] Rumors about possible Brazilian nuclear weapons ambitions evaporated when Lampreia met with General John Shalikashvili, chairman of the United States Joint Chiefs of Staff, and guaranteed that a fully safeguarded nuclear program was free of threats to international security.[16]

Washington was not the only partner in the nuclear field. Brasília continued to pursue several other collaborations for its nuclear program. The Russian Federation, with its profound expertise in the atomic field, could provide important support to the Brazilian plan. Talks with Moscow began in 1990, when the two countries signed a first agreement for collaborating in the nuclear realm. The collapse of the Soviet Union impeded further cooperation until 1994, when it resumed with a new agreement that became effective in early 1995, a few days after Shalikashvili's visit to Brasília. Russian support in the disarmament area was crucial for "normalizing" Brazil's presence in the nuclear and missile nonproliferation regimes. Even if the agreement did not produce the expected outcome, Brasília's diplomatic strategy of closer relations with Moscow eventually succeeded.[17]

The outcome of Lampreia and Cardoso's strategy for acceding to the NPT depended on the outcome of the NPT RevCon in New York in April 1995. The treaty was postponed indefinitely, and the final declaration of the conference renewed the invitation to the few nonparticipating states (including Brazil) to accede. Moreover, a consensual agreement over the future signing of the CTBT was reached.[18] It was a conclusion that several Brazilian diplomats had expected, and it generated an internal debate within Itamaraty about Brazil's future position in the nonproliferation regime.

Key Brazilian diplomats in the disarmament field, such as Antônio Guerreiro, head of Itamaraty's High Technologies and Intellectual Property Division, strongly criticized the NPT. Its indefinite extension would perpetuate the discrimination between haves and have-nots, with no real NWSs making a commitment to disarmament.[19] It was the beginning of a two-year internal debate over one of the most radical modifications of Brazil's foreign policy in the last thirty years. Being one of a few countries opposing an almost universal treaty was not acceptable to the Brazilian president.

The most significant steps toward acceptance of the NPT would be Brazil's accession to export control regimes, such as the MTCR and the NSG, and to active participation in the CTBT negotiations. Guaranteeing a deeper relationship with the United States was central to Brazilian diplomatic choices. Brasília aimed at cooperating with Washington in the areas of both nuclear energy and space, but it wanted to have autonomy in developing the two sectors, without intrusive or limiting demands.

The First Step: Brazil's Accession to the MTCR

The MTCR had been established in 1987 by the G-7 nations (Canada, France, West Germany, Italy, Japan, the United Kingdom, and the United States). It was an informal, voluntary association of countries that shared the goal of nonproliferation of unmanned delivery systems capable of carrying weapons of mass destruction. Adhering to common guidelines, MTCR members sought to coordinate their national export norms to impede the spread of dual-use technologies.[20] Brazil's missile program was a target of MTCR members, especially because of international suspicions of a possible cooperation between Brazil and Iraq. When the regime was established, Brazil and Argentina shared their opposition to the MTCR. Rumors about Brazil's possible weapons of mass destruction needed to be quelled to guarantee the country's international credibility. Brasília's satellite launch vehicle (SLV) program had suffered from the consequences of trade restrictions imposed by the MTCR partners, particularly the United States.[21]

Guaranteeing civilian control over the space program and access to the MTCR became a priority for Collor and his successors.[22] This was clear from 1992, when France refused to cooperate and the US Congress adopted restrictions on the trade of sensitive technologies with Brazil.[23] The signing of the Quadripartite Agreement, the full acceptance of Tlatelolco, and the accession to the Chemical Weapons Convention made Brazil more reliable in the eyes of some US authorities, but not reliable enough to forgo stricter control measures.[24] The US administration suspected that Brazil could use the technology developed for its space program to build ballistic missiles. The comparison with Argentina mattered, since Buenos Aires decided to shut down its space program to allay any international suspicions.[25] If Brasília wanted to become a recipient of sensitive goods and technologies, it needed to adjust its export control legislation to avoid transfers to proliferant countries.[26] As with the nuclear program, foreign authorities attempted to discourage a Brazilian SLV, arguing that it was economically unviable for the country.[27] Brazil could be an important partner for foreign space agencies. Since the late 1980s it had been clear that the base at Alcântara, in northern Brazil, had the ideal geographic conditions for launching space vehicles. In 1994, in a meeting with US space authorities, the Brazilian space agency (recently established to include all the space activities under civilian supervision) signaled its commitment to the MTCR norms.[28]

Adopting new legislation would be the answer to Brazil's limitations in importing sensitive technologies and in cooperating in the space field. The MTCR's partners had to be persuaded to admit Brazil to the regime. Cardoso and Lampreia were aware that the main hurdle would be the air force's opposition to possible restraints on its activities. Unlike those of the other military forces, the air force special projects were not under full civilian control. Some months after the beginning of his administration, President Cardoso discovered that part of the secret budget of the parallel program was still outside the complete control of the executive power. Cardoso resolved the issue, but another problem alarmed the partners of the MTCR, above all the United States: Brazil's acquisition of a missile guidance system from Russia and MAPO (a rocket propellant) from India, neither an MTCR member.[29] In early May 1995 missile proliferation concerns led Washington to issue sanctions on the air force's Aerospace Technical Center and the Aeronautics Institute of Technology, entities involved in the transfer.[30]

The United States would waive the sanctions permanently if Brazil took certain steps by 10 July 1995. After that, Moscow agreed to Brazil's adoption of the MTCR guidelines, and Brasília thus met Washington's condition.[31] Brazil provided Washington with a comprehensive list of all the items included in the MTCR guidelines that it had acquired or contracted from non-MTCR countries since November 1990.[32] After Brazil provided additional information on the cooperation with India on the SLV propulsion system and with Russia on software technology, the United States waived the sanctions. It represented a great advance in the negotiations with the United States, which in June 1995 was available to sponsor Brazil's entrance to the regime.[33]

After persuading the air force, Fernando Henrique Cardoso announced in the city of São José dos Campos (headquarters of the Aeronautics Institute of Technology) that Brazil did not intend to produce, acquire, or transfer ballistic missiles even if the country mastered the SLV technology.[34] After almost three years of discussion, Brazil's executive and legislative authorities agreed to approve legislation on the export of sensitive technologies and materials. The United States welcomed Brazil's decision. When Lampreia met the US secretary of state, Warren Christopher, Christopher underlined that acceding to the MTCR would be a "fundamental component of the international cooperation," including an expansion of the collaboration between American and Brazilian space agencies.[35] The US administration eventually supported Brazil's request to participate in the MTCR. Approving law 9112/95 on 10 October 1995, Brasília established a system of accountability for sensitive exports, adhering to the rules of the MTCR and the NSG. The plenary of the MTCR members decided in Bonn on 27 October to accept Brazil's application following an Argentine proposal.[36] It was a remarkable success for Brazil. During the process of negotiating and adjusting the domestic legislation to MTCR parameters, Brazil preserved its technological advances in the more sensitive areas: the SLV program; the domestic nuclear technology of centrifuge uranium enrichment; and submarine nuclear propulsion. The acceptance of Brazil as a full member of the MTCR sparked criticism from some experts.[37] While Argentina and South Africa gave up their space and missile programs to obtain US approval to accede to the regime, the case of Brazil was completely different: it retained the possibility of keeping its space program and cooperating with other countries in the field, such as the United States—an attempted cooperation between the two countries in 2000 failed because the Congress opposed ratification—or Ukraine.[38] The SLV program continued during the Cardoso and Lula da Silva administrations, but at the time of this writing it has not had a concrete result.

The Second Step: Brazil Joins the NSG

In order not to be prevented from acquiring crucial instruments for its nuclear program, in November 1995 Itamaraty filled out the application to accede to the NSG.[39] Despite Brazil's new legislation and its submission of nuclear activities to full-scope safeguards, many European countries and the United States conditioned the entrance of Brasília to the NSG upon the signing of the NPT.[40] Cardoso, who still faced domestic opposition to the treaty, adopted a cautious policy to achieve the necessary consensus on accepting the NPT.[41] Direct talks with the Clinton administration in late February 1996 guaranteed US support for Brazil's admission to the NSG without accession to the treaty. The United States recognized the significant steps Brazil had taken in the nuclear nonproliferation regime and were aware of the difficulties Cardoso's government faced in proposing NPT accession to the congress.[42]

Brazil was eventually welcomed as a full member of the NSG at the plenary meeting in Buenos Aires on 23 April 1996. With a technologically advanced nuclear program and with nuclear industrial ambitions, Brazil was able to enjoy the fruits of fully taking part in the nuclear trade.

The Last Step: Brazil's Signing of the CTBT

As seen in the previous pages, reaching a global agreement to ban nuclear tests was a long-standing goal for Brazil and represented a condition for accession to the NPT. The Latin American country joined a large community of countries, including the United States, Russia, and the United Kingdom, that sponsored the CTBT. The exceptions were China and France; while they confirmed their support for nonproliferation, they spurned the spirit of the negotiations of the global test ban treaty by conducting underground nuclear tests. Public opinion worldwide was vehemently critical of the actions taken by Beijing and Paris, and at the UNGA Australia condemned the tests. Foreign Minister Lampreia joined Australia in this. On the occasion of the fiftieth session of the UNGA he commented that the tests undermined efforts toward global disarmament and therefore the possibility of concluding a comprehensive nuclear test ban treaty.[43] An exchange of letters between Fernando Henrique Cardoso and Bill Clinton in which they agreed on the necessity of signing the CTBT by 1996 confirmed their countries' commitment.[44] Washington, however, was concerned about Brazil's decision to tie accession to the NPT to the success of the CTBT negotiations.

After three years of discussions within the Conference on Disarmament, 1996 was crucial for reaching a tangible result. The draft treaty was under attack. The lack of consensus on the text and deep criticism from some US political forces threatened global convergence over the treaty. Consequently, the CTBT-NPT connection was a sticking point in US-Brazilian relations in early 1996. The difficulties in approving the CTBT vanished in the following months, and Brazil played a role in achieving that positive outcome. While India vetoed the draft text within the Conference on Disarmament, Brazil cosponsored an initiative to escape the impasse. New Delhi criticized the text because it did not require the NWSs to dismantle their nuclear arsenals. Brazil shared India's concern. However, according to Brazil, the CTBT was a necessary precondition for promoting any global deal to ban and eliminate nuclear weapons. As a result of the discussion, in September at the UNGA 127 countries presented a draft resolution approved by two-thirds of the plenary. When the treaty was opened to signatures on 24 September 1996, Foreign Minister Lampreia was one of the first signatories in a ceremony collateral to the fifty-first UNGA.[45]

The next signature and ratification of the CTBT, in 1998, represented a point of continuity in Brazil's long-standing nuclear disarmament efforts. The successful negotiations and the possible creation of a regime for the complete ban of nuclear tests was a decisive outcome from the Brazilian perspective. Even though nuclear weapons countries had agreed on a moratorium on nuclear tests a few years earlier, the establishment of a regime was a concrete step toward general disarmament and denuclearization. Thanks to the CTBT, the NPT's inequality became less consequential. As Hedley Bull noted on the eve of the 1975 NPT Rev-Con, a complete ban on nuclear explosions could attract opposing states to the regime.[46] This was the case for Brazil, since it meant that one of its central reasons for not acceding to the NPT disappeared.

Brazil's Accession to the NPT

In early 1997 the Brazilian government began an internal debate over acceding to the NPT. The international pressure, the opportunity to establish a strong nuclear and space collaboration with the United States, and according to some authors the economic crisis that affected Cardoso's Brazil were important drivers for joining the treaty. Despite the expected criticism from Itamaraty and several other political forces, the president's determination to accede to the NPT eventually prevailed. The decision was made during meetings of the cabinet between March and May 1997. On 26 March Fernando Henrique Cardoso met with several Brazilian ambassadors at the Palácio da Alvorada, the presidential residence in Brasília. All the diplomats agreed with Cardoso's decision, although Ambassador

Sardenberg underlined the need to receive highly sensitive technologies from the United States in exchange for the accession.[47]

On 24 May the issue was debated for the last time by the Chamber for Foreign Relations and National Defense (Câmara de Relações Exteriores e Defesa Nacional, or Creden), a body of Brazil's government headed by the Brazilian president. An internal document presented by Lampreia justified joining the NPT and responded to any internal hostility to doing so. Accession to the NPT would be consistent with the recent acceptance of the more discriminatory MTCR and the much more rigid and less dynamic NSG. Participating in the NPT could provide Brazil with benefits for cooperating in the development of space and nuclear technologies.[48] Brazil had already provided all the needed nonproliferation guarantees, but acceding to the treaty would be highly symbolic.[49] Cardoso endorsed Lampreia's position. Creden approved the decision, although two members raised some doubts: Mauro César Pereira, minister of the navy, noted that Brazil would not receive any technology transfer; and Sardenberg was concerned that the congress could misread the new Brazilian foreign policy as representing submission to foreign interests.[50]

On 20 June, after almost twenty-nine years, Brazil made a U-turn in its foreign policy. Creden submitted Lampreia's proposal to accede to the NPT to the Brazilian congress.[51] Lampreia signed the NPT at the UN headquarters in New York the following day. The end of the long opposition was celebrated by the United States as well as by some sectors of the Brazilian population.[52] Brazil's decision did not imply more intrusive safeguards, such as those under discussion in Vienna. As in the case of Argentina, Brazil's nuclear program would be subject exclusively to the inspection regime imposed by the Quadripartite Agreement.[53] When Brazil's congress ratified the NPT on 2 July 1998, an amendment gave an additional political orientation to Brazil's nonproliferation policy. For the Brazilian congress, in fact, accession to the NPT was connected to the interpretation that following the terms of article 4 of the treaty, "effective measures would be taken" to bring about a rapid end to the nuclear weapons race, together with the full elimination of atomic weapons.[54] Brazil, consequently, would continue its effort in disarmament forums, but it would also refuse to accept further limitations to its nuclear program.

Acceding to the NPT meant the conclusion of a crucial phase of Brazil's foreign policy. The result of the accession was twofold. First, the regime appeared strengthened, leaving India, Pakistan, and Israel as the main opponents of the treaty. Brazil's accession to the NPT represented a continuation of the gradual process that, after the end of the Cold War, affected the main opponents to the treaty. Second, besides enjoying greater international credibility, as an insider

US Secretary of State Madeleine Albright (*center left*) meets Brazil's foreign minister, Luiz Felipe Lampreia, New York, 9 August 1997. To Lampreia's left is Ambassador Celso Amorim. (Luiz Felipe Lampreia personal archive, LFL foto 009_25, FGV/CPDOC)

Brazil was considered to be in a stronger position to criticize the remaining unequal aspects of the regime. It is important to note, in fact, that Brasília continued to speak out about the unfair nature of the treaty, but it tried to change this through initiatives from within. As it will be seen in the following section, Brazil's leaders perceived immediate benefits deriving from its accession.

Brazil: A Promoter of Disarmament

According to Lampreia's memoirs, Brazil enjoyed the advantages of acceding to the NPT, which became one of Cardoso's most important foreign policy decisions.[55] When Lampreia signed both the NPT and the CTBT, the US secretary of state, Madeleine Albright, recognized that "for Brazil, joining the Non-Proliferation Treaty cements its rightful place in the circle of the world's leading nations."[56] Another important outcome of the Brazilian decision was that it meant receiving the necessary IMF support to deal with the 1998 financial crisis, which deeply affected the country.

After Brazil's accession to the NPT, the government worked to preserve and strengthen the global nuclear order. The "golden age" of nonproliferation ended abruptly when India and Pakistan tested new nuclear weapons.[57] Twenty-four years on from the "Smiling Buddha" PNE, the Indian government—led since February 1998 by the nationalist Bharatiya Janata Party (BJP)—decided to test its ballistic and nuclear weapons capability. On 19 March 1998 the New Delhi government declared that it would not hesitate to provide the country with nuclear weapons to guarantee its national security, territorial integrity, and unity. After experimenting, as Pakistan did, with long-range ballistic missiles, India exploded five nuclear devices from 11 to 18 May. Despite the efforts of the US special envoy Strobe Talbott to deter Pakistan, Islamabad responded with five nuclear tests on 18 and 19 May.[58] The territorial dispute in which the two countries had been engaged since their independence became a nuclear rivalry that affected the stability of the nuclear nonproliferation regime. The attempts by New Delhi and Islamabad to reach a bilateral nonproliferation agreement in the early 1990s, taking as a model the Brazilian-Argentine experience, failed. The tension on the Indian subcontinent and the threat of North Korea and Iran demanded a strong reaction from countries that wished to preserve global nuclear order. The toughest response came immediately from the United States, which imposed extensive sanctions on both New Delhi and Islamabad in an effort to get them to reverse their nuclear stance. Other countries, including Brazil, adopted similar measures. Brasília took an active role in bilateral and multilateral actions to boycott and inflict sanctions on India and Pakistan. Unlike in the 1970s, Brazil condemned the nuclear tests in Asia.[59]

Brazil's dynamism in disarmament initiatives was strong. Following the Canberra Report, a plan promoted by the Australian government for achieving nuclear disarmament in 1996, Brazil joined a geographically disparate group of middle and small powers constituting the New Agenda Coalition (NAC). Brazil was one of the eight signatories of an eighteen-point joint declaration titled "Towards a World Free from Nuclear Weapons: The Need for a New Agenda." In Dublin on 9 June 1998 nine governments requested that NWSs, whether or not they had been recognized by the NPT, pursue "the elimination of nuclear weapons and assurance that they will never be produced again."[60] The NAC would play an important part in further negotiations and policies for achieving global nuclear disarmament. In the post–Cold War era, the NAC represented important southern and unaligned powers. Ireland, Mexico, New Zealand, and Sweden, for instance, had led in terms of denuclearization policies. Brazil, Egypt, and South Africa had given up their nuclear ambitions to assume a new role in the international disarmament effort. New political geometries were built around nuclear nonproliferation issues. Although the initiative was not viewed with favor by the NWSs, Brazil's policy gave it a new international status.

Some days after the NAC declaration, the British government, on behalf of the G-8 (G-7 + Russia), invited Brazil, along with South Africa, Argentina, the Philippines, and Ukraine, to discuss nuclear issues after the Indian-Pakistani nuclear tests and to create a task force made up of those countries that had given up their nuclear ambitions. The G-8 convened the expanded group on 12 June 1998 to implement UNSC resolution 1172, of 4 June 1998, sponsored also by Brazil, which condemned the nuclear tests.

In Birmingham, Lampreia requested the end of horizontal and vertical proliferation, particularly in South Asia. The solution could rest on immediate Indian and Pakistani accession to the CTBT. A multilateral approach was more efficient than the unilateral moratorium that India declared after the tests. Moreover, Lampreia proposed to ban producing and stockpiling fissile material. Such a ban, along with the prevention of an acceleration of missile programs in the two countries, was essential. According to Lampreia, the cooperation offered to North Korea for giving up its nuclear ambitions had been a significant mistake in great power diplomacy. Brazil vehemently opposed a solution (as did France at the 2000 NPT RevCon) that would undermine the NPT, namely, conceding NWS status to India and Pakistan.[61] Brazil saw it as a dangerous precedent, and it would be proposed again later more than once to fix the nuclear order. Clearly, considering India and Pakistan to be rogue states would be counterproductive. Even with strong sanctions, the two countries could not be isolated; they needed to be induced to eliminate their arsenals by joining a global effort toward nuclear disarmament or emulating the Brazilian-Argentine solution.[62]

Brazil's views on disarmament strongly impacted its relations with New Delhi. The two governments had recently renewed their cooperation in the nuclear field through a 1996 memorandum of understanding on the peaceful use of nuclear energy, signed after President Cardoso's visit to New Delhi. As we have seen, in 1968 the two countries attempted to share skills and knowledge to advance their respective nuclear sectors. It was part of Brazil's strategy to continue to collaborate with both developing and industrialized nations. The collaboration with India went beyond scientific and nuclear cooperation; it was also political. Both countries wanted to reform the global political order, and they were historical partners in disarmament forums, even if their positions over the CTBT did not coincide. The relationship was so intense that a few weeks before the nuclear test, Cardoso had a cordial meeting in Brasília with his Indian counterpart, President Narayanan. The nuclear tests ended the positive climate between both countries. As a form of sanction against Indian nuclear explosions, Brazil took diplomatic action. The Brazilian government not only promoted a resolution within the

UNSC but also imposed bilateral sanctions. As a reaction to the test, Brazil kept a chargé d'affaires rather than an ambassador in New Delhi for more than a year. Moreover, Brasília denounced the nuclear agreement signed two years earlier. Promising cooperative actions discussed in the latest presidential summits had not blossomed as expected, since Brasília wanted to avoid any possible association with India's nuclear weapons program. The Indian-Brazilian partnership would be the focus of new discussions several years later, when Luiz Inácio Lula da Silva referred to India as a possible strategic partner in his 2003 inaugural speech. Washington praised Brazil's reaction to this shock to the nuclear order. The United States, as became clear during a meeting between a Clinton envoy and Cardoso, welcomed the tough measures taken by Brasília, assessing them as evidence of a new commitment to nuclear nonproliferation.

The accession to the NPT and the strong action with the NAC over the elimination of nuclear weapons made Brazil a leader in the disarmament initiative. The NAC declaration of June 1998 became the basis of a resolution that the UNGA approved on 4 December 1998. It remained the main proposal for achieving the elimination of nuclear weapons until the 2000 NPT RevCon. Brazil, along with the NAC, made a clear commitment to fully respect the NPT and, above all, to a global accession to the CTBT, which was under attack from many countries after the tests in South Asia. Brazil continued to criticize what it saw as the regime's unfairness and the lack of commitment on the part of the haves.[63] Neither Russia nor the United States wanted to renounce its nuclear arsenal; in each case the arsenal continued to be central to the country's national security strategy. In 1998 the US Senate's rejection of the CTBT was a strong setback for global disarmament and for the Clinton administration, the main sponsor of the agreement.[64] Internal divisions after the tests in South Asia hindered reaching a sufficient consensus. The NPT was not thought to be reliable enough to guarantee US security. Brazil protested against the US policy both unilaterally and multilaterally despite guarantees from the US Department of State that it would respect the 1992 moratorium on nuclear tests.[65]

After the debacle of the last years of the Clinton administration, the nonproliferation regime was revitalized by the 2000 NPT RevCon. Despite doubts about the NPT's future, the gathering was a partial success. After an initial impasse, the treaty was strengthened. The RevCon's main outcome was the definition in practical terms of the NWSs' disarmament obligations. They were summarized in the "Thirteen Steps," an NAC initiative, in a paragraph of the final document of the conference. The Thirteen Steps were a set of "practical steps for the systematic and progressive efforts to implement Article VI of the NPT."[66] They confirmed Brazil's prominence as a country strongly involved in the disarmament process.

Brazil's Nuclear Program in the Cardoso Years

Brazil's acceptance of the NPT did not imply either scaling down Brazil's nuclear activities or accepting a safeguards regime considered more intrusive. Brazil did not give up the goal of mastering the nuclear fuel cycle. The lack of economic resources slowed down the implementation of the country's nuclear plans. At the beginning of Cardoso's administration, the Angra 2 and Angra 3 nuclear power reactors remained unfinished even though the agreement with Germany was still in place. The nuclear program became the object of further reform during the Cardoso years. Following the report of the 1986 Vargas Commission, the nuclear sectors of Furnas and Nuclen merged in 1997 to create Eletronuclear, a subsidiary of Eletrobrás. Its purpose would be to manage and supervise the construction of Brazilian nuclear power plants. In 2002, twenty-seven years on from the signing of the FRG-Brazil nuclear deal, Eletrobrás inaugurated the Angra 2 nuclear power reactor, leaving the construction of the third reactor for

President Cardoso (*right*) visits IPEN, São Paulo, 4 April 1996. To his right is José Israel Vargas, minister of science and technology. Behind them is Ronaldo Sardenberg, secretary of strategic affairs. (Getúlio Gurgel, Presidência da República, Secretaria de Imprensa e Divulgação, Acervo Histórico do Presidente Fernando Henrique Cardoso)

the future. It was an important achievement for the nuclear lobby, which during a year of exceptional drought was able to demonstrate nuclear energy's important role as a complement to hydroelectric production.

It was not the only accomplishment of Brazil's nuclear sector, since the Brazilian government decided to maintain the goal of enriching uranium on a commercial scale. Although the plan to build a nuclear-powered submarine had been suspended from 1996 to 2002, Brazil's nuclear military projects remained central to the work to master the nuclear fuel cycle. Uranium enrichment continued to be under the control of the navy at its facility in Aramar, where both centrifuges and enriched uranium were produced. Even though many protagonists of the autonomous program retired—Rear Admiral Othon Luiz Pinheiro da Silva left the navy in 1994—the Navy's Technological Center in São Paulo (Centro Tecnológico da Marinha em São Paulo, or CTMSP) became one of the main nuclear energy research centers, along with São Paulo's IPEN. The transfer of skills and equipment was an accomplishment of the nuclear project established in 1979. Army and air force projects in nuclear energy research continued, even if on a reduced scale. The technological details of the Brazilian centrifuges remained secret even though the military facilities were under full-scope international safeguards. While the main aim of the Aramar Experimental Center was to produce fuel for future nuclear submarines, the military research centers would also serve civilian activities.

In 1998, Brazil's National Congress approved the modernization of the INB facilities for nuclear fuel production in Resende (Rio de Janeiro) and, more importantly, decided to aim to enrich uranium for commercial purposes. Where Nuclebrás sought to enrich uranium using the jet-nozzle method of uranium isotopic separation, INB would establish a commercial plant with ultracentrifuges produced by the Brazilian navy. In the future Brazil would be able to produce the fuel, which at that moment it had to acquire abroad. A 1998 turnkey agreement between the navy and INB guaranteed the future provision of the enrichment equipment.[67] As with the centrifuges in Resende, the industrial secrets would be preserved under the conditions of the Quadripartite Agreement. As noted in the following chapter, Brazil refused to accept the Additional Protocol to the international safeguards agreements.

In the Cardoso years, refusing the Additional Protocol did not signify a lack of dialogue about possible modification to the Brazilian position on a new inspection regime. The dispute would last many years. Brazil's attitude toward the nuclear nonproliferation regime would not be dogmatic. The acceptance of further norms could be negotiated within the limitations imposed by national interests. In the case of Brazil's accession to the NPT, the main goal was to acquire international credibility and eventually eliminate doubts about the country's ambition to develop weapons of mass destruction. Acceding to the regime did not come at a high cost to Brazil. The possibility of developing and launching space vehicles and mastering the nuclear fuel cycle had been preserved. Cardoso did not dismantle the nuclear program, and as he recently revealed, if necessary a future president could decide to resume a nuclear weapons program.[68] While Brazil acceded to the NPT and reinforced its diplomatic action toward disarmament, it kept up its criticism of NWSs and what it perceived as the unfair nature of the treaty. The next pages discuss how this nuclear disarmament was maintained and how Brazil's nuclear ambitions were renewed over the years 2003 to 2018.

CHAPTER NINE

Brazil and the Nuclear Issue from Lula da Silva to Temer, 2003–2018

After exhausting talks and negotiations in Tehran, in May 2010 the leaders of Brazil, Turkey, and Iran presented to the world a proposal for resuming the dialogue between Iran and the P5+1 (the five permanent members of the UNSC and Germany) on the international dispute over sensitive aspects of the Iranian nuclear program. Since the 1990s, Iran had been suspected of cheating the NPT, secretly developing dual-use nuclear technologies and producing nuclear material with the final goal of building an atomic bomb. The agreement brokered by Turkish and Brazilian diplomats could succeed where the great powers had failed for several years. The illusion of a solution to a crisis for the nuclear nonproliferation regime lasted for a few days. In June 2010 the UNSC approved, with the exclusive opposition of Brazil and Turkey, further sanctions against Iran. However, even though the deal failed, owing mainly to US opposition, it demonstrated that the solutions to tense diplomatic crises did not lie exclusively with the traditional powers. Although an agreement on the issue was eventually and temporarily achieved in 2015, Brazil, in contrast to its stance a few years earlier, decided not to take part in further negotiations on the Iranian nuclear program. The foreign policy activism of a rising power—the world's seventh largest economy in 2014—was replaced by a chaotic economic and political situation that led to President Dilma Rousseff's impeachment in 2016. Despite its recent domestic troubles, Brazil sent a clear message to the world that it was not a marginal actor in the discussions on the global nuclear order. Middle and emerging countries manifested the capability to fix nuclear disorder with their initiatives, diverging from the solutions presented by the Global North. Many international observers and governments praised the Brazilian-Turkish action in Tehran as a sign of a possible new international order.

Brazil had acceded to the NPT, albeit belatedly and sparking some criticism, and had mastered sensitive nuclear technologies. "What Brazil can do, Iran can do as well," was an oft-repeated comment of Brazil's president, Luiz Inácio Lula da Silva, and his foreign minister, Celso Amorim, up until the Tehran declaration.[1] Brazil, however, did not keep nuclear activities secret after joining the NPT and was not at the center of grave, long-lasting regional conflicts, even if there were still some suspicions concerning the ultimate goal of its nuclear program.[2] Lula da Silva's rhetoric underestimated (or avoided considering) the risks of the Iranian nuclear program's advancement to the security of the Middle East and of the international system. What Brazil defended was Iran's right to enrich uranium and reprocess spent fuel under international safeguards and inspections for its peaceful use, but without international constraints. Brazil also shared with Iran (and with a large community of developing countries) a concern about the unfair nature of the nonproliferation regime. A leader in disarmament forums, Brazil criticized the limited efforts of the NWSs to reduce and ultimately give up their arsenals. Despite some unfortunate declarations by several Brazilian politicians and foreign policy officials—among them the vice president, José Alencar; the minister of science and technology, Roberto Amaral; and the secretary-general of the Foreign Ministry, Samuel Pinheiro Guimarães—Brazil kept its commitment not to develop a nuclear bomb.[3]

A new national defense strategy, the Estratégia Nacional de Defesa, and an ambitious energy plan (Eletrobrás's Brasil 2030), both announced in 2008, included nuclear energy as a priority for national development and excluded further commitments to unfair nuclear nonproliferation norms, at least until real steps were taken toward atomic disarmament. Brazil resumed the navy plan, partially abandoned in the 1990s, to build a nuclear-propelled submarine and decided to increase the number of nuclear power plants. It was part of a new strategy for Brazil to situate itself in the world in the second half of the 2000s. In a new international context, the members of the BRICS group (Brazil, Russia, India, China, and South Africa) appeared to be rising future great powers. Brazil would be a candidate for a permanent seat in the UNSC without a nuclear bomb, but in a state of latency, being the only NNWS with serious plans to build a fleet of nuclear submarines.

The recent troubles notwithstanding, Brazil's position in the global nuclear order is not to be downscaled since the country remains one of the main supporters of nuclear disarmament and has mastered uranium enrichment technologies. Together with other middle powers, Brazil is, in fact, one of the main proponents of a treaty banning nuclear weapons to fully realize article 6 of the NPT.[4]

Unlike the Tehran agreement, the initiative cosponsored by Brazil in 2017 did not make the headlines of major international newspapers and was substantially ignored and opposed by the NWSs. The treaty continued a longstanding thread in Brazil's diplomacy but was an important step toward further discussions within global nuclear diplomacy.

This chapter deals with Brazil's stance toward the nonproliferation regime from 2003, with the beginning of Lula da Silva's first presidential term, to 2018. The domestic and international debate over whether to accept or resist the Additional Protocol (AP) to the IAEA safeguards agreement is discussed. In June 2011, after six years of negotiations, the NSG temporarily accepted the ABACC system as a substitute for the IAEA Additional Protocol. Several countries raised doubts about Brazil's nuclear ambitions, including the construction of a submarine in domestic shipyards with a nuclear reactor built locally. The origins and consequences of the Brazilian-Turkish attempt to solve the Iranian nuclear crisis are also analyzed. In conclusion, the state of the nuclear program is discussed.

Brazil and Nuclear Disarmament

While it is true that Lula da Silva during his presidential campaign of 2002 strongly criticized the accession to the NPT and that later prominent members of his cabinet followed his example, these were exceptions to the rule.[5] Indeed, Lula da Silva and his successor and fellow PT member, President Dilma Rousseff, did not reverse Cardoso's decision to join the international regime. On the contrary, continuing the previous policy, Lula da Silva, Rousseff, and Michel Temer kept nuclear disarmament as a central goal of Brazil's foreign policy. Moreover, Itamaraty has continuously condemned North Korea (which has diplomatic relations with Brasília) for its nuclear tests and missile programs.[6] Brazil's activism was confirmed by the appointment of Ambassador Sérgio de Queiroz Duarte, an experienced Brazilian diplomat with a long career dealing with nuclear issues, first as president of the 2005 NPT RevCon and second as the UN high representative for disarmament (2006–11). Despite the resumption of nuclear talks between Brazil and India (a cooperation in the field of thorium was promising), Brasília was critical of the United States' failure to commit to nonproliferation and disarmament. It was clear after the signature of the 2008 US-Indian nuclear agreement, which allowed New Delhi to import atomic goods and technology.[7] As noted by William Walker, the US-Indian nuclear deal constituted an "exception from the NSG's restrictions on trade with states lacking full safeguards coverage." It created a dangerous precedent for treating some countries differently and allowing them to be informally admitted to the nuclear club because of Washington's ambiguous stance toward disarmament and nonproliferation.[8]

Brazil continued to be an active partner in several initiatives, such as Global Zero and the NAC. It also praised US President Obama's 2009 speech in Prague favoring reducing the number and size of the existing nuclear arsenals and the 2010 new US-Russian Strategic Arms Reduction Treaty, or START. However, as no NWSs moved to dismantle their arsenal, after the 2010 NPT RevCon Brazil and several other countries supported a new strategy: adoption of a legal instrument for prohibiting nuclear weapons. The NWSs judged the negotiations and the proposal ineffective and counterproductive for the NPT.[9] On 7 July 2017, 122 countries with no NWSs and not allies to NWSs agreed on the final text of the Treaty on the Prohibition of Nuclear Weapons.[10] It was a diplomatic achievement for Brazil, other middle powers, and international organizations such as the International Committee of the Red Cross and the International Campaign to Abolish Nuclear Weapons, the latter of which was awarded the Nobel Peace Prize in 2017. As noted, the treaty divided the international community but constitutes a tool for pressuring the NWSs and is consistent with the first UNGA resolutions that called for complete nuclear disarmament.[11]

Achieving a longtime goal of Brazil's foreign policy and confirming its constitutional commitment against nuclear weapons, the signing of the treaty represented a fundamental step toward a world free of nuclear weapons.[12] The initiative was in line with Brazil's foreign policy after accession to the NPT, and the TPNW is considered an important national diplomacy achievement.[13]

A Controversial Issue: Brazil and the Additional Protocol

While Brazil championed disarmament initiatives, several analysts considered its participation in the nuclear nonproliferation regime controversial. As anticipated in the previous chapter, starting in 1997, after several years of discussions in Vienna, an additional layer of safeguards was proposed: the IAEA Additional Protocol to the safeguards agreement (INFCIRC/540).[14] Even though both Brazil and Argentina had accepted full-scope safeguards to their nuclear activities in 1994, they refused to allow IAEA complementary inspection authority. According to the AP, the IAEA inspectors could provide to the agency assurances about both declared and possible undeclared nuclear activities. Above all, the IAEA was granted expanded rights of access to information and nuclear sites. It was a measure considered necessary after the United States and IAEA inspectors, during the first Gulf War, discovered that Iraq, an NPT member, had cheated the regime by developing a secret nuclear weapons program in undeclared facilities.[15]

Brazil, along with a large group of other countries, refused to accept the new inspection regime during the negotiations in Vienna and confirmed the position after a US request.[16] In early 1996, it justified its position with an argument that remains valid today. Brazil's representatives in Vienna considered the measures proposed by the United States and the IAEA director-general, Hans Blix, too intrusive. Brazil's congress would not accept further safeguard measures, especially after the difficult approval of the Quadripartite Agreement. IAEA inspections would be more invasive since they would cover not only facilities containing nuclear material but also other buildings, such as the centrifuge production plant, under the supervision of the Brazilian navy. In that case, according to the Brazilians, it would be challenging to preserve the country's industrial secrets.[17] It is important to note that INFCIRC/540 would allow international inspectors to have access to the facilities where rotors and centrifuges are assembled. However, article 7 permits the IAEA and the states to "make arrangements for managed access to protect proprietary or commercially sensitive information."[18] The issue, even if the costs of adjusting the inspection system are high, appears more political than technical. Cardoso's foreign minister, Luiz Felipe Lampreia, recently told this author that the reason for Brazil's position toward the AP was that the navy was opposed to it. The military force supervising the uranium enrichment program had eventually accepted the Quadripartite Agreement and needed to be persuaded to accept Brazil's accession to the NPT. Submitting Brazil's nuclear activities to intrusive inspection was unacceptable to the Brazilian navy and could cause serious problems within the Brazilian government.[19] As Lampreia confirmed in his document supporting Brazil's accession to the NPT, the country would not accept further commitment beyond ABACC and IAEA-ABACC inspections.[20] Any possible modification of the safeguards regime had to be agreed upon by Argentina and ABACC.

Brazil's participation became a matter of international concern in 2004, when Brazilian authorities denied full access to its centrifuges for enriching uranium at the INB enrichment plant. All of this, along with the statements of the science and technology minister, Roberto Amaral, in early 2003 about seeking the complete nuclear fuel cycle and the capacity to develop nuclear weapons, caused great concern among international analysts.[21] Nonetheless, after long negotiations Brazil granted the IAEA access to verify the nuclear material, although it preserved the centrifuges from visual inspections to protect industrial secrets.[22] According to US documents released by Wikileaks, Brazil's opposition may have been to hide that the enrichment technology had been illegally obtained from Germany in the past.[23] The United States mildly criticized Brazil's stance and continued to request, as other nuclear and nonnuclear states did, its acceptance of the protocol. During the 2005 NPT RevCon, several countries recommended linking the AP implementation as a standard for IAEA safeguards. Brazil and members of the Non-Aligned Movement, particularly the Middle Eastern countries, vehemently objected to the proposal.[24] The then foreign minister, Amorim, declared that the issue was not central to the reform of the NPT, and he underlined Brazil's right to maintain its industrial secrets.[25] Amorim's words are consistent with the current stance toward the issue, even if the possible acceptance of the AP has been the object of discussions within the Brazilian government and between Brazilian and Argentine officers.

As João Marcelo Galvão de Queiroz, a Brazilian diplomat, recently wrote, in 2001 Brazil and Argentina decided to begin preliminary talks with the Vienna agency about a possible additional protocol associated with the Quadripartite Agreement. In the middle of those discussions and as a consequence of the deep financial crisis affecting Argentina in the first years of the century, the Brazilian government discussed in 2002 the possible extinction of ABACC. According to several officials, ABACC's goal in putting the Argentine and Brazilian nuclear programs under full-scope safeguards had been fulfilled and the inspection and verification system could be left to the IAEA. The idea, however, was rapidly abandoned, above all because of the Argentine government's possible suspicions about Brazil's nuclear activities.[26] Thus, after a four-year analysis that also involved ABACC, and despite a positive declaration about a new agreement with the international agency in 2004 by the science and technology minister, Eduardo Campos, both Brazil and Argentina decided to reject the AP as a new verification system.[27] The final decision on the issue had probably been made by President Lula da Silva, but future evidence will have to confirm this statement.[28] The issue provoked a division within the Brazilian cabinet during Lula da Silva's second presidential term (2006–11). While the Ministry of Defense officially rejected the possibility of a new verification system in the 2008 national defense strategy, some members of the Foreign Ministry supported its adoption.[29] Although several politicians and diplomats both in Brasília and in Buenos Aires have recently supported a revision of the Brazilian position, Brazil and Argentina reached different solutions.[30]

The bilateral Brazilian-Argentine ABACC inspection system, like other regional verification agreements, could represent an alternative to the Additional Protocol. Argentine and Brazilian inspectors' twenty years of verifying the two countries' military and civilian nuclear facilities and materials was evidence of the peaceful nature of the atomic programs in the Southern Cone. Starting in 2006, the NSG discussed revising the export guidelines in order to strengthen controls over transfers of enrichment and reprocessing (ENR) equipment and technologies. In the initial proposals, signing an AP was a condition for importing sensitive items.[31] It would affect both Argentina and Brazil, who opposed the proposal. After five years of negotiations, the NSG in June 2011 temporarily accepted ABACC's request that its inspection system be an alternative to the Additional Protocol and "that ABACC and the Quadripartite Agreement [provide] assurances that enrichment and reprocessing [would not be] misused for nuclear weapons purposes."[32] Such a decision had several important consequences for Brazil.[33] It put an end, at least temporarily, to the international community's preoccupation with a supposedly ambiguous Brazilian nuclear attitude. The NSG decision also was significant for bilateral relations with Argentina. The recognition of the binational agency meant international approval of the cooperation between the two countries.[34] Finally, in the words of Itamaraty, the decision "opens new perspectives for international cooperation and greater access to the technologies relevant to the development of the Brazilian nuclear program."[35] This temporary victory notwithstanding, Brazil continues to face international pressure to sign the IAEA AP.

Industrial nuclear countries and several NWSs insisted, in fact, on universalizing the AP to promote nuclear nonproliferation. Moreover, the adoption of a state-level approach in IAEA verification, a proposal debated by the IAEA board of governors with no consensus, is highly controversial. As noted by Brazilian observers, the approach would rely more on subjective factors than on objective ones.[36] In the years to come it will be important to follow the decision the international community adopts. In deciding whether to adopt an AP, as in the case of the NSG decision, a nation could look to the Brazilian-Argentine decisions and the ABACC system. As Togzhan Kassenova, an expert on Brazil's nuclear issues, noted, the "NSG ENR transfer criteria includes an important caveat: it recognized regional safeguards arrangements [such as ABACC] *pending* adoption of an additional protocol."[37] In the future, Argentina and Brazil should either adopt an AP or at least adopt "key elements of the protocol that provide the highest level of confidence."[38] At this writing a modification of the stance toward international safeguards does not appear to be on the agenda of either country, but the issue is highly sensitive given the future need to safeguard the equipment and material of the nuclear-powered submarines.[39]

The 2010 Tehran Declaration

Another controversial aspect of Brazil's nuclear diplomacy in the last years has been the attempt to negotiate a nuclear agreement with Tehran. The Brazilian press has often strongly criticized Lula da Silva's decision to cooperate with an authoritarian regime.[40] However, it is essential to emphasize the parallels existing between Brazil's and Iran's nuclear programs. Both countries are members of the NPT. According to the letter of the treaty, they can fulfill their ambition and right to enrich uranium up to 20 percent (the threshold for high enriched uranium suitable for weapons) for medical, research, and naval-propulsion uses. Neither country accepted the AP, and both wanted to preserve their industrial secrets.[41]

As is known, Iran's nuclear activities since the beginning of this century have raised international suspicions about possible military nuclear ambitions. This concern increased after the IAEA's discovery in 2009 of an undeclared nuclear enrichment facility. Later, Iranian authorities stated that the plant had been constructed for the production of enriched uranium to supply medical research reactors or future nuclear submarines. This parallel with Brazil emerged in a broader context. Since 2006 Brazil has taken a favorable position toward Iran, with growing bilateral trade between the two countries and cordial personal relations between Lula da Silva and Iran's president, Mahmoud Ahmadinejad. In September 2009, when Iran reached an agreement with the IAEA and the so-called P5+1 for swapping the enriched Iranian uranium for the fuel for the Tehran research reactor (TRR), Brazil welcomed this outcome as a successful step toward mutual trust between Iran and the international community. However, Tehran refused to implement the deal because the necessary guarantees were lacking and because conservative elements in the regime were opposed to it.

It was at that very moment that Brazil began to play a central role in the Iranian conundrum. It was not the first time that Brasília had been involved in discussions about the Iranian nuclear crisis. Since the establishment of closer relations in 2006, with the visit of Celso Amorim to Tehran—the first visit by a Brazilian foreign minister since Francisco Rezek's visit in 1991—Brazil had been attempting to persuade Tehran to accept a political solution proposed by Western powers.[42] Brazil's mediation was requested by one of the main Western players, Germany. Brazil, as noted by Sean Burges, was considered a bridge between the North and the South.[43] The mediation between an emerging country and the great powers was the right occasion for Brazil to assist in solving a knotty problem.

Brazil's participation in the Iranian nuclear crisis until 2010 remained discrete and not always favorable to Iran's nuclear program. In 2006, when the IAEA board of governors decided to take the Iranian case before the UNSC, the Brazilian governor voted in favor. Brazil made the same decision when the Security Council issued economic sanctions in 2007. Celso Amorim, in his memoirs of his tenure as Lula da Silva's foreign minister, considered the Brazilian attitude as a mistake. On the occasion of the first round of sanctions, Brazil sent a special envoy to Tehran to persuade Iran to accept a Brazilian-Swiss solution to the nuclear crisis to avoid further sanctions. Tehran's firmness prevented a positive outcome.[44]

At that very moment, when a major international financial crisis shocked the Western countries, Brazil's accelerated growth allowed the country to take part in new forums made up of the main economies, such as the G-20. Brazil continued its criticism of the G-8 and of the attitude of the most developed countries but used the new forums to present its proposals. In May 2009, however, in a personal meeting between Lula da Silva and President Barack Obama during the G-8 summit in L'Aquila (Italy) a new issue was discussed: the possibility of a future nonpermanent member of the UNSC playing a major role in the negotiation with Tehran.[45] The US-Brazilian discussions continued in Brasília in August 2009 with meetings between a high-ranking representative of the Obama administration and Lula da Silva's leading advisers on foreign policy and nuclear issues. Brazil's representatives committed to promoting dialogue with Iran.[46]

Thus, Brazil praised the TRR "swap" agreement reached between Iran and the P5+1 in October 2009. Diplomacy preserved the Iranian nuclear projects and the production of fuel needed for medical purposes but limited the possibility of producing fissile material. When Iran refused to adhere to the agreement with the P5+1, Washington and other international community actors sought Brazil's assistance. Javier Solana (EU high representative for foreign affairs and security policy), Mohamed ElBaradei (IAEA director-general), and Hillary Clinton (US secretary of state) all asked Lula da Silva to persuade Iran to accept the deal. According to them, President Lula da Silva should persuade the Iranian president, Mahmoud Ahmadinejad, when he visited Brazil in November 2009.[47] To stress the importance of Brazil's position in the dialogue with Tehran, President Obama sent Lula da Silva a personal letter in which he restated American support for the October agreement.[48] The Brazilians perceived those signals as a form of mandate for opening a new channel of communication with Iran.

More than four decades after the visit of Shah Reza Pahlavi, Brazil, despite criticism from some US congressmen, former Brazilian diplomats, and a significant bloc of the domestic press, received Ahmadinejad. Lula da Silva publicly defended Iran's "right to develop uranium enrichment for the production of energy for peaceful purposes just as much as Brazil does."[49] However, during his conversation with Lula da Silva on 23 November 2009 Ahmadinejad declined the invitation to respect the deal signed in October. Because of Iran's lack of trust toward the P5+1, Tehran's parliament refused to ratify the diplomatic decision adopted in Geneva. Iran's president was not completely opposed to the idea of a "swap" agreement, but another formula was to be sought.[50]

When Germany presented a new "swap" agreement to the IAEA board of governors a few days after Ahmadinejad's meeting with Lula da Silva, the United States and France again sought Brazil's assistance in trying to persuade Iran to accept the proposal. Brazil and South Africa, another emerging-country member of BRICS, however, both abstained in the IAEA vote on the issue. It was not the end of Brazil's mediating role. Brazilian diplomats acted as a bridge between Tehran and the West on a proposal to freeze uranium enrichment at 20 percent in Iran. Fear of the international community then sparked Iran to accumulate a large stock of 20 percent enriched uranium, which could easily be enriched to weapons grade. Consequently, the swap agreement became useless for keeping Iran away from accumulating fissile material. The tension among the parties increased.

In December 2009 Brazil continued discussions over the Iranian dossier with the P5+1 (excluding Russia and China) to avoid a major crisis. At that moment, on the eve of Brazil's joining the UNSC as a nonpermanent member, Amorim began to construct a strategy for circumventing stricter measures against Iran. After the failure of the "swap" deal with Iran, US diplomacy tailored a strategy within the UNSC to obtain the support of all permanent members for stricter economic sanctions against the Asian country, an option that Brazil had opposed since September 2009.[51] In early January 2010 the US secretary of state, Hillary Clinton, obtained Russian and Chinese endorsements of sanctions (which would not affect Beijing's and Moscow's interest in Iran). However, the Brazilian diplomats were unaware of this at the time.[52] Brasília received mixed signals from Washington about resuming the talks between Tehran and the P5+1.

One possible initiative was Brazilian, even if the path to an agreement passed through Istanbul. Turkey, another country present as a nonpermanent member of the UNSC, a NATO member, and with ambitions to become a regional power in the Middle East, had strong reasons for brokering a deal on Iran's nuclear program. On the one hand, avoiding a neighbor with nuclear weapons capabilities would guarantee its national security, but on the other, it was necessary to strengthen the relationship with Iran. A new Turkish foreign policy, led by Foreign Minister Ahmet Davutoglu and Prime Minister Recep Tayyip Erdogan, aimed at taking leadership in the region, abandoning the past strong relationship with Israel, along with reaching a solution to the Kurdish problem and establishing friendly relations with Islamist movements. Brazil and Turkey had different reasons for finding a way out for the Iranian nuclear impasse but fostered a partnership to reach a solution satisfactory to both.[53] As a high-ranking Brazilian diplomat declared to the US ambassador, a "third-party engagement . . . would be a key to success given Iranian skepticism of the United States and Europe as primary messengers."[54] It was the appropriate moment to resolve a crisis over nuclear Iran. In the first quarter of 2010 the international community would gather on two occasions to discuss the future of the nuclear nonproliferation regime: at the 2010 NPT RevCon and the Global Nuclear Security Summit. It guaranteed Brazil and Turkey an opportunity to discuss the issue both bilaterally and multilaterally.

Brasília and Istanbul sought US support for a possible initiative in Tehran. However, as became clear at a summit between Amorim and Clinton in Brasília in March 2010, the United States suspected that any prorogation of the negotiations with Iran would allow Iran more time to accumulate fissile material. According to the US secretary of state, Iran would negotiate in "good faith" following a new round of UNSC economic sanctions against Tehran. Amorim diverged widely from his US counterpart and defended Brazil's position toward dialogue.[55]

Notwithstanding, the Brazilian-Turkish effort continued, and in early April 2010, on the occasion of Davutoglu's visit to Brasília, Brazilian and Turkish diplomats redoubled their efforts to tailor a deal with Iran and gain US backing for their initiative.[56] They could still hope for White House support despite Hillary Clinton's opposition to new negotiations. When President Obama convened the Global Nuclear Security Summit in Washington on 13 April, President Lula da Silva and Prime Minister Erdogan privately introduced a proposal to him for reviving the nuclear fuel swap deal with Iran.[57] The Brazilian and Turkish leaders received mixed signals from the White House. Obama's immediate reaction was cold, but in a letter to Lula da Silva after the meeting he explicitly mentioned that a swap deal with Tehran would strengthen US "trust and would reduce regional tensions."[58] In that context, Brazil and Turkey focused their attention on Iran.

On 17 May, after several visits to Tehran and long negotiations, and despite Moscow's opposition, Amorim and Davutoglu succeeded in obtaining a formal declaration from the heads of government of Turkey (Erdogan), Brazil (Lula da Silva), and Iran (Ahmadinejad). As with the deal of October 2009, Iran would

President Luiz Inácio Lula da Silva (*left*) is greeted by the president of Iran, Mahmoud Ahmadinejad, Tehran, 18 May 2010. (Ricardo Stuckert, Presidência da República, Agência Brasil)

accept the nuclear fuel exchange as the basis for cooperation and dialogue. Upon receiving a positive response from the Vienna Group (the United States, Russia, France, and the IAEA), within a month Iran would transfer 1,200 kilograms of low enriched uranium to Turkey in exchange for the delivery of 120 kilograms of fuel needed for the Tehran research reactor.[59]

The Tehran declaration had an important impact on the international community, hitting the headlines of major newspapers. The governments in Ankara and Brasília seemed to have succeeded where the major powers had failed. However, a few hours after the declaration, Clinton confirmed to Amorim that the United States would propose further sanctions against Tehran. Washington, differently from what the Brazilians and Turkish perceived about the US position, would not accept new negotiations with Iran based on the Tehran declaration. The US interpretation of the Obama letter to Lula da Silva was actually that the White House would be sympathetic toward new efforts with Iran but that a new round of sanctions would be issued. It is not clear whether this was a misinterpretation of Obama's words or whether the Tehran declaration was a victim of a battle within the US administration.

At the end of the month, Amorim and Davutoglu issued a public call for international support, above all from the members of the UNSC, for the Tehran declaration.[60] However, on 9 June the UNSC, through resolution 1929, with the sole opposition of Turkey and Brazil and the abstention of Lebanon, decided to issue severe sanctions against Iran and continued to request the closure of the enrichment plant.[61] The Brazilian-Turkish initiative has been considered a failure of Brazilian diplomacy. A deep crisis over nuclear Iran lasted for more than two years, with a final agreement between the P5+1 and Tehran. The Brazilian-Turkish action was not totally in vain. Several analysts and government representatives assessed the diplomatic initiative as a possible basis for resuming negotiations between the international community and Iran to avoid the dramatic consequences of strict economic sanctions.[62]

In January 2013, at the beginning of Obama's second term, his administration declared its willingness to resume talks with Tehran, and after two years a final agreement was reached. Brazil decided not to participate in those talks, but the 2010 diplomatic proposal remains an important effort of the Latin American country toward disarmament. As noted earlier, Brazil has always played the role of mediator in major crises in its neighborhood, but this was its first such action outside the region. Both Brazil and Turkey, proposing to fix the Iranian crisis where the major powers had failed, attempted to build mutual trust between the parties. Brazil's activism toward disarmament, as seen in its role in promoting the treaty to ban nuclear weapons, was not downscaled, and the Tehran accord constitutes a landmark, even if a highly criticized one, in Brazilian diplomacy. The legacy of the 2010 initiative is still to be considered. Recently, in fact, after the US decision to abandon the Iran deal, Tehran requested Brazil's assistance to save the 2015 agreement.[63]

Brazil's Current Nuclear Plans

While Brazil played a significant role in nuclear diplomacy, since 2004 the government has also made efforts to resume its civilian and military nuclear programs. With the world's sixth largest reserve of uranium and the scientific and technical capability to enrich uranium, the Lula da Silva and Rousseff administrations resumed the nuclear plans of the 1970s.[64] Brasília wanted to turn Brazil into a nuclear industrial country with energy from nuclear power plants, radio-isotope production, and a fleet of nuclear submarines to defend its Atlantic territorial waters, the so-called Amazônia Azul, or Blue Amazon.

In the area of civilian nuclear energy, the Brazilian government decided to complete Angra 3, to start the enrichment of national uranium on a commercial scale using Brazilian technology, to acquire the complete nuclear fuel cycle, and to build with Argentina a multipurpose reactor for medical and research aims. The new Brazilian nuclear policy could be considered part of the so-called nuclear renaissance.[65] During Lula da Silva's second term, after a long internal debate the administration approved Plano 2030, an energy plan that included building up to eight nuclear power plants by 2030. It would expand Brazil's nuclear energy production to up to 5 percent of the national energy matrix.[66] New financial troubles combined with slower economic growth prompted a revision of the Brazilian nuclear energy strategy. Angra 3's completion was authorized in 2001, but the work only began again in 2010, after the Brazilian Institute of the Environment and Renewable Natural Resources (Instituto Brasileiro do Meio Ambiente e dos Recursos Naturais Renováveis, or IBAMA) environmental licensing and CNEN nuclear licensing. The nuclear power reactor, which was to be built by the French company AREVA (now Orano), which absorbed the nuclear sector of Siemens in 2009, was supposed to have been connected to the electric grid in 2015. However, delays in its construction have led to an uncertain forecast.[67]

It is necessary to note that the suspension of the nuclear power plant construction was not a temporary measure in the wake of the Fukushima accident;[68] domestic problems paralyzed the work. The judicial operation Lava-Jato (Car-Wash) uncovered a major corruption scheme that shocked the Brazilian political system and directly included the nuclear program and Eletronuclear, the company that runs the two nuclear power plants and is managing the completion of Angra 3. Othon Luiz Pinheiro da Silva, the father of the navy's nuclear program from the late 1970s to the mid-1990s, was appointed in 2005 to chair Eletronuclear after Brazil's government decided to complete Angra 3 and increase the number of nuclear power plants.[69] Sentenced to forty-three years in prison for taking bribes from major construction companies and money laundering, Admiral Pinheiro da Silva was imprisoned in 2015 and released under a habeas corpus request in 2017.[70] Pinheiro da Silva's imprisonment was an earthquake for the past and present of the Brazilian nuclear program and one of the reasons for its suspension. As a consequence of the economic crisis affecting Brazil since 2014 and the Eletronuclear troubles, the Brazilian government proposed new measures to guarantee the completion of Angra 3, such as increasing the national energy tariff.[71] Despite that situation, Brazil continued to seek international partners for its nuclear activities.[72] On the other hand, Argentina could be a regional strategic partner in the atomic field. With developed nuclear sectors, Brasília and Buenos Aires have talked since 2008 about resuming plans for their nuclear industrial integration.[73] Improving upon the ABACC system, they could create a unique bilateral nuclear complex by following the example of Euratom.[74]

One of the main areas of cooperation between the two countries is the joint construction of two multipurpose reactors, the Argentinean RA-10 and the

Brazilian multipurpose reactor (Reator Multipropósito Brasieiro, or RMB). Relying on the model of the OPAL (Open Pool Australian Lightwater) reactor, designed and built by the Argentine company INVAP for Australia, the multipurpose reactor will perform three main functions: radioisotope production, fuel and material irradiation testing to support the Brazilian nuclear energy program, and provision of neutron beams for scientific and applied research. Buenos Aires and Brasília confirmed their joint effort in December 2017, at a meeting between the Brazilian president, Michel Temer, and his Argentine counterpart, Mauricio Macri.[75] The Brazilian government decided to invest heavily in the reactor and laboratories, to be built at the São Paulo navy experimental center, to face the world market crisis in radioisotope production and radiopharmaceuticals resulting from the shutdown of reactors in Canada and Europe. Brazil, consequently, will become an independent producer of radioisotopes (currently imported) and will own an important tool for improving the Brazilian nuclear program and for training new generations of nuclear scientists and technicians. When the reactor is turned on, it will operate for at least fifty years.[76] The RMB will double the quantity of available radiopharmaceuticals in Brazil, allowing the sale abroad of surplus material. Then the domestic nuclear industry will have the possibility of challenging important international players such as Canada, the Netherlands, and South Africa in another significant sector of the global nuclear market.

The pursuit of civilian nuclear ambitions is also confirmed by the construction of the INB civilian industrial facility for enriching uranium in Resende, mentioned earlier.[77] INB's goals, meanwhile, are first to provide the fuel for Brazilian nuclear plants and later to join the international market of nuclear suppliers.[78] Becoming a nuclear supplier certainly depends on the possibility of mastering the nuclear fuel cycle. Currently, Brazil commands almost all phases of the cycle, but it still lacks the crucial industrial capability to convert uranium dioxide into UF_6, the component used in uranium enrichment isotopic separation. According to the available data, in the future the Brazilian navy will build a pilot conversion facility, which will allow Brazil to create a basis for the future industrial capability to produce nuclear fuel autonomously. Thus, Brazil has the possibility to become a global player in the nuclear market. Except for the partially resolved issue of access to the centrifuges for visual inspection, the civilian program does not raise any international concern.

The resumption of the civilian nuclear program coincided with Lula da Silva's full support of the nuclear submarine project.[79] As seen in the previous chapter, the navy budget had been downscaled, leaving naval nuclear propulsion as an indeterminate future goal. At the beginning of Lula da Silva's first term, in 2003, the navy program cost about US$1 billion, and the Navy Technological Center in São Paulo required twenty years and US$500 million for the final development and delivery of a nuclear submarine.[80] Several observers considered the program a drain on resources that could have been directed elsewhere.[81] In July 2007 Lula da Silva announced his support for the construction of the nuclear vessel, which could lead Brazil to "be more valued as a nation."[82] While Brazil is an emerging power in the global civilian nuclear arena, international commentators have expressed their misgivings about the Brazilian plan to develop nuclear submarines by 2030.[83] In 2008 Brazil's national defense strategy underlined the necessity of achieving nuclear autonomy for economic development and for building a fleet of nuclear submarines in the context of the military modernization.[84] Brazilian strategists justified the decision to build nuclear submarines not only because they would bring the nation prestige but also because they would preserve the country's immense marine and undersea resources from possible enemies and, above all, defend the oil reserves off the coast of the states of Rio de Janeiro and Espírito Santo.[85] The nuclear submarine was not supposed to be a threat to Argentina, even if at the end of Lula da Silva's second term Argentine officials complained about his risky nuclear policy.[86] Brazilian and Argentine representatives mentioned in broader discussions over nuclear cooperation the possibility of collaborating on the construction of the atomic vessel, but the proposal led nowhere.[87]

After long consultations with the United States, Israel, Russia, and France, the latter agreed to a major strategic partnership with Brazil. Thanks to a technology transfer agreement with the French government signed on 23 December 2008, Brazil launched the Submarine Development Program (Programa de Desenvolvimento de Submarinos, or PROSUB).[88] The aim is to construct submarines using Brazilian nuclear reactors built at the Aramar Experimental Center in Iperó (state of São Paulo). Following lengthy negotiations, the French government agreed to provide Brazil with the capability to construct Scorpène-class submarines. The submarines would be built in Brazilian shipyards, thanks to the partnership between the French company Naval Group (formerly known as Direction des Constructions Navales, or DCNS), the Brazilian company Odebrecht, and the Brazilian government, and modified for naval nuclear propulsion. It is important to note that France would not provide nuclear technology, which is being developed in Brazil.[89] In July 2011 President Rousseff manifested her willingness to pursue Lula da Silva's goal by inaugurating the shipyard of a new state-owned firm, Amazul, in Sepetiba, state of Rio de Janeiro, for building conventional and nuclear submarines.[90] According to the announcements of Admiral Luis Ferreira Marques, the navy's head of the Nuclear Development and Research Directorate, by 2023 Brazil will own the prototype of the reactor for nuclear submarines, while the first nuclear vessel should be ready between 2028 and 2030.[91] As in the case of Angra 3, corruption scandals could also affect PROSUB given the accusations of bribery against Odebrecht and the French partner.

Joining the small group of countries that possess a nuclear-powered submarine fleet (the United States, the United Kingdom, Russia, China, and France) will be a historic outcome and the realization of a longtime dream for Brazil. Currently, only the permanent members of the UNSC possess this instrument of strategic defense. Other emerging countries, including India, which also is an NWS, are planning to build several nuclear-powered submarines, but Brazil is one of the most advanced in designing and developing its own nuclear technologies without possessing nuclear weapons.

As seen in the previous pages, in the last fifteen years Brazil has emerged as a significant actor in the global nuclear order. As an important industrial nuclear power, the country, thanks to its natural resources and technological capability, defends its full membership in the NPT but maintains a critical stance toward the unfair nature of the international nuclear nonproliferation regime. Two goals are significant for Brazil's diplomacy: nuclear disarmament and the peaceful use of nuclear energy. This was clear in April 2009 and May 2010, when Brasília supported the right of Tehran to pursue its nuclear program through an agreement with international support and eventually the TPNW. Finally, Brazil will raise its international status when it launches its first nuclear submarine, becoming the first NNWS with such capability.

Conclusion

While I was writing the final words of this book, Eduardo Bolsonaro, son of President Jair Bolsonaro and Brazilian congressman, asserted that Brazil's atomic arsenal should be taken more seriously in the international arena. "In the future," he stated, "the decision not to have atomic weapons could be an object of debate."[1] However, Brazil's reversal on the issue appears highly unlikely. The previous chapters have shown that since the beginning of the nuclear age the country has never decided to follow the path toward developing and testing nuclear devices. Eduardo Bolsonaro is not the first politician since Brazil's accession to the NPT in 1998 to criticize the surrender of the nuclear option. As we have seen, many members from across the whole political spectrum have agreed on this position, so no revision appears on the horizon.

The improbability of nuclear reversal is one of the implications of the analysis presented here. This leads us to reconsider many of the critical aspects of Brazil's nuclear and foreign policy of the last seventy years. Brazil kept the strategic objective of mastering the technology for producing nuclear energy, mainly to acquire the capability to enrich uranium. Thus, if we compare the atomic project based on the guidelines of Getulio Vargas with the policy adopted in the 1970s by Ernesto Geisel and the 1990 report of the parliamentary commission of inquiry on the secret nuclear program, we see that the purpose was always the same: Brazil's aim was to create a national and *autonomous* nuclear program, with full control over sensitive technologies.[2] As this work demonstrates, the Brazilian goal was not to develop a nuclear bomb but only to have the capability to produce it. On at least one occasion, in 1984, the Brazilian government refused a proposal from the air force minister to develop an atomic device. The rationale of the program was connected to the economic and industrial development of the country (as a source for supporting growth). The involvement of the military, particularly the Brazilian navy, was and is limited to the construction of a nuclear submarine and to the mastery of uranium enrichment technologies. The ambition, now as in the past, is to keep open the possibility of producing nuclear weapons in the future, relying exclusively on national technology, as achieving such a goal should be free from international constraints.

From 1968 to 1997 Brazil strenuously opposed the NPT, and presently it maintains a critical stance toward some aspects of the regime (e.g., the IAEA Additional Protocol to the international safeguards agreement). During the military governments, especially starting in 1967, and the first ten years of the new democratic rule (1985–95) Brazilian and international analysts saw that stance as one of the pillars of Brazilian foreign policy. This assumption was supported by continued denunciations of the regime by Itamaraty for its discriminatory nature, which mirrored an unjust distribution of international power. What this book demonstrates is that despite this rhetoric, Brasília acted in a pragmatic way. Even at the height of its fiercest opposition to the treaty, Brazil considered accepting some international norms. The first case was the nuclear agreement with the Federal Republic of Germany in 1975. From the very beginning of the negotiations with Bonn, Brazil accepted the incorporation of some norms of the international regime as "special" safeguards, and it agreed not to transfer technologies without West German consent and not to use any sensitive technologies without Bonn's prior approval in the first fifteen years of the cooperation. In the same way, at the very end of the administration of Gerald Ford, Brazil bargained with the United States over relinquishing spent-fuel reprocessing technologies. During Geisel's presidency (1974–79), the Brazilian cabinet also discussed the possibility of accepting nonproliferation norms, and eventually the NPT, in exchange for recognition of the country as capable of mastering the nuclear fuel cycle. Regarding Brazil's accession to the NPT in 1997, this book demonstrates that the decision did not undermine the country's ambitions to enrich uranium or even put a cap on them. Signing on to the NPT was a low-cost move that did not take the country off course but rather guaranteed that Brazil could maintain its nuclear complex.

The United States played a key role in the planning and in the history of the Brazilian nuclear program. This book tells the story of how nuclear decisions in Washington shaped Brazilian responses. A crucial factor was how US pressures played out domestically in Brazil. The presence of governments with a more or less cooperative attitude toward the United States determined the activity, or lack thereof, around autonomous nuclear projects. This was the case of the alternating nuclear policies adopted from the late 1940s to the mid-1960s. On the one hand, presidents such as Eurico Gaspar Dutra, João Café Filho, Humberto

Castello Branco, and to some extent Arthur da Costa e Silva, Emílio Garrastazu Médici, and Juscelino Kubitschek renounced developing autonomous nuclear projects and accepted the limitations set by Washington. On the other hand, during the years of Getulio Vargas (1951–54), the presidencies of Jânio Quadros and João Goulart (1961–64), the military regime from 1974, and the presidency of José Sarney (1985–90) Brazil had a more independent attitude, implementing an autonomous nuclear program distanced from the position of the United States. As this book shows, during its history Brazil has preferred to collaborate with the United States on nuclear issues. It was when Washington decided not to implement such a cooperation that Brazil sought another partner and set out a plan for becoming completely independent regarding nuclear energy.

Starting in 1951, when Brazil tried to purchase a synchrocyclotron from the Dutch company Phillips, it attempted to overcome the limitations of the United States' restrictive policies by looking for other partners among the most industrialized countries. Negotiations and contracts, above all with France and West Germany, were a strong response to continuous denials of cooperation from Washington. The Brazilian government established partnerships for peaceful uses of nuclear energy with these countries in order to acquire the complete nuclear fuel cycle.

Both in the mid-1950s and especially during the 1970s, Brazil's agreements with the Federal Republic of Germany and France created a dispute between those governments and Washington. The establishment of the Nuclear Suppliers Group in 1975, an additional informal institution created by nuclear industrial countries for preserving and strengthening the NPT with a common rule on sensitive technologies exports, was threatened after the FRG's decision to cooperate with anti-NPT governments, such as Brazil. It provoked a temporary fracture in the common front formed by Bonn and Washington against the spread of nuclear weapons and technologies. Commercial reasons, such as the enormous economic advantage for West Germany deriving from the deal with Brazil, were at the roots of the refusal to accept the guidelines proposed by the NSG.

However, when nonproliferation policies prevailed in the decisions of the countries of the Global North, Brazil collaborated with other countries opposing the NPT. Especially from 1979 to 1984 but also in the previous decade, Brazil collaborated or negotiated with actors such as Pakistan, Argentina, the People's Republic of China, Israel, South Africa, and India in order to receive, free from international safeguards, nuclear materials and technologies not available on the nuclear market. The ban on sensitive nuclear exports established by the US Congress with the 1978 Nuclear Non-Proliferation Act obliged Brazil and other countries to operate in the *black* nuclear market, where they obtained crucial elements for reaching nuclear autonomy.

The most important collaboration with an opponent to the NPT has certainly been the collaboration with Argentina. The existing literature reports that until 1979, when a dispute over the Iguaçu hydroelectric plant was resolved, Brasília and Buenos Aires had not engaged in nuclear-related negotiations. Furthermore, there was a dominant belief, supported by the US government, that Brazil and Argentina, like India and Pakistan, were involved in some form of nuclear competition. However, available documents demonstrate that this interpretation needs to be qualified. As we have observed, the two countries took a common stance toward the nuclear nonproliferation regime from the creation of the IAEA up until the establishment of the system of common account and control of reciprocal nuclear materials and facilities in the early 1990s. Both countries, with similar nuclear ambitions, dissipated their reciprocal suspicions, created mutual trust in the atomic field, and created common institutions that eventually generated the conditions for a regional and global regime of nuclear nonproliferation. The relationship between Brazil and Argentina became an example to follow in the disarmament field, even though both countries still oppose the Additional Protocol.

Brazil has been active in disarmament forums, both promoting and opposing initiatives for achieving nuclear nonproliferation, from the beginning of the nuclear age. Besides its multilateral engagement, on two occasions Brazil attempted to play a key role in resolving major nuclear crises. The first occasion was the Cuban Missile Crisis, when Brazil advanced a proposal for dismantling the bases in exchange for a firm commitment from the NWSs on the denuclearization of Latin America and the Caribbean. The second, more recent occasion was when Brazil attempted to broker an agreement over the Iranian nuclear program—one of the major crises in the global nuclear order—through a trilateral declaration by Brazilian, Turkish, and Iranian heads of state in May 2010. Both proposals, initially supported by the United States, failed and have been criticized domestically and internationally, but they nevertheless demonstrated Brazil's ambitions to resolve international nuclear disputes.

Nearly seventy-five years after the beginning of the nuclear age, Brazil has almost completed its third nuclear power reactor, owns an advanced program for constructing a nuclear submarine, and has mastered sensitive aspects of the nuclear fuel cycle. In the disarmament field, Brazil is a leading actor in supporting full denuclearization. Even though the country does not accept more intrusive international safeguards to its nuclear activities, Brazil is not seen as a threat to the nuclear nonproliferation regime. Its scientific, technological, and political attitude appears consistent with the long trajectory of Brazil's nuclear plans explored here.

1. Serra do Cachimbo (Pará): Air base and former underground nuclear test site
2. Resende (Rio de Janeiro): INB nuclear fuel fabrication plant
3. Angra dos Reis (Rio de Janeiro): Power plants Angra 1, Angra 2, and Angra 3 (under construction)
4. Itaguaí (Rio de Janeiro): ICN nuclear submarine shipyard
5. Rio de Janeiro (Rio de Janeiro): Institute of of Nuclear Energy (IEN)
6. Rio de Janeiro (Rio de Janeiro): Institute of Radiation Protection and Dosimetry (IRD)
7. Belo Horizonte (Minas Gerais): Center for the Development of Nuclear Technology (CDTN, former IPr)
8. Caetité (Bahia): INB Uranium Concentrate Plant
9. Abadia de Goiás (Goiás): Radioactive waste repository
10. Iperô (São Paulo): Aramar Experimental Center
11. São Paulo (São Paulo): Nuclear and Energy Research Institute (IPEN, former IEA)
12. São Paulo (São Paulo): Navy Technological Center in São Paulo (CTMSP)

AA/USP	Álvaro Alberto personal archive, University of São Paulo
ABACC	Agência Brasileiro-Argentina de Contabilidade e Controle de Materiais Nucleares (Brazilian-Argentine Agency for Accounting and Control of Nuclear Materials)
ACDA	Arms Control and Disarmament Agency
AHMRE-B	Arquivo Histórico do Ministério das Relações Exteriores—Brasília (Historical Archive of the Ministry of Foreign Affairs, Brasília)
AMAE-F	Archive du Ministère des Affaires Étrangères, France (Archive of the French Ministry of Foreign Affairs)
AN-B	Arquivo Nacional, Brasília (National Archive, Brasília)
AP	Additional Protocol
CBTN	Companhia Brasileira de Tecnologia Nuclear (Brazilian Nuclear Technology Company)
CEA	Commissariat à l'Énergie Atomique (French Atomic Energy Commission)
CNEA	Comisión Nacional de Energía Atomica (Argentine National Atomic Energy Commission)
CNEIC	China Nuclear Energy Industry Corporation
CNEN	Comissão Nacional de Energia Nuclear (National Nuclear Energy Commission, Brazil)
CNPq	1951–74, Conselho Nacional de Pesquisa (National Research Council); from 1974, Conselho Nacional de Desenvolvimento Científico e Tecnológico (National Council for Scientific and Technological Development)

CPDOC	Centro de Pesquisa e Documentação de História Contemporânea do Brasil (Center for Research and Documentation of Contemporary Brazilian History)
CSN	Conselho de Segurança Nacional (National Security Council, Brazil)
CTA	Centro Técnicológico da Aeronáutica (Aerospace Technical Center)
CTBT	Comprehensive Test Ban Treaty
EdSP	*Estado de São Paulo*
EM	Exposição de Mótivos (Explanatory Memorandum)
EMFA	Estado Maior das Forças Armadas (Joint Staff of the Armed Forces)
ENDC	Eighteen-Nation Disarmament Committee
Euratom	European Atomic Energy Commission
Eurodif	European Gaseous Diffusion Uranium Enrichment Consortium
FdSP	*Folha de São Paulo*
FGV	Fundação Getulio Vargas (Getulio Vargas Foundation)
FOIA	Freedom of Information Act
FRG	Federal Republic of Germany
HEU	High enriched uranium
IADA	International Atomic Energy Development Agency
IAEA	International Atomic Energy Agency
IEA	Instituto de Energia Atômica (Institute of Atomic Energy)
IEAv	Instituto de Estudos Avançados (Institute of Advanced Studies)
IEN	Instituto de Energia Nuclear (Institute of Nuclear Energy)
INB	Indústrias Nucleares Brasileiras (Brazilian Nuclear Industry)
INFCE	International Nuclear Fuel Cycle Evaluation
IPEN	Instituto de Pesquisas Energéticas e Nucleares (Nuclear and Energy Research Institute)
IPR	Informação para o Presidente da República (Information to the President of the Republic)
IPr	Instituto de Pequisas Radioativas (Institute of Radioactive Research)
JWG	Joint Working Group
LEU	Low enriched uranium

MME	Ministério de Minas e Energia (Ministry of Mines and Energy, Brazil)
MTCR	Missile Technology Control Regime
NAC	New Agenda Coalition
NARA	National Archives and Records Administration
NNWS	Non-nuclear-weapon state
NPT	Nuclear Non-Proliferation Treaty
NPT RevCon	Nuclear Non-Proliferation Treaty Review Conference
NSC	National Security Council (US)
NSG	Nuclear Suppliers Group
Nuclam	Nuclebrás Auxiliária de Mineração (Nuclebrás Mining Associate)
Nuclebrás	Empresas Nucleares Brasileiras (Brazilian Nuclear Enterprises)
Nuclei	Nuclebrás Enriquecimento Isotópico (Nuclebrás Isotopic Enrichment)
Nuclep	Nuclebrás Equipamentos Pesados (Nuclebrás Heavy Equipment)
NWFZ	Nuclear-weapon-free zone
NWS	Nuclear-weapon state
OPANAL	Organismo para a Proscrição das Armas Nucleares na América Latina e no Caribe (Agency for the Prohibition of Nuclear Weapons in Latin America and the Caribbean)
PA/AA	Politisches Archiv des Auswärtiges Amt (Political Archive of the German Foreign Ministry)
PMDB	Partido do Movimento Democrático Brasileiro (Brazilian Democratic Movement Party)
PND	Plano Nacional de Desenvolvimento (National Development Plan)
PNE	Peaceful nuclear explosion
PRC	People's Republic of China
RAC/JCL	Remote Archives Capture, Jimmy Carter Library
SCCC	Sistema Comum de Contabilidade e Controle (Common System for Accounting and Control of Nuclear Materials)
SNIE	Special National Intelligence Estimate
TPNW	Treaty on the Prohibition of Nuclear Weapons
UNAEC	United Nations Atomic Energy Commission
UNGA	United Nations General Assembly

Unicamp	Universidade Estadual de Campinas (State University of Campinas)
UNSC	United Nations Security Council
Urenco	Uranium Enrichment Consortium
USAEC	United States Atomic Energy Commission
WC	Wikileaks Cable

Introduction

1. "Brasil já domina enriquecimento de urânio, diz Sarney," *Folha de São Paulo* (hereafter *FdSP*), 5 Sept. 1987, A-6.

2. José Sarney, "Nossos propósitos, do governo e da sociedade, são e serão pacíficos," *FdSP*, 5 Sept. 1987, A-6; "Não vamos fazer a bomba, diz Nazareth," *FdSP*, 5 Sept. 1987, A-6.

3. "Bomba pode ser produzida em 5 anos, afirma reitor da USP," *FdSP*, 5 Sept. 1987, A-7.

4. On the US policy to prevent nuclear proliferation, see Francis J. Gavin, "Strategies of Inhibition: U.S. Grand Strategy, the Nuclear Revolution, and Nonproliferation," *International Security* 40.1 (2015): 9–46, https:/doi.org/10.1162/ISEC_a_00205; Gene Gerzhoy, "Alliance Coercion and Nuclear Restraint: How the United States Thwarted West Germany's Nuclear Ambitions," *International Security* 39.4 (2015): 91–129, https://doi.org/10.1162/ISEC_a_00198; William Burr, "A Scheme of 'Control': The United States and the Origins of the Nuclear Suppliers' Group, 1974–1976," *International History Review* 36.2 (2014): 252–76, https:/doi.org/10.1080/07075332.2013.864690; and Or Rabinowitz and Nicholas Miller, "Keeping the Bombs in the Basement: U.S. Nonproliferation Policy toward Israel, South Africa, and Pakistan," *International Security* 40.1 (2015): 47–86, https://doi.org/10.1162/ISEC_a_00207. Specifically on the US policy to prevent Brazil from acquiring sensitive nuclear technologies, see Carlo Patti and Matias Spektor, "'We Are Not a Nonproliferation Agency': Henry Kissinger's Attempt to Accommodate Nuclear Brazil, 1974–1977," *Journal of Cold War Studies* 22.2 (2020): 58–93, https://doi.org/10.1162/jcws_a_00940; Carlo Patti, "The Origins of the Brazilian Nuclear Programme, 1951–1955," *Cold War History* 15 (2015): 353–73, https://doi.org/10.1080/14682745.2014.968557; William Burr, "The 'Labors of Atlas, Sisyphus, or Hercules'? US Gas-Centrifuge Policy and Diplomacy, 1954–60," *International History Review* 37.3 (2015): 431–57, https://doi.org/10.1080/07075332.2014.918557; and William Glenn Gray, "Commercial Liberties and Nuclear Anxieties: The US-German Feud over Brazil, 1975–7," *International History Review* 34.3 (2012): 449–74, https://doi.org/10.1080/07075332.2012.675221.

5. On the cooperation in the field of sensitive technologies, see Eliza Gheorghe, "Proliferation and the Logic of the Nuclear Market," *International Security* 43.4 (2019): 88–127, https://doi.org/10.1162/isec_a_00344; Matthew Kroenig, *Exporting the Bomb: Technology Transfer and the Spread of Nuclear Weapons* (Ithaca, NY: Cornell University Press, 2010);

and Matthew Fuhrmann, *Atomic Assistance: How "Atoms for Peace" Programs Cause Nuclear Insecurity* (Ithaca, NY: Cornell University Press, 2012). The existing literature does not consider Brazil's cooperation or attempts to collaborate with other countries opposing the NPT. For exceptions, see Dani K. Nedal, "Brazilian Nuclear Cooperation with the People's Republic of China," *NPIHP Research Update,* accessed 10 Aug. 2020, https://www.wilsoncenter.org/publication/brazilian-nuclear-cooperation-the-peoples-republic-china; and Carlo Patti, "The Forbidden Cooperation: South Africa–Brazil Nuclear Relations at the Turn of the 1970s," *Revista Brasileira de Política Internacional* 61.2 (2018), https:/doi.org/10.1590/0034-7329201800206.

6. On an initial debate over the issue, see Bernard Brodie, ed., *The Absolute Weapon* (New York: Harcourt, Brace, 1946). For a recent and specific work discussing the nuclear order, see Sara Z. Kutchesfahani, *Global Nuclear Order* (London: Routledge, 2019). On the centrality of nuclear weapons in the discussions on international order, see Andrew Hurrell, *On Global Order: Power, Values, and the Constitution of International Society* (Oxford: Oxford University Press, 2007).

7. William Walker, *A Perpetual Menace: Nuclear Weapons and International Order* (London: Routledge, 2012), 10.

8. Walker, *Perpetual Menace,* 12.

9. Walker, *Perpetual Menace,* 12.

10. William Walker, "Nuclear Order and Disorder," *International Affairs* 76.4 (2000): 707–8.

11. Walker, *Perpetual Menace,* 24.

12. Hedley Bull, "Rethinking Non-Proliferation in International Relations," *International Affairs* 51.2 (1975): 175, https://doi.org/10.2307/2617231.

13. On the challenge to the nuclear order during the 1970s, see Leopoldo Nuti, "The Making of the Nuclear Order and the Historiography on the 1970s," *International History Review* 40.5 (2018): 965–74, https:/doi.org/10.1080/07075332.2017.1404484.

14. See Francis J. Gavin, *Nuclear Statecraft: History and Strategy in America's Atomic Age* (Ithaca, NY: Cornell University Press, 2012); and Shane J. Maddock, *Nuclear Apartheid: The Quest for American Atomic Supremacy from World War II to the Present* (Chapel Hill: University of North Carolina Press, 2010).

15. David James Gill, *Britain and the Bomb: Nuclear Diplomacy, 1964–1970* (Stanford, CA: Stanford University Press, 2014).

16. Avner Cohen, *Israel and the Bomb* (New York: Columbia University Press, 1999).

17. Rabia Akhtar, *The Blind Eye: US Non-Proliferation Policy towards Pakistan from Ford to Clinton* (Lahore: University of Lahore Press, 2018).

18. Itty Abraham, *The Making of the Indian Atomic Bomb: Science, Secrecy and the Postcolonial State* (London: Zed Books, 1998); George Perkovich, *India's Nuclear Bomb: The Impact on Global Proliferation* (Berkeley: University of California Press, 1999); Jayita Sarkar, "The Making of a Nonaligned Nuclear Power: India's Proliferation Drift, 1964–1968," *International History Review* 37.5 (2015): 933–50, https:/doi.org/10.1080/07075332.2015.1078393; Harsh V. Pant and Yogesh Joshi, *Indian Nuclear Policy* (New Delhi: Oxford University Press, 2018).

19. On the Italian, West German, and Japanese cases, see, respectively, Leopoldo Nuti, *La sfida nucleare: La politica estera italiana e le armi atomiche, 1945–1991* (Bologna: Il Mulino, 2007); Andreas Lutsch, "The Persistent Legacy: Germany's Place in the Nuclear

Order" (NPIHP Working Paper 5, May 2015, Wilson Center); Fintan Hoey, "Non-nuclear Japan? Sato, the NPT, and the US Nuclear Umbrella," in *Negotiating the Nuclear Non-Proliferation Treaty: Origins of the Nuclear Order*, ed. Roland Popp, Liviu Horovitz, and Andreas Wenger (London: Routledge, 2017), 161–77; and Yoko Iwama, "The Japanese Ministry of Foreign Affairs and the Decision to Join the Non-Proliferation Treaty," in *Joining the Non-Proliferation Treaty: Deterrence, Non-Proliferation and the American Alliance*, ed. John Baylis and Yoko Iwama (London: Routledge, 2019).

20. On West German nuclear ambitions in the 1960s, see Harald Müller, "German National Identity and WMD Nonproliferation," *Nonproliferation Review* 10.2 (2003): 1–20, https://doi.org/10.1080/10736700308436927.

21. Nicola Horsburgh, *China and Global Nuclear Order: From Estrangement to Active Engagement* (Oxford: Oxford University Press, 2015).

22. On nuclear restraint, see Harald Müller and Andreas Schmidt, "The Little-Known Story of Deproliferation: Why States Give Up Nuclear Weapons Activities," in *Forecasting Nuclear Proliferation in the 21st Century*, ed. William C. Potter with Gaukhar Mukhatzhanova, vol. 1, *The Role of Theory* (Stanford, CA: Stanford University Press, 2010), 124–58; Maria Rost Rublee, *Nonproliferation Norms: Why States Choose Nuclear Restraint* (Athens: University of Georgia Press, 2009); Ariel Levite, "Never Say Never Again: Nuclear Reversal Revisited," *International Security* 27.3 (2002): 59–88, https://doi.org/10.1162/0162288 0260553633; T. V. Paul, *Power versus Prudence: Why Nations Forgo Nuclear Weapons* (Montreal: McGill-Queen's University Press, 2000); Benoît Pelopidas, "Renunciation: Restraint and Rollback," in *Routledge Handbook of Nuclear Proliferation and Policy*, ed. Joseph F. Pilat and Nathan E. Busch (London: Routledge, 2014), 337–48; Etel Solingen, "The Political Economy of Nuclear Restraint," *International Security* 19.2 (1994): 126–69, https://doi .org/10.1162/isec.19.2.126; and Solingen, *Nuclear Logics: Contrasting Paths in East Asia and the Middle East* (Princeton, NJ: Princeton University Press, 2007). On Argentina, see Diego Hurtado, *El sueño de Argentina atómica: Política, tecnología nuclear y desarollo nacional (1945–2006)* (Buenos Aires: Edhasa, 2014); and Jacques E. C. Hymans, "Of Gauchos and Gringos: Why Argentina Never Wanted the Bomb, and Why the United States Thought It Did," *Security Studies* 10.3 (2001): 153–85, https://doi.org/10.1080/09636410 108429440.

23. On the South African case, see Martha van Wyk, "Sunset over Atomic Apartheid: United States–South African Nuclear Relations, 1981–93," *Cold War History* 10.1 (2010): 51–79, https://doi.org/10.1080/14682740902764569; Jo-Ansie van Wyk, "Atoms, Apartheid, and the Agency: South Africa's Relations with the IAEA, 1957–1995," *Cold War History* 15.3 (2015): 395–416, https:/doi.org/10.1080/14682745.2014.897697; and Jo-Ansie Van Wyk and Anna-Mart Van Wyk, "From the Nuclear Laager to the Non-Proliferation Club: South Africa and the NPT," *South African Historical Journal* 67.1 (2015): 32–46, https://doi.org/10.1080/02582473.2014.977337.

24. Thomas Jonter, *The Key of Nuclear Restraint: The Swedish Plans to Acquire Nuclear Weapons during the Cold War* (London: Palgrave Macmillan, 2016).

25. Maria Rost Rublee, "The Nuclear Threshold States: Challenges and Opportunities Posed by Brazil and Japan," *Nonproliferation Review* 17 (2010): 49, https://doi.org/10.1080 /10736700903484660.

26. Rublee, "Nuclear Threshold States," 49. On the possible Brazilian challenge and contribution to the global and regional nuclear orders, see also Etel Solingen, "Hindsight

and Foresight in South American Nonproliferation Trends in Argentina, Brazil, and Venezuela," in *Over the Horizon Proliferation Threats*, ed. James J. Wirtz and Peter R. Lavoy (Stanford, CA: Stanford University Press, 2012), 136–59; and Carlo Patti, "Weapons of Mass Destruction: Will Latin America Backtrack?," in *Routledge Handbook of Latin America Security*, ed. David Mares and Ariel M. Kacowicz (London: Routledge, 2015), 221–29.

27. On latency, see Scott D. Sagan, "Nuclear Latency and Nuclear Proliferation," in Potter and Mukhatzhanova, *Forecasting Nuclear Proliferation in the 21st Century*, 1:80–101; Joseph F. Pilat, ed., *Nuclear Latency and Hedging: Concepts, History and Issues* (Washington, DC: NPIHP, Wilson Center, 2017); and Matthew Fuhrmann and Benjamin Tkach, "Almost Nuclear: Introducing the Nuclear Latency Dataset," *Conflict Management and Peace Science* 32.4 (2015): 443–61, https://doi.org/10.1177%2F0738894214559672.

28. Målfrid Braut-Hegghammer, *Unclear Physics: Why Iraq and Libya Failed to Build Nuclear Weapons* (Ithaca, NY: Cornell University Press, 2016).

29. William Burr, "A Brief History of U.S.-Iranian Nuclear Negotiations," *Bulletin of the Atomic Scientists* 65.1 (2009): 21–34, https://doi.org/10.2968%2F065001004; Farzan Sabet, "The April 1977 Persepolis Conference on the Transfer of Nuclear Technology: A Third World Revolt Against US Non-Proliferation Policy?," *International History Review* 40.5 (2018): 1134–51, https:/doi.org/10.1080/07075332.2017.1404483.

30. For a general overview of Brazil's history after the Second World War, see Leslie Bethell, ed., *The Cambridge History of Latin America*, vol. 9, *Brazil since 1930* (New York: Cambridge University Press, 2008). On Brazil's diplomatic history, see Rubens Ricupero, *A diplomacia na construção do Brasil, 1750–2016* (Rio de Janeiro: Versal, 2017); and Amado Luiz Cervo and Clodoaldo Bueno, *História da política exterior do Brasil* (Brasília: Editora Universidade de Brasilia, 2002).

31. Ricupero, *A diplomacia na construção do Brasil*, 343.

32. On Brazil's history until the 1964 military coup, see Leslie Bethell, "Politics in Brazil under the Liberal Republic, 1945–1954," in Bethell, *Cambridge History of Latin America*, vol. 9, *Brazil since 1930*, 87–164; Thomas E. Skidmore, *Politics in Brazil, 1930–1964: An Experiment of Democracy* (New York: Oxford University Press, 1967); and Jorge Ferreira and Lucilia de Almeida Neves Delgado, eds., *O Brasil republicano. O tempo da experiencia democrática: da democratização de 1945 ao golpe civil-militar de 1964. Terceira república (1945–1964)* (Rio de Janeiro: Civilização Brasileira, 2019).

33. For a general overview of the history of the military regime, see Leslie Bethell and Celso Castro, "Politics in Brazil under the Military Rule, 1945–1964," in Bethell, *Cambridge History of Latin America*, vol. 9, *Brazil since 1930*, 165–230; Thomas E. Skidmore, *The Politics of Military Rule in Brazil, 1964–85* (New York: Oxford University Press, 1988); and Jorge Ferreira and Lucilia de Almeida Neves Delgado, eds., *O Brasil republicano. O tempo do regime autoritário: ditadura militar e redemocratização. Quarta república (1964–1985)* (Rio de Janeiro: Civilização Brasileira, 2019).

34. On the Castello Branco years, see Elio Gaspari, *A ditadura envergonhada* (Rio de Janeiro: Intrinseca, 2014). On the years 1967–74, see Gaspari, *A ditadura escancarada* (Rio de Janeiro: Intrinseca, 2014).

35. On Geisel's presidency, see Elio Gaspari, *A ditadura derrotada* (Rio de Janeiro: Intrinseca, 2014); Gaspari, *A ditadura encurralada* (São Paulo: Companhia das Letras, 2004); and Walder de Góes, *O Brasil do General Geisel* (Rio de Janeiro: Nova Fronteira,

1978). On the Figueiredo years, see Gaspari, *A ditadura acabada* (Rio de Janeiro: Intrinseca, 2016).

36. For an overview of the evolution of the Brazilian economy, see Werner Baer, *The Brazilian Economy: Growth and Development* (Boulder, CO: Lynne Rienner, 2008).

37. Tanya Harmer, "Brazil's Cold War in the Southern Cone, 1970–1975," *Cold War History* 12.4 (2012): 659–81.

38. The recent literature relying on primary sources includes Guilherme Camargo, *O fogo dos deuses: Uma história da energia nuclear; Pandora 600 a.C.–1970* (Rio de Janeiro: Contraponto, 2006); Carlo Patti, "Origins of the Brazilian Nuclear Programme"; Matias Spektor, "The Evolution of Brazil's Nuclear Intentions," *Nonproliferation Review* 23.5–6 (2016): 635–52, https://doi.org/10.1080/10736700.2017.1345518; and Renata H. Dalaqua, "'We will not make the bomb because we do not want to make the bomb': Understanding the technopolitical regime that drives the Brazilian nuclear program," *Nonproliferation Review* 26.3–4 (2019): 231–49, https:/doi.org/10.1080/10736700.2019.1630094. It is important to note that a growing number of think-tank analyses and theoretical works relied heavily on historical accounts based on primary sources. See, e.g., Togzhan Kassenova, *Brazil's Nuclear Kaleidoscope: An Evolving Identity* (Washington, DC: Carnegie Endowment for International Peace, 2014); and Alexandre Debs and Nuno Monteiro, *Nuclear Politics: The Strategic Causes of Proliferation* (New York: Cambridge University Press, 2017), 88–115.

39. Etel Solingen, *Industrial Policy, Technology, and International Bargaining: Designing Nuclear Industries in Argentina and Brazil* (Stanford, CA: Stanford University Press, 1994).

40. On Brazil's nuclear weapons ambitions, see Leonard S. Spector, *The New Nuclear Nations: The Spread of Nuclear Weapons* (New York: Vintage Books, 1985); Tania Malheiros, *Brasil a bomba oculta* (Rio de Janeiro: Gryphus, 1993); and Jean Krasno, "Non-proliferation: Brazil's Secret Nuclear Program," *Orbis: A Journal of World Affairs* 38.3 (1994): 425–36, https://doi.org/10.1016/0030-4387(94)90006-X.

41. On the Argentine-Brazilian nuclear rivalry, see Norman Gall, "Atoms for Brazil, Dangers for All," *Foreign Policy* 23 (1976): 177–89, https://doi.org/10.2307/1147877. US and Brazilian intelligence analyses of a nuclear rivalry are cited in chapters 3, 4, and 5.

42. On the nuclear rapprochement between Brazil and Argentina, see Rodrigo Mallea, "La cuestión nuclear en la relación argentino-brasileña (1968–1984)" (master's thesis, IESP-UERJ, 2012); Julio Cesar Carasales, "The Argentine-Brazilian Nuclear Rapprochement," *Nonproliferation Review* 2 (1995): 39–48; Tatiana Coutto, "An International History of the Brazilian-Argentine Rapprochement," *International History Review* 36.2 (2014): 302–23, https://doi.org/10.1080/07075332.2013.864987; Sara Z. Kutchesfahani, *Politics and the Bomb: The Role of Experts in the Creation of Cooperative Nuclear Non-proliferation Agreements* (London: Routledge, 2014); and Charles A. Kupchan, *How Enemies Become Friends: The Sources of Stable Peace* (Princeton, NJ: Princeton University Press, 2010).

43. Many of those interviews are published in Carlo Patti, *O programa nuclear brasileiro: Uma história oral* (Rio de Janeiro: FGV, 2014).

Chapter 1 · Origins of Brazil's Nuclear Ambitions, 1946–1955

1. Patrick McGilligan, *Alfred Hitchcock—A Life in Darkness and Light* (London: John Wiley & Sons, 2003), 235.

2. "Establishment of a Commission to Deal with the Problems Raised by the Discovery of Atomic Energy," UNGA, 24 Jan. 1946, https://digitallibrary.un.org/record/209570?ln=en.

3. On the Indian case, see Itty Abraham, *The Making of the Indian Atomic Bomb: Science, Secrecy and the Postcolonial State* (London: Zed Books, 1998). On South Africa, see Anna-Mart Van Wyk, "Ally or Critic? The United States' Response to South African Nuclear Development, 1949–1980," *Cold War History* 7.2 (2007): 169–225, https://doi.org/10.1080/14682740701284124.

4. On the US nuclear nonproliferation policy at the beginning of the atomic age, see Barton J. Bernstein, "The Quest for Security: American Foreign Policy and International Control of Atomic Energy, 1942–1946," *Journal of American History* 60.4 (1974): 1003–44, https://doi.org/10.2307/1901011; and Shane J. Maddock, *Nuclear Apartheid: The Quest for Atomic Supremacy from World War II to the Present* (Chapel Hill: University of North Carolina Press, 2010), 47–80.

5. Gerson Moura, *O alinhamento sem recompensa: A política externa do governo Dutra* (Rio de Janeiro: FGV/CPDOC, 1990); Rubens Ricupero, *A diplomacia na construção do Brasil, 1750–2016* (Rio de Janeiro: Versal, 2017), 367–96; Luiz Alberto de Vianna Moniz Bandeira, *Presença dos Estados Unidos no Brasil (Dois séculos de história)* (Rio de Janeiro: Civilização Brasileira, 1973), 354–453.

6. Jonathan E. Helmreich, *Gathering Rare Ores: The Diplomacy of Uranium Acquisition, 1943–1945* (Princeton, NJ: Princeton University Press, 1986), 49–57.

7. Guilherme Camargo, *O fogo dos deuses: Uma história da energia nuclear; Pandora 600 a.C.–1970* (Rio de Janeiro: Contraponto, 2007), 173.

8. *Foreign Relations of the United States, 1947*, vol. 1, *General, The United Nations*, ed. Ralph E. Goodwin, Neal H. Petersen, Marvin W. Kranz, and William Slany (Washington, DC: GPO, 1973), doc. 311, https://history.state.gov/historicaldocuments/frus1947v01/d311.

9. Camargo, *O fogo dos deuses*, 143–46.

10. On the UNAEC negotiations, see David W. Kearn Jr., "The Baruch Plan and the Quest for Atomic Disarmament," *Diplomacy & Statecraft* 21.1 (2010): 41–67, https:/doi.org/10.1080/09592290903577742; S. Schratstetter, "'Loquacious . . . and pointless as ever?' Britain, the United States and the United Nations Negotiations on International Control of Nuclear Energy 1945–48," *Contemporary British History* 16.4 (2002): 87–108, https:/doi.org/10.1080/713999478; Larry G. Gerber, "The Baruch Plan and the Origins of the Cold War," *Diplomatic History* 6.4 (1982): 69–96, https:/doi.org/10.111/j.1467-7709.1982.tb00792.x; Harald Müller, David Fischer, and Wolfgang Kötter, *Nuclear Non-Proliferation and Global Order* (New York: SIPRI / Oxford University Press, 1994), 15; and William Walker, *A Perpetual Menace: Nuclear Weapons and International Order* (London: Routledge, 2012), 45–46.

11. David Holloway. *Stalin and the Bomb: The Soviet Union and Atomic Energy, 1939–56* (New Haven, CT: Yale University Press, 1994), 161–66.

12. Richard G. Hewlett and Oscar E. Anderson Jr., *A History of the United States Atomic Energy Commission*, vol. 1, *The New World, 1939–1946* (University Park: Pennsylvania State University, 1962), 615–16; Camargo, *O fogo dos deuses*, 163; Maria Regina Soares de Lima, *The Political Economy of Brazilian Foreign Policy: Nuclear Energy, Trade, and Itaipu* (Brasília: FUNAG, 2013), 102–3.

13. *Foreign Relations of the United States, 1947*, vol. 1, *General, The United Nations*, doc. 344, https://history.state.gov/historicaldocuments/frus1947v01/d344; Álvaro Alberto (Brazilian delegate to UNAEC) to Ambassador João Carlos Muniz (Brazilian representative at the UN), 25 Nov. 1947, Confidential, Álvaro Alberto personal archive, University of São Paulo (hereafter AA/USP).

14. *Foreign Relations of the United States, 1947*, vol. 1, *General, The United Nations*, doc. 344.

15. *Foreign Relations of the United States, 1947*, vol. 1, *General, The United Nations*, doc. 344.

16. *Foreign Relations of the United States, 1947*, vol. 1, *General, The United Nations*, doc. 344.

17. On the support received by the CSN, see "Ata da décima sessão do Conselho de Segurança Nacional," 27 Aug. 1947, Secret, CSN, BR DFANBSB N8.0.ATA.1/10, f.31v-34v, Arquivo Nacional, Brasília (hereafter AN-B).

18. *Foreign Relations of the United States, 1947*, vol. 1, *General, The United Nations*, doc. 344. A copy of a document sent by Marshall to Frederick Osborne—George Marshall to Osborne, 8 Sept. 1947, Secret—is in AA/USP.

19. On the position at the 1948 UNGA First Committee, see United Nations, *The United Nations and Disarmament, 1945–1970* (New York, 1970), 22.

20. "Comissão de Energia Atômica das Nações Unidas," Alberto to Muniz, 25 Nov. 1947, Confidential, AA/USP.

21. *Foreign Relations of the United States, 1947*, vol. 1, *General, The United Nations*, doc. 433, https://history.state.gov/historicaldocuments/frus1947v01/d433.

22. For Marshall's instruction, see *Foreign Relations of the United States, 1948*, vol. 1, pt. 2, *General, The United Nations*, ed. Neal H. Petersen, Ralph E. Goodwin, Marvin W. Kranz, and William Slany (Washington, DC: GPO, 1976), doc. 86, https://history.state.gov/historicaldocuments/frus1948v01p2/d86. On Raul Fernandes's agreement not to export fissionable material to other foreign powers, see *Foreign Relations of the United States, 1948*, vol. 1, pt. 2, *General, The United Nations*, doc. 88, https://history.state.gov/historicaldocuments/frus1948v01p2/d88; doc. 89, https://history.state.gov/historicaldocuments/frus1948v01p2/d89; and doc. 105, https://history.state.gov/historicaldocuments/frus1948v01p2/d105.

23. *Foreign Relations of the United States, 1949*, vol. 1, *National Security Affairs, Foreign Economic Policy*, ed. Neal H. Petersen, Ralph E. Goodwin, William Slany, and Marvin W. Kranz (Washington, DC: GPO, 1976), doc. 167, https://history.state.gov/historicaldocuments/frus1949v01/d167.

24. *Foreign Relations of the United States, 1950*, vol. 1, *National Security Affairs, Foreign Economic Policy*, ed. Neal H. Petersen, John P. Glennon, David W. Mabon, Ralph R. Goodwin, and William Slany (Washington, DC: GPO, 1977), doc. 174, https://history.state.gov/historicaldocuments/frus1950v01/d174; AmEmbassy Rio to SecState, 30 Mar. 1950, Telegram 508, Top Secret, Box 2, Brazil, RG 84, Records of the Foreign Service Posts of the State Department, Series: Brazil, US Embassy, Rio de Janeiro, Top Secret General Records, 1944–1955, National Archives and Records Administration (hereafter Brazil, 1944–55 NARA).

25. Alberto to Muniz, 25 Nov. 1947, Confidential, AA/USP.

26. Alberto to Obino (chief of staff), 6 Oct. 1949, Secret, AA/USP; R. Bennet (Thorium Ltd.) to J. Thomson (undersecretary of state), 7 Mar. 1950, AB 16 1015, Brazil 1950, The National Archives, Kew Gardens, UK.

27. Brazil's nuclear policy was initiated on 20 January 1947, when the CSN established the Commission of Studies and Control of Strategic Minerals. On Alberto's plan, see Alberto to Muniz, 25 Nov. 1947, Confidential, AA/USP. For an account of the nuclear policies adopted in Brazil from 1947 to 1953, see Aguinaldo Caiado de Castro to Getulio Vargas, 25 Nov. 1953, EM 771, Secret, Energia Atômica, Tomo 1, 1951/1953, Arquivo Histórico do Ministério das Relações Exteriores—Brasília (hereafter AHMRE-B); "Ata da décima sessão do Conselho de Segurança Nacional," 27 Aug. 1947, Secret, CSN, BR DFANBSB N8.o.ATA .1/10, f.31v-34v, AN-B.

28. On the evolution of the scientific sector in Brazil, see Shozo Motoyama, ed., *Prelúdio para uma história: Ciência e tecnologia no Brasil* (São Paulo: Edusp, 2004).

29. "Comissão Brasileira de Energia Nuclear," Apr. 1946, AA/USP. The commission also included J. A. Alves de Souza, José Carneiro Felipe, Luiz Cintra do Prado, and Joaquim da Costa Ribeiro. Shozo Motoyama and João Carlos Vitor Garcia, eds., *O Almirante e o novo Prometeu* (São Paulo: Editora da Universidade Estadual Paulista, Centro Interunidade de História da Ciência, 1996).

30. In April 1946 a private Dutch company, the Technisch Bureau S.K.F., of Rijswijk, offered to sell nuclear power plants to Brazil. Ramiro Saraiva Guerreiro to the Head of the Political Division, Memorandum, 2 Apr. 1946, 524.25, Diversos do Ministério, 136/4/10, Divisão Política, Informações e Relatórios. 1939–47, Arquivo Histórico do Ministério das Relações Exteriores—Rio de Janeiro. I thank Alexandre L. Moreli Rocha for sharing this document. Furthermore, the French National Center of Scientific Research (Centre National de Recherche Scientifique) applied for a patent in Brazil for a device "purporting to utilize the energy of a chain reaction from the fission of uranium." AmEmbassy Rio to SecState, 30 Jan. 1947, Dispatch 1576, Top Secret, Box 1, 1944–1950, Entry Number UD 2134, Brazil, 1944–55 NARA.

31. Law 1310, of 15 January 1951, established the CNPq, which became operative on 17 April 1951, after the beginning of Vargas's presidency. Leandro Batista Pereira, "Vitória na derrota: Álvaro Alberto e as origens da política nuclear brasileira" (master's thesis, FGV, 2013), 55.

32. Brazilian nuclear scientists, along with other members of the CNPq, visited research centers in Canada and the United States and in France, Italy, West Germany, Great Britain, Belgium, Holland, Sweden, and Norway. There is a detailed but undated report on this mission in AA/USP.

33. Alberto to Vargas, 10 Nov. 1951, EM 723, Confidential, AA/USP.

34. On the 1951 amendment to the US Atomic Energy Act, see Byron S. Miller, "Atomic Energy Act: Second Stage," *Bulletin of the Atomic Scientists* 8.1 (1952): 14.

35. Miller, "Atomic Energy Act: Second Stage," 14.

36. Despite personal meetings between Alberto and the USAEC chairman, Lewis L. Strauss, in March and August 1953, the US government was not able to transfer research reactors and nuclear power plants to Brazil due to the limitations imposed by US legislation on atomic energy. Lewis Strauss to Sílvio Ribeiro de Carvalho, 24 Sept. 1953, Emb. Washington/1122/592.01(22)/1953/Anexo Único, Tomo 1, AHMRE-B.

37. Alberto to Vargas, 30 Oct. 1952, AA/USP.

38. On the Canadian-Brazilian talks, see "Reunião entre C. J. Mackenzie (Conselho Nacional de Pesquisa do Canadá), Álvaro Alberto e Orlando Rangel (CNPq)," 15 Oct. 1951, Confidential, AA/USP.

39. *Foreign Relations of the United States, 1951,* vol. 1, *National Security Affairs, Foreign Economic Policy,* ed. Neal H. Petersen, Harriet D. Schwar, Carl N. Raether, John A. Bernbaum, and Ralph R. Goodwin (Washington, DC: GPO, 1979), doc. 275, https://history.state.gov/historicaldocuments/frus1951v01/d275.

40. Alberto to Vargas, 30 Oct. 1952, AA/USP.

41. Alberto to Vargas, 30 Oct. 1952, AA/USP.

42. On Paul Harteck, see Mark Walker, *Nazi Science: Myth, Truth, and the German Atomic Bomb* (New York: Plenum Press, 1995), 208, 236.

43. In 1943, uranium enrichment to 5 percent was achieved in German laboratories. However, technical difficulties hindered large-scale production. Klaus Hentschel and Ann M. Hentschel, eds., *Physics and National Socialism: An Anthology of Primary Sources* (Stuttgart: Birkhäuser, 2011), appendix F, xxix. On the American reasons for dropping the research on ultracentrifuge enrichment method during the Second World War, see Arthur Compton to Alberto, 10 Dec. 1958, AA/USP.

44. Harteck to Alberto, 18 Aug. 1952, AA/USP.

45. Harteck to Alberto, 27 Feb. 1953, AA/USP. Two ultracentrifuges were installed at the University of Hamburg in 1948. AmEmbassy Bonn to SecState, 23 June 1954, Telegram 4023, Confidential, Box 2, Brazil, 1944–55 NARA.

46. While the CNPq chairman was visiting France, the French ambassador to Rio de Janeiro, Gilbert Arvengas, expressed in a dispatch to the Quai d'Orsay his skepticism about Alberto's optimism regarding the future Brazilian capability to develop a nuclear program given the limitations on the equipment to be acquired and the doubts about the presence of uranium in Brazil. French Embassy (hereafter FrEmbassy) Rio to Paris, 16 July 1953, Dispatch 708/AM, Amérique 1952–1963, Brésil—56—Brésil—Carton 15-6-2—Questions Atomique—1952–1963 (hereafter 1952–1963/56/15-6-2), Archive du Ministère des Affaires Étrangères (hereafter AMAE-F).

47. Brazilian Embassy (hereafter BrazEmbassy) Paris to CNPq, 17 July 1953, Cable 140/524.6, Secret, AA/USP.

48. "Aplicação da energia atômica no Brasil," CNPq, 1956, AA/USP.

49. Robert Terrill to R. Gordon Arneson, 31 Mar. 1953, Secret cable, 21.10 Country File: Brazil a. General, 1953–54, Box 79, Special Assistant to the Secretary for Energy and Outer Space, Records Relating to Atomic Energy Matters, Finding Aid A1, RG 59, NARA (hereafter S/AE). I thank Mara Drogan for sharing several documents of this collection.

50. Alberto to Vargas, 9 Nov. 1951, EM 722, Confidential, AA/USP.

51. "Água pesada da Noruega para as pesquisas nucleares do Brasil," *O Globo,* 9 Feb. 1953, Night Edition, 11.

52. Harteck to Alberto, 18 Aug. 1952, AA/USP; "Conversações com o Professor J. Robert Oppenheimer nos Estados Unidos da América," Aug. 1953, Confidential, AA/USP.

53. Arneson to Herschel V. Johnson, 15 Mar. 1953, Secret cable, 21.10 Country File: Brazil a. General, 1953–54, Box 79, S/AE; L. Denivelle (CEA) to J. Costa Riberio (CNPq scientific director), 19 Feb. 1953, personal letter, AA/USP.

54. After visiting France, Alberto went to Italy, where he signed an agreement for the exchange of researchers and scholars with the Italian National Research Council. Alberto to Vicente Rao (Brazilian minister of foreign affairs), 28 Sept. 1953, Secret, 1989.524.26 (96), Tomo 1, AHMRE-B. On the need to have several partners, see Alberto to Vargas (document approved by Vargas), 10 Nov. 1951, EM 723-1-1951, Confidential, AA/USP.

55. Alberto to Vargas (document approved by Vargas), 10 Nov. 1951, EM 723-1-1951, Confidential, AA/USP. The same document reports that the US general Walsh, who was responsible for the emigration of German scientists, supported the idea since Werner Heisenberg and his colleagues in that period could "be seduced by Soviet proposals."

56. On the episode, see Ruth Stanley, "German-speaking Armaments Engineers in Argentina and Brazil, 1947–1963," in *Revisiting the National Socialist Legacy: Coming to Terms with Forced Labor, Expropriation, Compensation, and Restitution,* ed. Oliver Rathkolb (Innsbruck: Studien Verlag, 2002), 213; and Diego Hurtado, *El sueño de la Argentina atómica: Política, tecnología nuclear y desarrollo nacional (1945–2006)* (Buenos Aires: Edhasa, 2014), 46–47.

57. Stanley, "German-speaking Armaments Engineers," 214.

58. Alberto to Vargas, 20 Nov. 1951, EM 737, Confidential, AA/USP.

59. Confirming the secrecy of the operation, the archive of Brazil's Foreign Ministry does not possess documents on Brazilian-German cooperation during the 1950s. This gap is also confirmed by a Brazilian diplomatic record. João Batista Pinheiro to the Secretary-General, 4 Jan. 1955, Memorandum, N. 4, Secret, Energia Atômica, Tomo 2, 1951/1953, AHMRE-B.

60. W. Mitchell Carse (British general consul in São Paulo) to G. H. Thompson (British ambassador to Rio de Janeiro), 13 June 1952, AB 16 1079, "Work on Atomic Energy in Countries other than UK, USA and Canada," The National Archive, Kew Gardens, UK.

61. Carse to Thompson, 18 June 1952, AB 16 1079, The National Archive, Kew Gardens, UK.

62. Carse to Thompson, 18 June 1952, AB 16 1079, The National Archive, Kew Gardens, UK.

63. Karl Friedrich Bonhoeffer to Alberto, 21 Aug. 1952, AA/USP.

64. Alberto to Caiado de Castro, 30 June 1952, EM 639/1952-2, AA/USP.

65. Caiado de Castro to Vargas (with Vargas's approval), 25 Nov. 1953, EM 772, Secret, AA/USP.

66. Major Wener Hjamar Gross to Alberto, 25 Dec. 1953, CNPq internal document, Secret, AA/USP.

67. Oppenheimer visited Brazil for several weeks in June and July 1953. On 18 August 1953 Alberto met him in the United States. Asked to reveal the secrets on how to produce an atomic device, Oppenheimer steadfastly refused to provide any details. "Conversações com o professor J. Robert Oppenheimer nos Estados Unidos da América," Aug. 1953, Confidential, AA/USP.

68. On the possible production of fissile material using West German technologies, see Alexander Glaser, "Characteristics of the Gas Centrifuge for Uranium Enrichment and Their Relevance for Nuclear Weapon Proliferation," *Science and Global Security* 16.1–2 (2008): 8, 17, https://doi.org/10.1080/08929880802335998.

69. R. Scott Kemp, "Nuclear Proliferation with Particle Accelerators," *Science and Global Security* 13.3 (2005): 184, https://doi.org/10.1080/08929880500357708.

70. Alberto to Walther Moreira Salles (Brazilian ambassador in the United States), 25 Mar. 1953, EM 29/53, Secret, AA/USP.

71. Harald Müller and Andreas Schmidt, "The Little-Known Story of Deproliferation: Why States Give Up Nuclear Weapons Activities," in *Forecasting Nuclear Proliferation in the 21st Century,* ed. William C. Potter with Gaukar Mukhatzhanova, vol. 1, *The Role of Theory* (Stanford, CA: Stanford University Press, 2010), 132.

72. Orlando Rangel, "Notas sobre a bomba atômica," 20 Aug. 1945, AA/USP.

73. Although in that period the two countries were trying to forge an alliance, revising the 1915 Argentine-Brazilian-Chilean (ABC) Pact of 1915, Brazil's program could represent a response to the Argentinian one, whose director in 1951 publicly announced having mastered the nuclear fusion process in a laboratory environment. But the announcement was a bluff: Peron's nuclear supposedly successful project was a failure. Jacques E. C. Hymans, *Achieving Nuclear Ambitions: Scientists, Politicians, and Proliferation* (New York: Cambridge University Press, 2012), 222–23. On the initial phase of the Argentine program, see Mario A. J. Mariscotti, *El secreto atómico de Huemul: Crónica del origen de la energía atómica en Argentina* (Carapachay: Lenguaje Claro Editora, 2016).

74. Wilhelm Groth was supposed to receive three Brazilian chemists in Bonn in March 1954. According to the contract between the CNPq and Groth, the ultracentrifuges were to be built in German laboratories and assembled later in Brazil by Groth and Konrad Beyerle, who were supposed to spend one year in a laboratory in Petrópolis training Brazilian scientists. Alberto to Groth, 20 Mar. 1954, Confidential, 139/1954-2, AA/USP.

75. Beyerle to Alberto, 16 May 1961, AA/USP.

76. Alberto to Bernard Baruch, 30 June 1954, Cable 866, AA/USP; "Comissão Parlamentar de Inquérito para Proceder a Investigações sobre o Problema da Energia Atômica no Brasil—Relatório," 1956, AA/USP, 40–45. On the meeting between Conant and Alberto, see William Burr, "The 'Labors of Atlas, Sisyphus, or Hercules'? US Gas-Centrifuge Policy and Diplomacy, 1954–60," *International History Review* 37.3 (2015): 435, https://doi.org/10.1080/07075332.2014.918557.

77. AmEmbassy Bonn to SecState, 23 June 1954, Telegram 4023, Confidential, Box 2, Brazil, 1944–55 NARA.

78. Odette de Carvalho e Souza (head of the Division of Political and Cultural Affairs) to José Carlos de Macedo Soares (foreign minister), 19 July 1956, Doc. 7, Secret, Tomo 2, AHMRE-B.

79. On Alberto's meetings with Conant and Lewis Strauss, see Álvaro Rocha Filho and João Carlos Vítor Garcia, eds., *Renato Archer: Energia Atômica, Soberania E Desenvolvimento: Depoimento* (Rio de Janeiro: Contraponto, 2006), 74–75.

80. Rocha Filho and Garcia, *Renato Archer*, 76.

81. Rocha Filho and Garcia, *Renato Archer*, 76.

82. Terrill to Gerard C. Smith, 7 June 1954, Top Secret, 21.10 Country File: Brazil a. General, 1953–54, Box 79, S/AE; Terrill to Smith, 11 June 1954, Top Secret, Box 2, Brazil, 1944–55 NARA; Smith to Terrill, 25 June 1954, Top Secret, Box 2, Brazil, 1944–55 NARA.

83. Burr, "'Labors of Atlas, Sisyphus, or Hercules'?," 432.

84. Smith to Terrill, 12 Oct. 1954, Confidential, 21.10 Country File: Brazil a. General, 1953–54, Box 79, S/AE.

85. Burr, "'Labors of Atlas, Sisyphus, or Hercules'?," 432.

86. US High Commissioner Bonn to SecState, 2 Dec. 1954, Dispatch 1176, RG 59, Central Decimal Files 1950–1954, 862A.19/12-254, Digital National Security Archive (hereafter DNSA).

87. "Resposta dada ao deputado Aliomar Bareiro pela Casa Militar no final de novembro de 1954," 1954-2, Secret, AA/USP.

88. "Resposta dada ao deputado Aliomar Bareiro pela Casa Militar no final de novembro de 1954," 1954-2, Secret, AA/USP.

89. Chief Minister of the Military Cabinet to the President of the Chamber of Deputies, 24 July 1956, Ofício n°0215/Gab./81Renato Archer personal archive, FGV/CPDOC, DF 1956.02.10-XVI-A10.

90. Chief Minister of the Military Cabinet to the President of the Chamber of Deputies, 24 July 1956, Ofício n°0215/Gab./81Renato Archer personal archive, FGV/CPDOC, DF 1956.02. 10-XVI-A10.

91. Smith to Terrill, 12 Oct. 1954, Confidential, 21.10 Country File: Brazil a. General, 1953–54, Box 79, S/AE.

92. On the US-Brazilian negotiations from 1947 to 1953, see Alberto to Vargas, 5 Oct. 1953, EM 29-1953-2, AA/USP. On the new Brazilian nuclear policy approved by Brazil's president Café Filho, see Távora to Café Filho, 5 Apr. 1955, N.98, Secret, Tomo 2, AHMRE-B.

93. Terrill to Smith, 10 Dec. 1954, 12G Power and Research Reactors, 6, Reactors (Contribution of Aid to Other Countries) 1954, S/AE; Apud Mara Drogan, "Atoms for Peace: US Foreign Policy and the Globalization of Nuclear Technology, 1953–1960" (PhD diss., SUNY-Albany, 2011), 225.

94. Terrill to Smith, 5 July 1955, 21.10 Country File: Brazil m. d. General 1955–56, S/AE.; Drogan, "Atoms for Peace," 228.

95. Terrill to Arneson, 4 Mar. 1953, Confidential, 21.10 Country File: Brazil a. General, 1953–54, Box 79, S/AE.

96. Terrill to Arneson, 26 Feb. 1953, Restricted, 21.10 Country File: Brazil a. General, 1953–54, Box 79, S/AE. When the US government began to discuss Alberto's "Americanism," at least three different opinions were expressed. The US ambassador to Brazil, Johnson, considered Alberto an ultranationalist, while the USAEC chairman, Dean, declared the opposite, that he was pro-American. Terrill took an entirely different position and noted a latent anti-American attitude on the part of Alberto. John A. Hall to Arneson, 9 Feb. 1953, Memorandum, Confidential, 21.10 Country File: Brazil a. General, 1953–54, Box 79, S/AE.

97. Drogan, "Atoms for Peace," 226.

98. Richard G. Hewlett and Jack M. Holl, *Atoms for Peace and War: Eisenhower and the Atomic Energy Commission, 1953–1961* (Berkeley and Los Angeles: University of California Press, 1989), 245.

99. Raul Fernandes (Brazilian minister of foreign relations) to James Clement Dunn (US ambassador to Brazil), 3 Aug. 1955, DE/DAI/524.26, Secret, Tomo 2, AHMRE-B. Brazil's president, Café Filho, immediately approved the exchange of notes. Bina Machado (chief minister of the Military Cabinet) to Café Filho, 2 Aug. 1955, EM 286, Secret, Tomo 2, AHMRE-B.

100. Comissão de Energia Atômica to BrazEmbassy Washington, 13 May 1955, Portaria 46, Reserved Dec/De/Dpo, Secret, 2085, Tomo 2, AHMRE-B. On the first attempts to negotiate the transfer of a nuclear research reactor, see Fernandes to Juarez Távora, 22 Mar. 1955, G/DE/524.26, Secret, Tomo 2, AHMRE-B.

101. Heitor Grillo (temporary chairman of the CNPq) to Café Filho, 30 July 1955, EM 286, Secret, Tomo 2, AHMRE-B; Bina Machado to Café Filho, 2 Aug. 1955, EM 286, Secret, Tomo 2, AHMRE-B.

102. French General Consulate São Paulo to FrEmbassy Rio, 29 Feb. 1956, Dispatch 41, 1952–1963/56/15-6-2, AMAE-F.

103. Grillo to Café Filho, 30 July 1955, EM 286, Secret, Energia Atômica, Tomo 2, 1951/1953, AHMRE-B; Bina Machado to Café Filho, 2 Aug. 1955, EM 286, Secret, Tomo 2, AHMRE-B; FrEmbassy Rio to Paris, 7 June 1955, Dispatch 498, 1952–1963/56/15-6-2, AMAE-F.

Chapter 2 · *Brazil a Promoter of Nonproliferation Norms?, 1955–1964*

1. For an overview of Kubitschek's foreign policy, see Rubens Ricupero, *A diplomacia na construção do Brasil, 1750–2016* (Rio de Janeiro: Versal, 2017), 396–407; Amado Luiz Cervo and Clodoaldo Bueno, *História da política exterior do Brasil* (Brasília: Editora Universidade de Brasilia, 2002); and Alexandra de Mello Silva, *A política externa de JK: A Operação Pan-Americana* (Rio de Janeiro: FGV/CPDOC, 1992).

2. Ricupero, *A diplomacia na construção do Brasil*, 407.

3. On the inclusion of nuclear energy in the Plano de Metas, see Guilherme Camargo, *O fogo dos deuses: Uma história da energia nuclear; Pandora 600 a.C.–1970* (Rio de Janeiro: Contraponto, 2006), 255–60; and Leandro Batista Pereira, "Vitória na derrota: Álvaro Alberto e as origens da política nuclear brasileira" (master's thesis, FGV, 2013), 117. On Kubitschek's developmentalism, see Catherine Sikkink, *Ideas and Institutions: Developmentalism in Brazil and Argentina* (Ithaca, NY: Cornell University Press, 1991).

4. "Lieferung von 3 Gaszentrifugen an den Nationalen Forschungerst," Bonn to FRG Embassy in Rio, 10 Jan. 1957, Deutsch-Brasilianische Zusammen Arbeit auf dem Atomgebiete und der Nuclearforschung, Vom 5-9-1951 Bis 30-5-1958, Bd. 1346, Politisches Archiv des Auswärtiges Amt (hereafter PA/AA).

5. Groth visited Brazil in November 1958 and gave a lecture on the development of atomic energy in Germany and on the installation of the centrifuges in Brazil. See CNPq to FRG Embassy Rio, 28 Dec. 1958, Atomfragen und kernenergie—Versorgung Hier: Brasilien, Vom 1-12-1951 Bis 3-11-1961 (hereafter Bd. 849), PA/AA.

6. CNPq to FRG Embassy Rio, 28 Dec. 1958, Bd. 849, PA/AA.

7. Francis J. Gavin, "Nuclear Proliferation and Non-proliferation During the Cold War," in *The Cambridge History of the Cold War*, ed. Melvyn P. Leffler and Odd Arne Westad, vol. 2, *Crisis and Détente* (Cambridge: Cambridge University Press, 2010), 400.

8. The synchrocyclotron, not used in Rio, was moved to Porto Alegre and used for research purposes by the Federal University of Rio Grande do Sul. See Ana Maria Ribeiro De Andrade and R. P. A. Muniz, "The Quest for the Brazilian Synchrocyclotron," *Historical Studies in the Physical and Biological Sciences* 36.2 (2006): 311–27.

9. Despite the centrality of nuclear energy in the Plano de Metas, Kubitschek's government abandoned the atomic plans in 1960. "A Mensagem Presidencial," *Jornal do Brasil*, 16 Mar. 1960, 4.

10. BrazEmbassy Washington to Itamaraty, 28 Feb. 1956, Telegram 81, Confidential, G/DPo/DE/624.26(04), Folder: "Acordo internacional da energia nuclear, ONU, De agosto de 1955 a agosto de 1956" (hereafter AIEN-1955/6), AHMRE-B.

11. Terrill to Smith, 14 Oct. 1955, Confidential cable, Official—Informal, 21.10 Country File: Brazil a. Agreements, 1955–56, Part 1 of 2, S/AE.

12. Cecil B. Lyon (Bureau of Inter-American Affairs) to Smith, 6 Dec. 1955, Memorandum, Secret, 21.10 Country File: Brazil a. Agreements, 1955–56, Part 1 of 2, S/AE. See also Mara Drogan, "Atoms for Peace: US Foreign Policy and the Globalization of Nuclear Technology, 1953–1960" (PhD diss., SUNY-Albany, 2011), 233.

13. Terrill to Hall, 14 Dec. 1955, Memorandum, Secret, 21.10 Country File: Brazil a. Agreements, 1955–56, Part 1 of 2, S/AE.

14. Terrill to Hall, 14 Dec. 1955, Memorandum, Secret, 21.10 Country File: Brazil a. Agreements, 1955–56, Part 1 of 2, S/AE; Itamaraty to BrazEmbassy Washington, 1 Mar. 1956, Telegram 55, Confidential, DE/Dpo/624.26 (04), AIEN-1955/6, AHMRE-B. In his reply to Itamaraty, Muniz suggested starting parallel talks with the USAEC. BrazEmbassy Washington to Itamaraty, 1 Mar. 1956, Telegram 87, Confidential, DE/Dpo/624.26 (04), AIEN-1955/6, AHMRE-B.

15. BrazEmbassy Washington to Itamaraty, 1 Mar. 1956, Telegram 88, Confidential, DE/Dpo/624.26 (04), AIEN-1955/6, AHMRE-B.

16. "Discussion with Brazilians regarding power reactor agreement for cooperation," 4 Feb. 1956, Memorandum, USAEC, 21.10 Country File: Brazil a. Agreements, 1955–56, Part 1 of 2, S/AE.

17. "Discussion with Brazilians regarding power reactor agreement for cooperation," 4 Feb. 1956, Memorandum, USAEC, 21.10 Country File: Brazil a. Agreements, 1955–56, Part 1 of 2, S/AE.

18. "Announcement by Willard F. Libby, Acting Chairman of the US Atomic Energy Commission, and João Carlos Muniz, Brazilian Ambassador to the United States," 17 Apr. 1956, 21.10 Country File: Brazil a. Agreements, 1955–56, Part 1 of 2, S/AE; H. W. Belgooyan (executive vice president, American & Foreign Power Company) to Henry F. Holland (assistant secretary of state for inter-American affairs), 14 May 1956, 21.10 Country File: Brazil a. Agreements, 1955–56, Part 1 of 2, S/AE.

19. Drogan, "Atoms for Peace," 237–38.

20. The Plano de Metas proposed the construction of two nuclear power plants. The first nuclear power plant, sponsored by the federal government, was supposed to be built by the American & Foreign Power Company in Mambucaba, close to Rio de Janeiro. The second one, financed by the state of São Paulo, was to be built close to the Jurumirim Dam by the Glenn Martin Company for the Paulista Nuclear Energy Company (Companhia Paulista de Energia Nuclear, or COPEN). On the second plant, see the detailed "Nuclear Power Plant in Jurumirim—State of São Paulo. Preliminary Progress Report," 21 July 1957, 21.10 Country File: Brazil a. Agreements, 1955–56, Part 1 of 2, S/AE. On the Mambucaba project, see Camargo, *O fogo dos deuses*, 258–60.

21. "Secretary's Visit to Brazil. August 5–8, 1958. Status of Atomic Energy Power Reactor Project (Position Paper)," 22 July 1958, 21.10 Country File: Brazil a. Agreements, 1955–56, Part 1 of 2, S/AE.

22. "Secretary's Visit to Brazil. August 5–8, 1958. Status of Atomic Energy Power Reactor Project (Position Paper)," 22 July 1958, 21.10 Country File: Brazil a. Agreements, 1955–56, Part 1 of 2, S/AE.

23. "Ação do Brasil no CIRP e na Comissão Preparatória da Agência Internacional de Energia Atômica: Projeto sobre o centro regional de treinamento," BrazEmbassy Washington to Itamaraty, 12 Feb. 1957, Confidential, Folder: "Acordo internacional da energia nuclear. ONU. 1956–8" (hereafter AIEN-1956/8), AHMRE-B; French General Consulate São Paulo to Paris, 30 Jan. 1958, Dispatch 39, 1952–1963/56/15-6-2, AMAE-F.

24. FrEmbassy Rio to Paris, 29 July 1959, Dispatch 684, 1952–1963/56/15-6-2, AMAE-F.

25. FrEmbassy Rio to Paris, 12 Apr. 1958, Dispatch 286/AM, 1952–1963/56/15-6-2, AMAE-F. On the criticism from the nationalist congressmen, see FrEmbassy Rio to Paris, 29 July 1959, Dispatch 684/SGL/CQA,1952–1963/56/15-6-2, AMAE-F.

26. FrEmbassy Rio to Paris, 30 Apr. 1958, Dispatch 83/SGL/CQA, 1952–1963/56 /15-6-2, AMAE-F.

27. Camargo, *O fogo dos deuses*, 260–61.

28. FrEmbassy Rio to Paris, 24 Apr. 1960, Dispatch 460/SGL/CQA, 1952–1963/56 /15-6-2, AMAE-F.

29. Cervo and Bueno, *História da política exterior do Brasil*, 322.

30. Diego Hurtado, *El sueño de Argentina atómica: Política, tecnología nuclear y desarollo nacional (1945–2006)* (Buenos Aires: Edhasa, 2014), 97–98.

31. Alfred C. Stepan, *The Military in Politics: Changing Patterns in Brazil* (Princeton, NJ: Princeton University Press, 1971), 93.

32. Camargo, *O fogo dos deuses*, 263.

33. "Companies qualified to Bid on Brazil's South Central Nuclear Power Plant," AmEmbassy Rio to SecState, 23 Jan. 1962, Air Pouch, 2. Aid and Assistance Programs. 1. Equipment Grants Brazil, 1959–62, S/AE. The companies were selected by a working group headed by Damy and composed of nuclear engineers representing the Institute of Atomic Energy of the University of São Paulo, the Federal University of Minas Gerais, the School of Engineering of the University of Brazil (later Federal University of Rio de Janeiro), the Institute of Naval Research, and the Institute of Military Engineering. The companies qualified to bid were the US companies General Atomics, International General Electric Company, and Westinghouse Electric International Company; the British companies English Electric Babcock, Wilcox and Taylor Atomic Power Construction Company, United Power Company, and Nuclear Power Group; Groupement de Constructeurs Français de Centrales Nucleaires of France; and Agip Nucleare of Italy. On the Brazilian nuclear project, see also FrEmbassy Rio to Paris, 14 Aug. 1961, Dispatch 4012, 1952–1963/56/15-6-2, AMAE-F.

34. Buarque Netto (first secretary) to Sérgio Corrêa da Costa (secretary-general of Brazil's Foreign Ministry), 30 Aug. 1967, Memorandum, Secret, 592.30 (85), Diretrizes de Energia Nuclear 1966, AHMRE-B.

35. Marcelo Damy to Gabriel de Rezende Passos, 27 Feb. 1962, CNEN 71-62, Confidential, Energia Nuclear e Desnuclearização na América Latina 1962–1966, BR DFANBSB 2M.0.0.49, v.1, Fundo Estado Maior das Forças Armadas (hereafter EMFA), AN-B.

36. Presidência da República, Casa Civil, Subchefia para Assuntos Civis, Lei n. 4118, de 27 de agosto de 1962, http://www.planalto.gov.br/ccivil_03/Leis/L4118.htm.

37. David Fischer, *History of the International Atomic Energy Agency: The First Forty Years* (Vienna: IAEA, 1997), 30.

38. BrazEmbassy Washington to Itamaraty, 25 Aug. 1955, Telegram 688, Confidential, AIEN-1955/6, AHMRE-B.

39. Edmundo Barbosa da Silva (head of the Economic Division) to the Minister, 29 Sept. 1955, DE/624.26(04), Confidential, Urgent, AIEN-1955/6, AHMRE-B.

40. "Ante-Projeto do Estatuto da Repartição Internacional da Energia Atômica," BrazEmbassy Washington to Itamaraty, 10 Oct. 1955, Confidential, Dpo/624.26.14, AIEN-1955/6, AHMRE-B.

41. Fischer, *History of the International Atomic Energy Agency*; Brazilian Delegation to the United Nations (New York) to Itamaraty, 26 Aug. 1955, Telegram 526, Confidential, AIEN-1955/6, AHMRE-B.

42. BrazEmbassy Washington to Itamataty, 19 Oct. 1955, Telegram 4084, Confidential, AIEN-1955/6, AHMRE-B.

43. BrazEmbassy Washington to Itamataty, 19 Oct. 1955, Telegram 4084, Confidential, AIEN-1955/6, AHMRE-B.

44. In early December 1955 the UNGA approved the expansion of the eight-nation committee, which previously had discussed the IAEA draft statute, to include four new members: two developing countries, India and Brazil, and two socialist countries, the Soviet Union and Czechoslovakia.

45. BrazEmbassy Washington to Itamaraty, 9 Nov. 1955, Telegram 5282, Confidential, AIEN-1955/6, AHMRE-B. The agenda was confirmed in mid-January 1956. BrazEmbassy Washington to Itamaraty, 17 Jan. 1956, Telegram 393, Confidential, DPo/DE/624, AIEN-1955/6, AHMRE-B.

46. Itamaraty to BrazEmbassy Washington, 10 Feb. 1956, Memorandum, Confidential, DE/624.26 (04), AIEN-1955/6, AHMRE-B.

47. "Energia atômica: Criação de uma repartição internacional," BrazEmbassy Washington to Itamaraty, 21 Feb. 1956, C G/DE/DPo/, AIEN-1955/6, AHMRE-B.

48. BrazEmbassy Washington to Itamaraty, 22–23 Mar. 1956, Telegram 113, Confidential, DE/Dpo/624.26 (04), AIEN-1955/6, AHMRE-B.

49. BrazEmbassy Washington to Itamaraty, 15 Mar. 1956, Telegram 103, Confidential, DE/Dpo/624.26 (04), AIEN-1955/6, AHMRE-B; Itamaraty to BrazEmbassy Washington, 15 Mar. 1956, Telegram 73, Confidential, DE/Dpo/624.26 (04), AIEN-1955/6, AHMRE-B.

50. BrazEmbassy Washington to Itamaraty, 5 Apr. 1956, Telegram 145, Confidential, AIEN-1955/6, AHMRE-B.

51. José Carlos de Macedo Soares to Kubitschek, 24 Sept. 1956, Confidential, AIEN-1956/8, AHMRE-B.

52. The safeguards issue was a concern for the developing countries and for the Soviet Union. See Gabrielle Hecht, "Negotiating Global Nuclearities: Apartheid, Decolonization, and the Cold War in the Making of the IAEA," *Osiris* 21.1 (2006): 25–48; Elisabeth Roehrlich, "The Cold War, the Developing World, and the Creation of the International Atomic Energy Agency (IAEA), 1953–1957," *Cold War History* 16.2 (2016): 195–212, https://doi.org/10.1080/14682745.2015.1129607; and David Holloway, "The Soviet Union and the Creation of the International Atomic Energy Agency," *Cold War History* 16.2 (2016): 177–93, https://doi.org/10.1080/14682745.2015.1124265.

53. Macedo Soares to Kubitschek, 24 Sept. 1956, Confidential, AIEN-1956/8, AHMRE-B.

54. Carlos Alfredo Bernardes, "Comentários ao projeto de estatuto da Agência Internacional de Energia Atômica," n.d., AIEN-1956/8, AHMRE-B.

55. On the Swiss-French solution, see Bertrand Goldschmidt, "The Origins of the International Atomic Energy Agency," in *International Atomic Energy Authority: Personal Reflections* (Vienna: The Agency, 1997), 10–12. For the text of the statute, see IAEA, "Statute of the International Atomic Energy Agency," accessed 5 Apr. 2020, https://www.iaea.org/about/statute.

56. "Comissão Preparatória da Agencia Internacional de Energia Atômica," Brazilian delegation to the United Nations to the Foreign Minister, 9 Mar. 1957, Confidential, AIEN-1956/8, AHMRE-B.

57. BrazEmbassy Buenos Aires to Itamaraty, 30 Apr. 1957, Aide-mémoire, 331.663.80(oo)/1957/Anexo 1, Confidential, AIEN-1956/8, AHMRE-B. At first the Brazilian Foreign Ministry had discussed a possible trilateral rotation within the IAEA board of governors through the involvement of Mexico.

58. BrazEmbassy Buenos Aires to Itamaraty, 7 May 1957, Telegram 129, Confidential, AIEN-1956/8, AHMRE-B.

59. Preparatory Commission of the IAEA (New York) to Itamaraty, 13 May 1957, Telegram 13, Confidential, AIEN-1956/8, AHMRE-B.

60. "Presidência da Junta dos Governadores da Agência Internacional de Energia Atômica. Candidatura do Ministro Carlos Alfredo Bernardes," Itamaraty to the Brazilian Mission at the United Nations, 20 Aug. 1959, Confidential, AIEN-1956/8, AHMRE-B.

61. A/RES/1665 (XVI), of 4 December 1961, was the resolution on the Irish proposal that separated nonproliferation from other issues, with a Swedish addendum calling upon non-nuclear states to decide under what conditions they would abjure the deadly weapons. A/RES/1722 (XVI), of 20 December 1961, established the ENDC and its composition. The text of both 1961 UNGA resolutions is available at http://www.un.org/depts/dhl/resguide /r16.htm. The ENDC was composed of the following members: Brazil, Bulgaria, Burma, Canada, Czechoslovakia, Ethiopia, France, India, Italy, Mexico, Nigeria, Poland, Romania, the Soviet Union, Sweden, the United Arab Republic (Egypt), the United Kingdom, and the United States. On the ENDC, see Vojtech Mastny, "The Eighteen-Nation Committee, 1962–1969: Could It Have Done Better?" (paper, "Uncovering the Sources of Nuclear Behavior: Historical Dimensions of Nuclear Proliferation" conference, Zurich, 18–20 June 2010). For a Brazilian account, see "Notas taquigráficas da reunião do Conselho dos Ministros, realizada a 30 de março de 1962," Ernesto Geisel personal archive, FGV/CPDOC (hereafter EG), apr 1961.09.14.

62. Jânio Quadros, "Brazil's New Foreign Policy," *Foreign Affairs* 40.1 (1961): 19–27.

63. Paulo Wrobel, "A diplomacia nuclear brasileira: Não proliferação e o Tratado de Tlatelolco," *Contexto Internacional* 15.1 (1993): 31.

64. "Relatório de Afonso Arinos sobre as atividades da primeira parte dos trabalhos da ENDC," Del.Bras./Desarmamento/N°5/1962/SECRETO/2—Geneva (Afonso Arinos) to Minister San Tiago Dantas, 16 June 1962, Antônio Azeredo da Silveira personal archive, FGV/CPDOC (hereafter AAS), del 1966.01.27.

65. "Consideration of Africa as a Denuclearized Zone," 24 Nov. 1961, A/RES/1652 (XVI), http://daccess-ods.un.org/TMP/7531841.39728546.html. On the Brazilian support, see Conference of the Eighteen-Nation Committee on Disarmament (United Nations), "Final verbatim record of the Conference of the Eighteen-Nation Committee on Disarmament [Meeting 003]," Digital Collection of the Eighteen Nation Committee on Disarmament at the University of Michigan, 8, https://quod.lib.umich.edu/e/endc/4918260.0003.001/8 ?rgn=full+text;view=image.

66. Paulo Wrobel, *Brazil, the Non-proliferation Treaty and Latin America as a Nuclear Weapon–Free Zone* (Brasília: FUNAG, 2017), 219.

67. "Relatório . . . ENDC," 16 June 1962, AAS del 1966.01.27.

68. "Brasil—ENDC—Relatórios 1962–1966," AAS del 1966.01.27; Conference of the Eighteen-Nation Committee on Disarmament (United Nations), "Final verbatim record of the Conference of the Eighteen-Nation Committee on Disarmament [Meeting 003]," 8.

69. "Boletim da delegação do Brasil," 19–21 Mar. 1962, AAS del 1966.01.27.

70. Conference of the Eighteen-Nation Committee on Disarmament (United Nations), "Final verbatim record of the Conference of the Eighteen-Nation Committee on Disarmament [Meeting 008]," Digital Collection of the Eighteen Nation Committee on Disarmament at the University of Michigan, 34–36, https://quod.lib.umich .edu/e/endc/4918260.0008.001/34?rgn=full+text;view=image, and 7, https://quod .lib.umich.edu/e/endc/4918260.0003.001/7?rgn=full+text;view=image;q1 =reconversion.

71. "Notas . . . ," EG apr 1961.09.14.

72. James G. Hershberg, "The United States, Brazil and the Cuban Missile Crisis, 1962 (Part 2)," *Journal of Cold War Studies* 6.3 (2004): 5–67, https://doi.org/10.1162 /1520397041447364; Carlo Patti, "Nuclear Vulnerability, Security and Responsibility in the Crisis of 1962: A View from Brazil" (paper, Third BISA Annual Conference—Global Nuclear Order, Birmingham, Sept. 2015); Renata Keller, "The Latin American Missile Crisis," *Diplomatic History* 39.2 (2015): 195–222, https://doi.org/10.1093/dh/dht134; Carlos Federico Dominguez Ávila, "A crise dos mísseis soviéticos em Cuba (1962) um estudo das iniciativas brasileiras," *Vária História* 28.47 (2012): 361–89, https://doi.org/10.1590/S0104 -87752012000100017.

73. "Clarification of Recommended Role of Brazil in Pressuring Cuba to Accept Verification," 1 Nov. 1962, Top Secret, Cable State, DNSA.

74. "Brazil: Draft Resolution," ca. 8 Nov. 1962, Non-Classified, DNSA. The Brazilian delegation modified the text of the draft resolution after receiving American suggestions. "Disarmament: Brazilian Denuclearized Zone Resolution," 8 Nov. 1962, Confidential, Cable, New York City, DNSA.

75. "Cuban Position on Brazilian Denuclearization Proposal," Cuban Foreign Minister Raúl Roa to Cuban delegation to the United Nations, 11 Nov. 1962, DNSA. Another Caribbean republic also opposed the Brazilian proposal. "Complete Opposition to Denuclearized Zone Proposal Expressed by the Dominican Republic," 12 Nov. 1962, Confidential, Cable Santo Domingo, Excised Copy, 699, DNSA.

76. "Latin American Atom Free Zone," 30 Nov. 1962, Memorandum of Conversation, Secret, DNSA.

77. "Brazil Denuclearization Res.," 16 Nov. 1962, Confidential, Cable, New York City, Excised Copy, 1838, DNSA.

78. "México está contra bases nas Américas," *Jornal do Brasil* 16 Oct. 1962, 1.

79. Marcos Castrioto de Azambuja, interview by author, 20 Feb. 2014, Rio de Janeiro.

80. "Opposition to Brazilian Proposal for Denuclearization of Latin America among Uruguayan Military," 13 Nov. 1962, Secret Cable, Montevideo, DNSA.

81. Damy to João Goulart, 29 Nov. 1962, EM 7/62, Secret, Maço 692.30 (00), Energia Nuclear: Universo 1954/66, Caixa 47, Secret, AHMRE-B.

82. Damy to João Goulart, 29 Nov. 1962, EM 7/62, Secret, Maço 692.30 (00), Energia Nuclear: Universo 1954/66, Caixa 47, Secret, AHMRE-B.

83. Damy to João Goulart, 29 Nov. 1962, EM 7/62, Secret, Maço 692.30 (00), Energia Nuclear: Universo 1954/66, Caixa 47, Secret, AHMRE-B.

84. "Denuclearization of Latin America," 27 Nov. 1963, A/RES/1911 (XVIII). Eleven Latin American governments submitted the resolution and then proposed a resolution by the Brazilian government. There were 91 votes in favor and 15 abstentions, from Cuba and the socialist countries.

Chapter 3 · Against the Regime(s) and Brazil's Renewed Nuclear Ambitions, 1964–1974

1. José Honório Rodrigues, "Nota liminar," in "Politica Nuclear Brasileira," special issue, *Revista Brasileira de Política Internacional* 37–38 (1967): 3.

2. João Augusto de Araújo Castro, "The United Nations and the Freezing of the International Power Structure," *International Organization* 26.1 (1972): 158–59.

3. Paulo Wrobel, *Brazil, the Non-proliferation Treaty and Latin America as a Nuclear Weapon–Free Zone* (Brasília: FUNAG, 2017).

4. Damy to Goulart, 10 May 1963, EM 15/63, Secret, Maço 692.30 (00), Energia Nuclear: Universo 1954/66, Caixa 47, Secret, AHMRE-B.

5. João Augusto de Araújo Castro to Damy, 24 Jan. 1965, Secret, CNEN, in BR DFAN-BSB 2M.0.0.49, v.1, EMFA, AN-B.

6. Vojtech Mastny, "Eighteen-Nation Committee, 1962–1969: Could It Have Done Better?" (paper, "Uncovering the Sources of Nuclear Behavior: Historical Dimensions of Nuclear Proliferation" conference, Zurich, 18–20 June 2010), 13.

7. "NonProliferation of Nuclear Weapons," 19 Nov. 1965, A/RES/2028 (XX), http://daccess-dds-ny.un.org/doc/RESOLUTION/GEN/NR0/217/91/IMG/NR021791.pdf?OpenElement.

8. Conference of the Eighteen-Nation Committee on Disarmament (United Nations), "Final verbatim record of the Conference of the Eighteen-Nation Committee on Disarmament [Meeting 224]," Digital Collection of the Eighteen Nation Committee on Disarmament at the University of Michigan, 17, https://quod.lib.umich.edu/e/endc/4918260.0224.001/14?rgn=full+text;view=image.

9. Conference of the Eighteen-Nation Committee on Disarmament (United Nations), "Final verbatim record of the Conference of the Eighteen-Nation Committee on Disarmament [Meeting 244]," Digital Collection of the Eighteen Nation Committee on Disarmament at the University of Michigan, 15–16, http://quod.lib.umich.edu/e/endc/4918260.0244.001/15?page=root;rgn=full+text;size=100;view=image.

10. Conference of the Eighteen-Nation Committee on Disarmament (United Nations), "Final verbatim record of the Conference of the Eighteen-Nation Committee on Disarmament [Meeting 244]," 17, https://quod.lib.umich.edu/e/endc/4918260.0244.001/17?view=image&size=100.

11. Brazil informed Argentina about the NPT negotiations beginning in 1966. Rodrigo Mallea, "La cuestión nuclear en la relación argentino-brasileña (1968–1984)" (master's thesis, IESP-UERJ, 2012), 44.

12. José Sette Camara, "Nota entregue pelo plenipotenciário brasileiro ao presidente da Commissão Preparatória para a desnuclearização da América Latina, ao assinar no México, em 9 de Maio de 1967, o tratado para a proscrição das armas nucleares na América Latina," *Revista Brasileira de Política Internacional* 37–38 (1967): 95.

13. Humberto de Alencar Castelo Branco, "Trecho do discurso do Presidente Castelo Branco, pronunciado em 14 de março 1967," *Revista Brasileira de Política Internacional* 37–38 (1967): 95.

14. Scott Kaufman, *Project Plowshare: The Peaceful Use of Nuclear Explosives in Cold War America* (Ithaca, NY: Cornell University Press, 2013).

15. "Ata da Quadragésima Sessão do Conselho de Segurança Nacional," 4 Oct. 1967, Secret, CSN, BR DFANBSB N8.o.ATA.3/5, f.104-133, AN-B.

16. John R. Redick, "The Tlatelolco Regime and Nonproliferation in Latin America," *International Organization* 35.1 (1981): 106, https://doi.org/10.1017/S0020818300004100.

17. Redick, "Tlatelolco Regime and Nonproliferation in Latin America."

18. "Brazilian Delegation Balance of Mutual Responsibilities and Obligations," 30 May 1967, Confidential, PNB pn a 1967.02.24.

19. "Brazilian Delegation Balance of Mutual Responsibilities and Obligations," 30 May 1967, Confidential, PNB pn a 1967.02.24.

20. "Non-Proliferation of Nuclear Weapons," 19 Dec. 1967, A/RES/2346 A (XXII), http://www.un.org/depts/dhl/resguide/r22.htm. The episode was recently recalled by Ambassador Sérgio Duarte, who during that period integrated the Brazilian delegation in Geneva. Sérgio de Queiroz Duarte, FGV/CPDOC interview, 13 Dec. 2011, Rio de Janeiro.

21. Conference of the Eighteen-Nation Committee on Disarmament (United Nations), "Final verbatim record of the Conference of the Eighteen-Nation Committee on Disarmament [Meeting 335]," Digital Collection of the Eighteen Nation Committee on Disarmament at the University of Michigan, 4, https://quod.lib.umich.edu/e/endc/4918260.0335 .001/4?rgn=full+text;view=image.

22. Mastny, "Eighteen-Nation Committee, 1962–1969," 17.

23. "Política Nuclear do Brasil 6/10/1967," PNB pn a 1967.02.24.

24. "Evolução prevista da potência total instalada na Argentina," 28 May 1965, Secret, in Ofício Sec. N.5 / Sec 2, 30 June 1965, Diretório de Estudos e Pequisas Tecnológicas, Ministério da Guerra, BR DFANBSB 2M.o.o.49, v.1, AN-B.

25. H. Jon Rosenbaum, "Brazil's Nuclear Aspirations," in *Nuclear Proliferation and the Near-Nuclear Countries*, ed. Marwah Onkar and Ann Schulz (Cambridge: Ballinger, 1975), 266.

26. "Política Nuclear do Brasil 6/10/1967," PNB pn a 1967.02.24.

27. "Ata da Quadragésima Sessão do Conselho de Segurança Nacional," 4 Oct. 1967, Secret, CSN, BR DFANBSB N8.o.ATA.3/5, f.104-133, AN-B.

28. FrEmbassy Rio to Paris, 5 Apr. 1967, Dispatch 67/099, Amérique 1964–1970, Brésil—124—Défense Nationale—Questions Atomiques (hereafter 1964-1970-124), AMAE-F.

29. Maria Regina Soares de Lima, *The Political Economy of Brazilian Foreign Policy: Nuclear Policy, Trade, and Itaipu* (Brasília: FUNAG, 2013), 117.

30. "Estudo Especial 2S-SG/CSN-BSB," 24 Oct. 1967, Secret, PNB pn a 1967.02.24.

31. José de Magalhães Pinto to Arthur da Costa e Silva, 12 Feb. 1968, IPR 45, series IPR 1968, AHMRE-B.

32. Magalhães Pinto to Arthur da Costa e Silva, 12 Feb. 1968, IPR 45, series IPR 1968, AHMRE-B.

33. "Diretivas para o preparo de instruções sobre a tática brasileira na reunião de Genebra sobre não-proliferação nuclear," 2 Jan. 1968, Secret, PNB pn a 1967.02.24.

34. On the reference to UNGA resolution 2028, see Magalhães Pinto to Costa e Silva, 5 Feb. 1968, IPR 50, series IPR 1968, AHMRE-B; and Araújo Castro to Magalhães Pinto, 21 Mar. 1968, Memorandum, Secret, PNB pn a 1967.02.24.

35. Araújo Castro to Magalhães Pinto, 21 Mar. 1968, Memorandum, Secret, PNB pn a 1967.02.24.

36. Araújo Castro to Magalhães Pinto, 21 Mar. 1968, Memorandum, Secret, PNB pn a 1967.02.24, 15.

37. "Alterações introduzidas no projeto soviético-americano pela nova redação apresentada ao Comitê do Desarmamento, no dia 11 de março de 1968, pelas delegações dos Estados Unidos da América e da União Soviética," internal document of the Brazilian Foreign Ministry, n.d., PNB pn a 1967.02.24.

38. "Texto do Relatório do Comitê de Desarmamento XXII Assembléia-Geral da ONU," PNB pn a 1967.02.24.

39. On the Magalhães Pinto statement in New York, see Paulo Fagundes Visentini, *A política externa do regime militar brasileiro* (Porto Alegre: UFRGS Editora, 2004), 116.

40. A/RES/2373 (XXII) and annex, "Treaty on the Non-Proliferation of Nuclear Weapons," 12 June 1968, https://www.un.org/ga/search/view_doc.asp?symbol=a/res/2373(xxii).

41. Marcos Castrioto de Azambuja, interview by author, 20 Feb. 2014, Rio de Janeiro.

42. Brazil abstained to support nuclear disarmament and in order not to cause a diplomatic crisis with the United States. Magalhães Pinto to Costa e Silva, "XXII Assembleía Geral das Nações Unidas. Tratado de Não Proliferação de Armas Nucleares. Secreto. Abril 1968" and "Texto em inglês da declaração de voto, feita no plenário da I Comissão, no dia 10 de junho, expondo as razões determinantes da abstenção do Brasil na votação da resolução n° 2372," PNB pn a 1967.02.24.

43. Security Council resolution 255, "Question relating to measures to safeguard non-nuclear-weapon States parties to the Treaty on the Non-Proliferation of Nuclear Weapons," 19 June 1968, http://unscr.com/en/resolutions/255.

44. Mastny, "Eighteen-Nation Committee, 1962–1969," 20.

45. "Instruções para a Delegação do Brasil Conferência dos Estados Militarmente Não Nucleares," Itamaraty to Brazilian Delegation in Geneva, 16 Aug. 1968, Secret, PNB pn a 1967.02.24. For Paulo Nogueira Batista's speech, see "Discurso proferido pelo Ministro Paulo Nogueira Batista, na ocasião da Conferência dos Países Militarmente Não Nucleares," PNB pn a 1967.02.24; and UNGA resolution 2456 (XXIII), "Conference of Non-Nuclear Weapon States," http://www.worldlii.org/int/other/UNGARsn/1968/78.pdf.

46. H. Jon Rosenbaum and Glenn Cooper, "Brazil and the Nuclear Non-Proliferation Treaty," *International Affairs* 46.1 (1970): 89, https://doi.org/10.2307/2614211.

47. Itamaraty to BrazEmbassy Bonn, 30 Jan. 1968, Telegram 30, Secret-Urgent, AHMRE-B.

48. "Besprechingem im Brasílianishen Aussenministerium waehrend Besuchs Bundesaussenminister am 24.10.68," FRG Embassy Rio de Janeiro to Bonn, Telegram 598, Akt IB2—82.20 Besuch Bundesminister Willy Brandt 1967.

49. On the report of the National Planning Association, see Moeed Yusuf, "Predicting Proliferation: The History of the Future of Nuclear Proliferation," Brookings Institution Foreign Policy Paper No. 11 (Jan. 2009), 17, https://www.brookings.edu/research/predicting-proliferation-the-history-of-the-future-of-nuclear-weapons/.

50. "Remarks by Dr. Glenn Seaborg, Chairman US Atomic Energy Commission at Rio de Janeiro—The New World," 3 July 1967, 6, Maço 592.30 (22), Energia Nuclear 4333, AHMRE-B. On the failure of the negotiations between Seaborg and the Brazilian Foreign Ministry, see "Resultado dos Entendimentos havidos durante a estada do Sr Glenn Seaborg no Brasil," BrazEmbassy Washington to Itamaraty, 4 July 1967, Confidential, Maço 592.30 (22), Energia Nuclear 4333, AHMRE-B. For an account of the visit, see also Glenn Theodore Seaborg, *Stemming the Tide: Arms Control in the Johnson Years* (Lexington, MA: Lexington Books,1987), 258. On the meeting between CNEN and USAEC over possible cooperation in the field of Plowshare, see CNEN, MME, *Relatório Annual: Ano 1967* (Rio de Janeiro, 1967), 49, 166.

51. SecState to USUN New York, 7 May 1968, Telegram 2762, Confidential, Subject-Numeric Files 1967–1969, Box 1739, Folder DEF 18-6 5-1-68, RG 59, NARA; "Brazilian Opposition to NPT Draft Likely to Continue," Thomas L. Hughes to Dean Rusk, 19 Apr. 1968, Intelligence Note 290, Secret, DNSA.

52. *Foreign Relations of the United States, 1964–1968*, vol. 11, *Arms Control and Disarmament*, ed. Evans Gerakas, David S. Patterson, and Carolyn B. Yee (Washington, DC: GPO, 1979), doc. 289, https://history.state.gov/historicaldocuments/frus1964-68v11/d289. The Argentine opposition to the NPT was not as solid as the Brazilian. The chairman of the Argentinean Nuclear Energy Commission (CNEA), Admiral Oscar A. Quihillalt, favored accession to the treaty but met the opposition of the Argentine president and of the foreign minister, who "refused to accept 'a diminution of our dignity.'" Jacques E. C. Hymans, *The Psychology of Nuclear Proliferation: Identity, Emotions, and Foreign Policy* (Cambridge: Cambridge University Press, 1996), 145.

53. On the approval of the new safeguards system, see Harald Müller, David Fischer, and Wolfgang Koetter, *Nuclear Non-Proliferation and Global Order* (New York: SIPRI / Oxford University Press, 1994), 17; and Elisabeth Roehrlich, "Negotiating Verification: International Diplomacy and the Evolution of Nuclear Safeguards, 1945–1972," *Diplomacy & Statecraft* 29.1 (2018): 39, https:/doi.org/10.1080/09592296.2017.1420520.

54. "Relatório do grupo de trabalho encarregado de examinar o projeto de convênio tripartite de transferência de salvaguardas," 18 Jan. 1966, BR DFANBSB 2M.0.0.49, v.1 EMFA, AN-B.

55. "AIEA. Salvaguardas. Acordo trilateral," 24 Aug. 1965, BR DFANBSB 2M.0.0.49, v.1, EMFA, AN-B.

56. "Brasil e França concordam em colaborar no campo atômico," *Jornal do Brasil*, 16 Oct. 1964, 3; "Coopération Nucléaire—Production d'electricité d'origine nucléaire," FrEmbassy Rio to Paris, 23 Nov. 1964, Confidential, 1964-1970-124, AMAE-F. On the provision of heavy water, the thorium group, and the cooperation with France, see Guilherme Camargo, *O fogo dos deuses: Uma história da energia nuclear; Pandora 600 a.C.–1970* (Rio de Janeiro: Contraponto, 2006), 267–69; Carlo Patti, *O programa nuclear brasileiro: Uma história oral* (Rio de Janeiro: FGV, 2014), 212; and "Collaboration franco-brésilienne sur les reacteurs au Thorium," FrEmbassy Rio to Paris (CEA), 2 Mar. 1966, 1964-1970-124, AMAE-F.

57. CNEN, MME, *Relatório Anual: Ano 1967*, 49. I thank Dr. Laercio Vinhas for clarifying, in an email to the author of 11 June 2019, the possible mistakes present in the beforementioned 1967 CNEN report.

58. US Consul São Paulo to SecState, "Brazilian Centrifuge Program," 16 May 1968, History and Public Policy Program Digital Archive, RG 59, Subject-Numeric Files

1967–1969, Box 1169, Inco-Uranium Brazil, NARA, https://digitalarchive.wilsoncenter
.org/document/145012.

59. A few months after the military coup, the French Embassy encouraged CEA to submit a bid for the construction of a nuclear plant in the state of São Paulo. FrEmbassy Rio to Paris, 30 Oct. 1964, Telegram 1227/1231, 1964-1970-124, AMAE-F. Moreover, an IPr study requested by Centrais Elétricas do Pará to the IPr, concluded in January 1967, suggested that new studies be conducted in the period 1970–75 regarding the possible introduction of two small nuclear power plants by 1981. Camargo, *O fogo dos deuses*, 269; CNEN, MME, Relatório Anual: Ano 1967, 30.

60. CNEN, MME, Relatório Anual: Ano 1967, 24.

61. CNEN, MME, Relatório Anual: Ano 1969 (CNEN: Rio de Janeiro, 1969), 42.

62. CNEN, MME, Relatório Anual: Ano 1968 (CNEN: Rio de Janeiro, 1968), 1.

63. Itty Abraham, *The Making of the Indian Atomic Bomb: Science, Secrecy and the Postcolonial State* (London: Zed Books, 1998), 91–95.

64. "Política Nuclear do Brasil," 6 Oct. 1967, Unclassified, PNB pn a 1967.02.23; "Política Nacional de Energia Nuclear—Diretrizes," Presidência da República, n.d., Top Secret, in Aviso 2-2S-SG/CSN-BR from General Jayme Portella de Mello (secretary-general of CSN) to Magalhães Pinto, 1 Sept. 1967, Confidential, PNB ad 1967.02.23. See also "Ata da Quadragésima Sessão do Conselho de Segurança Nacional," 4 Oct. 1967, Secret, CSN, BR DFANBSB N8.0.ATA.3/5, f.104-133, AN-B, 6.

65. Even if Itamaraty proposed to resume cooperation with France, Paris did not participate in the international bid of 1969 for construction of Brazil's first nuclear power plant. FrEmbassy Brazil (Jean André Binoche) to French Foreign Ministry, 22 Sept. 1967, Telegram 417/19, 1964-1970-124, AMAE-F; "Projeto de associação com Israel na construção de uma usina piloto de água pesada," 27 Aug. 1971, Confidential, Maço 592.30 (00), Energia Nuclear: Universo (00 a 56) 1967 (hereafter 592.30/67), AHMRE-B.

66. Brasil, Ministério da Ciência e Tecnologia, *Relatório da visita à Índia da Comissão Nacional de Energia Nuclear, 1970*, 5–18 Oct. 1970, Confidential, 37, http://memoria.cnen
.gov.br/manut/ImprimeTR.asp?Codigo=60.

67. William Burr and Avner Cohen, "The Quest for Yellowcake: The Secret Argentina-Israel Connection, 1963–1966," *NPIHP Research Updates*, https://www.wilsoncenter.org
/publication/israels-quest-for-yellowcake-the-secret-argentina-israel-connection-1963-1966.

68. On the 1966 agreement, see "Accord Nucléaire Brésil-France," FrEmbassy Rio to Paris (Jean Renou, CEA), 16 May 1966, 1964-1970-124, AMAE-F. On the 1967 meetings, see "Influences extérieures au Brésil dans le domaine nucléaire," n.d., Amérique 1964–1970, Brésil—125—Défense Nationale—Questions Atomiques, AMAE-F. On the visit, see also CNEN, MME, *Relatório Annual: Ano 1967*, 111. On the possible collaboration on heavy-water plants, see CNEN to Itamaraty, 19 Oct. 1971, CNEN internal document, CNEN-74/71, Secret, Maço 592.30 /67, AHMRE-B; and Hervásio de Carvalho to Jorge de Carvalho e Silva (secretary-general, Brazilian Ministry of Foreign Affairs), 5 Sept. 1973, CNEN-56/73, Secret, AHMRE-B.

69. "Fornecimento pelo Brasil de minérios atômicos à RFA e Israel," 25 June 1973, Memorandum, Secret, AHMRE-B; Luiz Augusto de Castro Neves, FGV/CPDOC interview, 23 Jan. 2012, Rio de Janeiro.

70. "Report, Argentinian Ministry of Foreign Relations, 'Nuclear Energy,'" 15 Jan. 1968, History and Public Policy Program Digital Archive, Caja Brasil AH0124,

Archives of the Ministry of Foreign Affairs and Worship, Argentina, obtained and translated by FGV, https://digitalarchive.wilsoncenter.org/document/116852; "Tratado de Não Proliferação de Armas Nucleares, Entendimentos Brasil-Argentina," Brazilian Foreign Ministry to Argentine Embassy in Brazil, 17 Apr. 1968, Secret, AHMRE-B.

71. Arthur da Costa e Silva, "Compromisso com o Brasil: Satisfazer suas aspirações democráticas," April 1967, Biblioteca da Presidência da República, https://www.biblioteca .presidencia.gov.br/presidencia/ex-presidentes/costa-silva/discursos/1967/07.pdf/@@ download/file/07.pdf.

72. "Suposto acordo atômico entre Brasil e Argentina," BrazEmbassy Vienna to Itamaraty, 25 Mar. 1967, Secret, 592.30/67, AHMRE-B. On the request for authorization to increase the talks with the Argentines, see "Utilização pacífica de energia nuclear: Possibilidade de cooperação Brasil-Argentina," DCA/DAM/365/692.30 (04); and Sérgio Corrêa da Costa (secretary-general, Ministry of Foreign Relations) to Jayme Portella de Mello (secretary-general, National Security Council), 31 Aug. 1967, Secret, AHMRE-B. See also Visentini, *A política externa do regime militar brasileiro*, 116. On the possible continuation of talks in 1970, see "Acôrdo Brasil-Argentina nos usos pacíficos da energia nuclear," 12 Nov. 1970, Telegram 709, Secret, DOA/DBP/592.30 (41), Maço 592.30 /67, AHMRE-B; and Mallea, "La cuestión nuclear," 56.

73. On the debate within West Germany, see Francis J. Gavin, "Nuclear Proliferation and Non-proliferation During the Cold War," in *The Cambridge History of the Cold War*, ed. Melvyn P. Leffler and Odd Arne Westad, vol. 2, *Crisis and Détente* (Cambridge: Cambridge University Press, 2010), 410–11. On Italy and the NPT, see Leopoldo Nuti, *La sfida nucleare: La politica estera italana e le armi atomiche, 1945–1991* (Bologna: Il Mulino, 2007).

74. BrazEmbassy Tokyo to Itamaraty, 14 Sept. 1967, Telegram 324, Secret, 592.30/67, AHMRE-B.

75. "Cooperação Brasil-Japão nos usos pacíficos da energia nuclear," Itamaraty to BrazEmbassy Tokyo, 27 Sept. 1967, Secret, 592.30/67, AHMRE-B.

76. "Cooperação Brasil-Japão na utilização pacífica da energia nuclear," Itamaraty to BrazEmbassy Tokyo, 23 Jan. 1968, Secret, 592.30/67, AHMRE-B.

77. BrazEmbassy Bonn to Itamaraty, 19 Sept. 1968, Telegram 203, Secret, 592.30/67, AHMRE-B.

78. Paulo Nogueira Batista to Magalhães Pinto, "Viagem do Ministro Paulo Nogueira Batista à RFA, em setembro de 1968: Relatório ao Senhor Ministro de Estado," 11 Oct. 1968, Secret, PNB ad 1967.02.23.

79. R. B. Kehoe, *The Enriching Troika: A History of Urenco to the Year 2000* (Marlow, UK: Urenco, 2002), 23.

80. From 1969 to 1973 more than eleven Brazilian nuclear engineers were trained at Jülich.

81. Kehoe, *Enriching Troika*, 33.

82. Susanna Schrafstetter and Stephen Twigge, "Spinning into Europe: Britain, West Germany and the Netherlands; Uranium Enrichment and the Development of the Gas Centrifuge, 1964–1970," *Contemporary European History* 11. 2 (2002): 253–72, https://doi .org/10.1017/S0960777302002047. The three governments participated in Urenco through the national companies URANIT (Federal Republic of Germany), Ultra-Centrifuge Nederland NV (the Netherlands), and Enrichment Holdings Ltd. (United Kingdom).

83. Soares de Lima, *Political Economy of Brazilian Foreign Policy*, 141. At the same moment and for similar reasons, Argentina refused a similar West German offer. Jacques E. C. Hymans, "Of Gauchos and Gringos: Why Argentina Never Wanted the Bomb, and Why the United States Thought It Did," *Security Studies* 10.3 (2001): 148.

84. Paulo Nogueira Batista, "O acordo nuclear Brasil-República Federal da Alemanha," in *Sessenta anos de política externa brasileira*, ed. José Augusto Guilhon de Albuquerque, vol. 4, *Prioridades, atores e políticas (1930–1990)* (São Paulo: Annablume-NUPRI-USP, 2000), 39.

85. The commission was composed of Hervásio de Carvalho (CNEN), Leo A. Penna (Eletrobrás), John Cotrim (Furnas), Moacyr de Vasconcelos (DNPM), and Colonel Oswaldo M. Oliva (CSN General Secretariat). The final report was issued on 27 January 1969.

86. Camargo, *O fogo dos deuses*, 272.

87. Camargo, *O fogo dos deuses*, 269.

88. "Fuel Contract entre a Westinghouse e a Furnas para ANGRA 1," n.d., Confidential, PNB pn a 1955.08.03.

89. On the creation of the strategic stock of thorium, see "Ata da Vigésima Segunda Consulta ao Conselho de Segurança Nacional," 19 Feb. 1971, Secret, BR DFANBSB N8.0.ATA.7/12, p.83–86, CSN, AN-B. In 1975, on the eve of the nuclear agreement between Brazil and West Germany, the act was amended to include the uranium produced in Brazil in the strategic nuclear stock. "Ata da Trigésima Nona Consulta ao Conselho de Segurança Nacional," 25 Apr. 1975, Secret, BR DFANBSB N8.0.ATA.8/3, p.15–22, CSN, AN-B.

90. Aluisio Castanho Maciel, "A formação de geólogos no Brasil e sua influência na prospecção, pesquisa e descoberta de jazidas de urânio," in *Geologia USP 50 anos*, ed. Celso de Barros Gomes (São Paulo: Edusp / Instituto de Geociências da USP, 2007), 228.

91. "Enriquecimento de urânio," Nogueira Batista to Mário Gibson Barboza, 19 Apr. 1971, Secret, AHMRE-B.

92. Ricardo Bonalume Neto, "Pirataria ajuda marinha a construir centrifugas," *FdSP*, 9 Apr. 1988, A-17.

93. On the Nixon-Kissinger attitude toward nuclear proliferation, see Michael J. Brenner, *Nuclear Power and Non-Proliferation: The Remaking of U.S. Policy* (New York: Cambridge University Press, 1981); Francis J. Gavin, "Nuclear Nixon: Ironies, Puzzles, and the Triumph of Realpolitik," in *Nixon in the World: American Foreign Relations, 1969–1977*, ed. Fredrik Logevall and Andrew Preston (Oxford: Oxford University Press, 2008); and James Cameron and Or Rabinowitz, "Eight Lost Years? Nixon, Ford, Kissinger and the Non-Proliferation Regime, 1969–1977," *Journal of Strategic Studies* 40.6 (2017): 839–66, https://doi.org/10.1080/01402390.2015.1101682.

94. *Foreign Relations of the United States, 1969–1976*, vol. E-7, *Documents on South Asia, 1969–1972*, ed. Louis J. Smith (Washington, DC: GPO, 2005), doc. 300, https://history.state.gov/historicaldocuments/frus1969-76ve07/d300.

95. "National Security Implications of Alternative Forms of Ownership of Uranium Enrichment Plants," n.d., Secret, Folder: "Enrichment (private ownership)," RG 59, Entry P 108, Box 2, NARA.

96. BrazEmbassy Washington to SecState, 22 Sept. 1971, Aide-mémoire, Confidential, Folder: "AE 1971 Brazil (Aug.–Dec.)," RG 59, Entry P 108, Box 20, NARA.

97. Isabelle Anstey, "Negotiating Nuclear Control: The Zangger Committee and the Nuclear Suppliers' Group in the 1970s," *International History Review* 40.5 (2018): 975–95, https:/doi.org/10.1080/07075332.2018.1449764.

Chapter 4 · The Brazilian Nuclear Program in the Geisel Years, 1974–1979

1. "Nuclear Madness," *New York Times,* 13 June 1975, 36.

2. On the II PND, see Werner Baer, *The Brazilian Economy: Growth and Development* (Boulder, CO: Lynne Rienner, 2008), 79.

3. Shigeaki Ueki to Ernesto Geisel, 23 Apr. 1974, Dispatch, EG pr 1974.03.26/2. The nuclear industrial plan was drafted in early 1974. Proposal for a study on the initiation and development of a national fuel cycle and nuclear reactor component industry in Brazil, 28 Feb. 1974, PNB pn a 1975.01.09.

4. In that phase several of Brazil's nuclear scientists from CBTN received specific training by the NUS Corporation on negotiations. Carlo Patti, *O programa nuclear brasileiro: Uma história oral* (Rio de Janeiro: FGV, 2014), 75.

5. The feasibility study for a new nuclear policy was conducted by CBTN in 1973 and 1974. Patti, *O programa nuclear brasileiro,* 57. On the possible partnership with Westinghouse on the nuclear fuel cycle, see Beatriz Helena Domingues, *Reinventar a roda: A política nuclear no Brasil entre 1964 e 1978* (Rio de Janeiro: COPPE-UFRJ; Juiz de Fora: EDUFJF, 1997), 77.

6. EM 245/74, 23 Apr. 1974, MME, cited in EM 055/74, 13 Aug. 1974, CSN, Secret, AAS, mre pn 1974.08.15; "Programa Nuclear Brasileiro," document submitted on 6 May 1987 by Rex Nazaré Alves (chairman, CNEN) to the Subcommittee on Political Rights, Collective Rights, and Guarantees of the Committee on Sovereignty and of Rights and Guarantees of the Man and of the Woman of the National Constitutional Assembly.

7. For a summary of other types of foreign assistance from the British Nuclear Energy Society and the German market research institute GfK, see "II Plano Nacional de Desenvolvimento. Programa nuclear," 1974, CBTN, PNB pn a 1968.06.15. Brazilian nuclear scientists also collaborated with the Italian Comitato Nazionale per l'Energia Nucleare until 1987. See Carlo Patti, "An Unusual Partnership: Brazilian-Italian Forms of Cooperation in the Nuclear Field (1951–1986)," in *Nuclear Italy: An International History of Italian Nuclear Policies during the Cold War,* ed. Elisabetta Bini and Igor Londero (Trieste: Edizioni Università di Trieste, 2017).

8. FrEmbassy Brasília to Paris, 16 May 1974, Letter 715/QA, Amérique 1971–1975, 185, Carton 15-6-2, Coopération atomique, spatial, énergie solaire, 1975 (hereafter 185-15-6-2), AMAE-F.

9. EM 055/74, 13 Aug. 1974, CSN, Secret, AAS mre/pn 1974.08.15.

10. On the French decision on the reactor line, see Bertrand Goldschmidt, *Le complexe atomique: Histoire politique de l'énergie nucléaire* (Paris: Fayard, 1980), 370.

11. FrEmbassy Brasília to Paris, 8 Oct.1971, Letter 1799/QS, 185-15-6-2, AMAE-F.

12. BrazEmbassy Bonn to Itamaraty, 4 May 1971, AEO/430.1(81a)(42) 550.(81a), Secret-Urgent, PNB pn a 1968.06.15.

13. FrEmbassy Brasília to Paris, 3 May 1974, Telegram 454/55, Secret, 185-15-6-2, AMAE-F.

14. Paris to FrEmbassy Brasília, 21 May 1974, Telegram 328/33, 185-15-6-2, AMAE-F; FrEmbassy Brazil to Paris, 30 May 1974, Dispatch 779/QS, 185-15-6-2, AMAE-F; CEA to

Rio, 24 June 1974, Telegram 8693, 185-15-6-2, AMAE-F. On the Brazilian interest in cooperating with France in the complete nuclear fuel cycle, see FrEmbassy Brasília to Paris, 28 June 1974, Telegram 629/33, 185-15-6-2, AMAE-F.

15. Giraud visited Brazil from 5 to 12 August 1974. "Information on the visit of André Giraud to Brazil," FrEmbassy Brasília to Itamaraty, 9 July 1974, Secret, and "Programa de Visita para M. André Giraud," CNEN to Nogueira Batista, 31 July 1974, PNB pn a 1952.07.01.

16. French Consulate Rio to Paris, 5 Aug. 1974, Telegram 152, Reserved, 185-15-6-2, AMAE-F. On the denial, see Paris to FrEmbassy Brazil, 9 Aug. 1974, Telegram 570, 185-15-6-2, AMAE-F.

17. For a detailed account of the French proposal, see Carlos Syllus, "Análise da proposta francesa para conjuntamente estabelecer uma usina de enriquecimento no Brasil," CBTN, pn a 1952.07.01.

18. See André Giraud to Ueki, 13 Aug. 1974, Secret, and Ueki to Giraud, 18 Sept. 1974, PNB pn a 1952.07.01. For the French documentation, see FrEmbassy Brasília to Paris, 16 Aug. 1974, Dispatch 1259/QS, Confidential, and 16 Oct. 1974, Dispatch 1661/QS, Confidential, 185-15-6-2, AMAE-F.

19. Silveira to Geisel, 21 Aug. 1974, IPR 200, Secret, series IPR 1974, AHMRE-B.

20. Silveira clearly pressured France's ambassador, Fouchet, during a conversation a few days before the signing of a preliminary agreement with the West Germans. FrEmbassy Brasília to Paris, 3 Oct. 1974, Telegram 888/90, 185-15-6-2, AMAE-F.

21. CEA to FrEmbassy Brasília, 11 Dec. 1974, Dispatch 2065/DG, and FrEmbassy Brasília to Paris, 13 Dec. 1974, 185-15-6-2, AMAE-F.

22. "Compte-rendu des entretiens au C.E.A. de M. Nogueira Batista, Président de Nuclebrás, accompagné de Mm. Syllus Pinto et Forman, le 2 juillet 1975," PNB pn a 1952.07.01 (62).

23. FrEmbassy Brasília to Paris, 29 Nov. 1975, Telegram 1189/94, Strictly Reserved Diffusion, Amérique 1971–1975, Brésil—186, Brésil, Coopération atomique, spatiale, énergia nucléaire, 1975 (hereafter 1971-1975-186), AMAE-F.

24. FrEmbassy Brazil to Paris, 8 Oct. 1975, Dispatch 1984/QS/qa, 1971-1975-186, AMAE-F.

25. Aviso 475/75, 23 Dec. 1975, Secret, PNB pn a 1952.07.01 (62). Despite the governmental prohibition, Nogueira Batista continued discrete talks with the French CEA, whose representative, in a meeting in Rio de Janeiro, confirmed to be available to build, excluding the sensitive aspects, a CEA-Nuclebrás enrichment facility. Nogueira Batista to Ueki, 11 Feb. 1976, PR-032/76, Secret, PNB pn a 1952.07.01; Paris to FrEmbassy Brasília, 12 Dec. 1975, Telegram 1189/94, Strictly Reserved Diffusion, 1971-1975-186, AMAE-F.

26. AmEmbassy Paris to SecState, 9 July 1975, Cable 1975PARIS17726, Electronic Telegrams, Department of State, Central Foreign Policy Files, NARA (hereafter DOS/CFP); AmEmbassy Brasília to SecState, 10 July 1975, Cable 1975BRASIL05657, DOS/CFP. The US government monitored the French action and in a cable in October wrote that despite the deal with Germany, the French "appear to continue to aspire to a part of the Brazilian nuclear pie." AmEmbassy Paris to SecState, 20 Oct. 1975, Cable 1975PARIS27180, Confidential, DOS/CFP. In the same days, several US newspapers reported that Nuclebrás was planning to sign contracts with the United States for acquiring high-temperature gas-cooled reactors. SecState to USMission IAEA Vienna, 11 July 1975, Cable 1975STATE161924, and 15 July 1975, Cable 1975STATE166300, DOS/CFP.

27. Ueki to Geisel, 30 Apr. 1974, Dispatch, EG pr 1974.03.26/2.

28. Elio Gaspari, *A ditadura encurralada* (São Paulo: Companhia das Letras, 2004), 130–31; Beatriz Helena Domingues, *Reinventar a roda: A política nuclear no Brasil entre 1964 e 1978* (Rio de Janeiro/Juiz de Fora: COPPE-UFRJ/EDUFJF, 1997), 84.

29. On the conversation of 1971, see "Beziehungen zu Brasilien auf dem Anreicherungsgebiet," 24 Nov. 1971, Bd. 8440, PA/AA.

30. William Glenn Gray, "Commercial Liberties and Nuclear Anxieties: The US-German Feud over Brazil, 1975–7," *International History Review* 34.3 (2012): 453; "Deutsch-Brasilianische Zusammenarbeit in Kernforschung und Kerntechnischer Entwicklung," 12 Mar. 1974, Bonn to Brasília, Bd. 8440, PA/AA.

31. "Bericht über eine Dienstreise nach Brasilien vom 2–9 Juni 1973," 6 June 1973, Bd. 8440, PA/AA.

32. R. B. Kehoe, *The Enriching Troika: A History of Urenco to the Year 2000* (Marlow, UK: Urenco, 2002), 177.

33. "Zusammenarbeit mit Brasilien auf dem gebiet der kernenergie," 25 Sept. 1974, doc. 85, Bonn to Brasília, Deutsch-Brasilianische zusammenarbeit im nucklearen Bereich Nuklearpolitik 1974–1984, PA/AA. For the text of the protocol, see "Program for Industrial Cooperation between Brazil and the Federal Republic of Germany in the Field of Peaceful Uses of Nuclear Energy," n.d., Deutsch-Brasilianische zusammenarbeit im nucklearen Bereich Nuklearpolitik 1974–1984, PA/AA. The meeting between the Kraftwerk Union and the Ministry of Mines and Energy took place in Brasília from 29 September to 4 October. AmEmbassy Brasília to SecState, 1 Oct. 1974, Cable 1974BRASIL07476, Limited Official Use, DOS/CFP; Ueki to Geisel, 26 Sept. 1974, Dispatch, EG pr 1974.03.26/2.

34. On the KFU fear of possible competition with Mitsubishi, see Gerold Herzog (KWU) to Heinrich D. Dieckmann (FRG Embassy in Brasília), 6 Sept. 1974, Deutsch-Brasilianische zusammenarbeit im nucklearen Bereich Nuklearpolitik 1974–1984, PA/AA.

35. Kehoe, *Enriching Troika*, 29.

36. For a list of the countries that were recipients of US nuclear cooperation, see SecState to AmEmbassy Jiddah, 14 June 1974, Cable 1974STATE126853, Limited Official Use, DOS/CFP.

37. SecState to AmEmb Brussels, 9 July 1974, Cable 1974STATE147110, Confidential, DOS/CFP. In the same days Sigvard Eklund, the IAEA general director, talked with the US representative at the international agency about the future of the NPT and the threat from the countries opposing the NPT. USMission Vienna to SecState, 11 July 1974, Cable 1974IAEAV06175, Confidential, DOS/CFP.

38. Bonn to Brasília, 12 Feb. 1975, Top Secret, Very Urgent, PNB 1975.01.09. For a full and detailed account of Nogueira Batista's mission to West Germany, see "Relatório da Missão à Alemanha (RFA) (1 a 15 de Fevereiro 1975)," Secret, Nuclebrás, PNB 1975.01.09.

39. "Bericht über eine Dienstreise nach Brasilien vom 2–9 Juni 1973," 6 June 1973, Bd. 8440, PA/AA.

40. Ueki to Geisel, 24 Sept.1974, EG pr 1974.03.26/2; FrEmbassy Brasília to Paris, 1 Nov. 1974, Dispatch 1757/QS/qa, 185-15-6-2, AMAE-F. On 18 November Carvalho was reappointed chair of CNEN. Although he had lost some of his influence in Brazilian nuclear decisions, he remained a key actor in the sector. AmConsul Rio de Janeiro to SecState, 25 Nov. 1974, Cable 1974RIODE04381, Confidential, DOS/CFP. On the official decision on

Nuclebrás, see "Nuclebrás," Ueki to Geisel, 5 Dec. 1974, Ministério de Minas e Energia, EG pr 1974.03.26/2; AmEmbassy Brasília to SecState, 9 Jan. 1975, Cable 1975BRA-SIL00190, Confidential, DOS/CFP. On possible external investors in Nuclebrás, see AmEmbassy Brasília to SecState, 12 Nov. 1974, Cable 1974BRASIL08544, DOS/CFP.

41. FrEmbassy Brasília to Paris, 3 Sept. 1974, Letter 1357, 185-15-6-2, AMAE-F.

42. FrEmbassy Brasília to Paris, 21 July 1975, Dispatch 1425 QS/qa, 1971-1975-186, AMAE-F.

43. Patti, *O programa nuclear brasileiro*, 239–40; Gaspari, *A ditadura encurralada*, 134; "Besuch Brasilianischer Kritiker des deutsch-Brasílianischen Kernenergie Abkommens in der Bundesrepublik Deutschland," Bonn to FRG Embassy Brasília, 15 Sept. 1978, Deutsch-Brasilianische zusammenarbeit im nucklearen Bereich Nuklearpolitik 1974–1984, PA/AA.

44. See Carlos Syllus's interview in Patti, *O programa nuclear brasileiro*, 148–49; "Programa proposto pelo Eng° Dietrich Wilhelm Sontag para a implantação de usina de enriquecimento de urânio por centrifugação no Brasil," Secret, PNB pn c 1969.12.01; and "Considerações sobre um programa alternativo na área de enriquecimento," Secret, PNB pn c 1969.12.01.

45. James Cameron, "Technology, Politics, and Development: Domestic Criticism of the 1975 Brazilian–West German Nuclear Agreement," *Revista Brasileira de Política Internacional* 61.2 (2018), https://dx.doi.org/10.1590/0034-7329201800201.

46. Itamaraty to SNI/AC, FA-2/EMFA, 2ª Sec. EME, 2ª Sec. EMA, 2ª Sec. EMAER, 23 Feb. 1976, Informação DSI/809, Confidential, AN-B.

47. "Prospects for Further Proliferation of Nuclear Weapons," 24 Aug. 1974, Top Secret, Special National Intelligence Estimate (hereafter SNIE), DNSA, https://nsarchive2 .gwu.edu//NSAEBB/NSAEBB240/snie.pdf.

48. AmEmbassy Brasília to SecState, 20 May 1974, Cable 1974BRASIL03567, Secret, DOS/CFP.

49. BrazEmbassy Washington to Brasília, 6 Nov. 1974,Telegram 4237, Confidential Urgent, AAS mre be 1974.03.15. On the London Group and the Zangger Committee, see Isabelle Anstey, "Negotiating Nuclear Control: The Zangger Committee and the Nuclear Suppliers' Group in the 1970s," *International History Review* 40.5 (2018): 975–95, https: /doi.org/10.1080/07075332.2018.1449764. For a general overview of the history of the NSG, see Tadeusz Strulak, "The Nuclear Suppliers Group," *Nonproliferation Review* 1.1 (1993): 2–10, https:/doi.org/10.1080/10736709308436518. On the United States and the origins of the NSG, see William Burr, "A Scheme of 'Control': The United States and the Origins of the Nuclear Suppliers' Group, 1974–1976," *International History Review* 36.2 (2014): 252–76, https:/doi.org/10.1080/07075332.2013.864690.

50. FRG Embassy in Brasília to Itamaraty, 16 Dec. 1974, Confidential, PNB 1975.01.09; Batista to FRG Embassy Brasília, 9 Jan. 1975, Confidential, in "Draft agenda for discussion on government level—preparation of an agreement on collaboration between the Federal Republic of Germany and Brazil on the peaceful uses of nuclear energy," n.d., Secret, PNB 1975.01.09.

51. BrazEmbassy Bonn to Brasília, 12 Feb. 1975, Telegram 153/41800, Top Secret, Very Urgent, PNB pn a 1975.01.09.

52. SecState to AmEmbassy Bonn, 24 Mar. 1975, Cable 1975STATE066020, Secret, DOS/CFP.

53. For a more detailed account of US-Brazilian relations in the nuclear field in the period, see Carlo Patti and Matias Spektor, "'We Are Not a Nonproliferation Agency': Henry Kissinger's Failed Attempt to Accommodate Nuclear Brazil, 1974–1977," *Journal of Cold War Studies* 22.2 (2020): 58–93.

54. AmEmbassy Brasília to SecState, 4 June 1975, Cable 1975BRASIL04414, DOS/CFP.

55. Jaime Dantas, "URSS vê perigo no acordo Brasil-RFA," *Jornal do Brasil,* 20 June 1975, 6.

56. Michael J. Brenner, *Nuclear Power and Non-Proliferation: The Remaking of U.S. Policy* (New York: Cambridge University Press, 1981), 89.

57. "Nuclear Madness"; "A Message for President Scheel," *Washington Post,* 16 June 1975, A22; L. H. Diuguid, "Brazil Nuclear Deal Raises US Concern," *Washington Post,* 1 June 1975, A1.

58. SecState to AmEmbassy Brasília, 20 June 1975, Cable 1975STATE146237, Confidential, DOS/CFP.

59. FrEmbassy Washington to Paris, 13 June 1975, Dispatch 1086/AM, 1971-1975-186, AMAE-F. On the Soviet position, see SecState to AmEmbassy Tripoli, 3 July 1975, Cable 1975STATE157800, Secret, DOS/CFP. For a US assessment of Brazilian reluctance to contract Soviet enrichment services, see AmEmbassy Brasília to SecState, 14 July 1975, Cable 1975BRASIL05792, Confidential, DOS/CFP. On Brazilian authorities banning negotiations over purchases of enriched uranium from Moscow, see Patti, *O programa nuclear brasileiro,* 57.

60. Meeting between Henry Kissinger and Andrei Gromyko, Memorandum, 11 July 1975, Secret, National Security Council, DNSA.

61. Meeting between Kissinger and Gromyko, Memorandum, 11 July 1975, Secret, National Security Council, DNSA.

62. Ueki to Geisel, 3 July 1975, Dispatch, EG pr 1974.03.26/2; CSN to Geisel, 15 Oct. 1975, Secret, AAS, mre pn 1974.08.15.

63. US Mission New York to SecState, 23 Sept. 1975, Cable 1975USUNN04426, DOS/CFP.

64. US Mission Vienna to SecState, 3 Oct. 1975, Cable 1975IAEAV08465, DOS/CFP.

65. SecState to AmEmbassy Brasília, 24 Nov. 1975, Cable 1975STATE277689, Confidential, DOS/CFP.

66. CSN to Geisel, 6 Dec. 1975, Secret, AAS, mre pn 1974.08.15; "Opening Statement at Brazil/FRG/IAEA Negotiation," 12 Jan. 1976, Vienna, PNB pn a 1975.01.09.

67. AmEmbassy Paris to SecState, 23 Dec. 1975, Cable 1975PARIS33474, Secret, DOS/CFP; "Non-Proliferation—Coopération nucléaire germane-brésilienne," FrEmbassy United States to Paris, 29 Dec. 1975, Strictly Reserved Diffusion,, 1971-1975-186, AMAE-F.

68. SecState to US Mission IAEA Vienna, 18 Feb. 1976, Cable 1976STATE038742, Confidential, DOS/CFP.

69. SecState to US Mission IAEA Vienna, 18 Feb. 1976, Cable 1976STATE039078, Secret, DOS/CFP.

70. "Acordo entre o Governo da República Federativa do Brasil, o Governo da República Federal da Alemanha e a Agência Internacional de Energia Atômica, para a Aplicação de Salvaguardas," CNEN, accessed 12 May 2020, http://memoria.cnen.gov.br/manut/ImprimeTR.asp?Codigo=192.

71. Brazilian Mission Vienna to Brasília, 25 Feb. 1976, Very Urgent, PNB pn a 1975.01.09; US Mission IAEA Vienna to SecState, 10 Mar. 1976, Cable 1976IAEAV01878, Confidential, DOS/CFP.

72. "The Arms Export Control Act (P.L. 90-629)," Federation of American Scientists, accessed 10 Aug. 2018, https://fas.org/asmp/resources/govern/aeca00.pdf, 472–73; J. Samuel Walker, "Nuclear Power and Nonproliferation: The Controversy over Nuclear Exports, 1974–1980," *Diplomatic History* 25.2 (Spring 2001): 222, https://doi.org/10.1111/0145 -2096.00260; Michael A. Bauser, "United States Nuclear Export Policy: Developing the Peaceful Atom as a Commodity in International Trade," *Harvard International Law Journal* 18.2 (Spring 1977): 244–48.

73. Charles Mohr, "Carter Vows a Curb on Nuclear Exports to Bar Arms Spread," *New York Times*, 26 Sept. 1976, 1.

74. Brenner, *Nuclear Power and Non-Proliferation*, 117–18.

75. Brenner, *Nuclear Power and Non-Proliferation*, 117–18.

76. Ueki to Geisel, 4 Nov. 1976, Dispatch, EG pr 1974.03.26/2.

77. Winston Lord to Kissinger, "Your Meeting with Senator Ribicoff," Confidential, 4 Nov. 1976, CWR Memos to the Secretary, October 1976–January 1977, RG 59, Entry 5176, Lot 77D117, Box 5, NARA.

78. Charles W. Robinson, telephone interview by author, 1 July 2010. I was unable to retrieve any documents confirming the visit. On the meeting between Robinson and Geisel, see also a June 2010 personal communication from David Rossin to the author, which can be found in A. David Rossin's forthcoming book on US nuclear policy under Presidents Ford and Carter.

79. "Senador prevê que Brasil não reprocessará urânio," *Jornal do Brasil*, 29 Jan. 1977, 1. On Itamaraty's desire to avoid an open confrontation with the United States, see Walter de Góes, "Novas garantias para salvar o acordo," *Jornal do Brasil*, 29 Jan. 1977, 11.

80. Robinson to Kissinger, "Next Steps on Pakistan and Brazil," 11 Jan. 1977, Top Secret, and Robinson to Kissinger, "Non-Proliferation Letter to de Guiringaud," 11 Jan. 1977, Top Secret, CWR Memos to the Secretary, October 1976–January 1977, RG 59, Entry 5176, Lot 77D117, Box 5, NARA.

81. Craig R. Whitney, "Schmidt May Modify Rio Atom Pact," *New York Times*, 27 Jan. 1977, 4. See also BrazEmbassy Washington to Itamaraty, 27 Jan. 1977, Telegram 274, Top Secret, AAS mre pn 1975.09.25.

82. SecState to AmEmbassy Brasília, 20 Feb. 1977, Cable 1977STATE035757, Secret, DOS/CFP.

83. Charles W. Robinson, telephone interview by author, 2 July 2010.

84. "Analise tática da consulta com os norte-americanos," 25 Feb. 1977, Secret, AAS, mre 1974.08.15.

85. On the meeting in Brasília, see Silveira to Geisel, 2 Mar. 1977, IPR48, Top Secret, AAS, mre pn 1975.04.25. See also AmEmbassy Brasília to SecState, 3 Mar. 1977, Cable 1977BRASIL01616, Secret, DOS/CFP.

86. Geisel to President Carter, 9 Mar. 1977, AAS mre be 1976.00.00.

87. Memorandum, Cyrus Vance to Carter, 7 Apr. 1977, Secret Handwritten Approval by Carter of the Christopher-Simonsen meeting, Remote Archives Capture, Jimmy Carter Library (hereafter RAC/JCL), NLC-128-12-7-6-3.

88. Handwritten note by Carter, Vance to Carter, "Talks with the Brazilians on Nuclear Proliferation," 2 Mar. 1977, Memorandum, Secret, RAC/JCL, NLC-128-12-6-2-8; Warren Christopher to Zbigniew Brzezinski, 28 Apr. 1977, Memorandum, Secret, Warren Christopher Papers, RG 59, Box 7, NARA.

89. On the INFCE, see Philip Gummett, "From NPT to INFCE: Developments in Thinking about Nuclear Non-proliferation," *International Affairs* 57.4 (Autumn 1981): 549–67.

90. On Smith's appointment, see Brenner, *Nuclear Power and Non-Proliferation*, 166–67.

91. BrazEmbassy Vienna to Itamaraty, 3 May 1977, Telegram 199, Top Secret Very Urgent, AAS, mre pn 1975.04.25.

92. "National Security Affairs Calendar," Secret, RAC/JCL; Silveira to Geisel, 19 Apr. 1978, Roteiro 030/78, Secret. EG pr 1974.03.00/2.

93. Ueki to Geisel, 19 May 1977, Dispatch, EG pr 1974.03.26/2; "Política Nuclear Brasileira. Interesses Norte-Americanos," n.d., Secret, AAS, mre be 1977.04.29.

94. Memorandum for Zbigniew Brzezinski and the President from Jessica Tuchman, Subject: the future of the London Suppliers Group, 30 Mar. 1977, Jimmy Carter Library Donated Historical Material, White House Central File—Subject File, National Security—Defense, ND-18, Box ND-48, General, ND 16 / CO 172 1/20/77, through Executive, ND 18 3/1/77–3/31/77.

95. Silveira to Geisel, 25 May 1977, IPR126, Top Secret, AAS, mre d 1974.03.26. Cyrus Vance proposed that Brazil participate in the NSG in June 1977. DelGrenada to Brasília, 15 June 1977, Série Chanceler 37, Secret Urgent, AAS, mre be 1977.01.27; Vance to Silveira, 21 June 1977, AAS, mre be 1977.01.27.

96. Paul C. Warnke to Christopher, 25 Mar. 1977, Memorandum, DNSA.

97. Evening Report from Robert Pastor to Jimmy Carter, 5 May 1978, RAC/JCL, NLC-24-53-6-6-5.

98. For the text of the 1978 Nuclear Non-Proliferation Act, see Public Papers of the Presidents of the United States. Jimmy Carter, 1978 (in two books). Book I—January 1 to June 30, 1978 (Washington, DC: GPO, 1979), 498–502.

99. Allan S. Krass, Peter Boskma, Boelie Elzen, and Wim A. Smith, Uranium Enrichment and Nuclear Weapon Proliferation (Solna, Sweden: SIPRI, 1983), 223.

100. Present at the Palácio da Alvorada were President Geisel, Foreign Minister Silveira, Minister Ueki, General Gustavo Moraes Rego Reis (chief minister of the general secretary of the National Security Council), Professor Hervásio Guimarães de Carvalho (chairman of CNEN), Minister Nogueira Batista (chairman of Nuclebrás), counselors Ronaldo Sardenberg and Sebastião de Rego Barros Neto, and Lieutenant Colonel Glicério Vieira Proença Junior. Silveira to Geisel, 23 Feb. 1978, IPR 60, Top Secret, EG pr 1974.00.03.2.

101. Krass et al., *Uranium Enrichment and Nuclear Weapon Proliferation*, 223.

102. Leopoldo Nuti, "Italy as a Hedging State? The Problematic Ratification of the Non-Proliferation Treaty," in Bini and Londero, *Nuclear Italy*, 119–39.

103. Krass et al., *Uranium Enrichment and Nuclear Weapon Proliferation*, 223.

104. Krass et al., *Uranium Enrichment and Nuclear Weapon Proliferation*, 223.

105. Preeminent physicists such as José Goldemberg (USP) and Rogério Cerqueira Leite (Unicamp) criticized the deal in a long interview in *Estado de São Paulo* (hereafter *EdSP*) on 2 April 1978, "Interne Kritik am Brasílianischen Kernenergieprogram," FRG

Embassy Brazil to Bonn, 6 Apr. 1978, Deutsch-Brasilianische zusammenarbeit im nucklearen Bereich Nuklearpolitik 1974 1984, PA/AA.

106. AmEmbassy Buenos Aires to SecState, 23 Sept. 1974, Cable 1974BUENOS07083, Secret, DOS/CFP.

107. Silveira to Geisel, 3 June 1975, IPR 116, Secret, AAS, mre d 1974.03.26. In mid-June 1975 Lysaneas Maciel, a Brazilian congressman, declared that Argentina had developed its first atomic bomb and owned more than 150 kilos of plutonium. "L'Argentina ha l'atomica," *L'umanitá,* 20 June 1975, Archivio Achille Albonetti, Universitá Roma Tre.

108. Silveira to Geisel. 21 May 1975, IPR 108, AAS, mre d 1974.03.26.

109. "National Security Study Memorandum 202. US Nuclear Non-Proliferation Policy," 23 May 1974, National Security Council Institutional Files, Study Memorandums (1969–1974), Box H-205, Richard Nixon Presidential Library.

110. Sidney Sober to Henry A. Kissinger, 31 May 1974, Secret/Sensitive, Presidential Decision Directives Extras, Box 6, National Security Study Memorandums 156–165, DNSA, 13. A US document comparing the nuclear agreement between India and Argentina to the 1968 agreement between India and Brazil underlined that both agreements were "void of any reference to international safeguards or inspections." "Argentina-Brazil: Nuclear Cooperation Agreements with India," 1 Aug. 1974,Memorandum for the record, Secret, Department of State, Declassified Documents Reference System.

111. AmEmbassy Brasília to SecState, 24 May 1974, Cable 1974BRASIL03679, Secret, DOS/CFP; AmEmbassy Brasília to SecState, 5 June 1974, Cable 1974BRASIL03965, Confidential, DOS/CFP.

112. On the lack of implementation and the expiry of the agreement, see Silveira to Geisel, 7 Aug. 1975, p. 5, IPR 227, AAS, mre d 1974.03.26.

113. AmEmbassy Brasília to SecState, 5 June 1974, Cable 1974BRASIL03964, Limited Official Use, DOS/CFP; AmEmbassy New Delhi to SecState, 7 June 1974, Cable 1974 NEWDE07608, Confidential, DOS/CFP; Ueki to Geisel, Dispatch, 4 June 1974, EG pr 1974.03.26/2.

114. Gaspari, *A ditadura encurralada,* 155.

115. Silveira to Geisel, 17 Oct. 1974, IPR 253, series IPR 1974, AHMRE-B.

116. "Visita de funcionário da embaixada à central nuclear de Atucha," BrazEmbassy Buenos Aires to Itamaraty, 1 July 1974, Confidential, PNB pn a 1974.07.01.

117. Ueki to Geisel, 29 Aug. 1974, Dispatch, EG pr 1974.03.26/2; "Relações Brasil-Argentina," Silveira to Geisel, 14 Oct. 1974, IPR, Secret, EG pr 1974.03.00/2.

118. The idea of an agreement between Argentina and Brazil to solve a possible nuclear dispute in the area was later proposed by Cyrus Vance and Joseph Nye during the first year of the Carter administration. SecState to AmEmbassy Bonn, 7 June 1975, Cable 1975 STATE133585, Secret, DOS/CFP.

119. "Energia Nuclear. Cooperação entre o Brasil e a R.F. da Alemanha," BrazEmbassy Buenos Aires to Itamaraty, 9 June 1975, Secret Urgent, AAS, mre pn 1974.08.15.

120. Diego Hurtado, *El sueño de Argentina atómica: Política, tecnología nuclear y desarollo nacional (1945–2006)* (Buenos Aires: Edhasa, 2014), 168.

121. AmEmbassy Brasília to SecState, 11 July 1975, Cable 1975BRASIL05714, Confidential, DOS/CFP.

122. AmEmbassy Brasília to SecState, 11 July 1975, Cable 1975BRASIL05714, Confidential, DOS/CFP.

123. "Nota à reunião no MRE em 24 de Novembro de 1976," handwritten document, PNB pn a 1974.07.01.

124. "Acordo Brasil-RFA. Consulta alemã sobre entendimentos Brasil-Argentina," Geraldo Holanda Cavalcanti to Silveira, 14 Feb. 1977, Pró-Memória, Top Secret, AAS, mre pn 1974.08.15.

125. Warnke to Christopher, 25 Mar. 1977, Memorandum, Secret, DNSA. On the Argentine criticism, see "Argentina—Estados Unidos," n.d., AAS, mre be 1977.06.01.

126. "Package Solution for Brazil Nuclear Issue," Christopher to Vance, 21 Apr. 1977, Memorandum, Warren Christopher Papers, Box 7, NARA.

127. EMFA to Hugo Abreu, CSN minister, 22 Mar. 1977, Confidential, EG pr 1974.03.25/1.

128. "Visita do Embaixador da URSS ao Senhor Presidente da República," 24 May 1977, Confidential, EG pr 1974.00.03/2.

129. For a deeper analysis of the Findley initiative, see Carlo Patti and Rodrigo Mallea, "American Seeds of ABACC? Findley's Proposal to Create a Mutual Nuclear Inspections System between Brazil and Argentina," *International History Review* 40.5 (2018): 996–1013, https://doi.org/10.1080/07075332.2018.1441891.

130. Silveira to Geisel, 14. Nov. 1977, IPR 275, Secret, EG pr 1974.03.00/2.

131. "Conversation with Lionel Brizola, December 22, 1977," 10 Jan. 1978, Memorandum, Confidential, Presidential Papers of Jimmy Carter, National Security Affairs, Staff Material, North/South, Pastor, Country File, Collection 24, Box 2, Jimmy Carter Library.

Chapter 5 · *Between Autonomy and International Collaboration, 1979–1985*

1. "Brasil. Congresso Nacional. Senado Federal. Comissão Parlamentar Mista de Inquérito destinada a apurar o Programa Autônomo de Energia Nuclear, também conhecido como 'Programa Paralelo,'" *Relatório final*, 1990, Biblioteca do Senado, accessed 8 July 2017, http://legis.senado.leg.br/sdleg-getter/documento?t=66808&mime=application/pdf, 9.

2. Christopher to Carter, 16 Oct. 1978, Memorandum, Secret, Department of State, Declassified Documents Reference System; Saraiva Guerreiro to Figueiredo, 20 Mar. 1979, IPR 004, Secret, Ramiro Saraiva Guerreiro personal archive, FGV/CPDOC (hereafter SG); Walter Mondale to Carter, "My Trip to Venezuela and Brazil: Impressions and Suggestions for Follow-Up," 2 Apr. 1979, Memorandum, Secret, Walter Mondale Papers, Jimmy Carter Library.

3. *Foreign Relations of the United States, 1977–1980*, vol. 24, *South America; Latin America Region*, ed. Sara E. Berndt (Washington, DC: GPO, 2018), doc. 48, https://history.state.gov/historicaldocuments/frus1977-80v24/d48.

4. Saraiva Guerreiro to Figueiredo, 26 Dec. 1980, IPR 361, Secret, SG.

5. Saraiva Guerreiro to Figueiredo, 9 Oct. 1981, IPR 328, Top Secret, SG.

6. An important issue was possible missile proliferation. "US-Brazilian Space Cooperation," Brzezinki to Carter, 3 Oct. 1979, NSC Memorandum, Secret, RAC/JCL.

7. João Baena Soares (Brazil's representative in Geneva) to President Figuereido, 18 Sept. 1980, IPR 262, SG.

8. "Brazil's changing nuclear goals: Motives and constraints," 21 Oct. 1985, SNIE 93-83 (hereafter SNIE 93-83), Secret, CIA, https://www.cia.gov/library/readingroom/docs/DOC_0000787520.pdf.

9. "Construir usinas nucleares já não é prioridade, diz Cals," *FdSP*, 14 Dec. 1983, 7.

10. Silveira, Ueki, and Gustavo Moraes Rego Reis to Geisel, 12 Mar. 1979, EM 008/79, Secret, AHMRE-B.

11. The decision to start Project Conversão (the indigenous and unsafeguarded project of IPEN to convert yellowcake into uranium hexafluoride) was prescient, since the agreement with the French UPUK was never implemented because of the safeguards that the French government would impose. Luiz Augusto de Castro Neves, FGV/CPDOC interview, 23 Jan. 2012, Rio de Janeiro.

12. On the inclusion of the IEA in the National Nuclear Energy Plan, see Convênio CNEN 12/72, 7 June 1972, CNEN.

13. Débora Motta, *Rex Nazaré—Uma vida dedicada à energia nuclear* (Rio de Janeiro: Walprint Gráfica e Editora, 2014), 77.

14. Danilo Venturini to Saraiva Guerreiro, 14 Mar. 1979, Aviso 070/79, AHMRE-B.

15. Venturini to Saraiva Guerreiro, 18 June 1979, Aviso 135/79, Secret, AHMRE-B.

16. Jacques E. C. Hymans, "Of Gauchos and Gringos: Why Argentina Never Wanted the Bomb and Why the United States Thought It Did," *Security Studies* 10.3 (2001): 155–59.

17. "Guidelines for the Autonomous Brazilian Nuclear Program," Venturini to Figueiredo, EM 11/085, 11 Feb. 1985, History and Public Policy Program Digital Archive, https://digitalarchive.wilsoncenter.org/document/121361.

18. Venturini to Saraiva Guerreiro, 18 June 1979, Aviso 135/79, Secret, AHMRE-B.

19. In 1981 the Brazilian Society of Physics denounced the existence of civilian-military nuclear research activities. "Físicos formarão comissão sobre o uso bélico da ciência," *FdSP*, 15 July 1981, 12.

20. Motta, *Rex Nazaré*, 101.

21. "Guidelines for the Autonomous Brazilian Nuclear Program," Venturini to Figueiredo, EM 11/085, 11 Feb. 1985, History and Public Policy Program Digital Archive, https://digitalarchive.wilsoncenter.org/document/121361; Luiz Augusto de Castro Neves, FGV/CPDOC interview, 13 Jan. 2010, Rio de Janeiro.

22. Retired general Coutinho Dirceu, former director of Nuclei, in October 1979 severely criticized the jet-nozzle option and requested the adoption of the ultracentrifuge method for enriching uranium. AmEmbassy Brasília to State, 22 Oct. 1979, Cable 1979BRASIL09291, Confidential, DOS/CFP.

23. On Unicamp's scientific environment, see Simon Schwartzman, *Um espaço para a ciência: A formação da comunidade científica no Brasil* (Brasília: Ministério de Ciência e Tecnologia, 2001), chap. 9, p. 11. On Zeferino Vaz and the creation of Unicamp, see Stela Maria Meneghel, "Zeferino Vaz e a UNICAMP: Uma trajetoria e um modelo de universidade" (master's thesis, Unicamp, 1994).

24. Rogério Cerqueira Leite, telephone interview by author, 3 Mar. 2020.

25. Jack Boureston and Charles D. Ferguson, "Laser Enrichment: Separation Anxiety," *Bulletin of the Atomic Scientists*, Mar./Apr. 2005, 14–18. On the technique, see also F. S. Becker and K. L. Kompa, "The Practical and Physical Aspect of Uranium Isotope Separation with Lasers," *Nuclear Technology* 58 (Aug. 1982), PNB pi Becker, F.1982 .08.00.

26. Steven Hargrove, "Laser Technology Follows in Lawrence's Footsteps," *Science & Technology Review*, May 2000, https://www.nrc.gov/docs/ML1017/ML101790145.pdf.

27. Motta, *Rex Nazaré*, 77; Cláudio Rodrigues, interview by author, 23 Nov. 2015, IPEN–São Paulo.

28. João Paulo dos Reis Velloso, Maria Celina Soares d'Araújo, and Celso Castro, *Tempos modernos: João Paulo dos Reis Velloso; memórias do desenvolvimento* (Rio de Janeiro: FGV, 2004), 232.

29. Hervásio de Carvalho to Ueki, 9 Sept. 1977, CNEN 11/77, PNB pn c 1969.12.01.

30. Hervásio de Carvalho to Ueki, 9 Sept. 1977, CNEN 11/77, PNB pn c 1969.12.01.

31. Walker Antonio Lins de Santana and Olival Freire Junior, "Contribuição do físico brasileiro Sérgio Porto para as aplicações do laser e sua introdução no Brasil," *Revista Brasileira de Ensino de Física* 32.3 (2010): 1–10.

32. Hervásio de Carvalho to Ueki, 9 Sept. 1977, CNEN 11/77, PNB pn c 1969.12.01.

33. Hervásio de Carvalho to Ueki, 9 Sept. 1977, CNEN 11/77, PNB pn c 1969.12.01.

34. Luiz Francisco Ferreira to Ueki, 20 Sept. 1977, Processo MME/GM 181/77, Secret, PNB pn c 1969.12.01. On Geisel's support of the autonomous project, see Luiz Augusto de Castro Neves, FGV/CPDOC interview, 25 Mar. 2011, Rio de Janeiro.

35. "José Alberto Albano do Amarante," AEITA, accessed 22 Jan. 2017, http://www.aeitaonline.com.br/wiki/index.php?title=José_Alberto_Albano_do_Amarante.

36. AmEmbassy Brasília to AmEmbassy Tokyo, 23 Jan. 1979, Cable 1979BRASIL00661, DOS/CFP.

37. It is not clear whether the Brazilian navy's interest was in response to Argentina's possible plans to develop nuclear submarines with Italy.

38. Gaspari, *A ditadura encurralada*, 134; "Tecnologia Nuclear para a Marinha," 16 Nov. 1976, Aide-mémoire, Secret, EG pr 1974.03.19.

39. "Brasil. Congresso Nacional. Senado Federal. Comissão Parlamentar Mista de Inquérito destinada a apurar o Programa Autônomo de Energia Nuclear, também conhecido como 'Programa Paralelo,'" *Relatório final*, 1990, Biblioteca do Senado, accessed 8 July 2017, http://legis.senado.leg.br/sdleg-getter/documento?t=66808&mime=application/pdf, 4.

40. Luiz Augusto de Castro Neves, FGV/CPDOC interview, 19 Jan. 2010, Rio de Janeiro.

41. For Jordan's criticism of the jet nozzle, see Igor Veltman, "Docente analisa o setor nuclear," *FdSP*, 24 Jan. 1981, 15. On Jordan's expertise, see Laercio Vinhas, telephone interview by author, 25 May 2019.

42. Cláudio Rodrigues, interview by author, 23 Nov. 2015, IPEN–São Paulo.

43. As noted by Dr. Vinhas, IPEN had a deep experience of collaboration with private companies and the rest of the University of São Paulo. Laercio Vinhas, telephone interview by author, 25 May 2019.

44. Ricardo Bonalume Neto, "Pirataria ajuda Marinha a construir centrifugas," *FdSP*, 9 Apr. 1988, A-17.

45. Luiz Augusto de Castro Neves, FGV/CPDOC interview, 13 Jan. 2010, Rio de Janeiro.

46. Hélio Contreiras, "Espionagem à brasileira: Governo montou operação saber os segredos da tecnologia nuclear de países como Alemanha e Estados Unidos," *Istoé*, 9 May 1999, http://istoe.com.br/30749_ESPIONAGEM+A+BRASILEIRA/.

47. Mark Fitzpatrick, *Nuclear Black Market: Pakistan, A. Q. Khan and the Rise of Proliferation Networks; A Net Assessment* (London: International Institute for Strategic Studies, 2007), 58.

48. Mark Hibbs and Daniel Horner, "Bearing Design Prompted Brazil to Withhold Centrifuge Data from IAEA," *Nuclear Fuel*, 6 Dec. 2004; "Cnen vê novo tipo de 'ruido' em negociações," *FdSP*, 23 Oct. 2004, A-12.

49. See, e.g., Othon Luiz Pinheiro da Silva, "Um grande preconceito," *O Globo*, 27 Oct. 2004, 9, https://www2.senado.leg.br/bdsf/bitstream/handle/id/392446/noticia .htm?sequence=1&isAllowed=y.

50. Cláudio Rodrigues, interview by author, 23 Nov. 2015, IPEN–São Paulo.

51. "Brasil. Congresso Nacional. Senado Federal. Comissão Parlamentar Mista de Inquérito destinada a apurar o Programa Autônomo de Energia Nuclear, também conhecido como 'Programa Paralelo,'" *Relatório final*, 1990, Biblioteca do Senado, accessed 8 July 2017, http://legis.senado.leg.br/sdleg-getter/documento?t=66808&mime=application/pdf, 4.

52. On the end of the Nuclebrás activities, see SNIE 93-83, CIA, Freedom of Information Act (hereafter FOIA).

53. On the possible capability of producing plutonium, see Bernardo Kucinski, "Status of Nuclear Development Reported," *Guardian*, 29 Dec. 1981, 6. The article appears in "Worldwide Report. Nuclear Development and Proliferation," JPRS L/10343, 19 Feb. 1982, FBIS, https://www.cia.gov/library/readingroom/docs/CIA-RDP82-00850R000500030052 -6.pdf.

54. "Guidelines for the Autonomous Brazilian Nuclear Program," Venturini to Figueiredo, EM 11/085, 11 Feb. 1985, History and Public Policy Program Digital Archive, https://digitalarchive.wilsoncenter.org/document/121361.

55. See "Convênio de Cooperação CNEN/Ministério do Exercito," 9 Feb. 1972, CNEN 01/72.

56. A private company called TECMAT, owned by a former army officer, would provide pure nuclear graphite as specified in an agreement with CTEx; the heavy water would be provided by CNEN or by the company Peróxido do Brasil. Odete Maria de Oliveira, *Os descaminhos do Brasil nuclear* (Ijuí: Ed. Inuijuí, 1999), 332.

57. Brazilian nuclear scientist, interview by author, February 2012.

58. SNIE 93-83, CIA.

59. "Guidelines for the Autonomous Brazilian Nuclear Program," Venturini to Figueiredo, EM 11/085, 11 Feb.1985, History and Public Policy Program Digital Archive, https://digitalarchive.wilsoncenter.org/document/121361.

60. BrazEmbassy Canberra to Itamaraty, "Segurança/Militar, Brasil/Australia, Oferecimento de material bélico e combustivel nuclear," 15 Jan. 1979, Secret Urgent, AHMRE-B.

61. On Brazil's cooperation with other countries, such as Venezuela, see "Considerações preliminares sobre definição de uma política brasileira de cooperação com outros países na área nuclear," 2 July 1979, Secret, Nuclebrás document, PNB pn a 1973.05.18; Matthew Kroenig, *Exporting the Bomb: Technology Transfer and the Spread of Nuclear Weapons* (Ithaca, NY: Cornell University Press, 2010); and Matthew Fuhrmann, *Atomic Assistance: How "Atoms for Peace" Programs Cause Nuclear Insecurity* (Ithaca, NY: Cornell University Press, 2012).

62. For a general overview of relations between Brazil and Iraq, see Seme Taleb Fares, "O pragmatismo do petróleo: As relações entre o Brasil e o Iraque," *Revista Brasileira de Política Internacional* 50.2 (2007): 129–45.

63. On the Iraqi program, see Målfrid Braut-Hegghammer, *Unclear Physics: Why Iraq and Libya Failed to Build Nuclear Weapons* (Ithaca, NY: Cornell University Press, 2016).

64. Ueki to Rego Reis, 17 Jan. 1979, Avisos 28 and 29/79, Confidential, PNB pn a 1978.07.13.

65. Saraiva Guerreiro to Figueiredo, 17 Apr. 1979, IPR 37, Top Secret, SG; "Bras.-irakische Gesprache uber evtl. Uranlifierungen an Irak," Cable 373, 30 May 1979, Folder: "Geimensame uranprospektion-NUCLAM" (hereafter Bd. 13261), PA/AA.

66. Saraiva Guerreiro to Figueiredo, 19 Sept. 1979, IPR 191, Top Secret, SG.

67. On the agreement between Brazil and Iraq on the peaceful use of atomic energy, see Senado Federal, Decreto 8651, 27 Oct. 1981.

68. Motta, *Rex Nazaré*, 90.

69. Luiz Augusto de Castro Neves, FGV/CPDOC interview, 10 Jan. 2010, Rio de Janeiro.

70. For a detailed analysis of the possible cooperation between Brazil and South Africa, see Carlo Patti, "The Forbidden Cooperation: South Africa–Brazil Nuclear Relations at the Turn of the 1970s," *Revista Brasileira de Política Internacional* 61.2 (2018), https:/doi .org/10.1590/0034-7329201800206.

71. Luiz Augusto de Castro Neves, FGV/CPDOC interview, 23 Jan. 2012, Rio de Janeiro.

72. Feroz Hassan Khan, *Eating Grass: The Making of the Pakistani Bomb* (Stanford, CA: Stanford University Press, 2012), 153–54.

73. IPR 101, 4 Apr. 1984, Top Secret, SG; IPR 40, 13 Feb. 1984, Top Secret, series IPR 1984, SG; IPR 95, 28 Mar. 1984, Top Secret, SG.

74. BrazEmbassy Islamabad to Brasília, 26 Sept. 1981, Telegram 104, Secret, 664.2, Caixa 307, AHMRE-B.

75. Luiz Augusto de Castro Neves, FGV/CPDOC interview, 23 Jan. 2012, Rio de Janeiro.

76. Nicola Horsburgh, *China and Global Nuclear Order: From Estrangement to Active Engagement* (Oxford: Oxford University Press, 2015), 85.

77. "Secretary's Talking Points: US-China Relations," June 1981, History and Public Policy Program Digital Archive, National Security Archives, http://digitalarchive .wilsoncenter.org/document/122356.

78. Danielly Silva Ramos, "O Brasil e a República Popular da China: Política externa comparada e relações bilaterais (1974–2004)" (PhD diss., Universidade de Brasília, 2006).

79. In December 1981 Ambassador Marcos Castrioto de Azambuja, head of the Asia and Oceania section of the Foreign Ministry, met with the Chinese ambassador, Chang Te-Chun, in Brasília to discuss the possible supply of enriched uranium. "Perspectiva de fornecimento de urânio enriquecido ao Brasil por parte da República Popular da China (PRC)," 1 Feb. 1982, Memória da 1ª Subchefia do Conselho de Segurança Nacional, Confidential, BR DFANBSB N8.0.PSN,EST.121, AN-B.

80. "Compras de urânio enriquecido na República Popular da China," 29 Oct. 1982, Memória da 1ª Subchefia do Conselho de Segurança Nacional, Secret, BR DFANBSB N8.0.PSN, EST.121, AN-B.

81. "Compras de urânio enriquecido na República Popular da China," 29 Oct. 1982; IPR 101, 4 Apr. 1984, Secret, SG.

82. "Compras de urânio enriquecido na República Popular da China," 29 Oct. 1982.

83. "Compras de urânio enriquecido na República Popular da China," 29 Oct. 1982; Luiz Augusto de Castro Neves, FGV/CPDOC interview, Rio de Janeiro, 25 Mar. 2011.

84. In November 1983 Brazil paid the PRC almost US$2 million for nuclear material. See n. 03-SF/33381/83, 1 Nov. 1983, Conselho de Segurança Nacional, BR DFANBSB N8.o.PSN, EST.317, AN-B. On the possible acquisition of HEU, see Rodrigo Mallea, Matias Spektor, and Nicholas J. Wheeler, eds., *The Origins of Nuclear Cooperation: A Critical Oral History Between Argentina and Brazil* (Washington, DC: Wilson Center; Rio de Janeiro: FGV, 2015), 133. Doctor Laercio Vinhas, then working at IPEN, is unaware that any amount of HEU was imported from China. Laercio Vinhas, email to author, 25 May 2020.

85. "Zusammenarbeit mit Brasilien auf den gebiet der friedlichen nutzung der kernenrgie," Bonn to West German Embassy in Brasília, 23 Nov. 1982, Cable 0280, Kernenergie—Deutsche-Brasilianische zusammenarbeit 1982 (hereafter Bd. 13261), PA/AA.

86. The US government suspected an illegal trade between the PRC and other countries. In October 1985 the US senator Alan Cranston (D-CA) accused China of sharing nuclear technology with countries like Argentina, Brazil, Iran, Pakistan, and South Africa. "Telegram, Argentine Embassy in Brasilia, Brazil and China Deny Charges of Nuclear Proliferation," 24 Oct. 1985, History and Public Policy Program Digital Archive, Telegrama ordinario, Cable 1674, Historical Archive of the Ministry of Foreign Affairs and Worship, Argentina, obtained and translated by FGV, https://digitalarchive.wilsoncenter.org /document/116878.

87. IPR 101, 4 Apr. 1984, Secret, SG. On the invitation to China, see IPR 175, 13 June 1983, Secret, SG. On Figueiredo's approval, see IPR 125, 2 May 1984,Top Secret, SG. On the text of the agreement, see *Visita do Presidente João Figueiredo à República Popular da China, Maio—1984*, Presidência da República (Brasília: Imprensa Nacional, 1984), 67.

88. Saraiva Guerreiro to Figueiredo, 2 May 1984, IPR 125, Top Secret, SG.

89. Bundesnachrichtendienst (German Federal Service of Intelligence), "Brasilien/ VR China: Angebliche Geheimklausel zum Nuklearvertrag," 4 Oct. 1984,Wissenshaftlich-Technologische-Zusammen arbeit mit der VR China und Brasilien, Bd. 13261, PA/AA.

90. Michael Barletta reported that 200 kilograms of UF_6 were covertly imported from China for use at IPEN before Brazil developed its enrichment capacity. Barletta, "The Military Nuclear Program in Brazil" (CISAC–Stanford University Working Paper, 1997), 13.

91. Brasília to BrazEmbassy Beijing, 22 May 1985, Telegram 301, Secret, AHMRE-B.

92. Héctor Subiza (Departamento América Latina) to Dirección General de Política, "Cooperación con Brasil en el area nuclear," 23 Aug. 1979, Memorandum 227, AHC; Rodrigo Mallea, "La cuestión nuclear en la relación argentino-brasileña (1968–1984)" (master's thesis, IESP-UERJ, 2012); W. A. Selcher, "Brazilian-Argentine Relations in the 1980s: From Wary Rivalry to Friendly Competition," *Journal of Interamerican Studies and World Affairs* 27.2 (1985): 25–53.

93. Subiza to Dirección General de Política, "Cooperación con Brasil en el area nuclear," 23 Aug. 1979, Memorandum 227, AHC. On the posible Brazilian-Argentine cooperation, see also AmEmbassy Buenos Aires to State, 22 Aug. 1979, Cable 1979BUE-NOS6831, Confidential, DOS/CFP.

94. Saraiva Guerreiro to Figueiredo, 24 Jan. 1980, IPR 14, Secret, PNB pn a 1974.07.01; Saraiva Guerreiro to Figueiredo, 3 Mar. 1980, IPR 49, Secret, SG; Itamaraty to BrazEmbassy Buenos Aires, 12 Feb. 1980, Telegram 146, Secret, AHMRE-B.

95. Nogueira Batista to Saraiva Guerreiro, "Relatório enviado ao Ministro da Relações Exteriores. Assunto: Viagem a Buenos Aires," 23 Mar. 1980, Secret, PNB pn a 1974.07.01.

96. Nogueira Batista to Saraiva Guerreiro, "Relatório enviado ao Ministro da Relações Exteriores. Assunto: Viagem a Buenos Aires," 23 Mar. 1980, Secret, PNB pn a 1974.07.01.

97. Saraiva Guerreiro, Cesar Cals, and Venturini to Figueiredo, 24 Jan. 1980, IPR 14, Secret, PNB pn a 1974.07.01.

98. "Negociações com Argentina," 16 Apr. 1980, Unclassified—Unofficial Document of the Brazilian Ministry of Foreign Relations, PNB pn a 1974.07.01; Nogueira Batista to Saraiva Guerreiro, "Relatório enviado ao Ministro da Relações Exteriores. Assunto: Viagem a Buenos Aires," 23 Mar. 1980, Secret, PNB pn a 1974.07.01; Ney Freire to Nogueira Batista, 25 July 1980, Nuclebrás internal communication, Confidential, PNB pn a 1974.07.01. The leasing contract was signed on 20 August 1980. On the supply of yellowcake and the CNEA confirmation, see Itamaraty to Nuclebrás, 8 May 1980, Telegram, PNB pn a 1974.07.01.

99. Mallea, "La cuestión nuclear."

100. Julio César Carasales and Instituto del Servicio Exterior de la Nación, eds., *De rivales a socios: El proceso de cooperación nuclear entre Argentina y Brasil* (Buenos Aires: Grupo Editor Latinoamericano, 1997).

101. "Acuerdo de cooperación entre el Gobierno de la República Argentina y el Gobierno de la República Federativa del Brasil, para el desarrollo y la aplicación de los usos pacíficos de la energía nuclear, Brasília, 02.11.80," Aviso 059/80, Secret, 5 Feb. 1980, AHMRE-B.

102. "Argentine-Brazilian Nuclear Cooperation: More Form than Substance," 22 June 1980, Top Secret, RAC/JCL.

103. Rubens Ricupero, *A diplomacia na construção do Brasil, 1750–2016* (Rio de Janeiro: Versal Editores, 2017), 543–45.

104. "Questão das Malvinas. Energia nuclear. Declarações do Presidente da Comissão Nacional de Energia Atômica," Unclassified and undated telegram from the Brazilian Embassy in Buenos Aires, signed Carlos. F. Duarte, PNB pn a 1974.07.01. On the British deployment of nuclear submarines in South America during the Falklands War, see Lawrence Freedman, *Official History of the Falklands Campaign*, vol. 2, *War and Diplomacy* (London: Routledge, 2005), 48–52.

105. Itamaraty to CNEN, 16 June 1982, Telegram, PNB pn a 1974.07.01.

106. "Relatório sobre visita à unidade de reprocessamento da CNEA, em Novembro 1982," Nuclebrás internal document, Confidential, PNB pn a 1974.07.

107. Roberto Esteves to Nogueira Batista, "Fornecimento de serviços de enriquecimento à Argentina," 13 Dec. 1982, Nuclebrás document, PNB pn a 1974.07.01; Nogueira Batista to Venturini, "Fornecimento de urânio enriquecido à Argentina," 23 Dec. 1982, Nuclebrás document, Confidential, PNB pn a 1974.07.01.

108. In 1981 Argentina purchased the heavy-water facility from the Swiss company Sulzter. "CNEA Informa," Feb. 1981, Unclassified, PNB pn a 1974.07.01. The contract was viewed with suspicion by the United States and partially by Brazil. On the Soviet sale of enriched uranium, see Itamaraty to CNEN, 16 June 1982, Telegram, PNB pn a 1974.07.01.

109. "Argentina's Nuclear Policies in Light of the Falklands Defeat," 8 Sept. 1982, SNIE 91-2-82, Secret, CIA, https://www.cia.gov/library/readingroom/docs/DOC_0001265543

.pdf. On Alfonsín's awareness of the enrichment capability, see Itamaraty to BrazEmbassy Buenos Aires, 1 Dec. 1983, Telegram 2327/83, AHMRE-B.

110. "Cartas enfatizam o uso pacífico da energia nuclear," *FdSP*, 19 Nov. 1983, 4.

111. BrazEmbassy Buenos Aires to Itamaraty, 18 Nov. 1983, Telegram 3172, Secret, AHMRE-B.

112. Saraiva Guerreiro to Figueiredo, 17 May 1984, IPR 156, Secret, SG.

113. Richard Kessler, "Argentine Enrichment Pronouncement Characterized as Startling," *Nucleonics Week* 24.47 (1983): 1; "Argentina's Nuclear Policies Under Alfonsín," 31 July 1984, Secret, SNIE 91/5-84, CIA, FOIA, https://www.cia.gov/library/readingroom /docs/DOC_0001265542.pdf.

114. "Argentina's Nuclear Policies Under Alfonsín," 31 July 1984, Secret, SNIE 91/5-84, CIA, FOIA, https://www.cia.gov/library/readingroom/docs/DOC_0001265542.pdf.

115. The United States reported that since November 1983 Brazil had proceeded with construction of a pilot centrifuge uranium enrichment plant, increasing funding for all indigenous research activities at the expense of the nuclear power program, and tightened security measures at its nuclear research centers. "Argentina's Nuclear Policies Under Alfonsín," 31 July 1984, Secret, SNIE 91/5-84, CIA, FOIA, https://www.cia.gov/library /readingroom/docs/DOC_0001265542.pdf.

116. Itamaraty to BrazEmbassy Buenos Aires, 1 Dec. 1983, Telegram 2327/83, AHMRE-B.

117. "Brasil-Argentina: Energia Nuclear," Roberto Abdenur to Saraiva Guerreiro, 10 Jan. 1985, Secret, Rubens Barbosa personal archive, FGV/CPDOC (hereafter Rba), mpc c 1985.01.10.

118. "Brasil tem capacidade para fabricar a bomba, afirma brigadeiro," *FdSP*, 14 Dec. 1983, 7. For the CIA estimates on Brazil's lack of capability in the design of nuclear weapons, see SNIE 93-83, 21 Oct. 1983, CIA, https://www.cia.gov/library/readingroom/docs /DOC_0000787519.pdf.

119. "Abertura nuclear," *FdSP*, 14 Oct. 1984, 2.

120. The secret proposal was revealed by Ambassador Luiz Augusto de Castro Neves, then a member of CSN. See Mallea, Spektor, and Wheeler, *Origins of Nuclear Cooperation*, 132.

121. Mallea, Spektor, and Wheeler, *Origins of Nuclear Cooperation*, 132.

122. On the rumors concerning a possible Brazilian bomb, see Jean Krasno, "Nonproliferation: Brazil's Secret Nuclear Program," *Orbis: A Journal of World Affairs* 38.3 (1994): 425–36. The opposition to Brazilian participation in the nuclear arms race was confirmed by President Figueiredo in May 1984. "Statements of President Figueiredo on the Treaty of Tlatelolco," AmEmbassy Brasília to SecState, 21 May 1984, Confidential, DNSA.

123. SNIE 93-83, CIA.

124. Saraiva Guerreiro to Figueiredo, 17 May 1984, IPR 156, Secret, SG.

Chapter 6 · Brazil's Re-democratization and Continuation of the Nuclear Program, 1985–1989

1. "Declaração de Iperó. Declaração conjunta sobre política nuclear," 8 Apr. 1988, ABACC, https://www.abacc.org.br/en/wp-content/uploads/2016/09/Declaração-de-Iperó -português.pdf.

2. On the support of the review of Brazil's nuclear policy, see "Físicos apóiam tese da revisão do acordo nuclear," *FdSP*, 20 Aug. 1984, 4. On the US intelligence analyses, see SNIE 93-83, Secret, CIA. For the CIA assessment of Neves's attitude toward nuclear energy, see "Brazil: The Civilians Return to Power; An Intelligence Assessment," Feb. 1985, ALA 85-10015, CIA Directorate of Intelligence, CIA, FOIA, 9, https://www.cia.gov/readingroom/docs/CIA-RDP86T00589R000100060002-9.pdf.

3. "Brazil: The Civilians Return to Power; An Intelligence Assessment," Feb. 1985, ALA 85-10015, CIA Directorate of Intelligence, CIA, FOIA, 9.

4. "Brazil: The Civilians Return to Power; An Intelligence Assessment," Feb. 1985, ALA 85-10015, CIA Directorate of Intelligence, CIA, FOIA, 9.

5. Leonard S. Spector, *The New Nuclear Nations: The Spread of Nuclear Weapons* (New York: Vintage Books, 1985), 178–80; John Redick, "Latin America's Emerging Non-Proliferation Consensus," *Arms Control Today* 24.2 (1994): 3–9; "Energia Nuclear. Relações Brasil Argentina," Information to the Director of the Economic Affairs and Trade Division of the Ministry of Foreign Affairs, 30 Apr. 1985, Secret, Rba mpc c 1985.01.10.

6. National Intelligence Daily, 15 Mar. 1985, Cable, Top Secret. CIA, FOIA, https://www.cia.gov/readingroom/docs/DOC_0000259006.pdf.

7. Leila Reiss, "Brasil deverá ter sua primeira bomba atômica em 1990," *FdSP*, 28 Apr. 1985, 25.

8. "Deputado vai a Bonn para denunciar pesquisa paralela," *FdSP*, 28 Apr. 1985, 25.

9. "Para Cerqueira Leite, não existe a 'vontade' de se chegar à arma," *FdSP*, 28 Apr. 1985, 25.

10. José Goldemberg publicly praised IPEN's effort to master uranium enrichment through the centrifuge method and requested the creation of a commission in a personal meeting with President Sarney on 10 July 1985. "Goldemberg quer rever acordo nuclear," *FdSP*, 14 July 1985, 27; Aureliano Chaves to José Sarney, EM 87/85, in "Avaliação do Programa Nuclear Brasileiro. Relatório ao Presidente da República. April 1986—Brasília," Academia Brasileira de Ciência, accessed 28 Feb. 2018, http://ecen.com/para_imprimir/relatorio_vargas.pdf.

11. The Vargas Commission was composed of the physicists José Israel Vargas (chairman), Oscar Sala (vice chairman), José Leite Lopes, Marcelo Damy de Souza Santos, Fernando Claudio Zawislak, and Ramayana Gazzinelli; the biologists Luiz Renato Caldas and Eduardo Penna Franca; and the economist José Pelúcio Ferreira. José Mindlin, Caspar Erich Stemmer, and Alberto Pereira de Castro represented the private industrial and entrepreneurial sectors, while Luiz Augusto de Castro Neves represented the CSN secretary-general, Roberto Rodrigo Krause represented the Ministry of Foreign Affairs, José Walderley Coêlho Dias represented Nuclebrás, and José Guilherme Araújo Lameira Bittencourt represented the Brazilian Institute of Nuclear Quality (Instituto Brasileiro da Qualidade Nuclear). "Avaliação do Programa Nuclear Brasileiro. Relatório ao Presidente da República. April 1986—Brasília," Academia Brasileira de Ciência, accessed 28 Feb. 2018, http://ecen.com/para_imprimir/relatorio_vargas.pdf.

12. Carlo Patti, *O programa nuclear brasileiro: Uma história oral* (Rio de Janeiro: FGV, 2014), 116.

13. "Relatório da 'Comissão Vargas' completa vinte anos," *Economia e Energia* 59 (Dec. 2006–Jan. 2007), http://ecen.com/eee59/eee59p/relatorio_comissao_vargas.htm.

14. SNIE 93-83, Secret, CIA, FOIA.

15. "Brasil. Congresso Nacional. Senado Federal. Comissão Parlamentar Mista de Inquérito destinada a apurar o Programa Autônomo de Energia Nuclear, também conhecido como 'Programa Paralelo,'" *Relatório final*, 1990, Biblioteca do Senado, accessed 8 July 2017, http://legis.senado.leg.br/sdleg-getter/documento?t=66808&mime=application/pdf, 105–9.

16. SNIE 93-83, Secret, CIA, FOIA.

17. On the refusals, see Olavo Setúbal to Sarney, 29 Oct. 1985, IPR 198, Confidential, Informações para o Senhor Presidente da República, Caixa 56—1985 (hereafter IPR 56-1985), AHMRE-B.

18. José Luiz de Santana Carvalho, telephone interview by author, 7 Apr. 2020.

19. Diego Hurtado, *El sueño de Argentina atómica: Política, tecnología nuclear y desarollo nacional, 1945–2006* (Buenos Aires: Edhasa, 2014), 264.

20. Hurtado, *El sueño de Argentina atómica*, 264.

21. Hurtado, *El sueño de Argentina atómica*, 265.

22. "Brasil já domina enriquecimento de urânio, diz Sarney," *FdSP*, 5 Sept. 1987, A-6.

23. José Sarney, "Nossos propósitos, do governo e da sociedade, são e serão pacíficos," *FdSP*, 5 Sept. 1987, A-6; "Não vamos fazer a bomba, diz Nazareth," *FdSP*, 5 Sept. 1987, A-6.

24. "Bomba pode ser produzida em 5 anos, afirma reitor da USP," *FdSP*, 5 Sept. 1987, A-7.

25. Itamaraty to BrazEmbassy Washington, 1 Oct. 1987, Telegram 2267, Confidential, Maço Ener-Política energética—AIEA 10.01.1987, AHMRE-B.

26. The United States refused to sell Brazil pressure transducers from the US firm MKS and also informed other US firms and subsidiaries of West German and British firms, such as Leybold-Heraus and Edwards Vacuum, of the US export requirements. "Talking points. Brazilian attempt to purchase nuclear proliferation related equipment," Az. 431, Bonn to FRG Embassy in Brasília, 30 Oct. 1987, Nuklearforshung 1987–1988, PA/AA.

27. "Talking points. Brazil nuclear program," 23 July 1987, Nuklearforshung 1987–1988, PA/AA.

28. "Brazil's decision to abandon Becket jet nozzle enrichment technology," Az. 431, Bonn to FRG Embassy in Brasília, 7 Nov. 1988, Nuklearforshung 1987–1988, PA/AA.

29. Itamaraty to BrazEmbassy Washington, 1 Oct. 1987, Telegram 2267, Confidential, Maço Ener-Política energética—AIEA 10.01.1987, AHMRE-B.

30. For a report of the West German–Brazilian cooperation in the R&D sector, see "Nuclear Research and Development," n.d., Nuklearforshung 1987–1988, PA/AA.

31. "In May 1983, a generally reliable source reported that the reprocessing project has been cancelled altogether." SNIE 93-83, Secret, CIA.

32. Renata H. Dalaqua, "'We will not make the bomb because we do not want to make the bomb': Understanding the Technopolitical Regime That Drives the Brazilian Nuclear Program," *Nonproliferation Review* 26 (2019): 231–49, https:/doi.org/10.1080/10736700.2019.1630094.

33. On the constituent assembly, see Leslie Bethell and Jairo Nicolau, "Politics in Brazil, 1985–2002," in *The Cambridge History of Latin America*, ed. Leslie Bethell, vol. 9, *Brazil since 1930* (New York: Cambridge University Press, 2008), 237–42.

34. *The Radiological Accident in Goiânia* (Vienna: International Atomic Energy Agency, 1988), 1.

35. Argentina, the Soviet Union, the United States, France, and the Federal Republic of Germany sent specialists to Brazil to help. Similarly, Israel, the Netherlands, Hungary, and the United Kingdom offered CNEN machinery for dealing with the emergency. ResbraViena to Itamaraty, 6 Nov. 1987, Telegram 1428, Confidential, Maço Ener-Política energética—AIEA 10.01.1987, AHMRE-B. On the occasion of the accident, the 1986 international convention on radiological emergency was implemented, along with Protocol 11 of the Declaration of Iguaçu on Argentine-Brazilian assistance in the case of nuclear and radiological accidents. On the spread of wrong information about the accident, such as the possible contamination of the Uruguay River, see Abreu Sodré to Sarney, 29 Oct. 1987, IPR 359, Confidential, Série Informação para o Senhor Presidente da República, Caixa 57-A, Ano 1987, AHMRE-B.

36. Deputy Fernando Cunha (PMDB) proposed the amendment on 3 September 1987. See Emenda ES27954-8 in Senado Federal, *Projeto de Constituição: Emendas oferecidas em plenário substitutivo do relator*, vol. 3, *Emendas 27037 a 311127* (Brasília: Centro Gráfico do Senado Federal, 1988), 1743. Other members supporting the proposal were Sarney Filho (son of Brazil's president) and Fábio Feldmann (PMDB). Cunha also proposed a plebiscite over the continuation of the nuclear program. Emenda ES28346-4 in Senado Federal, *Projeto de Constituição*, 3:1832. On the debate on nuclear energy in the constituent assembly, see Rodrigo Morais Chaves, "O programa nuclear e a construção da democracia: Análise da oposição ao programa nuclear brasileiro (1975–1990)" (master's thesis, FGV, 2014), 134–39; and Ricardo Lopes Esteves, "A constitucionalização da questão nuclear no Brasil" (master's thesis, Federal University of Goiás, 2018).

37. Emenda ES27380-9 in Senado Federal, *Projeto de Constituição*, 3:1610.

38. Guilherme Camargo, interview by author, 20 Oct. 2016, Rio de Janeiro. Rex Nazaré Alves, chairman of CNEN, proclaimed the peaceful nature of the nuclear program in assembly hearings and defended congressional involvement in the decision over the atomic projects. "CNEN jura que programa nuclear é pacífico," *FdSP*, 11 June 1987.

39. For the outcome of the vote in the constituent assembly on the ban of nuclear weapons, see "Artefatos Nucleares," BR DFANBSB N8.0.PSN, EST.62, AN-B.

40. José Luiz de Santana Carvalho, telephone interview by author, 7 Apr. 2020.

41. "Artefatos Nucleares," Acervo do Conselho de Segurança Nacional, BR DFANBSB N8.0.PSN, EST.62, AN-B.

42. "Análise sobre o relatório da Comissão de Avaliação do Programa Nuclear Brasileiro," n.d., EG dpr 1979.05.16; Brasil, Senado Federal, "Decreto n. 96621 de 08/31/1988," http://legis.senado.gov.br/legislacao/DetalhaSigen.action?id=519261.

43. Setúbal to Sarney, 22 May 1985, IPR 40, Rba mpc c 1985.01.10. On the possible Neves-Alfonsín convergence, see Sara Z. Kutchesfahani, *Politics and the Bomb: The Role of Experts in the Creation of Cooperative Nuclear Non-Proliferation Agreements* (London: Routledge, 2014), 58.

44. "Energia nuclear. Relações Brasil-Argentina," Rego Barros to Francisco Thompson Flores Neto (undersecretary of economic and trade affairs), 6 May 1985, Memorandum, Secret, Rba mpc c 1985.01.10.

45. "Subsídio para a reunião sobre temas nucleares com autoridades argentinas, preparatória do encontro em Foz do Iguaçu de Nov/85," 11 Nov. 1985, Confidential, Maço Ener-Política Nuclear Argentina 1985–86, AHMRE-B.

46. BrazEmbassy Buenos Aires to Itamaraty, 15 May 1985, Telegram 1282, Secret, and Itamaraty to BrazEmbassy Buenos Aires, 15 Nov. 1985, Telegram 3134, Secret, AHMRE-B; Setúbal to Sarney, 22 May 1985, IPR 40, Rba mpc c 1985.01.10.

47. José Goldemberg, "Cooperação Brasil-Argentina na área nuclear," Sarney to Setúbal, 10 July 1985, Encaminhamento, IPR 56-1985, AHMRE-B.

48. Setúbal to Sarney, 22 May 1985, IPR 40, Rba mpc c 1985.01.10.

49. "Visita do Senhor Ministro do Estado à Argentina; 20 a 21 de maio de 1985. Nova Versão—Fabricação da Bomba Atômica," 15 May 1985, Itamaraty internal document, Rba mpc c 1985.01.10.

50. "Pronunciamento do presidente José Sarney, por ocasião da abertura do debate geral da XL Assembleia Geral da ONU," 23 Sept. 1985, Biblioteca Presidência da República, http://www.biblioteca.presidencia.gov.br/presidencia/ex-presidentes/jose-sarney /discursos/1985/94.pdf/view.

51. Abreu Sodré in a message to US Secretary of State Shultz requested US support of the project. Sodré to Shultz, n.d., Informações para o Senhor Presidente da República, Caixa 57-1986 (hereafter IPR 57-1986), AHMRE-B.

52. On the submission of the proposal and its approval by President Sarney, see Sodré to Sarney, 22 May 1986, IPR 180, Secret, IPR 57-1986, AHMRE-B. On the UNGA approval and its consequences for Brazil, see Paulo Tarso Flecha de Lima to Sarney, 30 Oct. 1986, IPR 378, Confidential, IPR 57-1986, AHMRE-B.

53. Setúbal to Sarney, 29 Oct. 1985, IPR 198, Confidential, IPR 56-1985, AHMRE-B.

54. "Subsídio para a reunião sobre temas nucleares com autoridades argentinas, preparatória do encontro em Foz do Iguaçu de Nov/85," 11 Nov. 1985.

55. "Memorandum from the Argentine General Directorate for Nuclear Affairs and Disarmament, 'Overflight by Brazilian Military Plane at Pilcaniyeu Uranium Enrichment Plant,'" 10 Oct. 1985, trans. FGV, History and Public Policy Program Digital Archive, Historical Archive of the Ministry of Foreign Affairs and Worship, Argentina, https:// digitalarchive.wilsoncenter.org/document/117520. On the Argentine decision makers' comments on the issue, see Rodrigo Mallea, Matias Spektor, and Nicholas J. Wheeler, eds., *The Origins of Nuclear Cooperation: A Critical Oral History Between Argentina and Brazil* (Washington, DC: Wilson Center; Rio de Janeiro: FGV, 2015), 181.

56. "Declaração do Iguaçu," 29 Nov. 1985, ABACC, https://www.abacc.org.br/es/wp -content/uploads/sites/3/2016/10/1985-Declaração-do-Iguaçu-espanhol-assinada.pdf.

57. "Declaração Conjunta sobre Política Nuclear," 29–30 Nov. 1985, ABACC, https:// www.abacc.org.br/wp-content/uploads/2016/10/1985-Declaração-conjunta-sobre -Pol%C3%ADtica-Nuclear-português.pdf.

58. "Política Nuclear Brasil-Argentina. Declaração de Iguaçu. Implementação," July 1986, MRE, Information, Secret, AHMRE-B.

59. "Serra do Cachimbo pode ser local de provas nucleares," *FdSP*, 8 Aug. 1986, 6.

60. "Reações contra instalação de base para testes nucleares na Serra do Cachimbo, na fronteira do Pará com Mato Grosso," 29 Aug. 1986, ACE 6312786, Confidential, AN-B.

61. Michael Barletta, "Ambiguity, Autonomy, and the Atom: Emergence of the Argentine-Brazilian Nuclear Regime" (PhD diss., University of Wisconsin–Madison, 2000), 177.

62. Barletta, "Ambiguity, Autonomy, and the Atom," 178.

63. On the Argentine request, see Mallea, Spektor, and Wheeler, *Origins of Nuclear Cooperation*, 150.

64. "Informação sobre Perfurações Realizadas na Serra do Cachimbo," Rego Barros (Itamaraty) to Adolfo Saracho, Directorate for International Security and Nuclear and Space Affairs (Dirección de Seguridad Internacional, Asuntos Nucleares y Espaciales, or DIGAN), Argentine Foreign Ministry, non-paper delivered Oct. 1986, AHMRE-B.

65. Barletta, "Ambiguity, Autonomy, and the Atom," 178.

66. Mallea, Spektor, and Wheeler, *Origins of Nuclear Cooperation*, 149. On Caputo's positive reaction, see Barletta, "Ambiguity, Autonomy, and the Atom," 178.

67. Flecha Lima to Sarney, 24 Nov. 1986, IPR 408, Secret, IPR 57-1986, AHMRE-B.

68. Sodré to Sarney, 9 Dec. 1986, IPR 426, Secret, IPR 57-1986, AHMRE-B.

69. "Declaração Conjunta sobre Política Nuclear," 10 Dec. 1986, ABACC, https://www .abacc.org.br/wp-content/uploads/2016/09/1986-Declaração_Conjunta_sobre _Pol%C3%ADtica_Nuclear_1986_-_português_-_assinado1.pdf; "Protocolo n.17. Cooperação Nuclear," 10 Dec. 1986, ABACC, https://www.abacc.org.br/wp-content/uploads /2016/09/Protocolo-n°-17-português.pdf.

70. Flecha Lima to Sarney, 11 June 1987, IPR 210, Secret, Informações para o Senhor Presidente da República, Caixa 57-B, 1986, AHMRE-B.

71. Although the visit was meant to be kept secret, the information leaked to the press. Richard Kessler, "Brazil's President to Visit Top-Secret Argentine Nuclear Complex," *Nucleonics Week* 28.29 (1987): 3; Itamaraty to BrazEmbassy Buenos Aires, 29 June 1987, Telegram 896/87, Exclusive, AHMRE-B.

72. Kutchesfahani, *Politics and the Bomb*, 59.

73. "Declaração de Viedma," 17 July 1987, ABACC, https://www.abacc.org.br/wp -content/uploads/2016/09/Declaração-de-Viedma-Declaração-conjunta-sobre -Pol%C3%ADtica-Nuclear-português-assinada.pdf.

74. Rubens Ricupero, interview by author, 20 Sept. 2010, São Paulo. On the eve of the announcement, President Sarney informed his Argentine counterpart by phone. The details were provided by Ambassador Ricupero. On Alfonsín's letter, see BrazEmbassy Buenos Aires to Itamaraty, 4 Sept. 1987, Telegram 2506/87, Secret, AHMRE-B.

75. "Declaração de Iperó," 8 Apr. 1988, ABACC.

76. "Declaração de Ezeiza," 29 Nov. 1988, ABACC, https://www.abacc.org.br/wp -content/uploads/2016/09/Declaração-de-Ezeiza-português.pdf.

77. For example, the Brazilian physicist Luiz Pinguelli Rosa, an active opponent of the parallel nuclear program in Brazil, presented such a scenario in Washington in 1988. Kutchesfahani, *Politics and the Bomb*, 62.

Chapter 7 · *Giving Up the Bomb, 1989–1994*

1. "Brazil to Close Shaft Suited for Nuclear Test," *New York Times*, 19 Sept. 1990, A3.

2. Luiz Felipe de Seixas Corrêa, ed., *Brazil and the United Nations, 1946–2011* (Brasília: FUNAG, 2013), 638.

3. On Collor's foreign policy, see Guilherme Stolle Paixão e Casarões, "'O tempo é o senhor da razão?' A política externa do governo Collor, vinte anos depois" (PhD diss., Universidade de São Paulo, 2014).

4. On the meeting, see Fernando Collor de Mello, interview by author, 12 Feb. 2014, Brasília.

5. On the establishment of the GT-PRONEN and its objectives, see Brasil, Presidência da República, "Decreto N° 99,194, de 27 de março de 1990," http://www.planalto.gov .br/ccivil_03/decreto/1990-1994/D99194impressao.htm; Odete Maria de Oliveira, *Os descaminhos do Brasil nuclear* (Ijuí: Ed. Inuijuí, 1999), 485; and "Programa Nacional de Energia Nuclear. Grupo de Trabalho," Itamaraty to all diplomatic posts, 17 Apr. 1990, Secret, Folder: "Ener-Recursos energéticos Letras A.Z. 09.01.1985," AHMRE-B.

6. These included the Brazilian Association for the Development of Technical and Industrial Activities in the Nuclear Field (Associação Brasileira para o Desenvolvimento das Atividades Técnicas e Industriais na Área Nuclear, or ABDAN), the Brazilian Society for the Progress of Science (Sociedade Brasileira para o Progresso da Ciência, or SBPC), the Brazilian Society of Radiological Protection (Sociedade Brasileira da Proteção Radiológica, or SBRP), the Center for Nuclear Energy in Agriculture of the University of São Paulo, the Engineering Club (Clube de Engenharia), and the Coordination of the Graduate Program in Engineering of the Federal University of Rio de Janeiro (Coordenação dos Programas de Pós-Graduação de Engenharia, or COPPE/UFRJ). Oliveira, *Os descaminhos do Brasil nuclear*, 485. Guilherme Camargo, interview by author, 20 Oct. 2016, Rio de Janeiro.

7. Rodrigo Morais Chaves, "O programa nuclear e a construção da democracia: Análise da oposição ao programa nuclear brasileiro (1975–1990)" (master's thesis, FGV,2014), 140. Oliveira, *Os descaminhos do Brasil nuclear*, 485.

8. Michael Barletta, "The Military Nuclear Program in Brazil" (CISAC–Stanford University Working Paper, 1997), 11–12.

9. "Brasil. Congresso Nacional. Senado Federal. Comissão Parlamentar Mista de Inquérito destinada a apurar o Programa Autônomo de Energia Nuclear, também conhecido como 'Programa Paralelo,'" *Relatório final*, 1990, Biblioteca do Senado, accessed 8 July 2017, http://legis.senado.leg.br/sdleg-getter/documento?t=66808&mime=application /pdf.

10. Barletta, "Military Nuclear Program in Brazil,"12.

11. On the end of the Cold War and the superpowers' renewed efforts toward disarmament as a reason for Brazil's choice, see Itamaraty to BrazDelUN, 29 Nov. 1990, Telegram 1715/90, Secret, Folder: ENER—RECURSOS ENERGÉTICOS—Loo/Lo2 1990 (hereafter Loo/Lo2 1990), AHMRE-B.

12. "Energia Nuclear. Visita ao Brasil do Embaixador Richard Kennedy," Itamaraty to BrazDelUN, 1 June 1990, Telegram 873, Secret, Folder: Ener-Recursos energéticos Letras A.Z. 09.01.1985, AHMRE-B.

13. Gary Milhollin and David Dantzic, "Must the US Give Brazil and Iraq the Bomb?," *New York Times*, 28 July 1990, https://www.nytimes.com/1990/07/29/opinion/must-the -us-give-brazil-and-iraq-the-bomb.html.

14. Geraldo Lesbat Cavagnari Filho, "P&D Militar: Situação, Avaliação e Perspectivas," in *Ciência e Tecnologia no Brasil: Uma nova política para um mundo global*, ed. Simon Schwartzman (Rio de Janeiro: FGV, 1996), 321–55.

15. BrazEmbassy Bonn to Itamaraty, 17 Nov. 1986, Telegram 916, Secret, Maço Memorandos, 1986, Caixa 1TH, Secret, Estante G2, Prateleira 4, AHMRE-B.

16. FRG Embassy Brasília to Bonn, 12 Sept. 1990, Cable 666, Brennelementfertigung 25640 (hereafter Bd. 25640), PA/AA.

17. Francisco Rezek to Collor, 3 Sept. 1990, IPR 368, Série Informação para o Senhor Presidente da República, Caixa 62, Ano 1990-B (hereafter IPR 1990-B-62), AHMRE-B;

"Energia Nuclear. Visita ao Brasil do Embaixador Richard Kennedy," Itamaraty to Braz-DelUN, 1 June 1990, Cable 873, Secret, Folder: Ener-Recursos energéticos Letras A.Z. 09.01.1985, AHMRE-B.

18. Fernando Collor, interview by author, 12 Feb. 2014, Brasília.

19. Mark Hibbs, "Collor Moving to End Influence of Military in Nuclear Program," *Nucleonics Week*, 4 Oct. 1990, 6.

20. Mark Hibbs, "Looking Back at Brazil's Boreholes," *Arms Control Wonk*, 14 Apr. 2014, http://www.armscontrolwonk.com/archive/1102670/looking-back-at-brazils-boreholes/.

21. Santana Carvalho declared during a television interview that Brazil was close to detonating a nuclear bomb. The air force minister under President Sarney, Otávio Moreira Lima, contested the information. "Cientista confirma que País chegou perto de bomba," Portal Terra, 26 Aug. 2005, http://noticias.terra.com.br/brasil/noticias/0,,OI645737-EI306,00-Cientista+confirma+que+Pais+chegou+perto+de+bomba.html.

22. Fernando Collor, interview by author, 12 Feb. 2014, Brasília. On Socrates Monteiro's declaration, see Celso Castro and Maria Celina D'Araujo, eds., *Militares e política na Nova República* (Rio de Janeiro: FGV, 2001), 165.

23. Castro and D'Araujo, *Militares e política na Nova República*, 165.

24. Seixas Corrêa, *Brazil and the United Nations, 1946–2011*, 638.

25. "XLV AGNU. Discurso do Senhor Presidente da República. Tratado de Tlatelolco. Explosões Nucleares para Fins Pacíficos," Marcos Castrioto de Azambuja to Collor, n.d., IPR 1990-B-62, AHMRE-B. Brazil's intention to pursue the full development of nuclear energy was declared in a speech by the Brazilian delegate to the General Assembly, Ambassador Ronaldo Mota Sardenberg, on 15 October. BrazDelUN to Itamaraty, 12 Oct. 1990, Telegram 1367/90, Secret, Loo/Lo2 1990, AHMRE-B.

26. Azambuja suggested to Collor that he inform the Soviet Union and the United States, main signatories of the Partial Test Ban Treaty, and Mexico, promoter of the Treaty of Tlatelolco, about his announcement. "XLV AGNU. Discurso do Senhor Presidente da República. Tratado de Tlatelolco. Explosões Nucleares para Fins Pacíficos," Azambuja to Collor, n.d., IPR 1990-B-62, AHMRE-B.

27. Renata H. Dalaqua, "'We will not make the bomb because we do not want to make the bomb': Understanding the Technopolitical Regime That Drives the Brazilian Nuclear Program," *Nonproliferation Review* 26 (2019): 201, https://doi.org/10.1080/10736700.2019.1630094.

28. Michelangelo Durazzo, "História do Combustível Nuclear no IPEN," IPEN, accessed 20 July 2017, https://www.ipen.br/portal_por/portal/interna.php?secao_id=549.

29. Regina Eleutério, "Programa nuclear continua," *FdSP*, 19 Sept. 1990, A-6.

30. "Brasilianisches Nuklearprogram," Bonn to the FRG Ministries of Research and Economics, and to the General Consulates in Rio de Janeiro and São Paulo, 30 Aug. 1990, Telegram 629, Bd. 25640, PA/AA.

31. Harald Müller, David Fischer, and Wolfgang Kötter, *Nuclear Non-Proliferation and Global Order* (New York: SIPRI / Oxford University Press, 1994), 99–102.

32. Fernando Collor, interview by author, 12 Feb. 2014, Brasília.

33. "Deutsch-Brasilianische Zusammenarbeit auf dem Gebiet der friedlichen Nutzung der Kernenergie," Bonn, 431–466.21, BRA, 20 Oct. 1990, Bd. 25640, PA/AA.

34. The head of the Brazilian delegation, Sebastião do Rego Barros, met personally in Buenos Aires with President Menem and his foreign minister, Domingo Cavallo. IPR 261, 17 Aug. 1989, Confidential, IPR 1989-C-60, AHMRE-B.

35. Michael Barletta, "Ambiguity, Autonomy, and the Atom: Emergence of the Argentine-Brazilian Nuclear Regime" (PhD diss., University of Wisconsin–Madison, 2000), 187–88.

36. "Comunicado Conjunto," Buenos Aires, 6 July 1990, https://www.abacc.org.br/wp -content/uploads/2016/09/1990-Comunicado-Conjunto-de-Buenos-Aires_PT.pdf.

37. BrazEmbassy Buenos Aires to Brasília, 5 June 1990, Telegram 876/1990, Secret Urgent, L00/L02 1990, AHMRE-B.

38. On the Argentine-Brazilian meeting in June, see BrazEmbassy Buenos Aires to Brasília, 29 June 1990, Telegram 1035/90, Secret Very Urgent, L00/L02 1990, AHMRE-B; and Brasília to BrazEmbassy Buenos Aires, 16 Aug. 1990, L00/L02 1990, AHMRE-B.

39. Brasília to BrazEmbassy Buenos Aires, 16 Aug. 1990, L00/L02 1990, AHMRE-B. On the possible prohibition of nuclear-powered vessels, the Argentines were concerned about the application of article 16 of the Treaty of Tlatelolco to the IAEA special inspections. BrazEmbassy Buenos Aires to Itamaraty, 25 July 1990, Cable 1146, Secret–Very Urgent, L00/L02 1990, AHMRE-B.

40. BrazEmbassy Buenos Aires to Itamaraty, 25 July 1990, Cable 1146, Secret-Very Urgent, L00/L02 1990, AHMRE-B.

41. On the US proposal, see BrazEmbassy Buenos Aires to Itamaraty, 25 July 1990, Cable 1146, Secret–Very Urgent, L00/L02 1990, AHMRE-B.

42. BrazEmbassy Buenos Aires to Itamaraty, 25 July 1990, Cable 1146, Secret-Very Urgent, L00/L02 1990, AHMRE-B.

43. On the specifics of the Hexapartite Safeguards Project, see BrazEmbassy Buenos Aires to Itamaraty, 8 Aug. 1990, Telegram 307, Secret, L00/L02 1990, AHMRE-B.

44. Itamaraty to BrazEmbassy Buenos Aires, 2 Aug. 1990, Telegram 989, Secret Urgent, L00/L02 1990, AHMRE-B.

45. On Caputo's proposal, see chapter 5. Amorim also underlined that the revision of the Treaty of Tlatelolco would not include banning naval nuclear propulsion. BrazDelegation Geneva to Itamaraty, 24 Aug. 1990, Telegram 1123/90, Secret, L00/L02 1990, AHMRE-B.

46. BrazEmbassy Buenos Aires to Brasília, 6 Sept. 1990, Telegram 1052/90, Secret, L00/L02 1990, AHMRE-B.

47. On the role of the epistemic community, see Sara Z. Kutchesfahani, *Politics and the Bomb: The Role of Experts in the Creation of Cooperative Nuclear Non-proliferation Agreements* (London: Routledge, 2014), 24–54.

48. BrazEmbassy Buenos Aires to Itamaraty, 6 Nov. 1990, Telegram 1622/90, Secret Very Urgent, L00/L02 1990, AHMRE-B.

49. Rezek to Collor, 14 Nov. 1990, IPR 436, Série Informações para o Senhor Presidente da República, 1990-A, Caixa 61, AHMRE-B.

50. "Declaração sobre política nuclear comum brasileiro-argentina," 28 Nov. 1990, https://www.abacc.org.br/wp-content/uploads/2016/09/Declaração-de-Pol%C3%ADtica -Nuclear-Comum-português.pdf.

51. BrazEmbassy Mexico City to Itamaraty, 30 Nov. 1990, Telegram 1007/90, Secret Urgent, L00/L02 1990, AHMRE-B. On the domestic and foreign reactions to the

Declaration of Iguaçu, see BrazEmbassy Buenos Aires to Itamaraty, 17 Dec. 1990, Telegram 1365/90, Secret Very Urgent, L00/L02 1990, AHMRE-B; and Itamaraty to BrazEmbassy Buenos Aires, 22 May 1991, Telegram 445/91, Secret Urgent, L00/L02 1990, AHMRE-B.

52. BrazEmbassy Vienna to Itamaraty, Telegram 449/90, Secret Very Urgent, L00/ L02 1990, AHMRE-B.

53. BrazEmbassy Buenos Aires to Itamaraty, Secret cables 1390/87, 15 Sept. 1987, and 1146/90, 25 July 1990, AHMRE-B; Itamaraty to BrazEmbassy Buenos Aires, 29 Nov. 1990, Secret cable 1301/90, AHMRE-B.

54. BrazEmbassy Buenos Aires to Itamaraty, 7 Jan. 1991, Telegram 009, Secret, AIEA 09.01.1985, AHMRE-B.

55. Itamaraty to BrazEmbassy Buenos Aires, 22 May 1991, Telegram 445, Secret Urgent, L00/L02 1990, AHMRE-B.

56. Itamaraty to BrazEmbassy Buenos Aires, 25 May 1991, Telegram 458, Secret Urgent, L00/L02 1990, AHMRE-B.

57. "Acordo entre a República Federativa do Brasil e a República Argentina para o uso exclusivamente pacífico da energia nuclear," 18 July 1991, https://www.abacc.org.br/wp -content/uploads/2016/09/Acordo-Bilateral-original-português.pdf.

58. The ABACC-IAEA agreement of 1998 would suspend the 1967 and 1975 safeguards agreements between Brazil and the United States and Germany, respectively.

59. "Press briefing on the State Visit of President Collor de Mello of Brazil by Bernard Aronson, Assistant Secretary of State for Inter-American Affairs," 18 June 1991, National Security Council, Stack G, File System S, File Type OF, Code 73, Box OA/ID, No. CF1091, Charles A. Gillespie Files, Brazil (General) January 1991–June 1991(1), George H. Bush Presidential Library. On the possibility of signing an agreement on the transfer of sensitive technologies to Brazil, see Itamaraty to BrazEmbassy Buenos Aires, 23 May 1991, Telegram 441/91, Secret Urgent, L00/L02 1990, AHMRE-B.

60. Itamaraty to BrazEmbassy Buenos Aires, 23 May 1991, Telegram 441/91, Secret Urgent, L00/L02 1990, AHMRE-B.

61. Ambassador Azambuja recently declared that the South African accession to the NPT deeply influenced Brazil to make a similar decision. Marcus Castrioto de Azambuja, CPDOC interview, 19 Jan. 2010, Rio de Janeiro. On the French and the Chinese decision to sign the NPT, see BrazEmbassy Beijing to Itamaraty, 24 June 1991, Telegram 226/1991, Secret, Série Telegramas Recebidos Pequim 1991, AHMRE-B.

62. Gary Milhollin and Jennifer Weeks, "Keeping the Lid on Nuclear Arms," *New Scientist*, 17 Aug. 1991, 26–30, http://www.wisconsinproject.org/keeping-the-lid-on-nuclear -arms/.

63. The articles Brazil and Argentina wanted to modify were: 14, "Reports of the Parties"; 15, "Special Reports Requested by the Secretary-General"; and 16, "Special Inspections." The Brazilian and Argentine governments agreed to announce the modifications on the twenty-fifth anniversary of the treaty. The main Brazilian negotiator of full accession to Tlatelolco was Ambassador José Viegas Filho, who declared that that decision had been a "fundamental step on the path to accession to the NPT." José Viegas Filho, interview by author, 17 Feb. 2010, Rome.

64. Telegraphic Circular 19086, 14 Feb. 1992, Secret, Caixa 453, Tlatelolco. 25° aniversário, Declarações dos presidentes Brasil, Argentina. 1991–1992, AHMRE-B.

65. IAEA/INFCIRC/410, 21 Sept. 1992, IAEA, https://www.iaea.org/sites/default/files/infcirc410.pdf.

66. Cuban representatives participated as observers in the conference. Rezek to Collor, 12 Dec. 1990, IPR 488, Série Informações para o Senhor Presidente da República, IPR 1990-A, Caixa 61, AHMRE-B.

67. Luiz Felipe Lampreia, interview by author, 17 Mar. 2014, Rio de Janeiro.

68. Fernando Henrique Cardoso to Itamar Franco, 4 Feb. 1993, IPR 17, Caixa 70, IPR 1993-A, AHMRE-B.

69. Klaus Kinkel, "Alemanha quer cooperar com América Latina," *FdSP*, 3 Oct. 1993, 3; Mitchell Reiss, *Bridled Ambition: Why Countries Constrain Their Nuclear Capabilities* (Washington, DC: Woodrow Wilson Center Press, 1995), 70.

70. Luiz Alberto Moniz Bandeira, *O "milagre alemão" e o desenvolvimento do Brasil, 1949–2011* (São Paulo: Editora UNESP, 2011), 274, 281–82.

71. Celso Amorim to Franco, 10 Sept. 1993, IPR 205, Caixa 70, IPR 1993-A, AHMRE-B.

72. Lampreia, replacing Cardoso as foreign minister, insisted that Brazil needed to ratify both the Treaty of Tlatelolco and the Quadripartite Agreement at a cabinet meeting at the Palácio do Planalto chaired by President Itamar Franco. Luiz Felipe Lampreia, interview by author, 17 Mar. 2014, Rio de Janeiro.

73. Barletta, "Ambiguity, Autonomy, and the Atom," 189–90.

74. Celso Amorim to Itamar Franco, 23 May 1994, IPR 106, Caixa 73, IPR 1994-A, AHMRE-B. For the text of the treaty and Brazil's exemption from article 28, see "Legislação Informatizada—Decreto N. 1246, de 16 de setembro de 1994—Publicação Original," http://www2.camara.leg.br/legin/fed/decret/1994/decreto-1246-16-setembro-1994-449655-publicacaooriginal-1-pe.html.

75. Cavagnari Filho, "P&D Militar: Situação, Avaliação e Perspectivas," 328.

76. Cavagnari Filho, "P&D Militar: Situação, Avaliação e Perspectivas," 345.

Chapter 8 · Brazil's Accession to the Nuclear Non-Proliferation Treaty, 1995–2003

1. "Secretary's Remarks at Deposit of Brazil's Instrument of Accession to NPT," n.d., Luis Felipe Lampreia personal archive, FGV/CPDOC (hereafter LFL), pi 1998.08.18.

2. On nuclear latency, see Scott Sagan, "Nuclear Latency and Nuclear Proliferation," in *Forecasting Nuclear Proliferation in the 21st Century*, ed. William C. Potter with Gaukhar Mukhatzhanova, vol. 1, *The Role of Theory* (Stanford, CA: Stanford University Press, 2010), 80–101.

3. Sérgio Danese, *Diplomacia presidencial* (Rio de Janeiro: Topbooks, 1999).

4. Fernando Henrique Cardoso, "The Post–Cold War Era: A View from the South," in *After the Cold War: Essays on the Emerging World Order*, ed. Keith Philip Lepor (Austin: University of Texas Press, 1987), 24–37.

5. Luiz Felipe Lampreia, "A política externa do governo," *Jornal do Brasil*, 8 May 1995, 11.

6. Paulo Wrobel, "Brazil and the NPT: Resistance to Change?," *Security Dialogue* 27.3 (1996): 339; Julio C. Carasales, "A Surprising About-Face: Argentina and the NPT," *Security Dialogue* 27.3 (1996): 325–35, https://doi.org/10.1177/0967010696027003008.

7. Carasales, "Surprising About-Face," 334.

8. Luiz Felipe Lampreia to Fernando Henrique Cardoso, 24 Jan. 1995, IPR 26, LFL mrei 1995.01.24.

9. Luiz Felipe Lampreia, interview by author, 17 Mar. 2014, Rio de Janeiro.

10. Lampreia to Cardoso, 11 Jan. 1995, IPR 2, LFL mrei 1995.01.24; Luiz Felipe Lampreia, *O Brasil e os ventos do mundo: Memórias de cinco décadas na cena internacional* (Rio de Janeiro: Objetiva, 2009), 167.

11. Luiz Felipe Lampreia, interview by author, 17 Mar. 2014, Rio de Janeiro.

12. "Russian Report Says Brazil 'Closest' to Creating Its Own Nuclear Weapon," *BBC Summary of World Broadcast*, 25 Mar. 1995.

13. Lampreia, *O Brasil e os ventos do mundo*, 165.

14. The CTBT became a focus of Brazilian diplomats in 1988 thanks to efforts in the UN disarmament forums. On Lampreia's speech to the UN Conference on Disarmament, see "Statement by ambassador Luiz Felipe Lampreia, minister of external relations of Brazil, before the Conference on Disarmament, Geneva," 30 Jan. 1995, LFL pi Lampreia, L. F. 1995.01.30.

15. Brasil, Câmara dos Deputados, "Acordo de cooperação entre o governo da República Federativa do Brasil e o governo dos Estados Unidos da América sobre os usos pacíficos da energia nuclear," accessed 3 Aug. 2017, https://www2.camara.leg.br/legin/fed/decleg /1999/decretolegislativo-67-25-agosto-1999-358950-acordo-1-pl.html.

16. "Subsídios basícos para entrevista," 6 Mar. 1995, LFL mrei 1995.01.24.

17. Presidência da República, "Decreto n. 2750, de 26 de agosto de 1998," http://www .planalto.gov.br/ccivil_03/decreto/D2750.htm; Lampreia to Cardoso, 26 July 1995, IPR 236, Série Informações para o Senhor Presidente da República, Caixa 1995-A, AHMRE-B.

18. "Principles and Objectives for Nuclear Non-Proliferation and Disarmament—Adopted by the NPT Review and Extension Conference (New York, May 12, 1995)," http:// www.basicint.org/nuclear/NPT/1997prepcom/principl.htm. For recent analyses of the process that led to the NPT indefinite extensions, see Michal Onderco, "The Programme for Promoting Nuclear Non-Proliferation and the NPT Extension," *International History Review*, 23 June 2019, https:/doi.org/10.1080/07075332.2019.1631204; and Michal Onderco and Leopoldo Nuti, eds., *Extending the NPT—A Critical Oral History of the 1995 Review and Extension Conference* (Washington, DC: Wilson Center, 2020).

19. "Brazil does not intend to sign NPT," ITAR-TASS, 25 Apr. 1995.

20. On the MTCR, see "The Missile Technology Control Regime at a Glance," Arms Control Association, accessed 24 July 2017, https://www.armscontrol.org/factsheets/mtcr.

21. Washington to Brasília, 9 Sept. 1990, Cable 01C0141-01405, Confidential, History and Public Policy Program Digital Archive, Folha Transparência / Itamaraty Historical Archive (hereafter HPDA, FT/AHMRE-B), http://digitalarchive.wilsoncenter.org/document /121362.

22. "Letter from President Collor to President Bush on the Brazilian Space Program," 18 Oct. 1991, History and Public Policy Program Digital Archive, George H. Bush Presidential Library, http://digitalarchive.wilsoncenter.org/document/121363.

23. BrazEmbassy Washington to Itamaraty, 8 Feb. 1993, Cable 01C0144-00158, Confidential, HPDA, FT/AHMRE-B, http://digitalarchive.wilsoncenter.org/document/121380; Itamaraty to BrazEmbassy Washington, 5 June 1992, Cable 01C0144-00836, Confidential-Urgent, HPDA, FT/AHMRE-B, http://digitalarchive.wilsoncenter.org/document/121364.

24. BrazEmbassy Washington to Itamaraty, 11 June 1992, Cable 1309-51840, Confidential-Urgent, HPDA, FT/AHMRE-B, http://digitalarchive.wilsoncenter.org/document/121365; BrazEmbassy Washington to Brasília, 17 July 1992, Cable 1568-51800, HPDA, FT/AHMRE-B, http://digitalarchive.wilsoncenter.org/document/121367.

25. BrazEmbassy Washington to Brasília, 3 Sept. 1992, Cable 1900, Confidential, HPDA, FT/AHMRE-B, http://digitalarchive.wilsoncenter.org/document/121368; BrazEmbassy Washington to Brasília, Telegram 995/1992, Secret, Série Telegramas Expedidos Secretos 1992 Washington, AHMRE-B.

26. Itamaraty to BrazEmbassy Washington, 25 Sept. 1992, Cable DfCO144-02039, Confidential, HPDA, FT/AHMRE-B, http://digitalarchive.wilsoncenter.org/document/121369.

27. Fernando Henrique Cardoso, *Diários da Presidência: 1995–1996* (São Paulo: Companhia das Letras, 2015), 118; BrazEmbassy Washington to Brasília, 17 Apr. 1993, Cable 764, Confidential, HPDA, FT/AHMRE-B, http://digitalarchive.wilsoncenter.org/document/121370; Fernando Henrique Cardoso, interview by author, 11 Feb. 2020, São Paulo.

28. BrazEmbassy Washington to Itamaraty, 23 Aug. 1994, Cable 1757, Confidential, HPDA, FT/AHMRE-B, http://digitalarchive.wilsoncenter.org/document/121374.

29. Itamaraty to BrazEmbassy Washington, 17 Apr. 1995, Telegram 674, Secret-Very Urgent, Caixa: Memorandos 1995, AHMRE-B.

30. Itamaraty to BrazEmbassy Washington, 4 May 1995, Telegram 790, Secret-Very Urgent, Caixa: Memorandos 95, AHMRE-B.

31. Cardoso, *Diários da Presidência: 1995–1996*, 161.

32. Itamaraty to BrazEmbassy Washington, 30 July 1995, Telegram 1409, Secret–Very Urgent, Caixa: Memorandos 95, AHMRE-B.

33. Itamaraty to BrazEmbassy Bonn, 14 July 1995, Série Chanceler, Telegram, Secret Very Urgent, LFL mrei 1995.01.10/1; Cardoso, *Diários da Presidência: 1995–1996*, 165.

34. Cardoso, *Diários da Presidência: 1995–1996*, 165.

35. On the meeting between Lampreia and Christopher, see BrazEmbassy Washington to Itamaraty, 22 Sept. 1995, Série Chanceler, Telegram 10001, Confidential, LFL mrei 1995.01.10/1.

36. Lampreia to Christopher, 5 Oct. 1995, fax, LFL mrei 1995.08.12; Cardoso, *Diários da Presidência:1995–1996*, 270.

37. For a surprised reaction to the policy adopted by Washington, see Wyn Q. Bowen, "US Policy in Ballistic Missile Proliferation: The MTCR's First Decade (1987–1997)," *Nonproliferation Review* 5.1 (1997): 31. For an example of strong criticism of Brazil's accession, see Richard Speier, "Can the MTCR Be Repaired?," in *Repairing the Regime: Preventing the Spread of Weapons of Mass Destruction*, ed. Joseph Cirincione (London: Routledge, 2000), 209–10.

38. For a detailed account of Brazil's accession to the MTCR and the beginning of cooperation with Ukraine, see Wyn Q. Bowen, "Brazil's Accession to the MTCR," *Nonproliferation Review* 3.3 (1996): 86–91, https://doi.org/10.1080/10736709608436642.

39. Lampreia to Cardoso, 30 Oct. 1995, IPR 338 and Dispatch, Confidential, LFL mrei 1995.01.24.

40. "Brasil. Estados Unidos. Visita do Secretário de Estado. Pontos de Conversação," BrazEmbassy Washington to Brasília, 26 Feb. 1996, Confidential Urgent, LFL mrei

1995.01.10/1. It is relevant to note that the Russian Federation did not raise the question of the NPT accession. Lampreia to Cardoso, 26 May 1995, IPR, Confidential, LFL mre1 1995.01.24.

41. Cardoso, *Diários da Presidência:1995–1996,* 675.

42. John Holum (director, ACDA) to Luiz Felipe Lampreia, 16 Feb. 1996, Letter, LFL mre1 1995.01.10/1; Warren Christopher to Luiz Felipe Lampreia, n.d., Letter, LFL mre1 1995.01.10/1.

43. For Brazil's support of Australia and the antinuclear testing movement, see Itamaraty to BrazDelUN, 16 Aug. 1995, Telegram, Confidential, LFL mre1 1995.01.13/2; "Disarmament: Four Western States Join Anti-nuclear Move," Inter Press Service, 7 Nov. 1995.

44. Cardoso to President Bill Clinton, 19 Sept. 1995, Letter, LFL mre1 1995.01.24.

45. Lampreia to Cardoso, 17 Sept. 1995, IPR, Confidential, LFL mre1 1995.01.24.

46. Hedley Bull, "Rethinking Non-Proliferation in International Relations," *International Affairs* 51.2 (1975): 175.

47. According to Luiz Felipe Lampreia's personal notes, the participants in the meeting were Ambassadors Ronaldo Sardenberg (secretary of strategic affairs), Marcos Castrioto de Azambuja (ambassador to Argentina), Sebastião do Rego Barros (secretary-general of Itamaraty), Luiz Felipe de Seixas Corrêa, Paulo Tarso da Flecha Lima (ambassador to the United States), Rubens Barbosa, and Jório Dauster Magalhães e Silva (ambassador to the European Union), as well as Professor Celso Lafer and Mauro César Pereira (minister of the navy). "Reunião no Alvorada," 26 Mar. 1997, in Lampreia's personal notes, LFL mre1 1995.01.04.

48. Lampreia, *O Brasil e os ventos do mundo,* 166.

49. Fernando Henrique Cardoso, *Diários da Presidência, 1997–1998* (São Paulo: Companhia das Letras, 2015), 209–10.

50. On the position of Sardenberg and César Pereira, see Cardoso, *Diários da Presidência, 1997–1998,* 210; Luiz Felipe Lampreia, interview by author, 17 Mar. 2014, Rio de Janeiro; and Lampreia, *O Brasil e os ventos do mundo,* 167.

51. For the "Exposição de Motivos Interministerial n.252/MJ/MM/MEx/MAEr/EMFA /CC-PR/SAE-PR. 06.20.1997," see Câmara dos Deputados, Decreto Legislativo 65, 1998, accessed 25 July 2017, http://www2.camara.leg.br/legin/fed/decleg/1998/decretolegislativo -65-2-julho-1998-361728-exposicaodemotivos-143473-pl.html.

52. Roberto Campos, "Crítica da razão curta . . . ," *FdSP,* 29 June 1997, 4.

53. Câmara dos Deputados, Decreto Legislativo 65, 1998, accessed 25 July 2017, http:// www2.camara.leg.br/legin/fed/decleg/1998/decretolegislativo-65-2-julho-1998-361728 -exposicaodemotivos-143473-pl.html.

54. Câmara dos Deputados, Decreto Legislativo 65, 1998, accessed 25 July 2017, http:// www2.camara.leg.br/legin/fed/decleg/1998/decretolegislativo-65-2-julho-1998-361728 -exposicaodemotivos-143473-pl.html.

55. Luiz Felipe Lampreia, "A política externa do governo FHC: Continuidade e renovação," *Revista Brasileira de Política Internacional* 41.2 (1998): 13, https://doi.org/10.1590 /S0034-73291998000200001.

56. "Secretary's Remarks at Deposit of Brazil's Instrument of Accession to NPT," n.d., LFL pi 1998.08.18.

57. On the idea of a golden age, see William Walker, "Nuclear Order and Disorder," *International Affairs* 76.4 (2000): 710, https://doi.org/10.1111/1468-2346.00160.

58. George Perkovich, *India's Nuclear Bomb: The Impact on Global Proliferation* (Berkeley: University of California Press, 1999).

59. Luiz Felipe Lampreia, "Armas nucleares: Brasil diz não à proliferação," *O Globo*, 17 May 1998, LFL pi Lampreia, L. F. 1998.05.17/1.

60. For the text of the declaration, see "Joint Declaration by the Ministers for Foreign Affairs of: Brazil, Egypt, Ireland, Mexico, New Zealand, Slovenia, South Africa and Sweden (The 'New Agenda' Coalition)," 9 June 1998, Canadian Coalition for Nuclear Responsibility, http://www.ccnr.org/8_nation_declaration.html. For the text of the Brazilian communiqué, see "Towards a World Free from Nuclear Weapons," 9 June 1998, LFL mre1 1995.04.21.

61. "Reunião de consultas políticas Brasil-França," 24 Feb. 1999, LFL mre2 1999.02.24/2.

62. "Reunião dos chanceleres do Grupo dos Oito e da África do Sul, Argentina, Brasil, China, Filipinas e Ucrânia," 12 June 1998, LFL mre1 1995.04.21; Etel Solingen, "Middle East Denuclearization? Lessons from Latin America's Southern Cone," *Review of International Studies* 27 (2001): 375–94.

63. On the evolution of the NAC initiative after 1998, see Robert D. Green, *Fast Track to Zero Nuclear Weapons* (Cambridge: Middle Power Initiative, 1999).

64. On the new agenda at the 54th Session of the UNGA in 1999, see "Desarmamento Nuclear—Nova Agenda," n.d., Confidential, LFL mre2 1999.09.14. On the US Senate's rejection of the CTBT, see William Walker, *A Perpetual Menace: Nuclear Weapons and International Order* (London: Routledge, 2012), 702.

65. "Visita ao Brasil do Senhor William S. Cohen, Secretário da Defesa dos E.U.A.," 12 Nov. 1999, Confidential, LFL mre2 1999.09.14.

66. "2000 NPT Review Conference Final Document," Arms Control Association, accessed 28 July 2017, http://www.armscontrol.org/act/2000_06/docjun.

67. On the negotiations between INB and the Brazilian navy, see Renata Hessman Dalaqua, "Atómos e democracia no Brasil: A formulação de políticas e os controles democráticos para o ciclo do combustível nuclear no período pós-1988" (PhD diss., FGV, 2017), 200–208.

68. Fernando Henrique Cardoso, interview by author, 11 Feb. 2020, São Paulo.

Chapter 9 · Brazil and the Nuclear Issue from Lula da Silva to Temer, 2003–2018

1. AmEmbassy to SecState, 20 Apr. 2006, Wikileaks Cable (hereafter WC): 06BuenosAires894_a, https://search.wikileaks.org/plusd/cables/06BUENOSAIRES894_a.html.

2. AmEmbassy Tel Aviv to SecState, 20 Jan. 2006, WC: 06TELAVIV293_a, https://search.wikileaks.org/plusd/cables/06TELAVIV293_a.html.

3. Marta Salomon, "Ministro critica tratado nuclear às vésperas de revisão," *FdSP*, 18 Feb. 2010.

4. Aloysio Nunes Ferreira, "Rumo a um mundo sem armas nucleares," *FdSP*, 17 July 2017, https://www1.folha.uol.com.br/opiniao/2017/07/1901508-rumo-a-um-mundo-sem-armas-nucleares.shtml.

5. Plínio Fraga, "Na escola de guerra Lula muda discurso para agradar a militares," *FdSP*, 14 Sept. 2002. The US Congress was concerned about Lula's declaration, but both

the Workers' Party and the Brazilian Embassy in Washington guaranteed Brazil's commitment to the NPT. See "Informal translation of an October 4th letter to US Ambassador to Brazil Donna Hrinak from Workers' Party President José Dirceu," 4 Oct. 2002, Rba mpe.w.2000.03.17. On Alencar's declaration, see M. Sibaja, "José Alencar, Brazil VP, says Country Should Build Nuclear Arms," *Seattle Times*, 25 Sept. 2009, https://www.seattletimes.com/nation-world/brazil-vp-says-country-should-build-nuclear-arms/. Alencar's statement differed from his declaration to US emissaries a few years earlier in which he defended Brazil's effort toward denuclearization. AmEmbassy Brasília to SecState, 25 Apr. 2005, WC: 05Brasília1044_a, https://search.wikileaks.org/plusd/cables/05BRASILIA1044_a.html.

6. AmEmbassy Brasília to SecState, 26 May 2009, WC: 09BRASILIA667_a, https://search.wikileaks.org/plusd/cables/09BRASILIA667_a.html.

7. Togzhan Kassenova, *Brazil's Nuclear Kaleidoscope: An Evolving Identity* (Washington, DC: Carnegie Endowment for International Peace, 2014), 59.

8. William Walker, *A Perpetual Menace: Nuclear Weapons and International Order* (London: Routledge, 2012), 151.

9. Michal Onderco, "Why Nuclear Weapon Ban Treaty Is Unlikely to Fulfil Its Promise," *Global Affairs* 3.4–5 (2017): 391–404, https://doi.org/10.1080/23340460.2017.1409082.

10. "Treaty on the Prohibition of Nuclear Weapons," UNGA, 7 July 2017, A/CONF.229/2017/8, https://undocs.org/en/A/CONF.229/2017/8.

11. "Establishment of a Commission to Deal with the Problems Raised by the Discovery of Atomic Energy," UNGA, 24 Jan. 1946, https://digitallibrary.un.org/record/209570?ln=en.

12. Sérgio de Queiroz Duarte, "The Role of Brazil in Multilateral Disarmament Efforts," *Revista Brasileira de Política Internacional* 60.2 (2017): e013, epub 21 Dec. 2017, https://dx.doi.org/10.1590/0034-7329201700213.

13. Nunes Ferreira, "Rumo a um mundo sem armas nucleares."

14. "INFCIRC/540—Model Protocol Additional to the Agreement(s) between States and the International Atomic Energy Agency for the Application of Safeguards," IAEA, accessed 29 May 2020, https://www.iaea.org/sites/default/files/infcirc540.pdf.

15. Carlo Patti, "Brazil: An Emerging Nuclear Power," in *Emergent Brazil: Key Perspectives on a New Global Power*, ed. Jeffrey D. Needell (Gainesville: University of Florida Press, 2015), 264.

16. John. D. Holum to Luiz Felipe Lampreia, 16 Feb. 1996, ACDA document, LFL mre1 1995.01.10/1.

17. "Visita do Secretário de Estado dos Estados Unidos da América ao Brasil. Maço de Apoio. 3 a 5 de março de 1996," LFL mre1 1995.01.10/1.

18. "INFCIRC/540," 9. I thank Professor Laércio Vinhas, Brazil's representative at the IAEA from 2011 to 2016 and former director of international relations (1996–2007) and of the safeguards division (1994–96) of CNEN, for calling my attention to this point. Laércio Vinhas, email to author, 25 May 2020.

19. Luiz Felipe Lampreia, interview by author, 17 Mar. 2014, Rio de Janeiro.

20. Relations between ABACC and the IAEA were governed by a 1998 agreement between the two agencies. "Acuerdo de cooperación entre el Organismo Internacional de Energía Atómica y la Agencia Brasileño-Argentina de Contabilidad y Control de Materiales

Nucleares," ABACC, accessed 28 July 2017, https://www.abacc.org.br/wp-content/uplo
ads/2016/09/1998-Acordo-de-cooperação-entre-a-ABACC-e-a-AIEA-espanhol-assinado
.pdf.

21. Liz Palmer and Gary Milhollin, "Brazil's Nuclear Puzzle," *Science* 306.696 (2004):
617. On Roberto Amaral's declaration and Brazil's guarantees regarding its nuclear nonproliferation commitments, see AmEmbassy Brasília to SecState, 25 Apr. 2005, WC:
05Brasilia1044_a, https://search.wikileaks.org/plusd/cables/05BRASILIA1044_a.html.

22. Gabriela Wolthers, "Governo cede, mas mantem restrição à inspeção da AIEA,"
19 Oct. 2004, https://www1.folha.uol.com.br/fsp/brasil/fc1910200402.htm.

23. AmEmbassy Brasília to SecState, 23 Oct. 2009, WC: 09Brasilia1261_a, https://
search.wikileaks.org/plusd/cables/09BRASILIA1261_a.html.

24. William Potter and Gaukhar Mukhatzhanova, *Nuclear Politics and the Non-Aligned
Movement: Principles vs Pragmatism* (London: IISS-Routledge, 2012), 65.

25. "Chanceler Amorim no Canal Livre," 13 Apr. 2014, Ministério das Relações Exteriores, https://www.youtube.com/watch?v=mITSUfmKDVI.

26. Osmar V. Chofi (secretary-general, Ministry of Foreign Relations) to Cardoso,
23 Sept. 2002, IPR 120, Confidential-Urgent, IPR 2002, AHMRE-B.

27. João Marcelo Galvão de Queiroz, "O modelo Abacc: Um balanço," in *O modelo
Abacc: Um manco no desenvolvimento das relações entre Brasil e Argentina*, ed. Odilon Antonio Marcuzzo do Canto (Santa Maria: Editora UFSM, 2016), 74. On Eduardo Campos's
public statement, see AmEmbassy Brasília to SecState, 26 Aug. 2004, WC 05Brasilia2151_a,
https://search.wikileaks.org/plusd/cables/04BRASILIA2151_a.html.

28. AmEmbassy Brasília to SecState, 25 Apr. 2005, WC: 05Brasilia1044_a, https://search
.wikileaks.org/plusd/cables/05BRASILIA1044_a.html.

29. AmEmbassy Brasília to SecState, 20 Aug. 2009, WC: 09Brasilia1038, https://
search.wikileaks.org/plusd/cables/09BRASILIA1038_a.html.

30. Carlo Patti, "Brazil and the Nuclear Issues in the Years of the Luiz Inácio Lula
da Silva Government (2003–2010)," *Revista Brasileira de Política Internacional* 53.2
(2010): 186.

31. Mark Hibbs, "New Global Rules for Sensitive Nuclear Trade," 8 July 2011, Carnegie Endowment for International Peace, http://carnegieendowment.org/2011/07/28/new
-global-rules-for-sensitive-nuclear-trade/4avp.

32. David S. Jonas, John Carlson, and Richard S. Goorevich, "The NSG Decision on
Nuclear Transfers: ABACC and the Additional Protocol," *Arms Control Today*, 5 Nov. 2012.
On the discussions on ENR, see AmEmbassy Brasília to SecState, 8 June 2009, WC:
09BRASILIA725_a, https://search.wikileaks.org/plusd/cables/09BRASILIA725_a.html.

33. "Nuclear Suppliers Group (NSG) Recognizes the Quadripartite Agreement as an
Alternative Criterion to the Additional Protocol," *ABACC News*, 28 June 2011, http://www
.abacc.org.br/?p=3846&lang=en.

34. "ABACC's Existing Safeguards Agreement Provides the Highest Guarantees Regarding Nuclear Safeguards," *ABACC News*, 12 Aug. 2011, http://www.abacc.org.br/?p
=4431&lang=en; Mariana Oliveira do Nascimento Plum and Carlos Augusto Rollemberg
de Resende, "The ABACC Experience: Continuity and Credibility in the Nuclear Programs
of Brazil and Argentina," *Nonproliferation Review* 23.5–6 (2016): 587–88, https:/doi.org/10
.1080/10736700.2017.1339402.

35. "ABACC's Existing Safeguards Agreement Provides the Highest Guarantees Regarding Nuclear Safeguards," *ABACC News*, 12 Aug. 2011, http://www.abacc.org.br/?p=4431&lang=en.

36. Galvão de Queiroz, "O modelo Abacc," 77.

37. Togzhan Kassenova, "Brazil, Argentina, and the Politics of Global Nonproliferation and Nuclear Safeguards," 29 Nov. 2016, Carnegie Endowment for International Peace,http://carnegieendowment.org/2016/11/29/brazil-argentina-and-politics-of-global-nonproliferation-and-nuclear-safeguards-pub-66286#comments.

38. David S. Jonas, John Carlson, and Richard S. Goorevich, "The NSG Decision on Sensitive Nuclear Transfers: ABACC and the Additional Protocol," Arms Control Association, https://www.armscontrol.org/act/2012-11/nsg-decision-sensitive-nuclear-transfers-abacc-additional-protocol.

39. Eugenio Pacelli Lazzarotti Diniz Costa, "Brazil's Nuclear Submarine: A Broader Approach to the Safeguards Issue," *Revista Brasileira de Política Internacional* 60.2 (2017): e005, epub 19 Oct. 2017, https://dx.doi.org/10.1590/0034-7329201700205.

40. "Uma aposta perigosa em Teerã," *Luis Felipe Lampreia* (blog), *O Globo*, 7 May 2010, https://blogs.oglobo.globo.com/lampreia/post/uma-aposta-perigosa-em-teera-289871.html; Paulo Sotero, "Lula's Teheran Misadventure," *Foreign Policy*, 11 May 2010, https://foreignpolicy.com/2010/05/11/lulas-tehran-misadventure/.

41. Iran signed the AP in December 2003 but for political reasons decided not to ratify it.

42. Celso Amorim, *Teerã, Ramalá, Doha: Memórias da política externa ativa e altiva* (São Paulo: Benvirá, 2015), 18.

43. Sean W. Burges, "Brazil as a Bridge between Old and New Powers?," *International Affairs* 3 (2013): 577–94.

44. Amorim, *Teerã, Ramalá, Doha*, 13.

45. Amorim, *Teerã, Ramalá, Doha*, 28; Alexei Barrionuevo, "Obama Writes to Brazil's Leader about Iran," *New York Times*, 24 Nov. 2009, https://www.nytimes.com/2009/11/25/world/americas/25brazil.html.

46. AmEmbassy Brasília to SecState, 20 Aug. 2009, WC: 09Brasilia1038, https://search.wikileaks.org/plusd/cables/09BRASILIA1038_a.html.

47. Amorim, *Teerã, Ramalá, Doha*, 16.

48. Barrionuevo, "Obama Writes to Brazil's Leader about Iran."

49. Barrionuevo, "Obama Writes to Brazil's Leader about Iran."

50. AmEmbassy Brasília to SecState, 27 Nov. 2009, WC: 09BRASILIA1371_a, https://search.wikileaks.org/plusd/cables/09BRASILIA1371_a.html.

51. AmEmbassy Brasília to SecState, 23 Sept. 2009, WC: 09BRASILIA1186_a,https://search.wikileaks.org/plusd/cables/09BRASILIA1186_a.html.

52. AmEmbassy Brasília to SecState, 29 Jan. 2010, WC: 10BRASILIA33_a, https://search.wikileaks.org/plusd/cables/10BRASILIA33_a.html.

53. Luiz Felipe Lampreia, *Aposta em Teerã* (Rio de Janeiro: Objetiva, 2014).

54. AmEmbassy Brasília to SecState, 19 Feb. 2010, WC: 10BRASILIA59_a,https://search.wikileaks.org/plusd/cables/10BRASILIA59_a.html.

55. "Brasil e EUA reafirmam diferenças sobre Irã na visita de Hillary," *BBC Brasil*, 3 Mar. 2010, http://www.bbc.com/portuguese/noticias/2010/03/100303_hillarycoletiva_fp.

56. Lampreia, *Aposta em Teerã*, 72.

57. "Obama se reúne com Lula e Erdogan para conhecer proposta sobre Irã," *EdSP*, 13 Apr. 2010.

58. "Antes de acordo, Obama disse a Lula que pacto com Irã criaria confiança," *EdSP*, 21 May 2010, https://internacional.estadao.com.br/noticias/oriente-medio,antes-de-acordo-obama-disse-a-lula-que-pacto-com-ira-criaria-confianca,554803; Lampreia, *Aposta em Teerã*, 75.

59. "Joint Declaration by Iran, Turkey and Brazil," 17 May 2010, https://fas.org/nuke/guide/iran/joint-decl.pdf.

60. Ahmet Davutoglu and Celso Amorim, "Giving Diplomacy a Chance," *New York Times*, 26 May 2010, https://www.nytimes.com/2010/05/27/opinion/27iht-eddavutoglu.html.

61. Lampreia, *Aposta em Teerã*, 86.

62. It is important to note that by September 2012 the Brazilian, Turkish, and Swedish foreign ministers had agreed that the likelihood of the Tehran declaration's acceptance by the international community had increased. See Leonencio Lessa and Gustavo Chacra, "Brasil e Turquia avaliam retomar pacto da era Lula sobre Programa Iraniano," *EdSP*, 25 Sept. 2012.

63. "Iran Sends Message to Brazil on JCPOA," *Tasmin News Agency*, 29 June 2018, https://www.tasnimnews.com/en/news/2018/06/29/1763258/iran-sends-message-to-brazil-on-jcpoa.

64. Mônica Herz, Layla Dawood, and Victor Coutinho Lage, "Brazilian Nuclear Policy during the Workers' Party Years," *Nonproliferation Review* 23 (2016): 559–73, https:/doi.org/10.1080/10736700.2016.1246100.

65. On the nuclear renaissance, see AmEmbassy Brasília to SecState, 28 Dec. 2007, WC: 07Brasilia2335_a, https://search.wikileaks.org/plusd/cables/07BRASILIA2335_a.html.

66. Ministério de Minas e Energia, *Plano Nacional de Energia 2030* (Brasília, 2007); AmEmbassy Brasília to SecState, 10 Oct. 2008, WC: 08Brasilia 1354_a, https://search.wikileaks.org/plusd/cables/08BRASILIA1354_a.html.

67. "Areva construirá o terceiro reator de Angra," Consulado-Geral da França no Brasil, accessed 14 June 2018, https://riodejaneiro.consulfrance.org/Areva-achevera-le-troisieme,893.

68. Yuriy Humber, Sangim Han, and Shinhye Kang, "Nuclear Industry Says Back on Track after Fukushima 'Speed Bump,'" 25 Mar. 2012, Bloomberg, http://www.bloomberg.com/news/2012-03-25/nuclear-industry-says-back-on-track-after-fukushima-speed-bump-.html.

69. Togzhan Kassenova, "Turbulent Times for Brazil's Nuclear Project," 29 Oct. 2015, Carnegie Endowment for International Peace, http://carnegieendowment.org/2015/10/29/turbulent-times-for-brazil-s-nuclear-projects-pub-61800.

70. Mônica Bergamo, "Militar condenado na Lava Jato diz que foi preso por interesse internacional," *FdSP*, 7 Nov. 2017, https://www1.folha.uol.com.br/poder/2017/11/1933381-militar-condenado-na-lava-jato-diz-que-foi-preso-por-interesse-internacional.shtml.

71. Manoel Ventura, "Governo deve elevar tarifas para Angra 3," *O Globo*, 12 June .2018, https://oglobo.globo.com/economia/governo-deve-elevar-tarifa-de-angra-3-22769206.

72. Since 2004, for instance, Brazil and China have discussed a possible collaboration in the nuclear field. AmEmbassy Brasília to SecState, 18 June 2004, WC, 04Brasilia1503_a,https://search.wikileaks.org/plusd/cables/04BRASILIA1503_a.html; "Japan, Brazil Likely to Agree to Resume Talks on Nuclear Development," 20 June 2013, House of Japan, http://www.houseofjapan.com/local/japan-brazil-likely-to-agree-to-resume-talks-on-nuclear-development.

73. AmEmbassy Buenos Aires to SecState, 26 Feb. 2008, WC: 08BuenosAires236_a,https://search.wikileaks.org/plusd/cables/08BUENOSAIRES236_a.html.

74. Irma Arguello, "Brazil and Argentina's Nuclear Cooperation," 9 Jan. .2009, Carnegie Endowment for International Peace, http://carnegieendowment.org/2009/01/08/brazil-and-argentina-s-nuclear-cooperation/3jqa.

75. "Argentina y Brasil profundizan cooperación nuclear," Ministerio de Relaciones Exteriores y Culto—República Argentina, accessed 14 June 2018, http://cancilleria.gob.ar/argentina-y-brasil-profundizan-cooperacion-nuclear.

76. J. A. Perrotta and I. J. Obadia, "The RMB Project Development Status" (paper, International Conference on Research Reactors: Safe Management and Effective Utilization, Rabat, Morocco, 14 Nov. 2011); José Maria Tomazela, "Temer dá início a testes de submarino nuclear e pede 'otimismo' em Iperó," *EdSP*, 8 June 2018, https://politica.estadao.com.br/noticias/geral,temer-inaugura-testes-de-submarino-nuclear-e-pede-mais-otimismo-no-pais,70002343057.

77. Roberto Godoy, "Meta do programa nuclear é expandir conhecimento," *EdSP*, 17 May 2018, https://politica.estadao.com.br/noticias/geral,analise-meta-do-programa-nuclear-brasileiro-e-expandir-conhecimento,70002312058.

78. AmEmbassy Brasília to SecState, 27 Nov. 2007, WC: Cable 07Brasilia2185_a, https://wikileaks.org/plusd/cables/07BRASILIA2185_a.html.

79. On the resumption of the nuclear submarine program, see Fernanda das Graças Corrêa, *O projeto do submarino nuclear brasileiro: Uma história de ciência, tecnologia e soberania* (Rio de Janeiro: Capax Dei Editora, 2012), 166–90.

80. AmEmbassy Brasília to SecState, 28 Apr. 2004, WC: 04Brasilia1018_a, https://search.wikileaks.org/plusd/cables/04BRASILIA1018_a.html.

81. AmEmbassy Brasília to SecState, 28 Apr. 2004, WC: 04Brasilia1018_a, https://search.wikileaks.org/plusd/cables/04BRASILIA1018_a.html; AmEmbassy Brasília to SecState, 15 Jan. 2008, WC :08Brasilia93_a, ttps://wikileaks.org/plusd/cables/08BRASILIA93_a.html.

82. AmEmbassy Brasília to SecState, 15 Jan. 2008, WC :08Brasilia93_a, ttps://wikileaks.org/plusd/cables/08BRASILIA93_a.html.

83. José Maria Tomazela, "Submarino nuclear 'terrestre' ficará pronto em 3 anos, diz Marinha," *EdSP*, 17 May 2018, https://politica.estadao.com.br/noticias/geral,submarino-nuclear-terrestre-ficara-pronto-em-3-anos-diz-marinha,70002312057.

84. Ministério da Defesa, *Estratégia Nacional de Defesa* (Brasília, 2008).

85. Talita Bedinelli, "Brasil gasta miles de millones en blindar su costa para proteger el presal," *El País*, 14 Feb. 2014, http://internacional.elpais.com/internacional/2014/02/13/actualidad/1392329113_953453.html.

86. AmEmbassy Buenos Aires to SecState, 24 Dec. 2009, WC: 09BUENOSAIRES1305_a, https://search.wikileaks.org/plusd/cables/09BUENOSAIRES1305_a.html.

87. AmEmbassy Buenos Aires to SecState, 26 Feb. 2008, WC: 08Buesaires230_a, https://wikileaks.org/plusd/cables/08BUENOSAIRES230_a.html.

88. AmEmbassy Brasília to SecState, 15 Jan. 2008, WC: 08Brasilia93_a, https://wikileaks.org/plusd/cables/08BRASILIA93_a.html.

89. Simone Sanches, "Submarino nuclear brasileiro começa a ser desenvolvido em julho," *Cruzeiro do Sul*, 18 Mar. 2012, http://www.cruzeirodosul.inf.br/materia/372768/submarino-nuclear-brasileiro-comeca-a-ser-desenvolvido-em-julho.

90. "Construção de submarinos terá efeito estratégico, defende Dilma," *Agência Estado*, 18 July 2011.

91. Tomazela, "Submarino nuclear 'terrestre' ficará pronto em 3 anos, diz Marinha."

Conclusion

1. Ricardo Della Coletta, "Eduardo Bolsonaro defende que Brasil possua bombas nucleares," *FdSP*, 14 May 2019, https://www1.folha.uol.com.br/mundo/2019/05/eduardo-bolsonaro-defende-que-brasil-possua-bombas-nucleares.shtml.

2. For a comparison of the key documents on Brazil's nuclear program, see Carlo Patti, "Origins and Evolution of the Brazilian Nuclear Program (1947–2011)," *NPIHP Research Updates*, 15 Nov. 2012, Wilson Center, https://www.wilsoncenter.org/publication/origins-and-evolution-the-brazilian-nuclear-program-1947-2011.

Non-US government agencies and nongovernmental organizations are listed under their names in English translation.

Abraham, Itty, 4–5
Abrão, Alcídio, 111
abstinence principle, 3–4
Acheson, Dean, 19
Acheson-Lilienthal Report, 19
AEG, 76
Aeronautics Institute of Technology (ITA), 114, 179, 180
Aerospace Technical Center (CTA), 113–14, 115, 116, 135, 161, 179
Africa, as denuclearized zone, 233n65
Agency for the Prohibition of Nuclear Weapons in Latin American and the Caribbean (Opanal), 167, 170, 171, 172
Ahmadinejad, Mahmoud, 198, 199–200, 201–2
air force, 159, 162, 177, 189; Aerospace Technical Center, 113–14, 115, 135, 161, 179; PATN participation, 113–14, 115, 116–17, 118, 119, 122, 135; Project Solimões, 116–17, 122, 141, 159, 162, 163
Akhtar, Rabia, 4
Alberto da Motta e Silva, Álvaro, 40, 86; CNPq and, 24–25, 35, 36, 225n46; first nuclear plan, 25–32; France-Brazil nuclear collaboration, 27–28; Italy-Brazil nuclear collaboration, 225n54; UNAEC and, 18–19, 20, 21, 22, 25; US-Brazil nuclear collaboration, 18–19, 25, 36–37; West Germany-Brazil nuclear collaboration, 31–32
Albright, Madeleine, 174, 184
Alencar, José, 192
Alessandri, Jorge, 52

Alfonsín, Raúl, 1, 133–35, 137, 138, 140, 142; Argentina-Brazil nuclear cooperation, 147–56
Algeria, 51, 65, 123
Alliance for Progress, 61
Amaral, Roberto, 192, 195
Amarante, José Alberto Albano, 115, 116, 118
Amazul, 206
American & Foreign Power, 41, 42
American Machine and Foundry Company, 36
Amorim, Celso, 166, 172, 173, 184, 192, 196, 199, 200, 201–2
Angola, 8, 82
anticommunism, 7, 61
antinuclear movement, 100, 144–46, 270n43
Arab oil-producing states, Brazil's relations with, 8, 10
Aramar Experimental Center, 137, 142, 143, 146, 155, 160, 161, 163, 168, 189, 206, 212
Aramburu, Pedro Eugenio, 49
Araújo Castro, João Augusto de, 50, 56, 58, 64, 67, 91–92
AREVA (Orano), 204
Argentina, 1, 3, 5, 44, 71, 91, 97, 98, 104, 205; Falklands War, 132–33; IAEA AP opposition, 196–97, 211; IAEA creation and, 48, 49; nuclear power plants, 62–63; nuclear program, 31, 103–8; nuclear rivalry with Brazil, 10, 103–7, 211, 221n41; secret "parallel" nuclear program, 133–34; Treaty of Tlatelolco and, 59, 60; uranium enrichment technology, 112, 133, 134